The Skills of Management
Fifth Edition

This book is the fifth edition of a highly successful introduction to management. Starting with the transition to a managerial role, it deals with core skills involved in management. These include delegation, communication, appraisal, staff development, disciplinary handling, employee relations, negotiation and handling meetings. These are discussed alongside the key themes of prioritisation and the need for the thorough identification of objectives and diagnosis of problems before action. It is relevant to all those with line management responsibilities, particularly responsibility for people.

The book has been restructured to make it even more readable. Each chapter includes a statement of learning outcomes, and self-assessment questions. Account is taken of the many recent developments in management theory and practice. The increasing involvement of managers in negotiating over a wide range of issues has necessitated a new chapter on negotiating skills.

Real-life examples are offered throughout, with the variation in styles of management required by different organisations and national cultures taken into consideration. The authors draw on their wide academic and industrial experience to provide a sound blend of theory and practice which is useful and highly readable.

W. David Rees is a visiting lecturer at the University of Westminster where he was formerly a principal lecturer in human resource management. He has extensive international experience in management consultancy in both the private and public sectors and is a member of the ACAS Panel of Independent Arbitrators. He worked in industry before joining the University of Westminster.

Christine Porter is chair of the Human Resource Management Department in the Westminster Business School at the University of Westminster. She worked in industry and consultancy before joining the university and has undertaken several overseas assignments.

THE SKILLS OF
MANAGEMENT

5ᵀᴴ EDITION

W. David F

THOMSON

Australia • Canada • Mexico • Singapore • Spain • United Kingdom • United States

The Skills of Management ,5ᵗʰ Edition

Copyright © 1996 W. David Rees

For more information, contact Thomson Learning, High Holborn House; 50-51 Bedford Row, London, WC1R 4LR or visit us on the World Wide Web at:
http://www.thomsonlearning.co.uk

British Library Cataloguing-in-Publication Data
A catalogue record for this book is available from the British Library

ISBN 1-86152-550-8

First edition published 1984 by Routledge
Second edition published 1988 by Routledge
Third edition published 1990 by Routledge
Fourth edition published 1996 by Routledge
Fourth edition reprinted 1998 and 1999 by International Thomson Business Press
Fifth edition published 2001 by Thomson Learning
Reprinted 2003 by Thomson Learning

Typeset by Dexter Haven Associates, London

Printed in China by C & C Offset Printing Co. Ltd

Contents

List of Figures

Preface to the 5th edition

Perhaps the best way of explaining the rationale for this edition is to liken the writing of the book to the production of a car. Car design has to take place within a changing environment – particularly with technology and market conditions. However, if a car is to be produced, at some stage the design has to be frozen so that production can start, even though opportunities for improvement continue to emerge. Note is taken of these opportunities for further improvement, however, so that they can be incorporated into the next model. This is just the process that has taken place with this book. It has been repeated with each new edition. Also, use has been made of the information about the performance of the product after it has been launched. A particularly important source of information in this respect has been discussions about the content of the book with mature students in managerial jobs.

The scale of change between the fourth (1996) and fifth edition is the largest since the book was first published. Also, the book is now co-authored by Christine Porter, who has collaborated on it from the outset. Each chapter starts with a statement of the expected learning outcomes. This has helped focus on the precise way in which the material should be of benefit to readers. Extensive use is made of sub-headings, bullet points and boxed examples. This has led to a clear topic sequence. Self-assessment questions have also been introduced to enable readers to check their comprehension of the material at the end of each chapter.

Website access has also been created for readers for the first time so that they can work through exercise material specific to each chapter. This is over and above the exercise material included in the book itself. Tutors' notes can also be accessed for this extra material. These arrangements are explained in more detail in the section 'How to use the book'. Much of the material has been generated by the involvement of the authors in consultancy and related activities in a wide range of organisations.

Every chapter has been revised in the light of recent developments. The increased pace of change means that managers have to negotiate more frequently and over an ever-widening range of issues. This has led to a separate chapter on negotiations, which covers many important issues that are generally ignored. These include identifying and dealing with differences within negotiating teams, the dangers of misunderstanding about what has been agreed, how this is caused and how it can be avoided. The impact of culture on negotiations and the effective development of negotiating skills are also covered. The former chapter on appraisal, training and counselling has been divided into three separate chapters to make consideration of these topics more manageable. The material on training has been greatly expanded. This is necessary because the increasing pace of change and the amount of capital equipment operated by employees have increased both the need for training and the consequences of failure in this area. Also the national framework of training has radically changed, particularly because of the impact of National Vocational Qualifications (NVQs).

The book has been revised in light of the continuing impact of information technology and globalisation on organisations and managerial jobs. There is also an increased emphasis on the impact of national culture on management. The growth of individual employment protection, particularly because of European initiatives, has been extensive. This has led to a systematic updating of the law, particularly with regard to selection (chapter 9), discipline, dismissal and redundancy (chapter 13) and more generally in the context of employee relations (chapter 14).

There are some important issues with regard to writing style. We have dealt with the issue of the use of the personal pronoun 'he' by simply not using it unless it refers to a specific person. Language conventions have changed so that we have followed the practice of some other writers by using the term 'they' in a singular as well as a plural context to avoid sexist connotations. We have preferred to stay with the term 'skills' rather than use the term 'competencies'. This is because the term 'competencies' refers to a particular approach to the identification, development and assessment of skills, and we believe the term 'skills' is more generic. This is also in line with our aim to express ourselves as clearly as possible and to avoid using long words if there are shorter alternatives. The slightly narrower concept of 'competencies' is dealt with, however, where appropriate. The consistent feedback we have received about the previous editions has been that they have above all else been readable and we have been determined to keep it that way.

W. David Rees
Christine Porter

Acknowledgements

Particular acknowledgement is due to the countless number of management students who, in different classes and organisational workshops, have allowed us to test out and develop our ideas and have contributed both ideas of their own and many invaluable illustrative examples which appear in this book. The classes have been on a wide variety of courses – especially at Westminster Business School, University of Westminster and at the University's Diplomatic Academy both in London and at the American University in Paris. Particular thanks are due to students on the MA courses in international business and management, human resource management, personnel and development (and its predecessors), and diplomatic studies. They have given us very useful insights about management in a variety of cultural settings. A revelation that has been put to good use is the overlap between the skills needed in diplomacy and management. Further cultural insights were gained from the students on the various management development workshops we have run in Malaysia and Indonesia. We have gleaned innumerable valuable ideas from current and former colleagues at the University of Westminster and also by in-house training and consultancy in a wide variety of organisations, especially the Bass Group and in a range of London Borough Councils. We also gratefully acknowledge the University of Chicago Press for permission to reproduce the rectangles diagram in chapter 8 and the magazine *Private Eye*, for allowing us to reproduce the cartoon that appears in chapter 9.

We have received direct help in writing the various editions of the book from a wide range of people. Whilst it is perhaps invidious to name just some of them we must pay particular thanks to Angela Rice of ITE Corporate Training and Recruitment and Sue Miller of the University of Westminster, for their help in developing chapter 11 on training. Kath Brady of the University of Westminster gave significant help with chapter 13 on disciplinary handling and dismissal. Simon Marsh of the Chemical Industries Association helped develop chapter 14 on the manager and employee relations. Thanks are also due to Jaafar El-Murad, Reece Evans, Les Galloway, Bob Lea, Ralph Rees, John Ring, Gill Sudgen and Fraser Tuddenham. A particularly useful practical example regarding the need for specialist representation was provided by Denys Groves and is included in chapter 15 on negotiating skills. Thanks are also due to Matthew Rees and Priscilla Zanella for their considerable assistance with the data inputting.

Acknowledgements are due to GEE Publishing Ltd for the material adapted from the chapter on management skills written by David Rees in the CD-Rom *Personnel Management Factfinder*. Some of this material was adapted from the fourth edition of the book and has now been re-adapted from the CD Rom for use in the fifth edition. The experience gained in writing for GEE was also particularly useful in developing an even more user-friendly format for the fifth edition of the book. However, the responsibility for the content of the book lies with the authors.

W. David Rees
Christine Porter

Introduction

During the time that we have taught management subjects we have become aware of the dearth of books that address a reasonable range of core issues, let alone tackle such topics in an appropriate way. Most books about management are written from the perspective of a particular discipline or function and are intended for a specialist rather than a person with a range of management responsibilities. A further complication has been that the language in many of these books is not particularly accessible. By taking a marketing approach to our teaching and trying to establish the areas in which those with management responsibilities actually needed help, we have built up a fund of relevant material. We have also sought to use clear language and practical illustrations to facilitate learning.

After prompting from some student groups, including one in particular at the Royal College of Nursing, David Rees eventually converted some of his material into a book about practical management skills. As explained in the preface to this edition, it has been systematically developed through various editions, with help from Christine Porter. We have endeavoured to keep to the original idea of writing a user-friendly book that is of practical benefit to those who have acquired, or who expect to acquire, a range of management responsibilities.

Over the years we have become fascinated with the way in which people from widely different organisations and countries seemed to be grappling with similar fundamental issues and problems. This enabled David Rees to initially identify a core of basic issues that match the syllabus requirements of a wide range of courses as well as being relevant to the non-student practitioner. We have been able to draw on the contributions made in hundreds of classroom discussions and in-house workshops to provide appropriate practical examples to illustrate and help explain relevant theoretical concepts and practical skills. Such examples, and continuous contact with those facing management problems on a day-to-day basis, has enabled us to write a relevant book with an appropriate blend of theory and practice.

Providing this blend is critical, as this book is not intended to supply a set of prescriptive remedies. Action needs to be preceded by careful diagnosis. Mary Parker Follett's concept of the 'law of the situation', explained in chapter 1, is all-important. Decisions and action need to take account of the variables in a situation. By providing both a basic theoretical analysis of concepts and an explanation of the skills that are likely to be useful, the intention is to provide readers with the ability to judge when and how to use specific skills and remedies and not to apply them as a knee-jerk reaction to problems. Many of the issues dealt with are also crucial life skills. The need for accurate problem definition, effective communication, the resolution of conflict, negotiation and the development of practical strategies in these areas are not confined to the workplace. Development of skills in these areas may bring considerable advantages in one's personal life as well as at work.

It is increasingly recognised that people who train as specialists are likely to accumulate considerable managerial responsibilities in the course of their career. As explained in chapter 1, few people start their careers as managers. Organisations usually have a departmental structure. The normal career progression is for one to start off as a specialist and then progressively acquire responsibility for supervising or managing other specialists. Even business studies graduates usually find they have to be placed initially in a specialist job, despite the general nature of the training they have received. If that is the pattern, it is just as well to prepare people for what is to come. If the specialism requires training, why not also the managerial aspects? The trend to devolution of authority and decision-making within both private and public sector organisations, accompanied by flatter organisational structures, has emphasised this by increasing the range of responsibilities and the speed with which people acquire them. Recognition of this phenomenon meant that the first edition was very nearly called *Management – For Those Thrust Into It*. Logically, the syllabuses of most professional and specialist courses have now been adapted to include management. Many people, however, do not have the benefit of management training, and it is hoped that this book will be of assistance to them as well as those who are engaged in the formal study of management.

We have generally not made a distinction between management and supervision, although we have referred to the role of the first-line supervisor in chapters 13 and 14. We have used the term 'management' generically to incorporate supervision. Our general scepticism of the value of the distinction has been reinforced when we have run management courses or workshops for people at different levels within the same organisation. On one occasion, David Rees was involved in running management courses simultaneously at three different levels in the National Health Service. These were for ward sisters, middle managers and senior nursing officers. The, perhaps heretical, conclusion he came to was that many of the basic management problems facing the employees at these different levels were the same. Status issues required that the programmes be written up in distinctly different ways, and there were some genuine differences. However, it was the common nature of the problems rather than the differences that was more noticeable.

People in senior positions may perceive their management development needs as being very sophisticated, by virtue of their position, when the reality often is that they, for whatever reason, can't or don't get the basics right. The general problem is not one of establishing new insights but of getting people to convert key concepts into effective action. This also applies to management syllabuses on formal courses. Any introduction to key concepts is going to have to cover much the same general ground, whether it be on an undergraduate, professional or postgraduate course, or a National Vocational Qualification (NVQ) at any level. It is only when the key concepts have been mastered in practice as well as theory that it is appropriate to consider identifying and meeting advanced needs.

The range of topics covered includes general management and the management of people. The range does not extend to areas such as finance and marketing. These areas are not only outside our own particular area of expertise but are also subjects where there are likely to be considerable variations of responsibility between managers. What we believe we have done is to identify a core range of topics that is of relevance to all persons studying or involved in management. The potential scope of managerial responsibility is so wide that the coverage cannot be exhaustive. However, no person with managerial responsibilities can escape the need, for example, to consider such issues as the identification of objectives, prioritisation, managerial style, delegation, motivation, remuneration, communication, selection, training, disciplinary handling, negotiation, employee relations, and chairing and conduct in meetings.

In writing this book we have taken into account the needs of managers and students in and from countries other than the UK. We have for a long time been concerned that teaching and writing should be understandable to people from other countries without detracting from its value to British students. The avoidance of long words when short ones will do is very much in keeping with the theme of the chapter on communication. It means that readers, whether from the UK or from other countries, do not have to translate unnecessary jargon in order to understand the contents of the book. The aim is to help, not to impress.

In considering the needs of readers from other countries we have been able to capitalise on our experience in teaching and discussing management issues in the UK with people from a wide variety of countries. This has particularly included diplomats on the MA in diplomatic studies at the University of Westminster, studying both in London and Paris. We have also been able to capitalise on our own overseas working experience. This approach is also of benefit to British readers because of the increasing likelihood of their working or dealing with people from different cultural backgrounds or working in different cultural environments. These issues are particularly addressed in the sections dealing with culture in chapters 3 and 4. The places where one or both of us have worked, and thus gained insights into other cultures, include the University of Guyana; a range of private and public sector organisations in Malaysia, including the Mara Institute of Technology; Ngee Ann Polytechnic in Singapore, where David Rees was external examiner in business studies; and Pertamina – the national oil company of Indonesia. Our exposure to different cultures and to different nationalities has led us to the conclusion that the bulk of the material in this book is about skills that are needed in a wide range of cultures. Globalisation has increased the international relevance of the material.

How to use the book

The topics that we have chosen are core management skills that most managers are likely to have to confront at some time or other. The theme has been to write about what readers need to know, not what the authors know. However, some topics, such as marketing and finance, have not been covered, because these are outside the range of expertise of the authors. What is covered is a range of management issues relating to the management of people from the perspective of the line manager. The book may also be of interest to specialists in the human resource management area because of the core issues covered and their user-friendly treatment.

The book is arranged in a logical sequence of topics. The material covered in the first chapter explains the nature of management and the process by which people get involved in management. Subsequent chapters deal with core management skills. The material in the last nine chapters (8–16) all have a particular bearing on communication. Consequently, chapter 8 on communication skills is a foundation for the ones that follow.

There could be other ways of sequencing the chapters, but the one used is likely to be most useful to readers. Each chapter, however, is also written as a freestanding item. Consequently, if readers want to study a particular topic they will find a comprehensive treatment in the relevant chapter. Where cross-references are needed to other chapters, they are given in the text. Further reading material is also given. This is done either by starring general texts in the references and/or listing them separately.

Each chapter has a similar structure and contains the following elements:

- learning outcomes,
- introduction,
- main text,
- summary,
- self-assessment questions (one for each learning outcome),
- specific and general references.

The style of the book is to link theory and practice in an accessible way. There is no all-encompassing theory of management. However, there is a range of concepts from a variety of disciplines that can be very useful to readers in analysing management problems and developing problem-solving strategies. The many practical examples are meant to illustrate general issues and to help show the link between theory and practice. They are also useful for generating interest and helping readers remember particular issues. The concepts and examples included are also intended to form a link with the problems that readers have to deal with. These issues may be of an academic or practical nature or both.

NOTE TO TUTORS

Tutors who adopt the book for specific courses can obtain relevant teaching material free of charge from the publishers. The teaching material has been provided by the authors and successfully used by them in conjunction with the book. Material is available for each chapter and includes case studies, exercises and diagrams.

The authors recommend that students read specific chapters of the book either before or after individual teaching sessions. This frees up time in the classroom for the use of participative exercises and discussion. The supporting teaching material is designed to fit with each chapter. There is little point in simply presenting the material in class that can easily be read in the book. This is particularly so given the reader-friendly way in which the book is written. The usual pattern is to ask students to read a set case study for discussion in class and read the relevant chapter after it. Classroom discussions can generate considerable interest, enable people to test out their ideas and share experiences.

The book can be used at a number of different levels of management and the level of discussion adjusted in accordance with the sophistication of the student group. Many of the ideas and examples incorporated in the book are the result of classroom discussions. If groups have a particular orientation, the discussion can be centred on their particular needs.

As well as being successfully used on a variety of examination courses, the book has also been used as a manual for in-house courses for organisations wishing to develop key management skills amongst its managers. Discounts can be obtained on bulk orders direct from the publisher.

There are also particular uses to which the book can be used with students who have difficulty with English. Students can discuss the supporting teaching material at their own pace in syndicates with others helping them with their English when necessary. When teaching students who are all of the same nationality, they can have syndicate discussions or conduct exercises in their own language. They can then reinforce classroom work by reading specified material in the book in their own time and at their own pace. One of the advantages of the user-friendly style of the book is that the language needs of those whose first language is not English have been taken into account.

To make the case studies, available on the web-site, easier to follow, people's initials often coincide with those of their roles. For example, Stanley Marsden is a Site Manager.

SUPPLEMENTARY RESOURCES AVAILABLE AT http://www.thomsonlearning.co.uk

Supplementary material is available on the Thomson Learning website. This includes overhead projector slides, and the following case studies and exercises relevant to each chapter.

Chapter 1   The trade commissioner (the problems of a specialist handling managerial responsibilities)
Architects of a new era (managerial roles and organisational structure)

Chapter 2   Twelve hours in the life of Mr Perry (prioritisation and delegation)
see also briefing sheet for preparing a role set analysis diagram

Chapter 3   In search of sparkle (organisational structure)
At your service (TQM)
Architects of a new era (managerial roles and organisational structure)
Faith, hope and charity (organisation structure and staffing costs in a charity)
Marriage of convenience (conflict in a charity merger)
The peninsular bank (the employee relations implications of merging two branches)
see also Jean-Louis Barsoux, 'Group behaviour in French business: quality circles à la française', Case study no. 13, in David C. Wilson and Robert Rosenfeld (1990), *Managing Organisations*, McGraw-Hill

Chapter 4   Question of harmony (an attempt to impose Japanese-style working practices in a British manufacturing company)
Trouble abroad (problems with overseas posting)
The peninsular bank (the employee relations implications of merging two branches)
see also Jean-Louis Barsoux, 'Group behaviour in French business: quality circles à la française', Case study no. 13, in David C. Wilson and Robert Rosenfeld (1990), *Managing Organisations*, McGraw-Hill

Chapter 5   Twelve hours in the life of Mr. Perry (prioritisation and delegation)
Trouble in store (discipline/delegation, manual worker)
Mission of trouble (discipline/delegation, white-collar worker)

Chapter 6   The new broom (the impact of restructuring on motivation and staffing needs)
Market reality (reconciling labour market reality with managerial demands)

Chapter 7   Incentive for trouble (the organisational impact of an incentive scheme)
Grades of trouble (job evaluation)
Availability or activity (job evaluation)
Money for value (equal value claim)

Chapter 8   Practical exercise: draw a flow chart (or sociogram) of a meeting or other group activity that you attend (see chapter 16). Use the chart to analyse and evaluate the effectiveness of the communication processes you have observed.
Rectangles exercise (one-way vs two-way communication)

chapter one

Managers and their background

There are case studies and exercises at
http://www.thomsonlearning.co.uk
(for full details, see the listing at the
start of this book).

LEARNING OUTCOMES

When you have worked through this chapter you will be able to:

- Identify key management processes

- Understand how people become managers

- Identify the limitations of specialist career structures

- Understand the nature and causes of conflict between specialist and managerial work

- Identify where you are or are likely to be on the managerial escalator

- Develop a strategy for getting the right balance between specialist and managerial work, both for yourself and others

Introduction

This chapter sets the theme for the whole book. First, the nature of management is examined, and then the way in which people become managers. People usually have an escalator-type progression into management. They are likely to have to combine specialist with managerial responsibilities for much of their career and therefore become managerial hybrids. Unfortunately, people may neglect their managerial responsibilities in favour of specialist activity. If this happens, their personal priorities conflict with organisational priorities. There are four main reasons why such conflict can arise. These are because of lack of attention to:

- job definition,
- managerial selection,

- training and development,
- effective monitoring.

To be effective, managers need to be prepared to meet organisational rather than personal priorities. If they concentrate on doing specialist work, they are likely to find their career prospects severely limited because of the difficulty that organisations have in providing career structures only involving specialist work. Whilst much of the material used to illustrate this point is British, the problem of converting specialists into being managers of other specialists is an international phenomenon.

Other issues covered are the concept of managerial competencies and the remedial strategies for improving the quality of management. The remedial strategies are linked to dealing with the four basic causes of poor management already identified. The first issue to be developed is the actual nature of management.

The nature of management

THE MANAGERIAL CYCLE

Management has been defined by Mary Parker Follett as 'the art of getting things done through people' (Graham 1988).

The elements involved in the process of management were identified by Henri Fayol as 'to forecast and plan, to organise, to command, to co-ordinate and to control' (Gray 1988).

Synthesising Fayol's view with later writers, one can identify the basic elements in terms of the managerial cycle as shown in Figure 1.1.

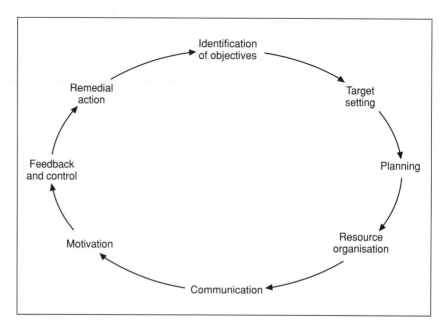

FIGURE 1.1 *The managerial cycle*

Management in practice

Some writers see the managerial cycle as a simplistic model with too rational a view of the manager. Mintzberg's study of how managers actually operate challenged the concept of the totally rational manager. He observed five American chief executives at work and also reviewed the results of studies of managers at generally lower levels in other Western countries. The overall pattern of managerial work appeared to him to be a hectic and fragmented one with little opportunity for reflective thought. Mintzberg also found decision-making was often abrupt, intuitive and incremental rather than strategic. It was often influenced by soft information, including internal and external gossip (Mintzberg 1989).

Another writer, Watson, also has spent time observing managers at work (1994). His observations of UK managers in the electronics industry led him to conclude that individuals view the process of management as being interrelated with their identity, values, status, development, self-esteem and material rewards. He also saw these managers' daily activities as particularly concerned with

> *feeling one's way in confusing circumstances, struggling to make sense of ambiguous messages, reading signals, looking around, listening all the time, coping with conflicts and struggling to achieve tasks through establishing and maintaining a network of relationships.*
>
> Watson 1994: 8

Another recent view of the role and skills of the manager was provided in a study of management in local government in the UK. There is a general relevance in their observation:

> *Management is best defined not as a limited number of 'top' or 'leading' positions, but as a set of competencies, attitudes, and qualities broadly distributed throughout the organisation. Management skills are not the property of the few. Effective local authorities will recognise that many jobs which have not conventionally borne the tag 'manager' rely none the less on that bundle of actions – taking charge, securing an outcome, controlling affairs – which amounts to 'managing'.*
>
> Local Government Management Board 1993: 8

How people become managers

RELATIONSHIP WITH ORGANISATIONAL STRUCTURE

The structure of organisations is usually such that most employees are engaged in a specialised activity. The number of general jobs involving the co-ordination of the work of a number of different specialist departments, for example, tends to be very limited.

The entry into organisations is usually into specialised activity. People may be engaged at a lowly level in a specialised department. Alternatively, they may have advanced specialist skills that they have acquired either by experience or training or a combination of both. This specialist background is the pedigree of the vast majority of managers. This can be demonstrated by probing into the background of almost anyone you know who has managerial responsibilities. Engineering managers, for example, come from the ranks of specialist engineers. Ward sisters or nursing officers will inevitably have a professional nursing qualification. A head teacher will normally have a teaching qualification. Football managers are invariably ex-professional players. Small business entrepreneurs are usually running a business based on their initial technical skill, for example, in computing, in the building trade or as a motor mechanic.

THE MANAGERIAL ESCALATOR

The concept of the managerial escalator seeks to explain how specialists become managers. Initially a specialist may be employed 100 per cent of the time on specialist activity. This may well be after professional training as an accountant, engineer or whatever. The competent specialist may gradually acquire minor supervisory responsibilities, perhaps quite informally. For example, this could be helping newcomers with their job. After five years of competent performance it would not be unusual for a specialist to be promoted. Given the structure of organisations, this usually involves an element of managerial responsibility. An engineer could become a section leader or a sales person a sales manager. After five more years there could be a further formal promotion, either within the same or another organisation. This may have been preceded by a certain amount of accumulation of managerial responsibility on an informal basis. People tend to be carried along this escalator and may finish with most or even all of their time on the managerial side of the axis. The exact course of progress will vary widely from one person to another. However, the escalator-type progression is very common. The managerial activity may well be in a specialist context, but the crucial change is that former specialists may have to spend most of their time managing other specialists, rather than engaging directly in specialist activity themselves.

Figure 1.2 demonstrates, in a rather simplified form, how specialists can, and often do, become managers. The amount of time spent on managerial activity by a specialist is indicated by reading off the level of the shaded area on the vertical scale on the left-hand side of the diagram. The balance of activity, much of which may be of a specialist nature, is calculated simply by subtracting the managerial element from 100 per cent. The difference between the amount of time that a person should be spending on managerial activities and the amount of time actually spent is defined as the managerial gap.

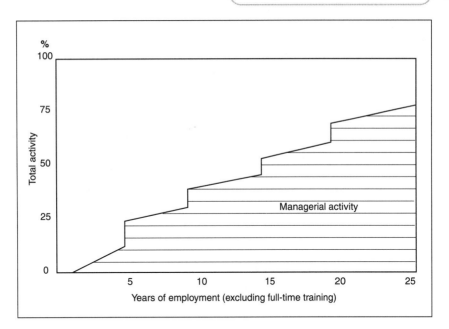

FIGURE 1.2 *The managerial escalator*

The conflict between specialist and managerial activity

NATURE OF THE PROBLEM

The possession of specialist skills is normally an asset and in many cases quite indispensable. If the person who manages in a specialist environment does not understand it, they will be under a great, and perhaps insurmountable, handicap. *Management does not take place in a vacuum but in a particular set of circumstances – usually requiring specialist knowledge.* This knowledge may be necessary so that instructions are sensible but may also serve to inspire respect in others. However, the specialist pedigree of most managers is at the root of many of the problems that confront them, *particularly the danger of getting the wrong balance between specialist and managerial activity.*

Some of the problems that are likely to arise may now be obvious. A person may have embarked on a career and acquired specialist skills that they are increasingly less able to use. A person may also have an emotional commitment to their specialist area and a confidence in that area which may be backed up by several years of formal training. Conversely, the commitment to, and training and aptitude for, the managerial side of the job may be low. *It would not be unusual for a manager in a specialist environment to have had years of specialist training but only days of management training.* This inexorably creates the temptation for managers to adjust the balance of their activity so that they concentrate on what they like doing and what they feel equipped to do at the expense of the managerial aspects of their job.

JOB TITLES

The conflict between specialist and managerial roles can sometimes be revealed by the job titles people use. A consultant working in the civil engineering industry found that the approach of the senior person on site was often indicated by whether they used the title 'site engineer' or 'site manager'. Job titles can be revealing in many other occupations as well, for example, the choice of the term 'buyer' or 'department manager' in a department store. It could also be that the use of the term 'head teacher' indicates a traditional orientation around teaching rather than the management of other teachers. This can be reinforced by a perception that the specialist activity is more important and has more status than managerial activity. *The specialist culture that exists in so many organisations is perhaps the biggest single obstacle to effective management.*

Specialist career structures and their limitations

THE GENERAL PROBLEM

The dilemma of the specialist who is forced into management is accentuated by the difficulty that organisations have providing alternative career progressions. In some cases, it may be possible to get around the dilemma by providing the opportunity for specialist career progression. However, the extent to which this can be done seems to be severely limited in practice as it frequently proves impractical to separate managerial and specialist duties. Managerial responsibility usually flows from specialist expertise. If a person has to run a specialist unit they are unlikely to be able to do this unless they understand what their subordinates are doing and can give appropriate guidance about working methods and end results. The development of the concept of 'team leaders' can lead to specialists acquiring significant management responsibilities despite occupying a junior position.

MANAGERIAL RESPONSIBILITIES OF THE HYBRID

The problems of disentangling specialist and managerial work can be demonstrated by identifying the managerial-type activities that specialists may need to get involved in. Consequently, they may need to act as hybrids, being involved in both specialist and managerial activity. Activities that specialists may need to become involved in are:

- anticipating, planning and allocating workload,
- identification of priorities,
- establishing and reviewing work methods,
- quality control,
- management of budgets,
- management of physical resources,

- trouble-shooting,
- supervision of staff (including selection, on-the-job training, appraisal, counselling, motivation, control and grievance handling),
- liaison with senior management, colleagues at a similar level and ancillary staff,
- external liaison.

The flattening of many organisational structures has tended to increase the speed at which specialists accumulate managerial responsibilities. Reductions in the numbers of specialist advisers can also lead to a broadening of managerial roles. Conventional specialist and managerial careers and work boundaries are often breaking down so that both specialists and managers are having to become multiskilled. These developments and flexible management structures can also lead to greater lateral movement of personnel in organisations.

Ironically, it may be more feasible to have a person without specialist knowledge at the top of an organisation than in less senior positions. A chief executive can rely on a raft of specialist departmental heads and concentrate on co-ordinating their work. Even then, however, the chief executive would need a good understanding of the environment in which the organisation was operating and of the internal resources and constraints within their organisation.

EMPLOYEE PRESSURES

The pressures for specialist career structures are often employee driven. Specialists may want to obtain the rewards usually associated with accepting managerial responsibility without actually accepting such responsibilities. Problems that this can cause for the organisation are:

- the demand for highly paid specialist jobs may greatly exceed their availability,
- the more highly paid specialists there are, the more the problems of integrating their work with that of colleagues,
- the incentive for and availability of other specialists to accept management responsibilities can be reduced.

The above issues have arisen with regard to the teaching and nursing professions. In 1998 the UK government announced plans for nursing consultants and 'superteachers'. Whilst this might be popular with members of the nursing and teaching professions who get appointed to these positions, organisations will still be left with the problems of finding enough capable specialists to undertake crucial managerial responsibilities. The concept of 'superteachers' appears to have since become incorporated with performance-related pay for teachers. Substantial rewards for good teachers may deter people from taking on positions with greater responsibility and will not ease the chronic shortage of capable head teachers and deputies. However, the introduction of 'super-nurses' may have the advantage of reducing the pressures on scarce and expensive medical staff.

EXPERIENCE IN THE AREA OF INFORMATION TECHNOLOGY

The area of information technology is one in which organisations do recognise that it is sometimes necessary to retain people with commercially important expertise without forcing them to accept management responsibilities. As with other specialist areas, the person with a high level of technical expertise will not automatically make a good manager or have managerial aspirations. However, even in this area a mix of managerial and technical expertise is often necessary.

A partner in a selection consultancy commented:

Everyone is crying out for project managers, desktop service managers – to keep the system up and running and to talk through problems – and call centre managers... They are looking for the hybrid manager: someone who has more than just technical skills, but knows how to create a customer-orientated culture within an organisation.

Coles 1997

Even when information technologists are hired out to other organisations they still need to have the people skills to interact effectively in client organisations. The essential point is that there are limits to the extent to which specialist and managerial activity can be disentangled. This is not to suggest though that there should not be experimentation in this area.

ADMINISTRATIVE SUPPORT

Sometimes the response to more explicit management pressures has been to give more administrative support to professionals. A diary study of the work of head teachers interestingly showed that they spend much of their time on boring, irrelevant or trivial tasks (Lever and Blease 1992). An example of administrative support being provided is the introduction of 'partnership administrators' in professional partnerships, e.g. firms of solicitors, general medical practitioners and accountants. However, partners cannot expect the administrators to determine policy, future strategy and financial priorities, to resolve conflict between partners or to supervise specialists in the professional aspects of their work. More competitive market conditions, including the emergence of more multiprofessional partnerships, mean that effective management is bound to become an increasingly important factor in determining success or failure. However, even if appropriate support is given, the dilemma of specialists as managers remains a general problem.

Reasons for people opting out of managerial responsibilities

FAILURE TO IDENTIFY THE MANAGERIAL ELEMENT IN A JOB

One reason why managers sometimes engage in an inappropriate balance of activities may simply be that they have failed to identify that they are doing so. If the general style is for over-concentration on specialist activity, an imbalance may not be easily recognised by others either, far less be the subject of constructive comment and advice.

Example

Sometimes managers can find out the right balance between specialist and managerial activity literally by accident. The player-manager of a football club did this when he broke his leg. He then found that, after a little while, the team actually performed better without him in the side. His enforced absence from the side caused him to concentrate on his managerial responsibilities. This more than compensated for his absence from the team. When his leg healed he refrained from playing again and acted as a full-time manager.

It is easy to see why professional footballers may try to combine the daunting tasks of playing and managing. Their reputations will be as players and, if they step down a division or two, they may find that for a while they can cope with both tasks. However, there is a danger that they will fail in both directions. Their playing ability will be on the decline because of age, just as technical specialists moving up the managerial escalator will find that their technical skills are declining. Their selection and support by club directors may be such that they have limited help, and perhaps limited aptitude, for the jobs for which they have been chosen. Under these pressures, and those of trying to learn a new job, probably with a new club, they may 'regress' into doing what they have been historically good at. The more they try in this direction, the more may be their physical exhaustion and retreat from the key area of management. Perhaps a few player-managers can cope with this for a while; others try and fail, and still others accept that they have to 'cross over the line' and concentrate full-time on management. The same logic applies when players move into the more restricted role of coach.

The football example is meant to help explain a general problem. When people are experiencing strain in the managerial part of their job they may seek to avoid this by regressing into their former specialist role. This may provide a temporary refuge, or comfort zone and restore confidence by enabling the person to do what they feel good at. However, like much avoidance behaviour, it is likely to make matters even worse in the long term. A symptom of this may be the eagerness with which a manager insists on 'acting down' when a subordinate is away.

A pressure to take promotion may include an antipathy to being supervised by any of the other people who may be appointed to the boss job. Some people may be reconciled to this shift and be able to cope with it. Others may not be reconciled to it and/or may not be equipped to handle it. This may lead to them over-concentrating on the specialist area – either through conscious design or, more likely, because they have never really reasoned it through. The problems may be compounded by the actions and perceptions of their bosses. If the boss has not reasoned it through either, a pattern may be created down the line. Alternatively, even if bosses have reasoned it through for themselves, the appointment of subordinate managers may still be faulty.

REWARDS

The reasons why people strive to obtain positions that they cannot or will not handle properly needs some explaining. A basic cause is that the structure of most organisations is such that this may be the only way for employees to gain promotion with the associated increases in pay, status and authority. Employees may accept promotion without appreciating the shift in emphasis to managerial activity that is required. On other occasions, people may have a calculated strategy of obtaining as many benefits as possible from a job but doing as little as possible of the work involved.

Example

An academic was attracted to the job as principal of a college because of the many tangible benefits on offer. However, once he had been appointed he announced that, as he was an academic, he would only undertake academic work. He deemed managerial tasks (or 'administrative work' as he called it) to be beneath his intellectual status. The position then arose that the only work he would do (academic) he was not given and the only work he was given (managerial) he would not do. Needless to say, senior colleagues were very unhappy about this blatant contract violation, particularly as they had to do the principal's job for him whilst he enjoyed all the benefits of the position. The principal did, at least though, provide a perfect example of how not to run an organisation.

Employers may need to give some attention as to how they reward 'knowledge' workers. As explained in chapter 7, if a particular expertise really is critical to the success of an organisation, it may be necessary to pay accordingly. Care needs to be taken that this is not done on spurious grounds or that any advantages are greater than the disadvantage of discouraging people from accepting managerial responsibilities. The worst thing to do is to promote people into managerial jobs while letting them think that they need not take their managerial responsibilities seriously.

WORK PREFERENCES

Frequently, managers concentrate unduly on what they simply enjoy doing (i.e. their specialisation). This can happen in many, if not all, managerial environments. When this was explained to a group of transport managers they responded by saying that not only did they recognise the phenomenon, but they also had a name for it. Supervisors who insisted on driving, ostensibly to 'keep their hand in', were described by them as being 'cab happy'. Ex-pilots are notorious for this, and the tendency is reinforced by the requirement that a minimum number of hours must be flown to retain a licence. If this type of activity only happens occasionally, perhaps one should not worry too much. When it forms a regular pattern, though, there is likely to be a serious problem.

Another problem can arise people with a background in a particular management specialism. Like other specialists, they may pay too much attention to their area of historic specialisation. Consequently, they may give too much priority in terms of time and decision making to issues in their specialised area.

Examples

A cost accountant was promoted into a position as a general manager. Unfortunately, instead of taking a broader view in his new job, he still concentrated on cost control. He neglected the marketing aspects of his job in particular and was reluctant to authorise expenditure that could have generated significant net income. He should instead have concentrated on optimising the difference between income and expenditures.

PERSONALITY FACTORS

The ability or willingness of people to handle managerial activity can be influenced by powerful psychological factors relating to individual personalities. Some people may strive for the power that managerial authority can give, regardless of whether or not they are competent to exercise that authority wisely. Sometimes people may actually be in flight from their specialism because they are not very good at it or because they have 'burnt out' in that area.

This does not mean that there are not also perfectly valid reasons why people aspire to positions of greater responsibility. One has sympathy for people who are sucked into management but who are concerned that, if for any reason they lose their jobs, they will have difficulty in returning to their specialist sphere unless they have kept up to date. The point being made, however, is that it is necessary at the selection stage to try and identify the real reason why people want a particular job and to distinguish between valid and invalid reasons.

The fundamental nature of some of the personality factors that may discourage people from applying for managerial positions, or regressing when they are in such jobs, needs examination. One basic possibility is that extroverts prefer the managerial role and introverts the specialist activity. To appoint or not to appoint just on that basis would be somewhat simplistic. However, the value system that specialists develop in their formative occupational years and their self-image may be much more bound up with specialist rather than managerial activity. This, in turn, may conflict with organisational values.

Keenan points out that several authors have noted how the professional values of engineers and scientists – emphasising technical accomplishment, autonomy and public availability of knowledge – are at a variance with the goals of profitability, marketability of products and safeguarding of knowledge which might be useful to competitors (Blackler and Shimmin 1984: 23). The conflict between these sets of values may be precipitated by promotion and create considerable stress. Blackler and Shimmin comment that promotion to supervisory or management positions of specialists 'may reduce or remove the opportunity to do the work for which they were trained and with which they identify. Professional and skilled manual workers are particularly prone to this type of conflict, for example, nurses whose contact with patients lessens with increasing seniority and engineers for whom advancement means abandoning technical work for management' (1984:23). They add:

> The perfectionist, for example, whose self-esteem is tied closely to the idea of a job well done, is likely to be more subject to stress of this kind than someone who is happy-go-lucky in his or her approach.
>
> 1984: 25

As Keenan says of professional engineers, 'the successful accomplishment of meaningful technical work is at the centre of their perception of themselves in their jobs' (1980). Consequently, neither work that underutilises their technical skills nor work that is so demanding that they feel unable to complete it successfully is satisfactory from their point of view.

Those with professional or scientific training may also, according to Pedler and Boydell, have developed norms of carefulness and certainty, and learnt to avoid conflict rather than develop skills to handle it (1985). There may also be little in their specialist culture to equip them to deal with that key variable – people.

Personality factors can, in turn, be reinforced by the uncongenial aspects of many managerial roles. This has led Scase and Goffee to coin the phrase 'reluctant managers', which is also the title of their book (1989). They refer to the 'emotional hardening' that may be necessary to handle managerial roles. They also comment about changing social values and the increasing desire of managers to balance their work and domestic roles. The stereotype of the male manager with the family's interests subordinated to his career is decreasingly representative. What is more common is for managers, as for others, to have significant domestic responsibilities. This can be for a variety of reasons including the career of a partner, dependent elderly relatives and single parenthood. There is also an increasing risk of divorce (Scase and Goffee 1989). Additionally, the actual work may be fragmented, managers can be expected to reconcile a mass of conflicting pressures, be poorly serviced and supported and in some cases even receive a lower salary than their subordinates. These unenviable aspects are considered further in chapter 14 under the sub-heading 'supervisory control'. There are still more reasons why those with managerial responsibilities might wish to shy away from the managerial aspects of their work. Pressures to reduce overall spending are another disincentive. Two further factors to be examined in detail are pressure from subordinates and inadequate training.

PRESSURE FROM SUBORDINATES

The traditions of a particular occupation may influence a manager's behaviour. In teaching, for example, there may be considerable direct and indirect pressure by junior teachers for senior or head teachers to concentrate on teaching. The person in a supervisory position may have to be prepared to resist the pressures of subordinates which could lead to them striking the wrong balance. Such a person may also feel that 'they should not give a job to a subordinate that they cannot do themselves' – a popular but dangerous maxim.

There may also be the fear that unless a direct specialist involvement is retained the manager will become out of date and perhaps ultimately unable to manage at all. The problem is that, if a person responds to these pressures, they may make matters worse. This can happen in two ways: by interfering in the work of subordinates and also by neglecting the critical managerial aspects of a job.

The pressures by subordinates for a manager to demonstrate competence and interest in their specialist activity can be real enough. According to research conducted by Adler (1989) this is particularly true in certain cultures especially Asian. As Mead (1998) comments:

> In a traditional Asian business, the superior should be able to provide specialist answers to technical questions... The Asian manager who cannot answer questions loses status.
>
> 1998: 33

However, subordinates may quite fail to comprehend the other aspects of a boss's job. Additionally, employees may resent the creaming-off of the more interesting parts of the job by a boss who wants to 'keep their hand in'. This may be particularly annoying if the boss does this on a random basis so that subordinates never quite know what their job is. Situations where there are 'two cooks in the kitchen' may generate more friction than where one cook leaves the other to get on with it and puts up with any adverse comments about the lack of specialist involvement.

EXPERIENCE IN DEVELOPING COUNTRIES

The problem of imbalance between specialist and managerial roles is not confined to any one country. Many specialists in developing countries enjoy speedy promotion. This can be caused by the shortage of staff with appropriate skills, the speed with which newly independent countries have had to assume responsibility for managing their own affairs, and the tendency for employees in state and parastatal organisations to be obliged to retire when they reach 55. This early retirement age not only reduces the pool of available talent, but also encourages managers to retain their specialist skills for a post-retirement career. As mentioned above, in many Asian countries the respect for specialist qualifications and expertise is even greater than in the UK and by implication the respect for managerial expertise less (Mead 1998). The following examples, all from developing countries, demonstrate the international nature of the problems identified in this chapter.

In two quite separate countries, medical doctors were appointed as permanent secretaries to the minister of health. There was nothing inherently wrong in that, but there was in their subsequent behaviour. They both spent about 90 per cent of their time on clinical medical work. In both cases they had to be quickly removed from their positions.

The chief executive of a national airline was an ex-pilot. He frequently flew passenger aircraft, particularly if there were prestigious people on board.

A commissioner of police would patrol highways checking unroadworthy vehicles. This left the staff, who should have been doing such work, free to take advantage of the lack of supervision.

An academic was appointed ambassador for his country. However, he continued to write academic books, leaving whatever embassy he was in charge of to run itself.

Often military dictators give high priority to military matters and sanction large defence budgets, even if there is no discernible threat to their country's security.

GENERAL CONSEQUENCES OF OPTING-OUT

Managers are likely to be judged ultimately by the results they achieve through constructive management of employees – not by possession of specialist knowledge. The specialist knowledge that managers require is that which enables them to supervise others. If subordinates can do a particular job better than the manager, the manager's skill is in arranging them to do so. To compete with the subordinate and then fail is hardly recommended.

There is a world of difference between a manager having no specialist competence and having sufficient specialist knowledge to supervise subordinates. The latter may be quite sufficient. It would be very nice if all managers knew more about every aspect of the subordinate's job than the subordinate, but it is not very realistic, particularly with changing technology. It may also not do a great deal for the esteem of subordinates. The manager may have to face up to being confronted by a specialist issue that they cannot deal with. Rather than worry about this, it may be that this is simply an instance when the manager reroutes the subordinate to a source where they may get the right information. The emphasis needs to be on seeing that the specialists maintain and develop their skill base rather than on the manager trying to do this.

A whole host of problems can arise if the weaning process, whereby those with managerial responsibilities get the right balance of specialist and managerial activity, is not satisfactorily accomplished. This is the recurrent theme of this chapter. Often managers show favouritism in the allocation of resources to their own area of interest and historical specialisation.

Remedial strategies

The remedial strategies needed to deal with the problem of poor managerial performance involve dealing with the four basic causes of ineffective performance identified in the introduction to this chapter. These issues are so important that they are worth repeating before being addressed in detail. They are:

- role definition,
- managerial selection,
- training and development,
- monitoring.

ROLE DEFINITION

When managers are reluctant to accept managerial responsibility, a key remedial strategy is to make such responsibilities crystal clear. This is also necessary if the other remedial strategies of selection, training and development, and monitoring are to be effective. This role clarification needs to be an integral part of selection, and the need to highlight the managerial aspects of a job are necessary for both applicants and those making appointments. This issue is given particular attention in the following section on managerial selection.

MANAGERIAL SELECTION

There are a variety of reasons why the wrong people are given managerial responsibility. Two key mistakes are considered in this section, viz. failure to recognise the managerial element in jobs and general selection incompetence. Intervention strategies need to be based on avoiding such mistakes.

Mistake No. 1: Failure to identify and select on the basis of the managerial element in a job

The easiest way to choose a manager is to look at their historical performance and appoint or reject on that basis. The danger in this approach is, however, that there may be critical differences between the duties that a person has performed in the past and those that they may be expected to perform in the future. Unfortunately, this point may not be properly grasped and, in any case, it is so much easier to assess historical performance rather than speculate about a person's managerial potential. It is, for example, far easier to count the number of international caps that a professional footballer has acquired than judge whether or not they have the appropriate range of skills to manage a football club. The likelihood of selection error is increased if selectors view an appointment as a reward for past specialist achievements, instead of a need to choose the right person for the future. In the police service this sometimes led to sergeants being regarded as 'constables with stripes on their arms'.

Examples

The dangers of over-reliance on specialist knowledge and interest as a job qualification are illustrated in the case of the Royal Opera House in London. A House of Commons committee called for the resignation of the entire board and the appointment of a new chief executive. They said:

> *The administrator must be chosen for his or her business skills... We would prefer to see the House run by a philistine with the requisite financial acumen than by the succession of opera and ballet lovers who have brought a great and valuable institution to its knees.*

(Commons Select Committee Report 1997)

Mistake No. 2: Incompetent selectors

The appointment of managers may prove to be a fairly random affair. The competence of the selectors may mean that it is often a question of luck as to whether the people with the right mix of skills and potential are appointed in the first place. However, those who find that they have emerged through the selection system as managers need to address themselves to the behaviour that will be appropriate, even if those appointing them did not. A further obstacle to appointment on the basis of suitability to the job in the UK has, historically at least, been the importance of social class. According to Scase and Goffee,

> *The 'skills' that have been traditionally, but perhaps erroneously, associated with leadership may be difficult to acquire, if only because they are derived through particular child-rearing patterns, education and class-based experiences. The persistence of such styles results from the tendency for senior managers to recruit successors with similar personal characteristics. Such processes militate against the career opportunities of those from working-class origins, of women and of others who have been unable to acquire the intangible but real personal attributes of class privilege.*

1989: 185–186

The problems that can arise as a result of selecting on the basis of historic performance are satirically and amusingly explained in the book *The Peter Principle* by Peter and Hull (1970). Their observations contain more than a germ of truth. The basic concept explained in the book is that if one looks backward in time instead of forward when selecting, people will rise up through organisational hierarchies until they pass their threshold of competence. Only when that has happened will there be no basis for appointment at a higher level of responsibility. The basic Peter Principle is stated to be that: '*In a hierarchy every employee tends to rise to his (or her) level of incompetence*'. Corollaries are:

- in time, every post tends to be occupied by an employee who is incompetent to carry out its duties;
- work is accomplished by those employees who have not yet reached their level of incompetence (Peter and Hull 1990: 22–24).

The material in chapter 9 on selection gives practical guidance on how to appoint on the basis of 'fit' with the job. It is crucial that the managerial ability or potential is included in selection criteria. It is also important that those undertaking the selection are competent in the techniques of selection, also explained in chapter 9.

TRAINING AND DEVELOPMENT OF MANAGERS

Whilst management training is a key intervention area, the quantity and quality of training development has often been neglected. Historically, managers have often received little management training. Charles Handy maintained that in the UK this had much to do with the amateur tradition:

> *Management, after all, was held by the British to be akin to parenting, a role of great importance for which no training, preparation or qualification was required: the implication being that experience is the only possible teacher and character the only possible qualification.*
>
> 1991: 122

There has been an increase in managers receiving training and a marked trend to including management throughout the world. In Britain there has also been a great expansion in business studies courses, and the annual output of MBA graduates is almost 10,000 (Thomson *et al.* 1997). Management training is also increasingly a core component of vocational university and professional courses. However, increases in the quantity of management training are one thing, ensuring that training is effective is another.

Management training can often be ineffective for a variety of reasons. These include inaccurate diagnosis of needs, poor selection and unsatisfactory training. A particular problem with management training is the need for those receiving the training to integrate what they have learnt with their personal behaviour. Sometimes the adjustments that managers need to make to manage are effectively beyond them. Also in-house training budgets can be amongst the first casualties in organisations seeking to economise. The problems of providing effective management training are considered further in chapter 11.

MONITORING

The fourth key intervention is monitoring. This applies whether a manager is managing others or reviewing their own performance. The good work in trying to ensure accurate role definition, selection, and training and development can easily be undone if there is no effective monitoring. A key feature of any strategy for correcting imbalance in the job is for those likely to experience the problem to be made more aware of it. They may do this for themselves by learning, perhaps on a trial and error basis. However, training and monitoring of performance can help to ensure that people do not have to learn everything the hard way – or even not at all. Unfortunately, if an organisation has too much of a specialist culture, it is particularly likely that those with managerial responsibilities will fail to see the need to monitor and then correct the performance of their subordinates or themselves.

Managers have a responsibility to see that the training and development of themselves and their staff fits into an integrated pattern. These are not activities that can be handled just by training departments or by sending people on courses. Performance management, on-the-job learning, appraisal, coaching and formal training need to be integrated. There is a particular responsibility for bosses to see that those who are given managerial responsibilities are also given help through appraisal, counselling and coaching. This is particularly necessary when people make critical moves up the managerial escalator. So often people are 'thrown in at the deep end' by managers who have not handled the transitional problems properly themselves and who blame subordinates for their shortcomings in a new job. The developmental strategies and techniques mentioned in this section are given more detailed attention in chapter 11.

SUMMARY

✔ The basics of management have been identified as a necessary prelude both to the chapter and the book. The essence of management is that it involves achieving results through others. Most managers gradually acquire managerial responsibility and change, in an escalator-like progression, from being specialists to being the managers of specialists. Most managerial activity is probably undertaken by hybrids (i.e. people who combine specialist and managerial activity). Unfortunately, there is often a conflict between the work that those with managerial responsibilities prefer to do and organisational priorities. Many specialists undertake managerial duties because of the lack of an alternative career structure. There are considerable practicable difficulties preventing organisations arranging specialist career structures.

✔ It is by understanding the above issues that individuals can understand the pressures on them to undertake managerial responsibilities and how they can handle them effectively. From an organisational point of view the four key remedial strategies are:

- the accurate definition of managerial roles,
- effective managerial selection,
- appropriate and adequate management training and development,
- the effective monitoring of those with management responsibilities.

✔ From an individual's point of view it is particularly important to define one's role accurately, plan appropriate training and development, and develop means of self-monitoring.

✔ Having identified the need for the proper definition of managerial roles as the first in this sequence of activities both organisationally and individually, it is appropriate that this forms the subject matter of chapter 2.

SELF-ASSESSMENT QUESTIONS

1. How did Mary Parker Follett define management?

2. Why are people with managerial responsibilities likely to have a specialist background?

3. Why do organisations find it difficult to provide specialist career structures?

4. Why might those with managerial responsibilities neglect them in favour of specialist activity?

5. Where are you on the managerial escalator? Where might you be in five years?

6. What are the four key areas where attention is needed to ensure that those with managerial responsibilities perform effectively?

📖 References

(Works of general interest in the specific references are marked with a star.)

Blackler, Frank and Sheila Shimmin, (1984) *Applying Psychology in Organisations*, Methuen. This paraphrases T. Keenan's (1980) work, which is contained in 'Stress and the Professional Engineer', in C.A. Cooper and J. Marshall (eds), *White-collar and Professional Stress,* Wiley, p.p. 23–24.

Coles, Margaret (1997) 'IT skills shortage stumps recruiters' (report of a survey by Theaker, Monro & Newman, *Sunday Times* appointments section, 16 November).

Commons Select Committee on Culture, Media and the Arts (1997), Chairman Gerald Kaufman, reported in the *Evening Standard*, London, 3 December.

Fayol, Henri, *General and Industrial Management*, revised by Irwin Gray (1988), Pitman.

Graham, Pauline (1998) *Dynamic Managing – The Follett Way*, Professional Publishing.

* Handy, Charles (1991) *The Age of Unreason*, Business Studies Books, 2nd ed.

Lever, D. and Blease, D. (October 1992) 'What Do Primary Headteachers Really Do?' *Educational Studies*.

Local Government Management Board (1993) *Managing Tomorrow*, Panel of Inquiry report.

* Mintzberg, H. (1989) *Mintzberg on Management*, The Free Press.

Mead, R. (1998) *International Management: Cross Cultural Dimensions*, 2nd ed., Blackwell Business.

M. Pedler and T. Boydell (1985) *Managing Yourself*, Fontana.

Laurence, Peter and Raymond Hull, (1970) *The Peter Principle*, Pan. Alternatively, see the Souvenir Press edition, 1969, reissued in 1992.

* Scase, Richard and Robert Goffee (1989) *Reluctant Managers: Their Work and Lifestyles*, Unwin Hyman.

Thomson, *et al.* (1997) *A Portrait of Management Development*, Institute of Management/ Open University Business School.

Watson, Tony J. (1994), *In Search of Management*, International Thomson Business Press.

chapter (two)

Identifying the manager's job

There are case studies and exercises at http://www.thomsonlearning.co.uk (for full details, see the listing at the start of this book).

LEARNING OUTCOMES

By the end of this chapter you will be able to:

● Distinguish between managerial activity and effectiveness

● Define appropriate work objectives

● Prioritise your work using the technique of role set analysis

● Manage your time effectively

● Sequence your work effectively

● Understand basic concepts of strategic planning and its importance for you as a manager

Introduction

It follows from the previous chapter that the first essential requirement for managers is to define their job carefully and accurately. Effectiveness depends upon the accomplishment of appropriate objectives rather than just being busy. Consequently, the methodology of objective setting is considered in this chapter. The technique of role set analysis is also explained. This can be a very effective way of identifying the priorities in a job, and it enables comparisons between model and actual time allocations. The technique can also be used on a departmental or organisational basis. Careful identification of the job is also a necessary foundation for effective time management. The basic elements of time management are explained.

It is not enough for managers to plan just their own work systematically. If this is to be accomplished they also need to help develop a rational framework within which to operate. Consequently, the need for effective strategic planning is also considered.

Activity vs effectiveness

PROACTIVE VS REACTIVE MANAGERS

Managers can fall into two groups: those who define what has to be done, get on with it and then go home; and those who create a flurry of physical activity and seek to justify their positions by the demonstrable effort they put into a job, rather than by the results they achieve. The latter group also tends to be reactive rather than innovative in their responses. The emphasis on effort tends to combine neatly with a reactive 'management by crisis' approach. There can, perhaps, be some of this in most managers but it is still useful to consider the different approaches.

Sometimes attempts at self-justification are a combination of humour, pathos and ineffectiveness. This can involve such managerial games as never going home until the chief executive has left, working overtime for the sake of it, and managers seeking to demonstrate to colleagues that they have worked longer and harder than them. Such stratagems may or may not work in the short term. It may even be that in some cases they are necessary political ploys, given that there will be political activity in any organisation. However, the great danger is that, if managers spend too much time simply justifying themselves, they may actually fail to diagnose what they should be doing and therefore fail to do it. Ultimately, managers are much more likely to be judged by results than by anything else. Activity-centred behaviour is in any case much more likely to spring from incompetence and/or insecurity rather than adroit political behaviour. Activity-centred behaviour is likely to aggravate the position of the manager in the long run rather than ameliorate it.

WHAT IS WORK?

One point that needs to be established at this stage is just how people define work. One view is that it is synonymous with physical activity. This misconception can have most unfortunate consequences, particularly when considering the job of a manager. An example of this misconception can occur when manual workers apply for white-collar jobs. They may find out too late that the mental activity can be far more demanding than the physical activity to which they have been accustomed. The mental activity of a clerk or supervisor simply may not be perceived by a person used to manual work, because such mental activity is not overt.

Example

A staff nurse working in a hospital noticed that a patient had fallen into a coma. She knew that the patient was on a special diet. Consequently, the staff nurse stopped what she was doing to try to puzzle out if the staff who would administer drip feeding to the patient would be aware of his special dietary needs. However, her mental activity was soon interrupted by the ward sister, who brusquely asked her what she thought she was doing just standing there and told her to get on with her work.

The recurring problem is that it is obvious when people are working at a physical level, but less obvious when they are engaged in what is likely to be more crucial mental activity. This is compounded by the fact that you can have staff just standing around day-dreaming and not engaged in mental problem-solving activity. Also, the tradition of judging manual workers by their rate of physical activity is something which can carry over into judgements about whether managers are working or not. It may be that to some extent managers have to respond to this type of pressure by demonstrating physical activity. It may be crucial to their effectiveness, though, that they do not overreact to such pressure. Managers also need to make this distinction when they are assessing, and perhaps pressurising, their own subordinates.

EFFICIENCY AND EFFECTIVENESS

It is necessary to distinguish between the concepts of efficiency and effectiveness at work. Efficiency can be defined as when people are working at or near their total capacity. Effectiveness is a different concept. It involves ensuring that people are doing the right things. Ideally employees should be working both efficiently and effectively. However, the two concepts can work against one another.

Example
> The funding authority for higher education colleges and universities in the UK introduced a requirement that all academic hours be accounted for. A consequence of this was the generation of activity by some academic staff to demonstrate that they were working to capacity regardless of how effective that activity was.

The Identification of the manager's job

Perhaps the first thing that any manager needs to do is actually to identify their job. This should be seen as a continuous process rather than a one-off activity. Organisations have to change in order to survive, and the jobs of managers need to alter accordingly. This is why if a manager has a job description it should be seen as a starting point for identifying the job rather than a definitive unalterable document. Job descriptions, whilst being useful, may leave considerable room for interpretation and will also need updating. They suffer too from the deficiency that they usually do not give a clear indication of the priorities in a job.

There are likely to be other ways in which managers identify and adjust their jobs. They are hardly likely to be left completely to their own devices as there will obviously be instructions from superior managers. In some cases the remit for a manager will be very specific, and the problem will primarily be one of doing the job rather than of identifying what needs to be done. In other cases – perhaps where there is significant internal and external change – the manager may need to spend a considerable amount of time defining and redefining what needs to be done. A further guide may be the way the work was performed by a previous job-holder. It would be folly to ignore the way a previous job-holder had performed a job, but perhaps equally foolish not to review their interpretation of a job nor to allow for changed circumstances.

There can be considerable misunderstanding about just what is done in a job before one gets to the question of what needs to be done. There may be significant surprises when the purpose and content of jobs are actually clarified. Often the job-holder will find that they are undertaking some tasks of which their boss is unaware. It is also likely that there will be some tasks that they are expected to do of which they are unaware. One of the reasons for these misunderstandings is that the boss may have never fully appreciated the demands of the job. Alternatively, they may have appreciated these demands at a previous time, or even have done the job at one stage, but may be basing their view on what was historically done rather than what is subsequently needed.

SHORT-TERM PRESSURES AND LONG-TERM NEEDS

Much of a manager's time will be devoted simply to responding to pressures and demands from other people. The in-tray tends to dominate the daily pattern of activity. Whatever a manager wants to do in the long term is all very well, but often cannot be contemplated until the short-term pressures have been dealt with. However, there are dangers that a manager will simply react to short-term pressures and not think out what they should be doing from a long-term point of view. This problem can be exacerbated by developments in information technology such as e-mail. These can make the manager too available, whether at work or at home. Managers are less likely than before to have personal secretaries to act as filters or, if they still do, it may be possible for people to bypass the secretary electronically. Consequently, there may be an even greater need for managers to consciously prioritise. Managers may also fall into a particular pattern of responding to certain short-term pressures and ignoring others. It is necessary to periodically review such patterns to see if they match the needs of the situation.

Responding to a predetermined selection of short-term issues can become a way of life for some managers. In some cases this may be because of the sheer pressure on a manager, in other cases because they want to avoid certain issues. One problem with this approach is that some of the issues that are left are important; moreover, if the manager thought things out on a long-term basis then some of the short-term pressures might be reduced or eliminated. Managers have to react to some, at least, of the short-term pressures. However, it can be very easy to fall into a pattern of just doing this, with possibly disastrous results on long-term effectiveness. Managers need to compare what they are doing with what they should aim to be doing. This issue is one that managers are not always prepared to face. In a study of the way 160 managers actually performed their jobs, Rosemary Stewart observed:

A fragmented day is often the laziest day; the day that demands the least in terms of mental discipline, though the most in nervous energy. It is easier to pass from one subject to a second when the first requires a difficult or unpalatable decision, or sustained thought. It is easier to respond to each fresh stimulus, to hare after the latest query, than to set an order of priorities and try to keep to it. This, of course, includes knowing when the latest query has priority. It is easier to be a grasshopper jumping from one problem to another, than a beaver chewing away at a tough task.

1988: 13

Stewart's analysis of managerial activity fits with and influenced the work of Mintzberg (1989) whose work was examined in chapter 1. He also found that the behaviour of managers in practice was hectic and fragmented. This led him to challenge the concept of the ordered rational manager.

THE IDENTIFICATION OF OBJECTIVES

As has already been indicated, the reverse of the reactive activity-centred approach of managers is one where objectives are carefully identified and then, hopefully, achieved. A consequential benefit can be that the manager's time is allocated in proportion to the priority of a task. Reactive managers may find, assuming they ever think in these terms, that they have failed to match the time available to the key elements in their jobs. Management writers who have made historically important contributions to this issue include Peter Drucker (1955) and John Humble (1979). Drucker appears to be the first person who used the term 'management by objectives'. Humble developed the idea into a systematic method of management, not just for the individual manager but for the total organisation of the concepts on which it was based. The crucial, and still very relevant, question it invited managers to ask was just why they were doing a particular job or task. It is all too easy to say what one is doing rather than why.

Example

Answering the question 'why?' can produce surprising results. The following *Evening Standard* report, whilst not an example of a managerial job, makes the appropriate point:

> *Night watchmen at Westminster Council House in Marylebone Road protecting the Council's silver plate, cost ratepayers £21,000 last year. Clever economists at the Council now think that the resident caretaker may be able to handle the job alone. They have discovered that the silver was moved elsewhere years ago.*

(1977)

The chief legal officer of a local authority was asked to explain his various activities during an annual appraisal. He described how he sought to minimise payments to claimants against the council. His technique included ignoring claims for liability the first time they were received. He estimated that this would dispose of 20 per cent of claims. If people persisted with their claims he would next send a complicated and threatening letter. He estimated that that would dispose of a further 20 per cent of claims. The remaining 60 per cent of claims would be contested with a view to

CONTINUED OVER ➤

CONTINUED FROM
PREVIOUS PAGE

paying as little as possible as late as possible. The legal officer was then asked by the chief executive *why* he resisted all claims and responded that it was to meet his objective of minimising payments made by the council. The chief executive then made the point that as the council had a responsibility to the local public, there was a case for simply accepting liability with regard to valid claims. The chief legal officer's response was this option had never occurred to him.

The identification of the key tasks that are contained in a job does present some advantages over the conventional type of job description. Job descriptions can, by their length and detail, obscure the key elements in a job. Humble (1979) also advocated that every manager needed to define the six to eight key tasks that needed to be accomplished if the overall job objective was to be achieved. It was argued that if this was done the residual detail in a job would fall into place. The minimum acceptable standards of performance were also specified. These were accompanied by quantitative and qualitative standards including cost limits and time deadlines. It may still be a useful exercise for managers to go through this type of exercise on an individual basis. Such a methodological approach needs to form the basis of performance management, as the essential first step is to have some criteria for judging what performance should be and then measuring it, either on an individual or collective basis. The concept of performance management and its links with appraisal are dealt with in more detail in chapter 10.

The management by objectives approach also has relevance, and in some ways broad similarities, to the establishment of organisational performance indicators. These are increasingly used, especially in the public sector. This has special relevance to the public sector because of the absence of the criterion of profit or loss. As is explained in the next chapter, there is much more emphasis now on ensuring that public services are customer-orientated. Consequently, key criteria are measures of customer satis-faction, e.g., with regard to service response times and the achievement of appropriate quality standards. Total Quality Management (TQM) initiatives also need to start from the basis of clearly defined objectives, and they involve the specification of product and, where appropriate, customer service performance standards. This topic is examined in more detail in the next chapter. Another similar approach is for organisations to produce mission statements. This involves defining the purpose of an organisation, where it plans to go, and the principles that will enable it to achieve its purpose. This may be supplemented by a statement of the organisational core values that underpin the mission statement.

The definition of objectives can present some problems. Key difficulties may be:

- they may not be easily defined;
- they may not lend themselves to quantification;
- they can conflict with one another;
- their relative importance to one another can change;
- organisational objectives may conflict with those of individual employees.

It is particularly important to recognise the potential for conflict between organisational and individual objectives.

A basic reason why management by objectives schemes failed was that they were applied in a simplistic manner. Many managers make the naive assumption that employees will automatically subscribe to the organisational objectives, strategies and priorities that are pronounced by senior management. This is in line with a 'unitarist' view of organisations which assumes that what is good for the corporate whole is good for all the constituent parts. Alan Fox (1965) very lucidly explains how, if one takes the pluralistic view of organisations, one can see that this is not necessarily the case. If, for example, labour-saving economies can be achieved, then those people who are going to be the subject of those economies may say that it will be all very well for those who remain in an organisation, but what about those who are made redundant as a consequence? The concepts of unitary and pluralistic frames of reference are considered in more detail in chapter 14, in the context of employee relations.

Other conflicts may be less obvious and dramatic, but nevertheless important. Staff may not, for example, co-operate in reorganising their work to accommodate new organisational priorities if that conflicts with individual priorities. This means that attempts to focus organisational activity, so that it is more effective, may be limited by the ability of managers to resolve such conflicts. This is particularly difficult if managers, because of their unitarist philosophy, can't see the potential conflict of interests. There may be some opportunity to coerce employees into accepting change, but organisational initiatives usually need active co-operation if they are to succeed, not minimalist grudging acceptance.

Whilst employee involvement is a feature of the TQM approach, other attempts to refocus organisational activity may be attempted with little or no regard on how to win the active co-operation of the staff. Consequently, many of the statements relating to organisational purpose may just be the rhetorical expression of what senior management *hopes* will happen, rather than effective planning tools to ensure that aspirations are actually achieved.

Another technique for identifying the priorities in a job or organisation is that of role set analysis. This technique is explained in the next section. The related concept of strategic planning is explained in the final section of this chapter.

Role set analysis

An alternative or additional technique that may help managers check whether they are using time effectively is role set analysis. The definition of role set used in this chapter is that it is those main activities and/or people that take up, or need to take up, most of a person's working time. Role set analysis involves comparing existing activities with current priorities. It can then though lead to a consideration or reconsideration of what the end objectives of a job should be.

POTENTIAL ADVANTAGES

The technique has five main advantages. These are:

- it is easy to apply;
- it is easy to update;
- it can enable managers to ask searching questions of themselves about their priorities and objectives;
- it can also be used on a work group basis to see if the activities of colleagues need to be adjusted;
- it can also be used on a departmental or organisational basis to review priorities with regard to resource allocation.

EXPLANATION OF THE TECHNIQUE

Role set analysis involves using a market research approach to one's job. The raw data consists of the expectations of the main individuals and interest groups with whom one has to interact. Instead of identifying one's job by asking 'what should I be doing?' the starting point is to ask 'what do others expect of me?'

In order to do that one first of all has to identify just what the main elements in the role set are. The process of identifying the expectations of the members in the role set may be undertaken by analysing data already available and, where appropriate, actually consulting with people about what the expectations are. The next stage is to synthesise this raw data, and the often conflicting pressures, into a coherent form. This is done by presenting the information in chart form, as shown in Figure 2.1.

The key activities, people and groups with whom a manager has to work must be identified. The chart needs to indicate the volume of work that is appropriate for each constituent part and also the priorities. It needs to be remembered that there may be some particularly influential members of the role set with whom contact is infrequent but very important. The diagram should be drawn so that the more important members of the role set are located closer to the person at the centre.

The next step is to see that the time and priority allocated to the elements in the role set are in line with what is actually needed. To do this effectively it is best for the person concerned to keep a diary of how they really spend their time over a few representative days. The actual time allocation to the individuals and groups in the role set can then be compared with what is considered desirable (see specimen figures in Figure 2.1).

Actual time spent is shown as a percentage with the model time given in accompanying brackets. Alternatively, time can be shown in hours and minutes. This enables planned reductions or increases in the total working time to be shown. The other numbers represent the rank order of importance of the individuals, groups or activities.

The company featured in Figure 2.1. employed 24 full-time and 30 part-time staff. The top priority was allocated by the director concerned jointly to accounts managers and company accounts. The role set analysis diagram immediately highlighted key issues. One was the lack of time devoted to strategic planning by board members. It emerged that there were unresolved difficult and controversial policy decisions. However, it was all too easy for the full-time board members in particular to maintain that pressure of work prevented them from addressing these issues. The small size of the board (the three directors in the chart and a non-executive director), and familiarity of the group, also meant that there was a lack of structure and focus for policy discussions when they did occur. This gave rise to the suggestion that the size of the group be widened when strategic planning issues were considered.

Another related key issue was the overload of the job-holder. It also demonstrated the dependence of the organisation on the director's skills, health and willingness to stay with the organisation. Immediate plans were made to reduce his workload by promoting one of the accounts managers to supervise the others. Other immediate plans were that he use the allocated 9 per cent slack time for emergencies and creative thinking and that he work fewer hours. Long-term plans were made to appoint a director of new business and to promote the production manager to become production director. Another issue addressed by the analysis was the lack of secretarial and administrative staff. The director was satisfied that they were not necessary because of the availability of word processors and other information technology. He was also satisfied that it was inappropriate to engage a full-time accountant as the data processing of accounts, use of accountancy computer packages and occasional use of an outside accountant meant that accounts were cost-effectively handled in-house (Rees 1997).

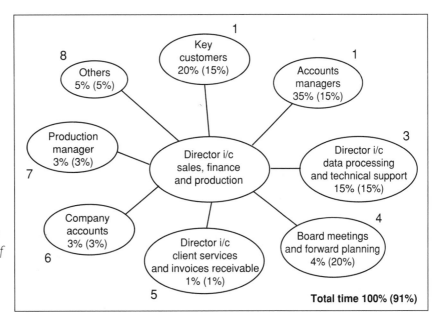

FIGURE 2.1 *Role set analysis for the director in charge of sales, finance and production in a marketing services organisation*

REASONS FOR POOR TIME ALLOCATION

There are many reasons why managers fail to identify their priorities and time allocations accurately. Role set analysis rapidly reveals how time can be used more effectively. Reasons for poor use of time may be:

- accessibility: some people may be both physically and psychologically more accessible than others. There is a danger of ignoring the needs of those who are not so easily available. Managers in turn may be too accessible to some who may take up more time with them than they should;

- congeniality: it is natural for people to want to spend time with those whose company they enjoy and who share the same values. If this is overdone, however, the activities of individual units within an organisation may become lopsided and not integrate well with overall organisational objectives;

- conflict: people vary in their ability to handle conflict. Most want to avoid it. However, it is often important to air differences of opinion to see if constructive solutions can be found. It may also be important to engage in some maintenance behaviour with colleagues where conflict is particularly likely. This may necessitate talking about non-contentious issues and, if appropriate, social issues, so that the relationship is maintained and, if possible, improved. This may help to preserve the working relationship when it is put under pressure by future conflict;

- work preferences: people may also want to concentrate on what they are good and confident at. The tendency for managers with a specialist background to spend too much time on their former specialism was examined at length in chapter 1. When students study for exams they may need to concentrate most on the subjects where they are weakest, but where the potential for improvement is greatest, rather than on the subjects they like the most;

- competence: some important tasks may be very demanding. It is important that people are carefully selected and developed to handle managerial responsibilities in particular;

- changing priorities: sometimes people are locked into historic priorities. Shifts in organisational priorities are not always formally announced. Managers need to examine the external pressures on an organisation in particular and to develop a 'feel' as to when new priorities have emerged.

In estimating the amount of time and attention that other individuals or groups require, it is necessary to remember that one can allocate too much time, as well as too little. Subordinates can feel over-supervised, and those in senior positions may not want to spend too much time with subordinate managers. However, having said this, it is obviously potentially damaging to spend less time with one's boss than they deem appropriate. It is also necessary to consider what time one needs for oneself, particularly for reflective thought. Diary analyses by managers usually reveal that it is very difficult for them to arrange periods when they can engage in concentrated work or reflective thought without interruption. Such time may, however, be essential if one is to do long-term planning. Appropriate refinements to the role set diagram are to allow a percentage of time for oneself as well as for those one occasionally interacts with who can be classified in the diagram as 'others'.

JOB STRUCTURE

Amongst the benefits that can be obtained from role set analysis is that it may show whether or not a job is viable as currently structured. There may be so many individuals and groups the manager has to interact with that the job may be impossible. Alternatively, the manager may be tackling their job in an inappropriate way. One example of this was the manager who, having used this technique, revealed that he was dealing directly with his subordinate's subordinates instead of just with his own subordinates!

Whether problems are organisational or of the manager's own making there may also be health implications if the manager has a pattern of interaction which is just too much to cope with.

Example

On a management development workshop one participant revealed that he suffered from angina. His role set analysis demonstrated that he was grossly overloaded and that his part of the organisation needed restructuring – a factor which cannot have helped his health problems and may have even precipitated them.

INDIVIDUAL PRIORITIES

A direct way in which individual managers can identify priorities is to ask themselves who is in the position to do them the greatest damage. The leader of an architectural group, when asked to do a role set analysis on this basis, likened it to the theory of damage limitation. The value of doing this is to see that those who can do the greatest damage are on top of the list in getting their share of the time. As will shortly be explained, it is also of value in working out what to do if one comes under conflicting pressures.

Alternatively, the question can be asked 'who can help the manager most?' and time allocated accordingly, though it is to be hoped that this approach is not used too opportunistically.

Establishing the order of importance in the role set is not always that simple. The hierarchy of importance is not always obvious in matrix structures, for agency workers, and with regard to important suppliers or other 'stakeholders'. It may not even be obvious in conventional organisations with a hierarchical structure. It is not the most senior person in an organisation who is necessarily the first in importance in one's role set. The view senior people have of you may well be important, but it is necessary to work out whose word they take into account when forming their opinion of you.

Example

One training officer gave the example of how he mistakenly thought the most important member of his role set was the managing director of a company he once worked for. The training officer had numerous differences of opinion with his immediate boss and sought to overcome the bad working relationship by going over the head of his boss, the company secretary, to the managing director. The company secretary became aware of this and as a counter-measure started giving bad reports about the training officer to the managing director. Consequently, the more the training officer went to the managing director the greater the number of bad reports there were of him. The managing director, faced with a choice, understandably preferred to accept the view of the more strategically placed company secretary. Ideally, of course, he should not have allowed the training officer to bypass the company secretary, but that is what actually happened. Eventually the training officer, prompted by good advice from other colleagues, came to realise that the most important person in his role set was the company secretary. In the end he did what he should have done in the first place in his particular case which was to work on improving his relationship with his immediate boss.

It isn't just people of high status who may be in a position to inflict 'damage' on a manager. Often people in low-status positions, but who control important and perhaps scarce services, can do the same. So too may those who control access to important information or who act as 'gatekeepers' to senior managers. Informal members of role sets may also need to be identified, assessed and handled in terms of their importance.

Example

A failure to give sufficient importance to an informal member of the role set allegedly contributed to the enforced resignation of President Reagan's chief of staff, Donald Regan, in 1987. The informal member of the role set was the president's wife, Nancy Reagan, and press reports suggested that on one occasion Donald Regan 'put the phone down on her'. It was also suggested that Donald Regan relied too much on his relationship with the president and not enough on the other powerful political figures in the role set. The other members may not have been individually as important as the president but collectively their influence was considerable, especially if it was reinforced by the views of Nancy Reagan (Regan, 1988). The extent to which these reports are true or untrue is unimportant as far as the basic point is concerned: the need for careful identification of the role set and appropriate responses based on that analysis.

It is also necessary to distinguish between short- and long-term aims in priorities.

Example

A freelance TV producer confessed that he only understood the need to identify long-term priorities after conducting a role set analysis in a management development workshop. He explained that on a recent assignment he had let the executive producer have all the contact with the broadcaster on whom his future contracts depended. Partly as a result of that he was now out of work.

ORGANISATIONAL PRIORITIES

The emphasis in this section has so far mainly been about working out appropriate time allocations on an individual basis. Role set analysis can also be used to consider how resources should be allocated on an organisational basis. Managers can also review their budget distribution in this way.

Example

An interesting example of establishing organisational priorities is the technique of crime-screening. This is a method of allocating resources for criminal investigative work that is sometimes formalised into a 'points system' by police forces. Offences that might realistically lead to successful detection and conviction are allocated resources in preference to cases where this is less likely. The amount of available evidence is considered particularly important in allocating points. Consequently, aspects such as the quality of the description of a person, the noting of a car number or the possibility of forensic evidence could be crucial in determining whether a crime is investigated or not. The severity of the crime is another important criterion as is the estimate of public priorities. Crimes with a low number of points might just be handled on the phone. The technique can also be used to review the allocation of resources between crime detection and crime prevention. The same type of issue arises with medical work in trying to strike the right balance between health cure and health care.

INFORMATION AND EVALUATION

There are many ways in which information can be collected about role sets. The technique can be a very useful device for getting people to talk about common problems during in-house management workshops. If syndicates of managers doing similar jobs are arranged, they can critically cross-examine one another about the appropriateness of one another's role set analysis. Workshops can provide a climate in which basic issues, which would not otherwise be discussed, are brought out into the open. The technique of role set analysis can have a powerful catalytic effect in this context. Another method of collecting information is for a manager to take a market research approach and ask colleagues just what their expectations are. Care has to be taken, however, about who is approached and the manner of the approach. One of the potential problems is that expectations are aroused which cannot be met. As a minimum, though, one should reflect on just what the expectations of you are by the other individuals and groups in your role set. This may reveal a variety of misunderstandings about what you expect from others and what they expect from you.

What also may be revealed by role set analysis is that some of the expectations are contradictory. This may happen if the manager is given incompatible tasks or if the sheer volume of work they are expected to do is unrealistic. The most practical way of handling such a dilemma is often for managers to try to gauge what the real priorities are amongst the welter of instructions they are given. They also need to be sensitive to changes in organisational priorities. Those senior to a manager may be reluctant to admit that the various expectations are in conflict.

The reality may be that the individual manager has to work out what the real priorities are at a given time. To do this the manager may need to judge just what the priorities are with others in the role set and the ways in which they may be changing. In an ideal world one would only work in organisations where job demands were compatible and all legitimate expectations could be met. However, as we live in an imperfect world there needs to be a method of resolving contradictory pressures. One should also recognise that when priorities change it is often politically too difficult for policymakers to say that a certain priority has been abandoned or even downgraded. The most one may get is an admission that a certain objective has been 'put on the back burner'. However, managers ignore these shifts in priority at their peril and need to adjust their pattern of activity to a new scale of priorities.

STRESS MANAGEMENT

The pressures for competitiveness in the private sector and for economy in the public sector are putting managers under increasing stress. Consequently, they usually cannot do all that is expected of them and have to develop some basis for deciding how their own time and the resources under their control are allocated. If everything cannot be done, it seems far more logical to consciously and systematically prioritise rather than do things on a random basis. Individual survival and organisational effectiveness are both likely to be served by conscious prioritisation. The best way of coping with managerial stress is to try and reduce it rather than simply deal with the symptoms. Techniques of prioritisation can be enormously useful in this context and also in relieving managers of guilt feelings about not meeting what may be impossible demands.

The issue of managerial stress is dealt with further in chapter 6, and the organisational problems caused by the mismatch between expectations and resources in the public sector in chapter 3. The issue of individual prioritisation is dealt with further in the next section of this chapter.

INDIVIDUAL INTERPRETATION AND APPLICATION

What has been explained is a progressively more sophisticated method of gathering data and developing insights about how to identify one's job. After all this has been done, it is up to the manager to evaluate and synthesise the material and stamp their own personality on their job. There is more to identifying a job than working out what those in strategic positions want of you, but it is prudent to take that into account before and then adding the essential ingredient – one's own personality.

The concept of role set analysis also stresses the interdependence of managers with others. The importance of the manager's role in creating and energising teams is examined in the context of organic structures in chapter 3, with regard to managerial style in chapter 4 and in handling meetings in chapter 16.

Time management

When the overall objectives, key tasks and role set have been clarified it may then be appropriate for a manager to consider how effectively their time is used. One view of the manager's job is that the only real resource is their time. There appear to be enormous variations in the ways in which managers either use their time effectively or waste it. Consequently, this topic deserves specific attention. Issues of particular importance are:

- identification of priorities,
- logical sequencing of work,
- avoidance of fatigue,
- need for managers to avoid wasting other people's time.

IDENTIFYING PRIORITIES

The reactive or 'grasshopper' manager's time management may be ineffective by failing to identify the priorities in their job. Perhaps the worst way of prioritising work is to deal with the last request first, whether it be made in person or be the item just received in the in-tray. Sadly, there are many examples of people who do this regularly. The priorities of a job need to be established quite consciously. To do this it may be necessary to write them down and then either to rank the priorities over a particular time period or to group them into bands of varying urgency. Even well organised managers find that they have to react to short-term crises and pressures, but they should have as a constant reference point a clear grasp of the priority issues that are accumulating and which merit attention.

Finding the time to think about the job may itself constitute a problem, particularly for managers who are already heavily involved in 'fire-fighting' activities. However, unless they somehow find the time to think their way through to a more rational pattern of activity, managers are unlikely to be effective. One of the problems in organisations is that managers find that they have to cope with so many interruptions that it is difficult to find time to think in a concentrated and systematic way about the job. It may be necessary to do this away from one's normal place of work or to use a secretary or other person as a screen to prevent interruptions. It may also be necessary to have a clear idea of who those people are who make unproductive claims on one's time with a view to reducing the time spent with them. It is one of the ironies of organisational life that so often the people with the most time to waste are those who insist on spending long periods telling you how busy they are! In such cases it may be particularly necessary to tell people at the start of a discussion how much time you have available for them.

Establishing the priorities in a job may well involve a careful look at the conflict between what a manager prefers to do and what they actually need to do. This is a necessarily recurring issue in this book. The consequences of inappropriate prioritisation can in some cases even threaten the survival of an organisation.

Example

One company was threatened with a hostile takeover. Unfortunately the senior executive responsible for objecting to this failed to turn up at the Government Takeover Panel meeting that could have blocked the change. Consequently, the takeover was approved without opposition!

The personnel policies of organisations unfortunately do not always help people take a balanced approach in their job.

Example

In a local authority building department all the charge-hand craftworkers were upgraded to be general trades supervisors. The idea was sound enough in principle – which was to avoid having a charge-hand craftworker on every site where craftworkers of that particular trade were working. Unfortunately, the idea was poorly implemented. There was no attempt to select who should be upgraded and who should not. Neither was there any attempt to train the newly appointed general trades supervisors, either in management or in the technical aspects of the new trades that were nominally under their control. Consequently, most of the newly appointed general trades supervisors were too frightened to supervise craftworkers in trades other than their own. This meant that, for example, the person who had previously been a charge-hand bricklayer spent nearly all their time with the bricklayers and rarely tried to supervise the craftworkers in the other groups, such as the electricians, plumbers and carpenters.

SEQUENCING WORK

Two interrelated issues should particularly influence the order in which work is done. One is the priority of importance and the other is the logical sequence. Not all issues need immediate attention. The following checklist may help in deciding work sequence.

- What needs to be done urgently? This can include minor tasks that have to be completed by an imminent deadline.
- What needs to be done to enable other people to get on with their job?
- What needs to be done when it is convenient, or within a non-urgent time-span?
- What can't be done until activities by others have been completed? Such work may be put in a pending tray, though a follow-up system may be necessary to monitor the progress of other people involved in the task.

- Information that is received but which requires no action.
- Issues that can simply be ignored.

Examples

A domestic example, which illustrates the need for work sequencing and its relationship to priorities is that it is more appropriate for people pressured for time in the morning to get dressed before they eat breakfast. It is much more practicable to run down the road for the train fully clothed but with breakfast unfinished rather than the other way around!

The need for careful sequencing is further illustrated by the following case of two delivery drivers working for the same firm. One driver would look at the first address and drive off and then look at the next address and so on. In the course of a day he was likely to retrace his route several times. The other driver would spend about an hour each morning planning his route so that, although he started his deliveries later, he covered his route with the minimum mileage.

Some work may need reflective thought before it is finalised. It is not just the speed at which issues are dealt with that is important, but also the quality of any decisions. The thought may not even need to be conscious, as ideas can suddenly fit into place after subconscious mental activity. Students can also find this when answering examination questions. A difficult question that is put on one side, whilst an easier one is tackled, may appear much simpler when it is read for the second time a while later. However, the manager needs to recognise the difference between procrastination and reflecting on difficult issues so that an appropriate decision is eventually taken.

Another issue is whether tasks are undertaken consecutively or simultaneously. The answer to this may depend on both personality and national culture. Monochronics may prefer to undertake tasks in a linear manner until they are completed. Polychronics often prefer to undertake a number of tasks simultaneously. Problems can arise when these two patterns clash. This can arise, for example, if a polychronic is busily engaged on a task and a monochronic wants something else done immediately. Hall (1987) maintains that these patterns correlate with national culture – for instance, mono-chronic work patterns are more common in Nordic countries than elsewhere.

CRITICAL PATH ANALYSIS

The concept of logical work sequencing can be developed further by the use of critical path analysis. This is of particular use in planning and controlling tasks where a number of activities need to be carried out simultaneously. The technique has been developed particularly for use on construction projects and in production planning. Its benefits did not live up to early expectations because of the unforeseen variables, failures in communication and competing agendas that can affect any project and frustrate mechanistic planning systems. If used carefully, however, critical path analysis often is a powerful planning tool and can also be of value for individual work planning. It is often used intuitively by people who have never heard of the term 'critical path analysis', for example, when the Sunday joint is put to roast whilst the rest of the dinner is prepared. Alternative titles for the same concept are 'network planning' and 'network analysis'.

An example of how critical path analysis can be used in launching a new product is shown in Figure 2.2. One assumes that the starting point is the announcement and launch of the new product, the market research and design having been previously undertaken. The packaging would then be designed and the dealers contacted at the same time to prepare them for the new product. When the packaging is designed it can then be ordered from the supplier. The publicity material can then be designed (not before, as one would want to see the packaged product first). When the packaging is received and orders received from the dealers the product can be delivered. A further step in the planning can be to show the time period during which each step of the process needs to be completed. Although the example is simple, the written explanation is complicated and difficult to follow. In contrast, the diagram is very clear (Lockyer 1991).

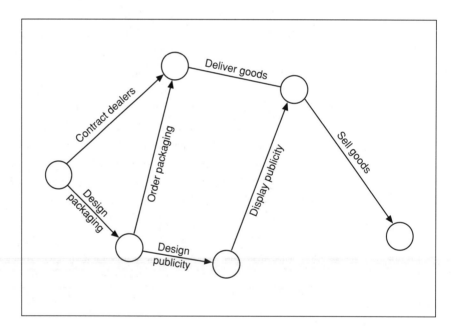

FIGURE 2.2 *Critical path analysis: launching a new product*

FATIGUE

It is also necessary for managers to take into account their own physical limitations in planning their workload. Individuals vary considerably in their propensity to fatigue, and fatigue also depends on the commitments a manager has outside the workplace. It can be very tempting to compare oneself to a person with an unusually high degree of energy, but the consequences may be disastrous if the workload is planned on an over-optimistic assessment of what one's physical capabilities really are. If this happens it seems likely that in the long term the quality and rate of work will suffer and the likelihood of illness increase.

RESEARCH EVIDENCE

Research studies demonstrate that long hours of work for manual workers can be counter-productive, and it would seem a common sense step to assume that the same pattern would affect managers.

Examples

Maier (1955a) reports on an interesting British Medical Research Council study of the effects of an increase in the working week in 1940 after the Dunkirk evacuation. Under the pressure of the World War II emergency, England increased the hours of its work-week. Before Dunkirk, the work-week was 56 hours; after Dunkirk it was increased to an average of 69.5 hours in the war industries. The first effect of this increase was a 1 per cent rise in production, but then production declined, and sickness, absenteeism, and accidents increased. By the end of a couple of months, the average work-week was 68.5 hours, but the average amount of time actually worked was only 51 hours, as compared with the period before Dunkirk when the average time was 53 hours. As a result, production was 12 per cent below that preceding Dunkirk. Six months later, the shorter week was restored, with the result that production steadily rose to a higher point than ever before.

Maier (1955b) also reports on Angela Masso's studies on fatigue. The results of these studies may have considerable implications for the way people, including managers, pace themselves at work.

One study on fatigue concerned the ability of a person to move a 6kg weight attached to a free finger by a length of string. It emerged that if the movement was repeated every two seconds an individual would cease to be able to lift the weight at all after about a minute. However, if the movement was only repeated every 16 seconds the weight could be raised and lowered almost indefinitely.

A particular point that needs stressing is that recovery time from fatigue tends to increase exponentially with the amount of the fatigue. What this means is that when practicable, one should rest as soon as there are signs of fatigue, otherwise recovery can take much longer. Performance may be unduly affected if one continues working once there are signs of fatigue.

What is crucial is that people take rest breaks before they get too tired. If they don't, recovery time may be much longer and the pace and quality of work significantly lower when they do resume.

SOCIAL NEEDS

It is also necessary to recognise that people may need to meet social as well as work needs when they are doing their job. An over-planned approach to the job may be too inflexible, and it can also make life dreadfully dull. Additionally, it may be necessary to spend some time maintaining working relationships by a certain amount of social conversation. There are obviously limits to the extent to which this should be done, but it could be foolish to ignore this aspect. Managers also need to pace themselves at work, and it may be necessary to have some periods in the working day when they relax a little. However, relaxation needs to be done in such a way that it does not interrupt those who are working effectively. The related issue of monotony at work is considered in chapter 6 on motivation.

SAVING OTHER PEOPLE'S TIME

Managers also need to help others use their time productively, as well as organising their own time management. This can, for example, mean careful preparation for discussions and interviews so other people's time is not wasted. Prior preparation is particularly important if one has to chair a meeting, as will be explained in more detail in chapter 16 on meetings and chairing.

Example

At a local government body 23 people from different parts of London were called to a meeting that had to be aborted because it had not been properly planned.

Strategic planning

NEED FOR PLANNING

The concepts explained so far in this chapter have focused mainly on how the individual manager can do their own job more effectively over a relatively short-term period. However, managers also need to take a long-term and corporate perspective. This inevitably means co-operating with other managers in order to anticipate and, where appropriate, shape the future. If an individual manager can help develop rational long-term policies, this can make their own job easier to perform and may also lead to improvements in other parts of an organisation that are even more important. It has already been explained how the techniques of setting objectives and role set analysis can be applied on a departmental or organisational basis as well as on an individual basis.

The essence of strategic planning is that it is the broad means of achieving overall objectives. However, it may necessitate careful thought about the nature of the organisational objectives. People in commercial organisations often take the view that they are in business to make a particular product or deliver a particular service when the reality is that their overall aim may need to be to optimise their return on capital investment. Although the literature on this topic is mainly based on the private sector, the concepts can and need to be adapted for use in the public sector. There the emphasis is likely to be on the need to provide cost-effective services in a changing market.

PLANNING MECHANISMS

Basic concepts and issues involved in strategic planning need to be explained. Even though most managers will not be involved in board level planning, long-term and strategic planning is also needed at a departmental level. For this to be done, it is necessary to involve the key decision-makers.

Experience with strategic planning groups made up of specialists outside the main power structure suggests that they are likely to fail because they do not have the 'clout' or often even the information and expertise with which to fashion long-term policies. The problem that has to be overcome with the key decision-makers is that they are invariably busy people. To complicate matters, such people may be reluctant to commit themselves to long-term strategies, particularly if there are sectional rivalries. Also, even if senior people are given responsibility for strategic planning, if they become distanced from operational reality, their plans may prove to be unrealistic.

The problem of creating time for such strategic planning with key, yet busy, people can be reduced by having a chair who is under less pressure and by the provision of specialist reports for consideration at corporate or long-term planning meetings. It can be inappropriate to include long-term planning with the business discussed at ordinary departmental or board meetings, as this inevitably leads to the short-term issues crowding out the long-term ones. In practice, often the only long-term planning that takes place is that associated with the annual financial budget.

Strategic planning can be a top-down or bottom-up process. In the former, the attempt is made to change the organisation in line with a centrally conceived master plan. With bottom-up planning, information is sought from the grassroots to help shape evolutionary development. In practice, there usually needs to be a fusing of these two approaches. Ideally, a long-term plan will be established and short-term plans integrated with it. This may involve 'gap analysis' to establish what has to be done to bring an organisation's activities into line with that which is planned. Any long-term plan will, however, need continuous adjustment, especially in turbulent environments (Johnson and Scholes 1999).

The increasing pace of change has caused a reaction against detailed centralised planning because such a process can be too cumbersome to react quickly and effectively. Now, the emphasis is much more on semi-autonomous business units which can react more quickly. Charles Handy (1994) has argued strongly for this 'federal' concept and for the associated idea of 'subsidiarity' of business in organisation. This involves decisions only being taken at the centre that cannot be sensibly taken lower down.

However, it is necessary to guard against fragmentation and the loss of a coherent organisational culture and purpose. Conversely, business units can be set up that are subject to such detailed central control that there is no real delegation. The more that strategic planning is pushed downwards, the greater the opportunity for individual managers to get involved in the process and to take initiatives. The impact of globalisation and information technology on organisation structure and the issue of semi-autonomous business units are considered in the next chapter.

FACTORS TO CONSIDER

In considering strategic planning, it is necessary to identify what the potential changes are in both the external and internal environments. Changes may be imposed on an organisation from outside, but opportunities for shaping the future through internal developments, such as product improvement, may also exist. It may be appropriate to establish what degrees of freedom are open to a unit or organisation in planning its future and what will happen if no positive decisions are taken. The lead time needed to alter activities must also be identified. It may also be useful to identify what an organisation's primary activity should be and to carry out an audit of its main strengths and weaknesses.

Another issue is the danger of identifying the future simply by extrapolating from the past. To paraphrase Marshall McLuhan (1997), it can be foolish to drive into the future looking in the rearview mirror. Perhaps Henry Ford had a point when he declared that 'history is bunk' – as that was the case with the way he revolutionised the car industry.

Example

The tendency for people to cling to fundamentally wrong assumptions based on experience elsewhere is also referred to by Bryson (2000: 29–30). He explains how successive early explorers in Australia dragged boats into the arid interior, in one case for 3000 miles, on the false assumption that they would encounter vast internal water systems.

It may be necessary to pay attention to what options are being created by developments in information technology in particular as well as market changes. A further issue is the need to identify the main ways in which an organisation is, or is likely to become, at risk. According to Porter (1998) the key need is to get the market positioning right and the organisational capacity to sustain competitive advantage. One simple model that incorporates some of these key issues is the SWOT analysis. The factors to be analysed are:

Internal
- Strengths
- Weaknesses

External
- Opportunities
- Threats.

Example

One UK conglomerate, centred on the brewing industry but with interests in many other areas, found that when they analysed the reasons for sometimes quite astonishing turn-arounds in the performance of subsidiary companies, they found that the key variable was the managerial talent that had been injected into these companies.

At whatever level strategic planning is undertaken the process needs to be reasonably broadly based – even if the lesson has been learned that one should avoid centralised prescriptive approaches that are too detailed. Many corporate plans revolve just around the financial and marketing dimensions. The whole move to strategic human resource planning, explained in more detail in chapter 14, necessitates considering the human resource dimension *before* and not after strategies are determined.

REALISTIC GOALS

One of the dangers in strategic planning is that unrealistic goals may be set. Although, there may be occasions when the circumstances are right to try and bridge the gap between heroic goals and existing resources, this is not always the case (Hamel and Prahalad, 1989). Whilst organisational capability can be developed, structures changed and cultures altered, there are limits to the change that is achievable. Also, technological achievements can be copied by competitors. What may be key is the web of working relationships within or even outside an organisation and its stock of intellectual capital. Incremental improvement may sometimes be the best option.

Example

One national social work charity embarked on an ambitious programme of expansion by taking over related charitable organisations. They ignored the legal obligations with regard to the employment rights of the employees they acquired and also lacked managerial capability. It was not long before the organisation ran into financial difficulties.

QUANTIFIABLE VS INTANGIBLE FACTORS

There is a great danger in planning processes that revolve too much around that which is relatively easily quantified. Denis Healey learned this lesson when he was chancellor of the exchequer. Admittedly, he was involved in planning on a macro scale, but his reflections are worth remembering with regard to smaller scale planning:

Economics has acquired a spurious respectability through the use of numbers, which appear to many people, like my old friend McNamara (Head of the World Bank), much more meaningful than mere adjectives or adverbs, because they appear to be precise and unambiguous. Unfortunately, I soon discovered that the most important numbers were nearly always wrong.

1990: 379–80

Denis Healey was even more forthright in commenting on the dangers of an over-reliance on numbers with regard to defence planning. Referring to an earlier stage in his career when he was defence secretary in the UK and Robert McNamara was his counterpart in the USA, and whilst acknowledging what he had learned from McNamara about the control of defence projects, he said:

> *McNamara, like the whizz-kids who had so much influence on his strategic thinking, demonstrated what I call the 'lamp-post fallacy' in its purest form. Late one night a policeman found a man on his knees under a lamp-post. 'What are you doing?' he asked. 'I dropped my keys at the bottom of the street,' was the reply. 'But that is a hundred yards away. Why are you looking here?' 'Because there's no light at the bottom of the street.'*

1990: 307

Denis Healey's concerns about the limitations and dangers of 'rational', numerically orientated strategic plans echo the concerns of the American consultants and writers Peters and Waterman whose views are explained and examined in the next chapter in the section on theories of organisations.

SUMMARY

✔ The importance of identifying realistic job objectives has been stressed in this chapter. Often managers justify themselves by the amount of work they do rather than the results they achieve. Objective setting can be a means of both targeting their activity and assessing their performance. There are many reasons why managers may get the balance of their job wrong.

✔ The technique of role set analysis was explained in detail because of its potential to help people organise their work effectively. It can be an easy and effective way of distinguishing between what managers are doing and what they should be doing. Role set analysis can also help managers prioritise, which will be particularly necessary if they are overworked. If that is the case, it is better that they consciously decide what is done and what is not done rather than engage in random prioritisation which can lead to important tasks being neglected. Managers also need to distinguish between short-term and long-term objectives. They need to create some time for reflective thought about the future.

✔ Time management was also explained. It includes sequencing work in a logical way. Some account also should be taken of social needs at work. Working too hard can be counter-productive because of the danger of cumulative fatigue.

✔ The need for managers to try and influence the framework in which they operate was explained. Managers should get involved in strategic planning at whatever level possible. This may help prevent their good work being undermined either by non-existent or faulty planning elsewhere. Their involvement may also be able to make overall strategic planning more effective.

SELF-ASSESSMENT QUESTIONS

1. How would you distinguish between managerial activity and managerial effectiveness?

2. Define appropriate work objectives either for yourself or for another person.

3. What are the advantages that role set analysis can have over other methods of identifying work content and priorities?

4. What are the essential elements of effective time management?

5. How would you ensure that you have sequenced your work logically?

6. Why might managers at all levels need to take an interest in strategic planning?

 References

(Works of general interest in the specific references are marked with a star.)

Bryson, Bill (2000) *Down Under*, Doubleday.

Drucker, Peter F. (1955) *Practice of Management*, Heinemann.

Evening Standard, 1 January 1977, London.

Hall, E.T. (1987) *Hidden Differences*, Anchor Press/Doubleday.

Hamel, G and C.K. Prahalad (1989) 'Strategic Intent', *Harvard Business Review*, May/June.

* Handy, Charles (1994) *The Empty Raincoat*, Hutchinson.

Healey, Denis (1990) *The Time of My Life*, Penguin.

Humble, John (1979) *Management by Objectives in Action*, McGraw-Hill in association with the British Institute of Management.

* Johnson, Gerry and Kevan Scholes (1999) *Exploring Corporate Strategy*, 5th ed., Prentice Hall Europe.

Lockyer, Keith and James Gordon (1991) *Critical Path Analysis and Other Project Network Techniques*, 5th ed., Pitman.

McLuhan, Marshall (1997) *Forward Through the Rearview Mirror*, MIT Press.

Maier, Norman, R.F. (1955) *Psychology in Industry*, Harrap, (a) p. 447, (b) p.p. 425–428.

Mintzberg, H. (1989) *Mintzberg on Management*, The Free Press.

* Porter, Michael (1998) *The Competitive Advantage of Nations*, 2nd ed., MacMillan.

Rees, W. David, (1997) 'Managerial Stress – Dealing With Causes, Not the Symptoms', *Industrial and Commercial Training*, 29(2): 25–30.

Regan, Donald T. (1988) *For The Record*, Arrow.

Royal Commission on Trade Unions and Employers' Associations/Alan Fox (1965), Industrial Sociology and Industrial Relations, research paper no. 3, HMSO.

* Stewart, Rosemary (1988) *Managers and Their Jobs*, 2nd ed., Macmillan.

chapter (three)

The manager and the organisation

There are case studies and exercises at
http://www.thomsonlearning.co.uk
(for full details, see the listing at the
start of this book).

LEARNING OUTCOMES

By the end of this chapter you will be able to:

● Understand the relevance of developments in organisational theory and practice to your own situation

● Identify the key variables that shape the structure and manner in which organisations operate, including information technology

● Identify the causes of the lack of effective integration of organisational activity and strategies for dealing with this

● Distinguish between role and personality behaviour in organisations

● Understand the key concepts involved in quality management schemes

● Identify differences and similarities between the private and public sectors

Introduction

In this chapter the organisational context in which those with managerial responsi-bilities have to work is examined. Managers need to appreciate this context and the way in which organisations need to establish structures to fit with the circumstances in which they have to operate. They may also need to help see that organisational structures and operational methods are adapted to take account of changed circumstances. Historical and recent theories of organisation are explained. Particular attention is paid to the impact of globalisation and technology and the development of more flexible organisational structures. Other key variables examined include the size of organisations, the need to identify the critical function and national culture. The problems of achieving effective integration of organisational activity are considered and strategies suggested for dealing with this issue. The need to distinguish between role and personality behaviour is also included. Innovations in the area of quality management and their popularity are such that a section has been devoted to this topic. General developments in the private and public sectors are covered and the similarities and differences between these two sectors considered.

Theories of organisation

SCIENTIFIC AND CLASSICAL MANAGEMENT SCHOOLS

The historical approach to management was that it consisted of a set of principles which were capable of definition and universal application. This was the approach of writers such as F. W. Taylor (1972, first published 1911) and Henri Fayol (1916). Taylor, along with Gantt and the Gilbreths, was a member of the Scientific Management School which conceptually overlapped with the classical management theorists, including Fayol. Those in the scientific management school concentrated on the organisation of manual work, production planning and time and motion study. Taylor advocated the systematic analysis of work and for management to take over decision-making about which methods of work were used, based on the principle that the average worker preferred a well-defined task and clear-cut standards.

The classical theorists developed the ideas of the scientific management theorists into a framework of organisational principles. The collective view of the classical theorists was that work could be so organised that the objectives of organisations could be accomplished with great efficiency. Organisations were viewed as the product of logical thought concerned largely with co-ordinating tasks through the use of legitimate authority. Employees were seen as rational beings whose interests coincided with those of the organisations in which they were employed. They were also seen as being capable of working to high levels of efficiency, provided they were properly selected, trained, directed, monitored and supported. Indoctrination and coercion would be used if necessary to achieve a rational approach by employees. This was presumed to lead to employees behaving exactly as they were told. Great emphasis was also placed on the need for careful and detailed explanation of organisational structure.

HUMAN RELATIONS SCHOOL

Later, the limitations of the classical writers became apparent, particularly their simplistic approach to people. The Hawthorne experiments conducted at the Western Electric Company in Chicago in the 1920s and 1930s revealed that groups can have a powerful effect on the way organisations work. It was recognised that people did not always do what employers wanted, nor did they always act in a way that was considered rational (Roethlisberger and Dickson 1939). The existence of informal networks and working relationships was also observed. This led to the evolution of the human relations school of organisational theory with which Elton Mayo in particular was associated. The work of occupational sociologists has subsequently emphasised the need to view organisations as social entities. As explained in the previous chapter, it is also necessary to recognise that there can be considerable conflict between the objectives of the organisation and those of the individuals employed in it. Informal and formal employee organisation can also lead to the sharing of power in organisations, so that there are limits to the authority of management.

SYSTEMS THEORY

Another school of thought which has emerged is the systems concept of organisations. This views organisations as dynamic organisms with interconnecting parts. Each part is dependent on integration with related parts if objectives are to be accomplished. Each part, however, has to operate in an environment which influences what the employees in that section want to achieve and are capable of achieving. An overlapping concept is that of 'socio-technical systems', according to which theory technical systems need to be effectively integrated with the social organisation at work, not simply imposed on it. The approach taken in this book is consistent with the systems theory of organisations.

MECHANISTIC AND ORGANIC STRUCTURES

A particularly useful classification of organisational structures is the extent to which they are mechanistic or organic. The ideas of the classical theorists were, and to a large extent still are, particularly appropriate to large-scale organisations operating in stable environments. Burns and Stalker (1972) have since suggested that such circumstances lend themselves to 'mechanistic' systems. This is in contrast to more rapidly changing environments where more adaptive 'organic' systems may be necessary. Although the research conducted by Burns and Stalker took place in the 1950s, it is still of great relevance. Later writers in this area have generally either used Burns and Stalker's work as a foundation or independently confirmed their conclusions even if they have identified further issues.

The features of mechanistic systems include a clear hierarchy of control, a high degree of specialisation of labour, and reference upwards for the reconciliation of differences within the organisation. This type of arrangement may be entirely appropriate where there is sufficient time to prescribe organisational arrangements and procedures in this type of detail, so that they match the environment in which the organisation operates. Where the technology and market are rapidly changing, however, it could be a recipe for disaster. A mechanistic system would simply not be adaptive, or its responses fast enough, to enable an organisation to remain competitive. Hence the need in some situations for 'organic' systems. These are characterised particularly by greater room for initiative, and for contact, co-operation and decision-making to be in accordance with the needs of particular situations rather than the formal organisation.

The work of Burns and Stalker was based on research into certain Scottish companies, particularly the electronics industry during 1953–7. Considerable success had been achieved in the application of scientific research findings within the Royal Air Force in the Second World War. This had been accomplished by the creation of organic structural arrangements that contrasted sharply with the mechanistic relationships between scientific departments and the Luftwaffe in Germany. The aim of Burns and Stalker's research was to investigate the extent to which organic arrangements needed to and could be introduced into organisations in peacetime.

A particular problem found in the firms in the Burns and Stalker study was that they often had arrangements for co-ordination between the research and development department and the production department that had more in common with the German wartime procedures than the British. However, it was clear that certain types of technical innovation, where know-how was diffuse and rapidly changing, demanded the reverse type of arrangements.

Unfortunately the lessons learned in wartime in Britain were not always applied afterwards.

Example

A British engine manufacturer unsuccessfully tried to introduce an improved engine. This led to the design and research and development staff blaming the production staff for being technically incompetent. The production staff in turn blamed the design and research and development staff for having been impractical, unrealistic and failing to communicate all their requirements. The company's response was not to create more organic relationships in this area (no-one was aware of this concept) but to establish three competing design teams. The view was that the best design would then be chosen for production. However, as the basic issue of the working relationships between the groups involved was not addressed, this approach did not prove to be very satisfactory either.

These mechanistic and organic approaches should be seen as different ends of a continuum rather than straight alternatives. Few, if any, organisations will be completely mechanistic or completely organic. However, it is important for the individual manager to be able to recognise the difference between the two. It is also necessary to recognise that market turbulence is likely to increase the emphasis needed for organic-type structures. Factors causing this are especially the increasing pace of technological change and the globalisation of markets. The ways in which a mismatch between organisational structure and needs can distort communication, and therefore organisational effectiveness, is examined in chapter 8 on communication.

MATRIX STRUCTURES

The matrix structure is a variation of organic arrangements. Essentially, this involves setting up more or less permanent project-type groups to which people are allocated from resource centres. The line, or command, structure is retained on the resource group side but the appropriate mix of specialists can then be allocated, full-time or part-time, to product-type teams. This arrangement is very often found necessary in high-technology organisations. It is also often found in colleges. It can assist in seeing that clients' needs are properly identified and met. If you have resource groupings only, as is often the case in universities, for example, the danger is that activity is focused on the development of the discipline alone without regard to the needs of clients. A feature of behaviour in many organisations, though, is that in any conflict between project groupings and the line structure it is the latter that usually wins. This is because of the power base of the command structure rather than because it necessarily has the better arguments.

HANDY'S CLASSIFICATION

A later writer who commented on the various different types of organisational structure was Charles Handy (1993). He identified the following four main organisational cultures:

- power: this type of organisational culture is said to be frequently found in small entrepreneurial organisations led by a dominant personality;
- role: this type of culture could be seen as similar to the concept of a mechanistic or bureaucratic structure;
- task: this could be seen as similar to the concept of an organic structure;
- person: this type of organisation culture is described as being a loose grouping of individuals who find it convenient to co-operate with one another without sacrificing too much of their independence, e.g., barristers' chambers or architectural practices.

THE WORK OF PETERS AND WATERMAN

Other writers to comment on the importance of the organic type of organisation include Peters and Waterman. Their book *In Search of Excellence* (1982) attracted much international attention. They based their work on the business practices of a number of leading American companies which they had been able to study whilst working for the management consultants McKinseys. They identified eight key attributes common to most of these successful companies:

- a bias for action,
- closeness to the customer,
- autonomy and entrepreneurship,
- productivity through people,

- hands-on and value driven,
- stick to the knitting (avoiding diversification into unconnected areas of business and technical specialisation),
- simple form, lean staff,
- simultaneous loose-tight properties (the co-existence of firm central direction and maximum individual autonomy).

This account by Peters and Waterman was of value in that it was an empirical attempt to explain what was actually happening in successful American companies. Their approach encouraged managers to beware of 'rational' planning models, to rely more on their subjective judgement, to consider the human element in organisations and to be aware of the virtues of organic-type structures. The book had considerable appeal in the business world, but there has been criticism by academics about the evidential base for the conclusions. These criticisms include the subjectivity of the data, its selective inter- pretation and the lack of a control group of less successful companies. Also many of the companies quoted as models of excellence fared badly in the subsequent economic downturn (Guest 1992). In addition there was no consideration at all of management issues in the public sector.

It may be that the type of characteristics described by Peters and Waterman tended to be particularly appropriate to large private sector organisations during a period of economic growth, but some of these attributes may actually have been handicaps when there was a recession. This illustrates a continuous theme of this chapter – that organisational structures need to fit with their objectives and circumstances. Whilst acknowledging the merits in the account by Peters and Waterman, it could have become a trap for those managers who based organisational structure on a prescriptive fashionable solution rather than undertaking the patient and intellectually demanding exercise of establishing which structure was right for their particular purposes.

Tom Peters' views have evolved further since *In Search of Excellence* was published. Subsequently, he claimed that the really key attributes were concern for customers, innovation, attention to the people in the organisation and, above all, leadership, which was a new explicit attribute (1985). Later, Peters emphasised the need for constant, rapid change to survive in a rapidly changing world (1988). He also embraced much of the philosophy of Total Quality Management, explained later in this chapter. Subse- quently, he has stressed the crucial importance of the impact of computer technology – particularly its effects on world markets – and globalisation (1992). Waterman has subsequently emphasised the importance of companies using their staff effectively and developing customer orientation even further (1992).

To reject the work of both Peters and Waterman because of its methodological limitations could well be a case of throwing the baby out with the bath water. The issues that they identified are of fundamental importance. However, particularly given the increasingly Messianic approach of Peters, managers should beware of blindly following his advice and instead carefully examine the extent to which Peters' ideas are useful in relation to their own particular circumstances. This contingency approach of matching behaviour with the actual situation is a topic that is considered further in chapter 4 on managerial style. The impact of information technology on organisational structure and behaviour is considered later in this chapter.

THE FLEXIBLE ORGANISATION

An extension of the concept of the organic organisation is the flexible organisation as illustrated by Atkinson (1985). It is particularly evident in Japan, where security of employment is often guaranteed only to a core of permanent employees. Other employees are engaged on a temporary basis. Potentially, an organisation is more likely to be able to adapt and survive if the outer core can be shed or replaced easily. This more easily guarantees the security of those in the inner core. Whilst people usually prefer to work in the inner core, those who are unemployed may regard a job in the outer core as better than no job at all. Employment in the periphery may provide opportunities for promotion to the core, and this can be a very useful way for employers to screen potential core employees. The requirement for some specialist skills may not be on a full-time basis, so cost-saving is made by employing some specialists part-time. These arrangements give the organisation *numerical* flexibility. However, this is at the cost of the job security of those who are only used when needed. Also, some of those with specialist skills may prefer to exploit the new options in the labour market by having non-standard working arrangements, particularly if that gives them tax advantages as well as greater freedom. This may include those who, having taken early retirement, are amenable to the idea of having their skills brought back in, for example, on a consultancy basis. This has led to an increasing number of people having 'work portfolios' rather than working for one employer. Where specialist skills are in short supply, however, employers may prefer to try and lock people with those skills into the organisation by employing them in the core.

Technological developments, such as those in electronic data processing, mean that practices such as working at home and subcontracting are possible in entirely new areas. Teleworking can be another option. Organisations that can predict their likely pattern of activity may also offer annual hours contracts so that employees' work attendance varies with, for example, the seasonal demand for their products. Employers may also want to employ some people at peak periods of the day only. Such arrangements could enable banks, for example, to have their counters fully manned at lunchtime, and thus overcome the problem of leaving some counters vacant at a peak time so that staff can have their lunch. Numerical flexibility can also be achieved by employing people on short-term contracts.

Another aspect of the flexible organisation is the benefits that may be derived in terms of *functional* flexibility. Staff may be contracted to perform a variety of different jobs and even to operate at varying levels of responsibility in accordance with the fluctuating needs of an organisation. Japanese companies in particular place much emphasis on multiskilling and generic job descriptions. Developments such as these are increasing functional flexibility within organisations.

Having explained the greater tendency for numerical and functional flexibility within organisations, it is necessary to say also that if taken too far this can create drawbacks. A sizeable core is needed to retain reasonable continuity and generate organisational synergy. Some able people may be discouraged from applying to organisations if, for example, only a fixed-term contract is on offer. Not all activities can be neatly packaged up and subcontracted. It is more difficult to develop an integrated organisational approach with a subcontractor who is only paid for what is strictly defined in the contract. Those in the peripheral work-force also need to be strategically managed. Inadequate attention to their supervision and training can easily lead to the alienation of the customers or clients on which the organisation depends. Also, some of the cost advantages of employing part-time staff have been reduced by improvements in their statutory protection. Part-time employees in the UK are now covered by dismissal and redundancy legislation. The European Part-Time Workers Directive also requires that part-time employees are not treated less favourably than full-time employees (see chapter 14) and the use of fixed-term contracts is to be limited by another European directive. In assessing the nature and importance of any trend towards more flexible working arrangements, it is probably best to view it as a series of *ad hoc* responses to labour market conditions rather than as an attempt to establish a conceptually different structure.

REVIEW OF THEORIES

It will be seen that organisational theory has gradually evolved. The formulation of one school of thought has facilitated the testing of that approach with actual organisational behaviour and the development of further schools of thought. The valid aspects of a particular approach have then been integrated with later views. The approach of the classical writers, in particular, needs to be seen in this light. Apart from its pioneering nature, much of what they had to say about organisations is still worth considering. However, their principles of organisations need to be seen as possible guidelines rather than definitive rules. The variety of managerial and organisational situations is such that it is impossible to set down universal principles. In any such list, the principles are platitudinous or have clear exceptions.

It is also necessary to have some understanding of the various approaches to management so that one can understand the views that colleagues may have about the way in which organisations should work. Such approaches may be reinforced or caused by an individual's cultural background. People tend to have beliefs and make value judgements about the ways organisations should operate. Even if these are never formally expressed, they may nevertheless be held with considerable conviction. Hopefully, such views will match the situations that arise. However, there are likely to be occasions when they do not, and it may be as well to recognise when a situation demands particular organisational arrangements that are in conflict with the beliefs of colleagues. It may even be appropriate to reflect on one's own ideology and the extent to which it is appropriate to the current situation.

Factors that determine organisation structure

There are many variables that will affect the structure and operation of an organisation. These may be within the organisation, outside it or a combination of the two. Managers need to determine which factors in their particular situation are likely to be important. These could include the impact of technology (including information technology), the size of their organisation, the identification of the critical function at a given time, and national culture.

TECHNOLOGY

One of the most critical factors is that of technology. The importance of information technology is such that a separate section is devoted to it. Organisational structure has probably always been influenced by the technology it deploys. One of the writers who made a historically important contribution to understanding this relationship was Joan Woodward (1965). She reported that organisations with mass-production technologies were found to lend themselves to mechanistic-type systems. Firms with process-type technologies appeared to be at that time best managed by less formal and more organic-type systems. The absence of the sheer physical effort involved in making items and co-ordinating thousands of small decisions, characteristic of large-batch and mass-production technology, meant that managers were left with much more time to initiate and co-operate with others. Consequently, the need for specialisation was found to be reduced in the process-type industries. The organic type of structure was also found to be more appropriate with small firms that were not making standard products. Some small organisations, though, tended to be informal and mechanistic – the routines being so well known that there was no need to formalise them. Technological developments since then, however, such as robotic technology, have enabled some of the traditional mass-production industries to acquire some of the characteristics of the process-type industries. More organic systems have therefore become appropriate for some mass-production systems with the consequent changes for managers described above.

The important point that emerged from the Woodward studies was the link between organisational structure, and organisation behaviour and technology. Related to this was Woodward's observation that many managers had as their model of organisation structure the old classical beliefs (1965: 256). Her work gave empirical support for the contingency approach which emphasises the need for managers to adapt organisation structures and behaviour to the situation in which they find themselves. As explained in the next chapter on managerial style, a mismatch between style and the needs of the situation can have unfortunate consequences. Given the general lack of management training, as explained in chapter 1, it is still likely that the options in organisational structure and behaviour are not fully understood by many managers.

INFORMATION TECHNOLOGY

The impact of technology on organisational structure and behaviour also has to be considered in relation to information technology. The rapid processing and retrieval of data can have a major impact. So too can computer-controlled production and other operational processes. Despite the increasing sophistication of information technology equipment, costs are falling and the general levels of computer literacy are rising.

The impact of information technology on markets

Rapid information access may increase an organisation's ability and need to respond quickly to market changes. It may also facilitate meeting individual customer requirements. This may necessitate flexibility within the organisational structure, and, especially in commercial organisations, the stakes are rising. The gains to be made by a rapid response may be high, and the penalties for a slow response correspondingly high as well. Many markets are becoming much more 'perfect' as information is more easily obtained and analysed and as the barriers of time and distance are reduced. This in turn means that product life cycles are tending to be shorter, and national and market boundaries less important and more permeable. The greater volatility of markets and knowledge about their behaviour means that customer and brand loyalty is likely to be less. Organisations may find that they have the knowledge and capacity to enter new markets but, conversely, this may mean that they have to face new sources of competition.

A related development is the use of software packages to automate processes previously done manually, for example many accountancy procedures and calculations. Such software packages facilitate the organisation of information, use of organisational memories, common databases throughout organisations while reducing internal barriers to communication. Given the increased emphasis on intellectual capital, explained later in this chapter, these processes assist in the creation of added value to an organisation's intangible assets (referred to contemporarily as 'knowledge management').

The use of electronic mail (e-mail) enables rapid and simultaneous transmission to any number of colleagues. Linking of e-mail to a wide area network enables messages to be exchanged and material accessed throughout the world. Other external contacts may involve more effective collaboration (as well as competition) with other organisations, shared information with buyers and sellers, and electronic market broking arrangements. Access is also available to an increasing number of public databases, e.g. copies of newspapers, magazines, journals and other archive material. Electronic Data Interchange (EDI) enables ordering to be done on a daily basis. Overnight orders to suppliers may reduce turn-around time. The same system also gives very accurate stock control. These internal and external developments may in turn mean that information is more readily available about new options and services that can be provided. Information technology may also facilitate 'business scope redefinition'.

Example

An example of how new technology created a business scope redefinition was the introduction by American Airlines of its computer reservation system (Sabre). This online system enabled reservations to be made directly from travel agents' offices. It also created the opportunity for the company to lease out the facilities to other airlines.

Impact on organisational strategy

The developments described above may enable organisations to use their expertise in information technology to creatively influence strategy rather than simply using technology in a supportive role. A dramatic example of this was how the Italian authorities were able to analyse the previously impenetrable wall surrounding many financial transactions involving the Mafia and then use the evidence obtained to secure criminal convictions. The information now available within the UK National Health Service enables comparisons to be made about the cost and quality of services at different locations. The technology can also be used to identify delays in treatment and the availability of space for those requiring treatment. Surprising spin-offs may be generated by new data.

Example

An example of how new data can cause spin-off improvements occurred in the social services directorate of a local authority in London. Details of external phone calls became available when all calls were electronically logged. Analysis of the data revealed, amongst other things, the times when homecare workers rang in to liaise with office staff. It emerged that the offices were overstaffed with support staff early in the morning, as the homecare workers generally rang in later than had been realised.

Impact on organisational structure

The changes so far identified may precipitate further internal organisational changes. Potential changes and actual examples are indicated below.

Centralisation

The rapid access to data can have a centralising effect and may enable senior managers to directly manage more people, leading to a flatter organisational pyramid. Sometimes, though, managers may centralise because they can do it more easily rather than as the result of a considered judgement as to whether decisions are better taken locally or not.

De-layering

Centralisation can also lead to de-layering, particularly by the elimination of tiers of middle managers. The overall scale of the organisational pyramid may also be shrunk in terms of the number of people employed, as many front-line tasks are automated or made easier.

Example An example of how front-line jobs may be eliminated in the service sector is the increasing use of electronic surveillance by the police to deter motorists from speeding and jumping traffic lights, and the possibility of using this method to detect illegal exhaust emissions.

Space savings

De-layering in turn can generate space savings. However, a host of other factors can also cause space savings. These include:

- computer controlled production and ordering systems which reduce the level of stock and work in progress;
- the easier storage of and access to data;
- hot-desking: employees may have a reduced need for their dedicated office space and may be able to operate effectively by utilising whatever space and facilities are available at the particular time that they are needed;
- teleworking: employees may choose or be asked to carry out their activities from home or elsewhere. This topic is explained further in the next section of this chapter.

Geographic dispersal of facilities

The use of internal communication systems, such as intranets, may increase the opportunities for economies by the geographic dispersal of facilities to areas with cheaper costs. A particularly dramatic example is the increased use of call centres usually located in low-cost areas. Airline reservations, for example, may be handled in a separate country, or even continent.

Employees may also be able to work more from home or wherever they happen to be by the use of laptop computers and modems. One of the disadvantages of this arrangement for the organisation, though, may be the decrease in face-to-face networking that is important for the co-ordination of organisation activities, problem-solving and the generation of new ideas. To a certain extent, the lack of formal interaction may be offset by the use of video-conferencing facilities or group decision-support systems (Laudon and Laudon, 2000: 478). However, these facilities will not replace casual conversations between employees which can result in the priceless exchange of organisation information.

Reduced numbers of employees

Organisations may be able to offer a considerable range of products or services with relatively few employees. The ultimate development is the virtual organisation which simply provides information and services electronically. Whilst there may be relatively few organisations that operate totally on that basis, some large organisations operate with surprisingly few people. Examples include sportswear houses such as Nike and Reebok whose core employees are designers and who undertake no production themselves.

Organisations can also operate without owning sophisticated information technology systems by hotelling at centres that provide those facilities.

Delegating work to the customer

A further way of reducing the numbers employed in organisations is by the delegation of work to customers. In some industries and services, customers are increasingly encouraged to access their files and give telephoned instructions that may require little or no contact with staff of the organisation. This is particularly so with telephone banking. Interest rates and bank charges are manipulated to encourage these developments. This trend is illustrative of the ways in which organisations are changing from face-to-face to electronic contact with their customers or members of the public. Pre-recorded telephone information messages and Internet information pages are also increasingly used. These changes reduce the number of employees needed whilst at the same time increasing the accessibility of the products and services on offer.

Changes in internal relationships

Power relationships in organisations are likely to be affected by who has access to particular data combined with the ability to handle that information and who does not have access. This means that some people in junior positions can acquire considerable influence. Some front-line jobs may be made much easier by developments in information technology. In other cases, ready access to data enables front-line staff to take decisions that would not have previously been thought possible or desirable. The ability of others to maintain power by their control of and ability to filter information will be correspondingly reduced. A further impact is the blurring of traditional distinctions between blue and white-collar employees, as new skills replace old ones and the shape of an organisation changes.

Skills development

The importance of developments in information technology make it essential for organisations to review what new skills need to be acquired by their staff. This involves more than exhortations that everyone become computer literate. A mix of skills is needed, including systems design, programming, data inputting and retrieval, the facility to use a keyboard and the ability to make use of the information processes effectively. The acquisition of these skills needs to be matched to individual requirements. The concept of the learning organisation (considered in chapter 11) may be particularly appropriate in this context. Organisations may need to have open systems of learning so that they are able to acquire knowledge about relevant developments on an ongoing basis, particularly in the area of information technology, and be able to apply these new developments as appropriate. However, the changes precipitated by information technology necessitate a range of other skills as well. A particular danger is that computer specialists only recognise the need for new skills in their area and not the range of managerial and other skills that are also necessary if information technology is to be harnessed effectively.

Constraints and dangers

The constraints of information technology also need to be recognised. Whilst there may be general qualitative gains in decision-making and product reliability, the cost and consequence of systems and programming errors may be greatly increased.

Examples

The London Ambulance Service installed a computerised system for dispatching vehicles to emergencies in 1992. However, the operating delays it created meant that it had to be quickly abandoned and the manual system reintroduced (Cane 1993). Another failure was the expenditure of £20 million by the Wessex Health Authority trying to develop a computerised system for storing and accessing patient data; this also had to be abandoned (UK Public Accounts Committee, 1994). In both cases, the problems of developing and testing an effective system were greatly underestimated.

Other constraints or dangers are:

- not all important information is readily quantifiable – a point stressed in the previous chapter;
- sometimes expensive systems are not integrated and are used on top of existing systems rather than instead of them;
- sometimes systems may be acquired that do not do the job any more effectively than previous arrangements, leading to a low or negative payoff on the investment;
- if the right equipment is acquired, a further adaptation that may be necessary is that of shift-working, so that full use is made of the new facilities;
- the dehumanising impact on certain jobs may also require consideration, for example, the even greater impersonalisation of relationships between staff and customers in supermarkets caused by new technology. Thought should be given to what remedial action can be taken in such cases;
- the security aspects of systems may need considerable attention. Dangers include accidental loss of information, systems failures, computer viruses, breach of confidential and statutorily protected information, sabotage and espionage.

The general implication of the change precipitated by information technology is that management needs to learn to live not only with continuous change, but also with change that may accelerate in pace. The use of fibre optics to enable massive amounts of information to be transmitted may be of particular importance in actually accelerating the rate of technological change. This will facilitate the development of information superhighways. Central to the need to capitalise on these developments is the need for managers, especially in the private sector, to learn to keep abreast of developments in information technology, so that they can take advantage of the new applications as they come on stream before their competitors. There is, though, a tendency for technology to race ahead of the ability of organisations to identify areas of application. Even when applications are identified, organisations may lack the ability to use them productively. A key need is for organisations to invest in technical support and in the training of managers and others so they can make good use of the equipment that is available. The issue of the impact of developments in information technology on patterns of organisational and individual communication is examined further in chapter 8 on communication.

SIZE

Another important factor that will affect the structure and operation of an organisation is size. You do not need much formality if you are engaged in constructing a small building, as to a large extent people can see what needs to be done for themselves. The mass production of vehicles, for example, requires much more formality because, amongst other things, people cannot easily grasp what has to be done. The number of variables that has to be co-ordinated in that situation creates enormous organisational problems. It may well be that these problems increase on an exponential rather than a linear basis. The solution of breaking the units down into manageable sizes may not be an option if your technology dictates that you need a large integrated plant.

Many organisations fail to grow because of their inability to develop a viable structure to cope with increased work. Larger organisations generally need an element of formality, clear reporting lines, delegation, managerial and specialist expertise, and control systems. Small organisations may also actually fail because they do not have the facilities to cope with extra work or the financial resources to wait until payment on large orders are made. A common constraint in family-controlled organisations is the unwillingness of family members to either bring in or make effective use of people with managerial expertise. They may also be very reluctant to bring in outside capital if that threatens their financial control. Very large organisations may need devolved structures so that the centre is not overloaded and too unresponsive to market conditions. This will particularly be the case if they have a wide range of products or services.

INTELLECTUAL CAPITAL

As explained in chapter 2, organisations can increasingly depend on their intellectual capital for survival and development rather than their physical assets. This is because more organisations are becoming knowledge-based and amorphous. It can be especially important to attract and retain the right mix of people who have the collective expertise and access to information networks to realise an organisation's potential. This is all the more so given the rapidity of many technological developments and the potential rewards in the private sector for organisations who are the first to exploit new market opportunities.

The importance of intellectual capital as a key factor in judging an organisation's worth has been reflected in stock market valuations. In the UK, for example, British Steel (before forming part of Corus) was no longer in the top 100 companies quoted on the stock exchange whereas Kingston Communications was. Kingston Communications was formerly the municipal telephone service owned and run by the local authority in Hull. A related development has been the tendency for share buying to sometimes be based more on a belief in the ability of organisations to exploit market opportunities with their expertise rather than their possession of physical assets or profit record. This has sometimes been the case with companies involved in exploiting the Internet. This in turn may involve a highly speculative view of the future value of a company.

The increased importance of the intellectual capital of organisations can also make them particularly dependent on the goodwill of their staff, raising the issue of vulnerability.

Example

A Portuguese bank (BCP) acquired an investment management firm despite this being against the wishes of the firm's employees. As soon as the merger was completed the staff handed in their notice in order to set up a rival investment company.

(Brealey and Myers 1996: 917)

IDENTIFYING THE CRITICAL FUNCTION

Another factor that needs to influence the structure of an organisation is the recognition of what is the critical function at a given time. Joan Woodward (1965) defined commercial success in part as stemming from the ability of those in organisations to identify the area where it was most important to get the correct decisions. If necessary, the views of the management in the critical function need to take precedence over the views of managers in less important areas. The critical function can vary over time, and in mechanistic structures especially such movement of influence from one function to another may be inhibited. The managers in a traditionally powerful function are not likely to take kindly to having a reduced say in major decisions in order to allow a rival function a greater say. The managers in the traditionally powerful function may, in any case, not fully appreciate that the critical focus of decision-making has moved. The success of managers in solving problems may be their very undoing in this respect. If, for example, difficult design problems are overcome, this removes a constraint. The problem then can be how to increase production or sales. However, a 'critical' function is still interdependent with the other functions in an organisation.

NATIONAL CULTURE

Another potentially important variable is national culture. As explained in the next chapter, care has to be used with the term 'national culture' because there are often wide cultural differences within a country. However, national or local culture is an increasingly important factor because of globalisation and increasing cultural diversity within countries. Indigenous organisations may not have to worry about it so much because they will normally know the local culture. However, even they need to pay attention to the issue if they are to interact effectively with other societies within and outside their own country. Particular attention needs to be paid to this issue by international organisations. Management structures and practices which appear to work well in a particular country may not be easily exported because the environment in which they operate cannot be transplanted. This also applies to the importation of practices from other countries. Local managers need to be able to adapt the structure, policies and procedures of an organisation in accordance with local conditions. Factors that may necessitate local adaptation may include:

- geography, climate and other environmental factors,
- levels of education and technology,
- economic infrastructure,
- social and political structures,
- local business practice,
- religion,
- law,
- language,
- history.

Historically, Western countries have tended to impose organisational structures on developing countries in particular based on Western rather than local needs. This includes an emphasis on large hospitals in health services, Western-style universities in the education sector and political systems as well as commercial organisation. An example of the difficulties that organisations can encounter in trying to import organisational practices is that of Western companies trying to copy Japanese methods. However, much of the industrial Japanese success was because of their highly developed work ethic, cultural homogeneity, outstanding technical achievements, long-term financing, effective and sophisticated system of governmental support for industry and import barriers. The social traditions of conformity and obedience, and the importance of the group or wider organisation compared with the individual, are also relevant. The importing of particular management practices and customs is not going to radically change organisational cultures in the West. That is not to say that some Japanese practices will not work elsewhere – the point is that much of their success stems from more fundamental causes. Another point that needs to be made is that the Japanese also need to adapt their organisations' structures and style when they have to operate in different cultures. The very success of countries such as Japan is also likely to precipitate social changes in their own societies. A further issue is that some of the apparent strengths in Japan have had built-in problems. The South East Asian economic crisis of the mid and late 1990s demonstrated that if banks have a large stake in the equity of a company, company failure can also jeopardise the bank.

An adaptation that some organisations have made is to become transnational. These organisations are structured so that they do not have their roots in any one country. The related issue of developing a managerial style, as opposed to organisational structure, to fit the local culture is considered in the next chapter on managerial style. The impact of national culture on motivation is considered in chapter 6 and on communication in chapter 8.

The interrelationship of organisational activity

DEPARTMENTALISM

As well as considering the nature of the organisation they are in and how appropriate that organisation is to its environment, managers need to consider how they relate to the other functions within their organisation.

Organisations may be arranged on neat departmental lines, but many of the problems that will have to be dealt with will not conveniently correspond to a departmental structure. Such structures, although usually necessary, are artificial. Problems may contain many different interactive dimensions. Managerial approaches to such problems will need to be integrated if they are to succeed. True, some problems may confine themselves to departmental boundaries, but this will not always be the case.

There are often considerable barriers to lateral contact between departments, especially in mechanistic-type organisations. Rivalries, role conflicts, different values and differing types of expertise may all act as impediments. Staff may prefer the security of contact with like-minded people within their own department to the often more hostile encounters with other departments. A lopsided approach to organisational problems may develop as a result. This may have a detrimental effect on the work of departments. It may also lead to problems that straddle departmental boundaries being ignored. It is all too easy for an ostrich-type managerial style to develop in organisations. Managers may keep a low profile and just deal with what is clearly in their own area. This tendency may be reinforced by their initial specialist training – as explained in chapter 1. Managers may be much more able to identify the problems that correspond with their specialism than those outside it.

The inherent problems of effective lateral communication can be reinforced by internal markets. These involve purchaser-provider relationships between departments. Service providers are financially dependent on the income they generate from internal purchasers. Whilst this can focus attention on the real needs of service users such arrangements can also have severe disadvantages. These include an emphasis on either minimising or maximising internal charges, according to whether you are a service provider or service user. This can distract attention from the needs of the organisation as a whole and encourage competitive rather than collaborative internal relationships. Experience in the National Health Service in the UK and the BBC suggests that these arrangements can easily become counter-productive and also generate vast amounts of paper work and other costly forms of control. Such arrangements may also ignore the costs of running down or closing existing internal activities. The same issues need to be faced with subcontracting. Whilst there is a clear logic for subcontracting ancillary services, the process can be carried too far. Hiving off core sections of the human resource function, for example, can ignore the importance of the lateral advisory and developmental links needed between this function and line management. Organisations are not the series of discrete functions that many accountants imagine. Developing an effective organisation is rather more complicated than assembling a permutation of Lego-style building blocks.

The problem of boundary-crossing can be particularly acute in the public sector, and it follows that there are many examples. The long established boundaries which define what is medical work and what is nursing work do not facilitate organisational change in the National Health Service.

The attempt to introduce corporate management in local government has been hampered by the professional orientation of individual departments and officers. The development of a corporate approach necessitates officers at all levels, not just those at the top tier, taking a wider approach. The legal profession provides a particularly glaring example of where well established professional traditions have led to fierce opposition to suggestions for change in working arrangements. The older and more established the profession, the greater seem to be the problems of altering occupational roles and associated training in line with changing organisational and societal needs.

To understand broader problems – particularly those which fall between different departments – managers need to have some understanding of overall activity in their organisations. Attempts to bring departments together may be frustrated, however, because of the conflict this can generate. The objectives of departments may not always be complementary nor will they all operate at the same level of performance. Consequently, much time and effort can go into justifying the activity of a particular department to others rather than developing common problem-solving approaches. The hidden agenda at interdepartmental meetings can be that nothing is to be proven wrong about one's own department. However, if everyone takes that approach the real issues to be discussed simply get lost in smoke-screens. One has only to look at the annual report of a company which has made a loss to see the standard smoke-screen that can be put out for public, if not internal, consumption. The list of causes for poor performance is likely to include inappropriate legislation, national and international trading conditions, unfair competition, government policy, failures by suppliers, acts of God, bad luck, trade unions and a deterioration in the standards of society. It might include incompetence by previous executives but is most unlikely to include admissions of failure that were within the current management's control.

The magnitude of the problem of departmentalism is compounded by the fact that the very nature of problems can often be identified only by an interdepartmental group with complementary skills and expertise. If the current objectives of an organisation, or the major constraints impeding the achievement of those objectives, are to be defined, this may be accomplished only by a pooling of knowledge. Even when the nature of a problem is identified, the causes may be far from obvious. One of the traps that people can fall into is to assume that the problems which emerge in particular departments have their causes in those same departments. Productivity levels may be influenced, for example, by production control, organisation structure, investment policy and personnel management policies. It may be pointless trying to recruit more and more labour to boost production if the production process or planning is inadequate. In some cases, problems, causes and solutions may all exist in the same department, but it is dangerous to assume that this is always the case. That is why the importance of the systems approach to organisations was stressed earlier in this chapter.

THE KNOCK-ON EFFECT OF DECISIONS

A further point of which managers need to be aware is the implications of their decisions for other departments.

> **Example**
>
> An example of how one department, in trying to improve its own performance, created greater problems elsewhere concerns a change in sales policy. The limit on the size of small orders in a soft drinks company was reduced and sales increased as a result. Unfortunately, the extra revenue was not sufficient to cover the extra transport costs involved.

The poet John Donne's observation that no man is an island can be applied to managers. They need to see their experience as something to be shared, to help identify and deal with problems facing the whole organisation, rather than simply a means of justifying the activity of their own department. They may not be capable of resolving the problems facing their own department alone anyway. This point is explained further in chapter 14 and illustrative examples are given from the field of employee relations. This is a function where the root cause of problems very often lie in other areas of management activity. Unfortunately, this is frequently not appreciated. Consequently, attempts to improve matters can erroneously take place entirely within the employee relations function when often the need is to remedy weaknesses elsewhere.

REMEDIAL STRATEGIES

There are preventative strategies which can reduce the problems created by poor inter-departmental liaison. As has previously been indicated, the most important strategy is to have the right fit between organisational structure and purpose. Whatever the formal structure, though, other means can be found to improve co-operation. Initiatives such as Total Quality Management (covered later in this chapter) and developments in information technology usually help interdepartmental co-operation. Broadly based management training may also be necessary. Positive steps can be taken to encourage team work by the creation of joint departmental teams or project groups containing staff from a range of departments. Contacts made in this way can help develop informal networks which are often the glue that holds organisations together and facilitates coherent activity. The geographic arrangement of work can also have an important and constructive impact if this dimension is given attention. Colleagues, especially those who are not in regular contact with one another, may find it very useful to meet in accessible communal areas such as coffee points. Unfortunately, this idea is often missed, with the consequence that work is physically arranged on the 'battery hen' model, with no thought given of the need to promote informal, and sometimes even formal, interaction. Even open-plan offices may be counter-productive in their effect, as relaxed or confidential exchanges may be discouraged by the 'goldfish bowl' atmosphere they can generate.

Whilst informal networks can sometimes work against the objectives of the organisation they can also be an essential supplement to its activity. In some cases they are mechanisms for coping with deficiencies in the formal organisation. They may also break new ground in demonstrating what needs to be encouraged and even formalised.

> **Example**
>
> The housing construction department of a local authority in London laid down concrete pathways on new estates. Unfortunately the residents often found shorter and more convenient routes to follow. This led to mud pathways being created that were used to supplement or replace the concrete pathways. Engineers came to the conclusion that it might be best to not lay any pathways when estates were built but instead to concrete over the mud pathways once it became clear which routes the residents preferred.

One could argue that the process of formalising informal arrangements is also evident in the way an increasing number of couples in the Western world live together before formalising their established relationships in marriage.

Role behaviour

PERSONALITY VS ROLE BEHAVIOUR

When interacting with colleagues it is important for managers to be able to distinguish between personality behaviour and role behaviour. Role behaviour occurs when a person acts in accordance with the requirements of the position that they hold. Managers may meet with opposition from colleagues that can be wrongly attributed to personality factors.

It would be foolish to pretend that personality factors never have an influence on people's behaviour, but it can be all too easy to miss the point that a person may feel obliged to behave in a particular way because of the demands of their job. The danger is that the issue can become personalised. Real role conflicts can thus be exacerbated by personality conflicts. Traditions of hostility can develop and spread through whole departments. It is, unfortunately, so much easier, and often more satisfying, to blame a particular dispute on the actual personality of a protagonist. Sometimes this will even be true – a role may be clumsily or wrongly interpreted by a particular person. It can be very difficult, in the heat of the moment, to reflect that there is nothing personal in the perhaps crucial conflict in which you are involved. The basis of the conflict, however, may be entirely to do with roles, and it may be possible to contain the area of conflict by putting one's case assertively, not aggressively. The concept of assertiveness is explained in detail in the next chapter. It is as well to remember, too, that whilst role conflicts can be incorrectly identified as personality clashes, it is rare for the mistake to be made the other way around. The constant danger is that conflict is wrongly attributed to personalities, rather than the reverse.

Failure to recognise that people's behaviour stems from their roles, rather than their personality, is particularly likely when the roles are informal. Often people adopt positions because, for example, they have particular information to hand which is not generally available or its significance may not be generally appreciated. This may drive them into conflict with others, even though their formal roles appear to be compatible.

REDUCING CONFLICT

The reason for distinguishing between role and personality behaviour is the need to contain the area of conflict to the minimum. It is also important to get the diagnosis right if one is attempting to resolve the conflict. If one makes the mistake of assuming that a conflict is personality-based when in reality it is because of roles, the false solution may emerge of changing the personalities involved. Thus, an 'awkward' person may be transferred or dismissed, only for the same 'awkward' behaviour to re-emerge with the next job-holder. The original solution, as well as having been wrong from an organisational point of view, may also constitute a grave injustice to the person who is removed. In some cases it may even be that a person is only doing their job correctly if they are being awkward. The creation of the job of traffic wardens was partly because of the need to avoid giving police the contradictory role of enforcing parking regulations and developing positive relationships with the general public.

In working out whether behaviour is a product of the role or the person, it is important to ensure that people are given viable roles. If people in managerial positions are expected to issue penalties, but no rewards, to their employees, it is unreasonable to expect them to have an easy working relationship with the same people. There is an inevitable tendency in organisations for there to be competition for the handing out of rewards – such as wage rises, good news and special privileges – and a great reluctance to get embroiled in, for example, disciplinary matters. A way of making it easier for a manager or supervisor to handle the disciplinary aspects of their job is to allow them to take the credit for distributing rewards when these are available.

The task of distinguishing between role and personality behaviour can demand considerable intellectual effort and emotional discipline. However, the rewards can be considerable, starting with the more accurate diagnosis of organisational problems. This can, in many situations, lead to real instead of false solutions. The amount of personal injustice can be reduced and last, but not least, the amount of personal aggravation for oneself diminished.

Quality management

QUALITY CIRCLES

An organisational development that has links with the organic system and project and matrix structures is that of quality circles. They have been defined as:

> *a small group of between three and 12 people who do the same or similar work, voluntarily meeting together regularly for about an hour per week in paid time, usually under the leadership of their own supervisor, and trained to identify, analyse and solve some of the problems in their work, presenting solutions to management, and where possible, implementing solutions themselves*

Hutchins 1985: 1

Quality circles, although American in origin, have attracted considerable attention because of their popularity in Japan since the 1960s and the economic success of that country. Consequently, they have been introduced into manufacturing and service activities in other industrial countries. The potential benefits are mainly improved quality, cost savings and the improved morale created by these achievements and the increased employee participation that is the essence of the process. Whilst the idea may be capable of useful application in other countries, one must always be wary of attempts to transplant management practices from one country to another – as was explained earlier in this chapter in the section on national culture. The greater emphasis on the group in Japan, compared with the emphasis on the individual in the West, is of particular importance. It is also necessary to beware, as is repeatedly stressed in this book, of management panaceas that so often turn out to be simplistic attempts to deal with complex issues. It is not surprising to learn that quality circles often fail and that even in Japan, according to one study, only one in three work (Collard and Dale 1985: 28–32). However, many apparently succeed, and it may be that the concept can work in selected situations, provided the conditions are right.

The way in which quality circles are implemented is also crucial, and the seven critical factors in their introduction have been identified by Collard and Dale (1985) as:

- commitment by the board and senior management,
- involvement of middle management and supervisors,
- trade union support,
- delegation of decision-making,

- adequate training,
- use of a pilot study,
- monitoring.

TOTAL QUALITY MANAGEMENT

A more recent development, Total Quality Management (TQM), adopts a broader approach to the continuous improvement of quality. TQM seeks to obtain everyone's commitment to satisfying customer expectations. Its originality lies in identifying the organisation as a set of linked processes with internal customers and suppliers all driven by what the external customer wants. The intention is to include quality at the earliest stages when designing a product or service – to get it right first time instead of relying on end-of-line activities such as inspection, quality control and assurance to remedy errors after they have occurred. The philosophy is of error prevention through careful specification of how to meet customer requirements, bringing to bear the knowledge and ideas of all the people involved in the process working as a team and accepting responsibility for a quality output.

Quality does not mean top-of-the-range excellence – a Mini car or a Rolls-Royce will both be quality products if they meet the specification, including price. In defining the quality standard, the question to answer is 'what does success look like?' Any gap between the quality standard and the quality actually achieved can then be identified. Organisational activity then needs to be directed towards eliminating this gap.

The concept of TQM was developed in Japan after the Second World War, particularly by an American industrial adviser, W. Edwards Deming. Deming used as a base the statistical process control techniques developed earlier by Walter Shewhart and promoted a method of review and improvement applicable to all activities (the 'plan-do-check-act' cycle). Other important exponents of TQM were Juran and Crosby.

Japan's quality revolution and export success caused organisations in other countries, especially competitors, to begin to look closely at what the Japanese had been doing. By the 1980s interest was widespread.

Ignored initially in the USA, Deming had found that Japan was a fertile ground for the development of TQM. Industry needed to be rebuilt, there was an adequate supply of labour, and raw materials were short, so waste urgently needed to be avoided. The Japanese culture particularly lent itself to TQM. The emphasis was on teams, not individuals, and organisation cultures were generalist rather than specialist. Trade unions had become weak and were organised on a company basis. Loyalty to the company and the work ethic were both high, and labour stability helped social control. Economic growth meant that work rationalisation did not create redundancies and the employment of a core workforce further guaranteed security for those with permanent jobs. Sophisticated long-term relationships evolved with suppliers so that quality was not threatened by supplies of faulty components. The concept of *kaizan* was developed too so that continuous improvement became part of organisational culture with work teams geared to constantly improving methods in order to produce innovative products attractive to customers.

There was not the same impetus for improvement in the West after the war. Manufacturers operated in a sellers' market, and some even developed cynical approaches to quality. The technique of 'just-in-time' production, which the Japanese developed so well, wouldn't work in overheated economies where the main concern was avoiding disruption to the production system. This could be caused by late or poor quality deliveries or industrial action. Consequently, components were often hoarded rather than only being fed in at the appropriate moment. When Western economies found that they had to operate much more in buyers' markets, many of their companies found it very difficult to compete with Japanese manufacturers, particularly on quality and price. The concept has also been applied in many parts of the public sector. This is in keeping with the increasing emphasis on consumerism and the increasing amount of work contracted out to internal or external clients.

Properly applied, TQM involves a major shift in organisational culture and a new decision-making structure so that all staff understand the strategic direction of the organisation and are empowered to 'own' problems and take actions to solve them and avoid recurrence. This can involve a fundamental organisational restructuring which is at variance with the traditional nature of so many organisations with strong functional and hierarchical boundaries. The potential benefits of TQM include cost reductions arising, for example, from the need for less inspection and rectification, and quicker introduction of innovative new products and services, leading in turn to greater market share and increased revenue. However, these benefits are only likely to be achieved if appropriate organisational adjustments and training investments are made. The key preconditions for success are generally seen to be:

- sustained commitment by the board and senior management, especially if the TQM initiative seems to be losing its momentum;
- strong emphasis on communication to the workforce;
- a determined attempt to improve and structure lateral communication and co-operation between departments;
- sound mechanisms for employee involvement and skills development with particular emphasis on problem-solving through teamwork.

It is also necessary to identify the specific qualitative standards and improvements that are required, mount a programme for their accomplishment, and measure and communicate progress. The development of skills by front-line staff is critical and, in turn, necessitates careful selection and appropriate training.

(Example)   An example of a fresh emphasis on the skills of front-line staff was the redefinition of the role of a delivery driver in a soft drinks company. In their redefined role

CONTINUED OVER ➤

CONTINUED FROM
PREVIOUS PAGE
drivers were expected to act as a representative of the company who, whilst undertaking deliveries, also accepted responsibility for developing and maintaining a
good relationship with the customer.

The role of front-line supervisors and managers is particularly important in TQM and
involves a change from keeping all authority and knowledge in their hands to one of
developing the skills of their team.

One important element of TQM is to have robust systems that ensure continuous
measurement of the achievement of quality standards and the basis for targeting
improvements to close the quality gap discussed earlier. Development of quality
standards requires working with customers to help clarify their needs. Having defined
the standards, the supplier needs to establish procedures to ensure that these standards
are consistently achieved. This has led to a wave of organisations seeking external
accreditation that they have done this and produced the appropriate operating quality
manual. The standard accreditation has become International Standards Organisation
(ISO) 5701. Accreditation does not involve any judgement about the quality level, just
that the organisation has detailed documented procedures to demonstrate that it is
consistently meeting the standards it has set for itself.

There is clearly felt to be a commercial advantage in gaining a quality kitemark, and
some customers, including many governmental departments, indicate that they expect
this in organisations tendering for business. The process can be bureaucratic, though,
and the costs of producing manuals, gaining accreditation and paying for this and
follow-up visits can be expensive. Critics claim that, in contrast to TQM, accreditation
does not focus on improving quality or exploiting new market opportunities (Halliday
1994). It remains to be seen if possession of a kitemark is a worthwhile investment
leading to quality improvements or simply a rigid bureaucratic on-cost. The answer will
vary according to the nature of the organisation and industry or service.

The potential gap between aspiration and achievement with regard to quality
standards is also an issue for the process of TQM as a whole. If organisations see it as a
quick cure for fundamental problems they are likely to be disappointed. Organisational
cultures are not that easily altered, and so often one 'quick fix' is tried after another and
all failing because the scale of the adjustment is not understood. There is also the
specific constraint in the public sector that, whilst TQM may reduce some costs and
improve service, it may not be easy to generate the revenue that would finance it. The
concept of TQM envisages all interested parties having a shared interest in organisational success, but for this to happen it is necessary to recognise sectional interests
when they arise and to address rather than ignore any potential conflict.

The difficulties that many organisations have encountered are documented in
research studies. Voss and O'Brien (1992) reported that many schemes were foundering
because of a lack of leadership by senior and middle management, and this was
exacerbated by a failure to understand customer needs. They also reported that cost-
cutting measures precipitated by recession were undermining quality initiatives and

that organisations often failed to realise the level of commitment and adjustment that needed to be made by the whole organisation The last failing featured prominently in a study led by Binney (1992) which also commented that change could be provoked but not imposed, and in the best examples TQM was working well. A further problem may be that organisations introduce what Deming would have seen as contradictory initiatives, such as performance-related pay (emphasising the contribution of the individual) and TQM (with its emphasis on teamwork). There is also the need, especially in the public sector, to carefully balance any measures of throughput with quality standards. However, there seems little doubt that TQM has the potential to release the energies of employees to regenerate and improve the effectiveness of their organisations considerably. Whether that potential is realised or not is clearly up to individual managements. If they do take it seriously, they will continually ask questions about whether a TQM initiative is working, paying back on the investment and moving the organisation forward.

General developments in the private and public sectors

Most of the major developments in the private sector have already been covered in this chapter. Developments relating to long-term and corporate strategy, including the relationship between operational units and the centre, were covered at the end of the previous chapter. Many of the issues covered also have considerable significance for the public sector. However, it is appropriate at this stage to explicitly cover important issues which apply to the private sector and which may also be relevant to the public sector. Developments specific to the public sector will then also be examined.

A recurring theme in the section on the public sector is how the changes in its framework and operation are creating a much more managerial, as opposed to administrative, culture. This is with a view to getting better 'value for money' with the resources available. This is also likely to apply to those organisations which do not fit into the category of private or public sector. Many can be categorised as non-governmental organisations (NGOs) and are likely to be independent charities. One example is that of Oxfam which provides relief to developing countries. The range in size of such organisations is considerable. They also vary in that some of them receive part of their income from public funds and others do not.

THE PRIVATE SECTOR

Competitive pressures have caused many private sector organisations to down-size and sometimes the concept of being 'lean and mean' has been carried to such an extent that organisations have become 'anorexic'. There has been a general tendency to move towards semi-autonomous business units with financial performance targets. This has reduced the potential for cross-subsidisation within organisations. These two developments have also been noticeable in the public sector. However, the move to semi-autonomous business units sometimes is contradicted by demands for detailed control information and prior approval on a range of matters large and small.

The concept of added value has been prominent, with units and individuals expected to justify themselves more in terms of their profitability. These developments in turn have led to a trend to much smaller head offices. There has been a reaction, too, to the Taylorist scientific management approach of division of labour, functional control and non-involvement of the workforce. This has partly been a consequence of more volatile markets. There is more emphasis now on flexibility and workforce involvement in process and product and service improvement. This in turn has necessitated more emphasis on training and creative human resource management. Of particular importance is the trend to relocate manufacturing processes away from high-cost economies. There is also likely to be increasing competition for the design work to be done in countries with low wage costs. One example of this is the use of satellite transmission to enable computer programming to be undertaken in Eire for American customers. The search for new markets and cost reduction opportunities is also causing more collaborative ventures. Another development has been for companies to plan international marketing strategies. As markets have become globalised, so it has become more possible and appropriate to market global or regional, as opposed to national, products.

THE CHANGING SHAPE OF THE PUBLIC SECTOR

In the UK and many other countries there has been a systematic attempt to redraw the boundaries between the public and private sectors so that many of the activities that were previously in the public sector could be run privately instead. As is so often the case, the shift in emphasis away from direct state spending and control seems to have started in the USA. Many of the interventionist and regulatory policies of the 1960s and before in America and elsewhere were seen not to have worked and had often become prohibitively expensive. Rising public expectations and reduced economic growth were further factors forcing a rethink of the role of the state, including an attempt to reduce the expectations of what the state should do for individuals. President Reagan in America and Margaret Thatcher in the UK were principal exponents of the need to roll back the frontiers of state ownership and regulation. One development of deregulation or divestment tended to lead to another until it became a flood. Associated developments were the opportunities this created for private business, the revenue generated by the sale of state assets and tax cuts. This is a route many countries in both the West and the developing world have followed. Some of these changes have also been introduced in the former Soviet bloc after the collapse of communism.

In the UK, successive Conservative administrations since 1979 have sought to create an 'enterprise' as opposed to a 'dependency' culture. Privatisation has been one important element in the UK government's strategy. This policy was continued by the

Labour government when it came to power in 1997. A political advantage for governments in devolving authority within the public sector is that sensitive decisions about prioritisation and resource allocation can be removed from central government.

COMPARISONS WITH THE PRIVATE SECTOR

As a corollary of reducing state ownership and control there has been a strong trend to the more effective use of those activities still financed or run by the state. There have been attempts to make the public sector operate more like the private sector. Whilst the public sector has undoubtedly had lessons to learn from the private sector, it would be a mistake to imagine that the differences between the two sectors can be ignored. It would also be a mistake to ignore the considerable variations within the private and public sectors. Public bodies are democratically accountable, have statutory obligations and often have to operate in a sensitive political environment, for example the National Health Service and local government. The aims of public sector bodies often cannot be easily defined and quantified. Often public sector organisations are very large. Much of the private sector, by contrast, is in small units with clear commercial goals. These differences enable private sector organisations often to behave in a way that would be quite inappropriate in the public sector, particularly with regard to risk-taking. The overall need in the public sector can perhaps best be described as for the various elements of that sector to become more businesslike without trying to operate as businesses.

Having defined the distinctive nature of the public sector, it is appropriate to examine the way in which it is adopting a more commercial approach. One way of explaining this is to examine the historic differences between management and administration. This has been done by a British civil servant associated with the Treasury Centre for Administrative Services. The emphasis, with management, is on results and on taking calculated risks; with administration it is on procedures, accountability and risk avoidance. These are not complete opposites but rather the ends of a continuum. The general thrust in the public sector has been to shift it more to the managerial end of the continuum. The full list is included as an appendix to this chapter.

Another basic change is that policy and budgeting is now much more finance-led instead of being on a needs or demand basis. This in turn has meant that managers have to make the best use of a given level of funding, which may necessitate making conscious priorities as explained in the previous chapter. Often the level of funding is geared to performance indicators. There are also attempts to generate cash from the private sector for the public sector, as for example with major transport projects. Publicly funded organisations are now expected to take less of a custodial approach to their assets and more of a market orientation of matching resources with demand. This is in keeping with greater customer orientation and focus on service delivery. A number of organisations have been required to produce citizens' charters guaranteeing standards of service to the public, and in some cases being obliged to make penalty payments if the standards are not met.

An increasing amount of work is organised on a contract basis, with public sector bodies being partly or totally financially dependent on the winning and retention of contracts, sometimes in competition with the private sector. The practice has now come to be known as market testing. This concept is often been applied to employment contracts, especially for senior positions. Renewal is logically likely to depend on performance. There has also been a general application of the concept of performance-related pay in the public sector, though, as explained in chapter 10, the results have been rather disappointing. Amongst the effects of the structural and operational changes in the public sector is the identification of much more explicit managerial roles than before. This means that there is a much clearer need for those in positions of authority to develop managerial skills.

An interesting development in the USA concerns the use of government purchasing power to influence business behaviour. The federal government has increasingly sought to impose ethical business practices on government contractors. An example of this happening in the UK is when those competing for public contracts are required or encouraged to have Investors in People accreditation. Additionally, the growing sensitivity of customers is likely to create a commercial pressure on an increasing number of private organisations to demonstrate that they have ethical business practices and also that they are behaving responsibly with regard to the local community and the environment. An example of this is the way in which consumer resistance to buying genetically modified food in the UK caused supermarkets to withdraw such goods from sale.

At one stage in the UK a massive shift in activity was envisaged by opening up work from the civil service and local government in particular to competitive tendering. Whilst there has been a significant increase in the amount of public sector work that has been subcontracted a constraint has been the European Union Acquired Rights Directive. This means that those who win contracts may assume responsibility for the workforce previously undertaking the work at their existing terms and conditions of employment. There is ongoing uncertainty however, about the circumstances under which the directive applies. A rough guide though is to distinguish between the disposal of an economic *entity* (which may involve acquired rights obligations) and an *activity* (which may not).

SUMMARY

✔ This chapter has attempted to set the scene within which those with managerial responsibilities have to operate. Key organisational theories have been examined. Organisational types that have been described and analysed include mechanistic and organic structures, matrix arrangements and the flexible organisation. Managers need to examine the fit between what is appropriate in terms of organisational design and operation and what actually exists. The factors that shape organisational structure have been identified. These include the impact of technology, particularly information technology; size; the extent to which the organisation is dependent on its intellectual capital; the nature of the critical function; and national culture. The importance of the market, and the way it needs to influence organisational structure, was stressed in the examination of key organisational theories.

✔ The dangers of sectional goals conflicting with broad organisational objectives has been examined and suggestions made as to how such conflicts may be handled. These particularly include developing lateral organisation links and broadening the base of training so that people can have a broader view of the organisation. The need for managers to distinguish between personality and role behaviour has also been covered. This is because of the unnecessary aggravation that can occur if managers fail to analyse the behaviour of colleagues in terms of their role. The frequency and importance of quality initiatives was also examined. Quality initiatives, if taken seriously, can significantly affect the way an organisation is structured.

✔ There are distinct differences in the nature of the private and public sectors. However, some trends have been common to both sectors. These include pressure for more market- or client-orientated structures with a generally greater devolution of authority for decisions in financial and other matters. Governments are under pressure to secure value for money in the public sector and often find it convenient to devolve authority for sensitive decisions about resource allocation. Whilst public sector organisations need to be run in a business-like way it is important to remember that they are not businesses, as they have constraints such as democratic accountability that businesses do not. The chapter is an essential prelude to considering the topic covered in the next chapter, managerial style.

SELF-ASSESSMENT QUESTIONS

1. Why is it important for managers to have an understanding of the options in organisational design?

2. What are the main factors shaping the structure and operation of an organisation with which you are familiar?

3. Why might units within an organisation pursue sectional rather than corporate aims? What can realistically be done to deal with this problem?

4. Why might role behaviour be mistaken for personality behaviour?

5. Why might quality initiatives fail?

6. Identify key similarities and differences between the private and public sectors.

References (Works of general interest in the specific references are marked with a star.)

Atkinson, J. (1985) *Flexibility, Uncertainty and Manpower Management*, IMS report no. 89, Institute of Manpower Studies.

Binney, George (1992) *Making Quality Work*, Economist Intelligence Unit.

Burns, T. and G. M. Stalker (1972) *Management of Innovation*, Tavistock Publications, first published 1961. For a summary of this work, see Honor Croome (1970), *Human Problems of Innovation*, Ministry of Technology pamphlet.

Brealey and Myers (1996) *Principles of Corporate Finance*, 5th ed., McGraw-Hill,

Cane, Alan (1993) 'Failure of Computers "May Kill"', *Financial Times*, 14 June.

Collard, Ron and Barrie Dale (1985) 'Quality Circles: Why They Break Down and Why They Hold Up', *Personnel Management*, February.

Fayol, Henri (1967) *General and Industrial Management*, transl. Constance Storrs, Pitman; first French edition published 1916; Storrs' translation first published 1949.

* Guest, David (1992) 'Right Enough to be Dangerously Wrong: An Analysis of the In Search of Excellence Phenomenon', in Graeme Salaman (ed.), *Human Resources Strategies*, Sage Publications in association with the Open University.

Halliday, Stephen (1994) *Which Business: Tested Ideas for Profitable Businesses*, Kogan Page.

Handy, Charles (1991) *The Age of Unreason*, 2nd ed., Business Books.

* Handy, Charles (1993) *Understanding Organisations*, 4th ed., Penguin.

House of Commons Public Accounts Committee (1994) 'Proper Conduct of Public Business', House of Commons paper no. 154, HMSO.

Hutchins, David (1985) *Quality Circles Handbook*, Pitman.

Laudon, Kenneth C. and Jane P. Laudon (2000) *Management Information Systems – Organisation and Technology in the Networked Enterprise*, Prentice Hall: New Jersey.

* Peters, Thomas J. and Robert H. Waterman Jr (1982) *In Search of Excellence, Lessons from America's Best-run Companies*, HarperCollins.

Peters Tom and Nancy Austin (1985) *A Passion for Excellence*, Random House.

Peters, Tom (1988) *Thriving on Chaos*, Pan Books in association with Macmillan.

Peters, Tom (1992) *Liberation Management*, Macmillan, Pan (1994).

Roethlisberger F. J. and W. J. Dickson (1939) *Management and the Worker*, Harvard University Press. For one of several abridged accounts see John Sheldrake (1996) 'Management Theories: From Taylorism to Japanization', chapter 11, *Elton Mayo and the Hawthorne Experiments*, International Thomson Business Press.

Taylor F. W. (1972) *Scientific Management*, Greenwood Press, first published 1911.

Voss and O'Brien (1992) *In Search of Quality*, London Business School.

Waterman, Robert H. Jr (1994) *The Frontiers of Excellence (Learning from Companies that Put People First)*, Nicholas Brealey.

Woodward, Joan (1965) *Industrial Organisation: Theory and Practice*, Oxford University Press. For a summary of this work see Joan Woodward, 'Management and Technology' (Ministry of Technology pamphlet, 1970), reprint.

General References

Currie, Wendy and Bob Galliers (eds, 1999) *Rethinking Management Information Systems*, Oxford University Press.

Handy, Charles (1994) *The Empty Raincoat, Making Sense of the Future*, Hutchinson: London.

Kennedy, Carol (1998) *Guide to the Management Gurus: Shortcuts to the Ideas of Leading Management Thinkers*, Century Business, 2nd ed.

Morton, Michael S. Scott (ed., 1991) *The Corporation of the 1990s*, Oxford University Press, (for a particularly useful series of papers on the impact of information technology on organisations).

Sheldrake, John (1996) *Management Theory: From Taylorism to Japanization*, International Thomson Business Press.

Appendix to chapter 3

THE DIFFERENT CHARACTERISTICS OF ADMINISTRATION AND MANAGEMENT

	Administration	**Management**
Objectives	• stated in general terms and reviewed or changed infrequently	• stated as broad strategic aims • supported by more detailed short-term goals and targets reviewed frequently
Success criteria	• mistake-avoiding • performance difficult to measure	• success-seeking • performance mostly measurable
Resource use	• secondary task	• primary task
Decision-making	• has to make few decisions but affecting many and can take time over it	• has to make decisions affecting few and has to make them quickly
Structure	• roles defined in terms of areas of responsibility • long hierarchies, limited delegation	• shorter hierarchies • maximum delegation
Roles	• arbitrator	• protagonist
Attitudes	• passive: workload determined outside the system; best people used to solve problems • time insensitive • risk-avoiding • emphasis on procedure • doing things right • conformity • uniformity	• active: seeking to influence the environment; best people used to find and exploit opportunities • time sensitive • risk accepting, but minimising it • emphasis on results • doing the right things • local experiments: need for conformity to be proved • independence
Skills	• literacy (reports, notes)	• numeracy, statistics, figures

chapter four

Managerial style

There are case studies and exercises at http://www.thomsonlearning.co.uk (for full details, see the listing at the start of this book).

LEARNING OUTCOMES

By the end of the chapter you will be able to:

- Understand the concept of managerial style and current trends

- Know the range of managerial styles that are commonly practised and the associated relevant theories

- Appreciate the need to adapt managerial style according to the needs of a situation

- Identify the organisational factors that influence managerial style

- Take account of the impact of national culture on managerial style

- Apply key skills involved in 'assertiveness'

- Evaluate the effectiveness of managerial style

- Identify and examine your own preferred managerial style

Introduction

Managerial style can be defined as 'the way in which a manager achieves results'. It overlaps with the concept of leadership. The range of commonly practised managerial styles is examined in this chapter. People need to be aware of their own preferred style but also of the need to adapt their style to the needs of the situation. Trends in management style are examined as are key factors which can influence it, such as organisational pressures and national culture. A style that is often required is the ability to behave assertively as opposed to being aggressive or non-assertive. This concept is examined, as are the key skills in assertive behaviour.

Finally the effectiveness of managers is considered. Whatever style or styles a manager uses though, they will ultimately by judged by results. Managerial style is a means to an end and not an end itself. A questionnaire is included as an appendix to the chapter so that readers can identify their own managerial style.

Trends in managerial style

THE CONCEPT OF MANAGERIAL STYLE

Managerial style was defined in the introduction as 'the way in which managers achieve results'. It overlaps with the concept of leadership. However, managers are appointed and are responsible to those who appoint them. In representative structures, in contrast, leaders are responsible to those who have allowed them to become their leader, often by election. The objectives of managers can sometimes conflict with those of the groups they have to manage. Not all managers are effective in achieving results and not all leaders are managers. Whilst leadership can be provided by managers, it can also be provided in a range of other roles.

The concept of effective management is often confused with 'charisma'. However, whilst charismatic leadership can be appropriate in some managerial situations this is not always the case. Sometimes it can be the reverse of what is needed, particularly if the manager needs to be primarily a facilitator and conciliator.

THE AUTHORITY OF THE MANAGER

Managers will normally have a certain amount of formal authority to do their job. This will usually have been delegated to them by a higher level of management. This will enable them to take decisions and commit organisational resources. They will also need to have some authority over their staff in the way of rewards and penalties. The extent of a manager's authority will vary considerably according to their seniority and from organisation to organisation. However, a number of factors have tended to limit the authority of individual managers. These are identified below.

ORGANISATIONAL DEVELOPMENTS

Organisations are often becoming more complex. This is because of factors such as accelerating change, technological development (particularly information technology) and globalisation. Levels of uncertainty are generally rising and knowledge within organisations is often becoming diffuse. Also, the process of management is increasingly becoming the management of 'intellectual capital' rather than that of physical resources. The ability of managers to control the flow of information is often greatly reduced. The cumulative effect of these changes is to make the manager more of a facilitator rather than a traditional authority figure.

LEGAL CONSTRAINTS

Increasingly managers are constrained in what they can do by the law. This is particularly so in the area of employment rights, e.g. unfair dismissal and anti-discrimination law. The ability of managers to hire and fire at will has been considerably curtailed.

SOCIAL DEVELOPMENTS

Social trends and rising levels of education have created pressures for people to manage in a more acceptable way. Managers are often also dependent on the information and expertise of their subordinates. Younger subordinates, for example, may be able to access and manipulate new information systems more easily than their bosses.

Whilst there are discernible general trends, the extent to which they have impacted on individual organisations and managers will vary widely. Some managers still rely significantly on their formal authority. Even managers who do not rely too much on their formal authority may need to use it when all else fails. Feelings of insecurity amongst employees may depend very much on their personal prospects of alternative employment.

SAPIENTIAL AUTHORITY

As organisations change so managers may be more dependent on their sapiential rather than their formal authority. Sapiential authority is that which derives from a person's expertise. The sapiential authority of a manager may lie in their specialist area or their organisational facilitating skills, or both. This concept is similar to that of expert power which is considered below.

POWER AND INFLUENCE

Whereas authority (the right to get something done) is officially sanctioned by the organisation, power is distributed throughout the organisation and may be invested in people at any level and not just managers. The determinants of power are also not only at the disposal of the organisation in the way in which authority is. Power can be defined as 'the ability to marshal human, informational, or material resources to get something done' (Lewis *et al.* 1995: 425). It can be used effectively even if the manager does not actually possess power but the party whom the manager is seeking to influence believes that they do. Power can be prescribed by a person's position in the organisation or as a result of their personal attributes. Position power can derive from the following four factors in particular:

- legitimacy: this exists when employees feel that the manager has the right to ask for particular tasks to be undertaken;
- coercion: this is the ability to discipline or penalise by withholding rewards. This type of power is more effective if used as a perceived threat rather than if penalties have to be imposed;

- rewards: these are the tangible benefits that a manager has at their disposal and will include not only salary increases but also other benefits that the employee values. These could include improved work schedules, promotion and formal recognition of a job well done;
- information: managers and others, by virtue of their position, often have access to information that people need in order to carry out their jobs. This information may be acquired in a variety of ways and not just by formal channels.

Personal power also derives from several sources:

- Expert power is similar to sapiential authority. This type of power stems from expertise in solving problems and performing important tasks. If a person is perceived as having expertise in a situation then they will exert more influence than someone who is not perceived in this way.
- Referent power is the ability to influence others based on personal liking, charisma or reputation. If an employee feels a deep personal loyalty to someone, then the employee may be influenced to do something that they might not otherwise have done. This is the basis on which high profile personalities are recruited to advertise products.
- Changes in the environment can affect the power balance. For example, in times of skills shortages particular employees may possess more power than they do when their skills are available in abundance. This change in power is determined by the state of the labour market and may not be within the organisation's control. The factors that determine the labour market are identified and examined in chapter 14.

LATERAL RELATIONSHIPS

Managers may need considerable political skills in negotiating their working arrangements with other departments. General organisational developments are such that fewer organisations have a traditional bureaucratic structure. The trend is to have more flexible and organic (as opposed to mechanistic) structures. In organic structures there will be a need for, and a pattern of, relatively open access to people in other parts of the organisation. This in turn can generate a greater need for work arrangements such as project teams and matrix structures. Managers and other employees may find that they often report to more than one boss.

MANAGERS AS FACILITATORS

Organisational trends are such that managers are increasingly likely to be the focal points for assembling the right mix of financial, physical and human resources to undertake specific tasks. This is particularly so in organisations with a high level of intellectual capital, as described in the previous chapter. These developments in turn affect managerial style. In explaining the concept of the triple 'I' organisation, based on the effective use of intelligence, ideas and information, Handy said:

> *It is this type of organisation which has given rise to what has been called the post-heroic leader. Whereas the heroic manager of the past knew all, could do all and could solve every problem, the post-heroic manager asks how every problem can be solved in a way that develops other people's capacity to handle it.*
>
> 1991: 132

The increasing need for managers to act as facilitators demonstrates that the charismatic approach to managing can have a downside as well as being a potentially effective way of managing. Working for a charismatic manager can be reassuring and exciting but it is heavily dependent on the judgement of the leader and the results can be disastrous if that judgement is flawed. The gap between followers and leader can become too great, rendering upward communication difficult and encouraging subordinates to surrender responsibility and independent thought. This in turn may create further opportunities or pressure on the charismatic leader to behave as though they are omniscient, thus further increasing the likelihood of failure. These views of the manager as facilitator fit with those expressed by the Local Government Management Training Board:

> *Among future management roles are those of the honest broker and negotiator, requiring qualities of peacemaking and peacekeeping between conflicting interests, and a temperament which maximises agreement and mutual benefits. Vital management skills, in short, include dealing with leading, motivating, handling people. Good management will more and more be seen as unlocking barriers to performance by colleagues and subordinates, enhancing their contribution and releasing their potential. Management involves simultaneously playing as a team member while pushing the team forward – not least in conveying a sense of direction, by successfully painting a picture of the future*
>
> 1993: 15

Options in managerial style

A number of writers have identified options in managerial style. Concepts such as Fox's (1965) unitary and pluralistic frames of reference also are relevant to this topic. Styles are generally viewed as being neutral, what matters is that the style used matches the situation. Trait theories are examined in the work by McGregor, as are the concepts of the managerial grid, contingency and management team mix.

TRAIT THEORIES

A traditional way of examining the broader concept of leadership is to identify the personality characteristics that are required by a leader. If this approach is used, one can quickly generate a long list of personality traits. This may include characteristics such as honesty, intelligence, consistency, integrity, firmness, ruthlessness, flexibility, vision, charisma and so on. It would be very difficult to find a person who possessed all these characteristics. Furthermore many of the characteristics can be the opposite of one another, such as consistency and flexibility.

If any value is be made of trait theories it is necessary to identify what traits are important in a given situation. The traits that are important in one situation may not be important in another or may even be a handicap. A matching exercise needs to be undertaken when selecting managers to try and ensure that the person appointed has those few critical traits required for a particular job. If the demands of the job change, the person appointed may no longer match the changed requirements. Consequently, it may be necessary to consider how a manager would be able to adapt to changed circumstances.

There are many examples from the world of politics of leaders not being able to adapt to changed circumstances. Great leaders can be thrown up in times of revolution or war who might otherwise have remained in relative obscurity. This is in keeping with the adage 'cometh the hour, cometh the man'. However, when the revolution or war is over a different style of leadership may be required. Often great revolutionary or war leaders have been unable to adapt to the demands of peacetime. One of many examples is that of Mao Zedong, the revolutionary communist Chinese leader.

Many successful business people have failed in the political world. Conversely, many politicians have failed in business adventures. A reason for this may be that business people operate in a hierarchical environment with an executive chain of command. Politicians need the skills to develop and retain grassroots support. Successful business people may particularly require financial acumen and politicians the power to impress an audience.

MCGREGOR'S THEORIES X AND Y

McGregor (1969) distinguished between managers who managed in a Theory X style and those who managed in a Theory Y style. Assumptions that Theory X managers made about employees were said to include:

- employees need and respond to close direction and control;
- people prefer to avoid work if they can;
- employees do not want to accept responsibility;
- employees have to be coerced to achieve organisational objectives.

The assumptions made by Theory Y managers about employees were said to include:

- individual and organisational goals can be integrated;
- work is a natural activity;
- employees will respond positively to objectives to which they are committed;
- emotional satisfaction can be achieved at work;
- employees will, under the right conditions, accept responsibility.

The value of this classification is to identify the assumptions of other managers and yourself. On the face of it, the Theory Y style is more enlightened, but the basic point is that the style adopted needs to fit the situation. The danger is that managers may have fairly fixed assumptions and consequently have difficulty in adapting their style to a situation that requires an approach different to their natural one. It is necessary to distinguish between genuine Theory Y styles and ones which are only superficial. Critics of Japanese techniques of employee involvement, for example, see them as attempts to create a coerced consensus, (Garrahan and Stewart 1992). The relationship between managerial assumptions about why people work and motivation is examined further in chapter 6.

TANNENBAUM AND SCHMIDT'S CONTINUUM OF LEADERSHIP STYLES

Tannenbaum and Schmidt (1957: 96) developed a model of leadership styles based on the concept of a continuum ranging from authoritarian behaviour at one end to democratic at the other. One can extrapolate a third style at the democratic end of the continuum, which is the *laissez-faire* leader who exercises little or no control and who may be a leader in name only. Leaders, or managers, can be at any point in the continuum. Their style can, and will need to, vary over time and according to situational requirements. See Figure 4.1.

BLAKE AND MOUTON'S MANAGERIAL GRID

The managerial grid is based on the concept of managers having two potentially conflicting centres of attention: employee needs and task needs. Blake and Mouton (1981) designed a questionnaire so that managers could identify where they were located on a grid. This would show the extent to which they were orientated around employee or task needs, or both. The effective manager was viewed as one who set out to reconcile these two sets of needs, rather than concentrating on meeting just one or the other.

CONTINGENCY THEORIES

Several theorists have examined the idea that the leadership style needs to be contingent on key factors in whatever situation requires leadership. John Adair (1982) identified three key factors: task, group and individual needs. He suggested that the

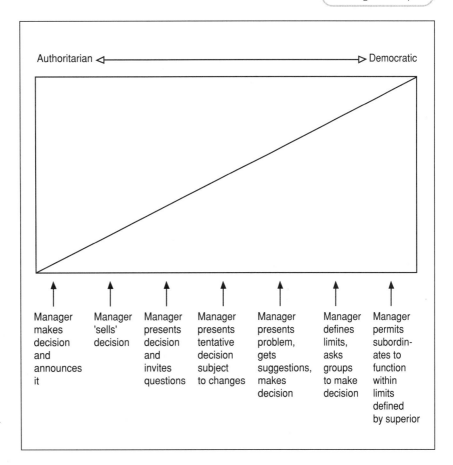

Authoritarian ←————————————————————————→ Democratic

| Manager makes decision and announces it | Manager 'sells' decision | Manager presents decision and invites questions | Manager presents tentative decision subject to changes | Manager presents problem, gets suggestions, makes decision | Manager defines limits, asks groups to make decision | Manager permits subordinates to function within limits defined by superior |

FIGURE 4.1 *A continuum of leadership styles*

effective manager will be the one who gives priority to these three overlapping interests according to the needs of the situation. If, for example, there was an emergency, the task needs would predominate. See Figure 4.2.

BELBIN'S MANAGEMENT TEAM MIX

Meredith Belbin's work (1981) focuses on the relationship between the membership of management teams and their effectiveness. He identified the right mix in a group as a key requirement for effectiveness. Belbin suggested that it is necessary for a management team to contain people prepared to play the various complementary roles. A group of talented individuals could fail because there could be too much competition to play some roles with no one prepared to play important but possibly less glamorous ones. The roles that he identified as being likely to be necessary are:

- chair,
- shaper (dominant, passionate, extroverted),
- plant (creative, intelligent, introverted),
- monitor/evaluator,

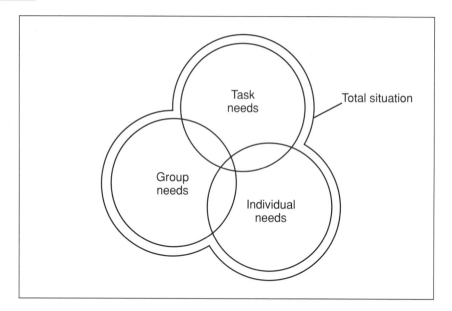

FIGURE 4.2 *John Adair's model of action-centred leadership*

- resource investigator (source of new contacts but not originator),
- company worker (the practical organiser),
- team worker (concerned with facilitating the work of the group),
- finisher.

This list needs to be viewed as only a set of guidelines for group membership as not all groups will require the exact permutation identified by Belbin. Also, people may need to and be able to play different roles according to the needs of a situation. People may also be able to switch from one role to another within a group. This is particularly important as managers may have to work with groups where they have little or no control over the membership.

A particularly important aspect of group activity is their potential creativity. Managers sometimes make the mistake of believing that they must be the ones who come up with the creative ideas and ignore the potential creativity with the rest of the team. This may be because they have concepts of managerial leadership that are old fashioned and egocentric. It can actually be counter-productive to have the senior manager also trying to play the role of creative thinker as this may detract from the effective organisation of the group. Groups also have to beware of unbalanced 'group think'.

(Example)

The importance of having the right mix of people in a group and the potentially disastrous consequences of unbalanced 'group- think' were sadly illustrated by a climbing disaster in 1995. Six climbers were blown to their death whilst trying to descend from the summit of the second highest peak in the world, K2 in the Himalayas. A seventh member of the team, who did not reach the top, died of pneumonia. The team included the British mountaineer Alison Hargreaves, who had recently climbed Mount Everest without oxygen. The lack of a person who was

CONTINUED OVER ➤

CONTINUED FROM
PREVIOUS PAGE

prepared to play the role of monitor/evaluator may have been crucial. Peter Hillary (1995) – another mountaineer and the son of Sir Edmund Hillary, one of the pair who first scaled Mount Everest – had abandoned his simultaneous attempt to climb K2. He commented:

> Summit fever had developed in that group. There was a chemistry in there that meant that they were going for the summit no matter what. They were all driving each other on... These people came together and, because of the place and the atmosphere and their personalities, they became blinkered and simply focused on the top... There was no careful awareness in the group and the most dangerous thing about groups is that people hand over responsibility for themselves to someone else... It means that no one is taking responsibility. There can be a false sense of security in numbers.

There can be occasions when managers and just one other colleague need to have complementary styles.

Example

A former British Royal Air Force officer commented about the relationship between the commanding officer of a unit and their adjutant. In his view it was necessary for the one to take a hard disciplinary line, and for the other a much softer line and be psychologically available so that they could find out what people really felt as well as soothe any hurt feelings. He also maintained that it did not matter who took the hard line and who the soft line as long as each took one and that they worked as a team. That way, effective control, based on reliable information and reasonable morale, could be exercised. If both the commanding officer and the adjutant adopted the same style he argued that either there would be an excess of control and lack of reliable information or the reverse.

Another example of the dovetailing of styles is the relationship between a fee-charging doctor or dentist and the receptionist.

Example

The doctor or dentist will usually leave the potentially embarrassing business of payment to the receptionist, so that it does not interfere with the relationship between the professional and their client.

A further example of how dovetailing can work, from recent political history, is the working relationship between Margaret Thatcher and William Whitelaw.

Example

Margaret Thatcher, as prime minister of the UK, played the role of the abrasive change agent, whilst William Whitelaw, as her deputy, played a conciliatory role, was approachable, brokered compromises and warned the prime minister when she was in danger of going too far. This led to Thatcher's unintended pun that 'every prime minister needs a Willie'. It was only after Whitelaw had to retire from active politics on health grounds that Thatcher got seriously out of step with her party, particularly over the introduction of the Poll Tax, and had to resign as prime minister in 1990.

UNITARY AND PLURALISTIC FRAMES OF REFERENCE

The ability of managers to handle internal organisational conflict may be largely determined by whether they have a unitary or pluralistic frame of reference (Fox 1965). Unitarists may be ill-equipped to handle such conflict because of their assumption that sectional interests will or should always be subordinated to overall organisation objectives. In the event of this not happening they may operate in an authoritarian manner. If this does not work they are likely to be both frustrated and ineffective. Those with a pluralistic frame of reference will be conceptually equipped to both recognise conflicts of interest and, when appropriate, to negotiate about them. This is in keeping with the view that the manager often needs to be a facilitator rather than simply an authority figure. This issue is examined in more detail in chapter 14 in the context of employee relations. The role of the first line supervisor is also examined in the same chapter. They often have to deal with significant conflicts of interest between the workforce and the organisation. Strategies are suggested as to how this can be constructively handled.

If you want to check on your own managerial style complete the questionnaire in appendix 1 to this chapter.

Organisational factors

Whilst managerial style will be influenced by the individual personality of a manager a number of external factors are also likely to influence their style and are outlined below.

NATURE OF THE WORK

The nature of the work may influence the managerial style. Of particular importance will be the knowledge gap between the manager and subordinates. The knowledge gap may be high if the work is predictable and routine. It may be small if the work is demanding and varied. The nature of the work will largely determine the level of skill needed in subordinates. The greater the gap, the more appropriate it may be for the manager to behave in an authoritarian way. If there is a small, or even reverse gap, the more consultative the manager will need to be.

The time pressures affecting the work are also likely to influence managerial style. Particularly in emergencies managers may need to behave in an authoritarian way. Organisations that are capital intensive, for example process-based plants such as oil refineries, may be able to have reasonable staffing ratios. This will reduce the time pressures on managers and enable them to consult more. Organisations in which labour costs are high may have to keep staff to a minimum, which in turn can mean that there is less time for consultation. The consequences of error may also be a factor. If the consequences are small, an authoritarian style may be appropriate. Conversely, if the consequences are high, managers will need to investigate and consult more fully.

ORGANISATIONAL VALUES

Organisations will have certain expectations of the way in which their managers behave. Managers may be selected and trained in such a way that these values are reinforced. They may also be rewarded or punished according to whether they conform or not to organisational values.

The values of organisations are sometimes enshrined in documents such as mission statements. These can be genuine statements about organisational values or statements of how the organisation would like to be viewed. In the latter case, managers need to be careful not to confuse the stated values with the real value system that may operate in an organisation. It is particularly important that prospective or new managers try and identify the real values in an organisation before they commit themselves to joining it or, if they have joined it, to see what adaptations in behaviour they may need to consider. Key questions are:

- attitudes to innovation: are you likely be rewarded or punished if you take initiatives?
- organisational protocol: how important is it to observe organisational protocol about approaching other employees?
- attitudes to risk: are you likely to earn disapproval for making mistakes, however small, or is a certain amount of risk-taking encouraged because of the need for commercial enterprise?
- ethical values: is the organisation one in which only success matters, or is this constrained by a need to behave ethically?
- constraints: to what extent is the organisation constrained in its actions by factors such as the law, image and public accountability?
- level of conformity: to what extent are non-conformity and dissent tolerated?
- customer/client orientation: do clients or customers really come first?
- developmental needs: to what extent will you be able to develop yourself in the organisation?
- values: what are the values of your immediate superior?

STYLE OF THE BOSS

Managers need to take into account the values of their boss as well as those of the organisation at large. The boss is usually in a powerful position to put pressure on a subordinate. Whilst some can see the value of having subordinates with complementary skills, many expect them to behave as 'clones'. Consequently, subordinates will need to work out the values and style of their boss and the extent to which they are expected to model themselves on it. One of the problems that organisations can have is that the 'cloning' process can go on throughout the managerial hierarchy. This may not necessarily be of benefit to the organisation, but it can reinforce the pressure on a subordinate to conform to established values and patterns of behaviour.

The managerial style of a boss can greatly influence the way in which issues entrusted to them are handled. One study showed how attempts to change the style was frustrated by the very style that was meant to be changed.

Example

The former Wales Gas Board had been statutorily obliged to consult with representatives of employees. Seventeen consultative committees were established, but eight of them collapsed. Ostensibly, this was because the employees stopped nominating representatives to serve on these eight committees. Detailed analysis of consultative committee minutes, however, showed that the managers who had chaired the eight defunct committee had taken a very reactive approach to discussions. They had also often ignored those issues raised by the employee representatives. This contrasted with the productive discussions at the nine other committees. These prospered because the managers who chaired them generally prepared for the meetings, actually raised more items for discussion than the employee representatives and took the issues raised by the representatives seriously. Ironically, the committees were most successful at those well-run establishments where they seemed to be least needed and vice versa.

(Rees and Porter 1998: 165–170)

The impact of national culture

National culture was identified, in the previous chapter, as one of the factors that determines organisational structure. It is now necessary to examine the impact of national culture on managerial style. The term 'national culture' is a crude one because of the cultural diversity within countries. However, the term is used instead of 'societal culture' because it is much more generally used and broadly understood. Care has to be used throughout in using the term 'national culture' because of the danger of stereotyping. This is all the more so because stereotypes tend to emphasise negative rather than positive characteristics.

Managers need to pay an increasing amount of attention to the impact of national culture. This is because of growing cultural diversity within countries and globalisation. Managers are also more likely to have to work abroad, even if only for short periods, which may require considerable adjustment on their part. It is important that managers avoid taking an ethnocentric approach and adapt appropriately to other cultures. The growth of international organisations in both the private and public sectors means that managers may have to deal with a number of different nationalities simultaneously.

KEY VARIABLES

Key variables which can affect the way in which managers need to work include:

- climate and geography,
- language,
- religion and general societal values,
- systems of government,
- attitudes to gender and age,
- patterns of doing business,
- attitude to time,
- level of technology,
- costs, particularly of labour,
- local law,
- work ethic,
- relationships with the manager's country,
- facilities for family members,
- history.

HOFSTEDE'S MODEL

The most important study to date on the impact of national culture on work was conducted in 1984 by Hofstede (1994). This was based on 116,000 IBM employees in 53 countries. Hofstede found that there were wide variations in values and behaviour between countries. Originally, he identified four dimensions for classifying key national differences that affected work behaviour.

- power distance: the lengths of hierarchies vary considerably. Low power distances encourage individualism and high ones conformity. This is because the fewer the levels in the hierarchy there are, normally the greater the opportunity and need for decision-making at the levels that do exist. High power distances are also associated with authoritarian managerial styles.
- uncertainty avoidance: some cultures encourage acceptance of ambiguity and uncertainty whilst others do not. A high need to avoid uncertainty can generate anxiety and a need to plan to reduce uncertainty levels. Low needs for uncertainty avoidance, such as in Sweden, can lead to low anxiety and a willingness to take risks.
- individualism vs collectivism: there are large variations in the extent to which the focus of work and society is the individual, as in the USA, or the group, as in Japan. This has major implications for the way work is organised. Initiatives such as Total Quality Management (TQM) which are dependent on group co-operation are more likely to work in societies such as Japan but are more likely to fail if transplanted into more individualistic cultures. The nature of the culture also has implications for payment arrangements, social control and attitudes to innovation. Attempts at social control may be relatively ineffective in individualistic countries, but individual merit schemes are more likely to be successful and innovation is likely to be higher.

- masculinity vs femininity: masculine cultures are characterised by strong gender distinctions and an emphasis on individual achievement and material possessions. Feminine cultures have greater equality between the sexes and a greater concern for people. In feminine cultures, collaboration is also valued more highly in comparison with competition.

Great Britain was classified by Hofstede (1991) as having:

- relatively small power distance,
- weak uncertainty avoidance,
- highly individualistic,
- moderately masculine.

Japan in contrast was classified as having:

- relatively large power distance,
- strong uncertainty avoidance,
- moderately collectivist,
- highly masculine.

Hofstede later identified a fifth factor – Confucianism. He, in common with other scholars, saw religious and philosophical values as helping explain economic success in many South East Asian countries. Key factors identified by Hofstede (1991: 165) were:

- the social stability that can be created by high power distance,
- the family being a role model for the rest of society,
- respect for others,
- a high work ethic accompanied by patience and perseverance.

As Mead (1998: 383–384) says, though, care has to be taken in using this model because of the variation of the success in the economies of South East Asia – even those with Confucian values. Also some of factors identified are also common to other religions, particularly Protestantism.

There are dangers in using any model too prescriptively, however. Hofstede's research work was undertaken in the 1970s and only on IBM employees. There are also the obvious dangers of assuming that everyone will conform to a pattern of national characteristics. However, the model is the best one currently available. If nothing else, it can give managers a checklist of the factors they may need to take into account when working with people from different national cultures.

(Example)

An example of the insights that can be generated by work such as Hofstede's is the ambivalence of the UK's attitude to the European Union. In many ways the UK has stronger ties and cultural similarities with the USA than with much of Europe. These include language, kinship, legal tradition, high individualism, low uncertainty avoidance and small power distance. These in turn are reinforced by a generally

CONTINUED OVER ➤

CONTINUED FROM
PREVIOUS PAGE Protestant individualistic tradition compared with the generally more Catholic tradition in many other parts of Europe. Such differences may also help explain the Nordic vs Mediterranean division within the European Union.

LOCAL CULTURE

As well as needing to adapt to national culture, managers may need to adapt to regional or local culture within their own or another country. Sometimes the cultural variations and mutual antagonisms within countries are very high. A related issue is that managers may have to also deal with 'third country nationals', i.e. employees who have been imported to work from countries other than the manager's. Managers may also need to beware of being too closely associated with a particular cultural group within a country.

Example

A national brewing company in the UK decided to build its biggest brewery on a green-field site in Merseyside. A reason for doing this was the government funding available for generating work in an area of high unemployment. Managers from the company's plant at Burton-on-Trent were transferred to help build and commission the new brewery. Initially, they concentrated on the technical aspects of their work. However, it soon became apparent that employee relations was of a much higher priority than was the case in Burton. This was because of the different regional culture in Merseyside. A key difference was the traditional antagonisms between management and employees in the area. The more amicable working relationships at Burton had not prepared the managers who had been transferred for this key aspect of their jobs.

MANAGING DIVERSITY

Workforces are increasingly culturally diverse and managers will need to respond to the characteristics of such workforces whether they are working at home or abroad if they are to both achieve organisational objectives and achieve some element of social justice. Benefits of managing diversity from the organisation's point of view include better utilisation of talent as well as increased market understanding. Cross-cultural team membership may present certain problems in terms of creating a shared understanding of a situation, including language differences and utilising different systems of communication, but they can also be more creative. In order to manage diversity effectively, the manager will find it necessary to develop cross-cultural knowledge and understanding. In addition, it will be necessary to develop an organisational climate that focuses on valuing diversity and an organisational culture that is tolerant of some of the differences in values and behaviour. An organisation can be seen as having a moral obligation towards members of all ethnic groups. At the same time, the benefits of managing diversity effectively from the organisation's point of view can include reduced labour turnover and absenteeism, improved problem solving and innovation, greater appeal to minority ethnic groups and a better public image.

WORKING ABROAD

The problems of cultural adjustment are likely to be magnified if a manager has to work abroad (Mead 1998: ch. 19). The natural temptation is for the manager to rely on their own national culture as a model and to judge all other cultures by that.

Ideally, managers should receive some cultural briefing before they go on an international assignment of any length and a preliminary visit if that is possible. However, even with good initial briefing, there will be much to learn once the manager starts to work in another country.

Example

An engineering manager was sent to Singapore on a three-year appointment. He paid no attention to how he might adjust to the habits, beliefs and expectations of local colleagues. Instead he plunged straight into the technical aspects of his work. After three weeks he was sent back to the UK.

A further danger for managers working abroad is that they may live and socialise in an 'expatriate ghetto'. If managers restrict their social contacts to other expatriates this may reinforce existing prejudices about the local community and inhibit learning about and appreciating the local culture. It may also not be very good public relations. If managers do try and adapt, however, even if they make mistakes people from the host community may well be understanding of a person who is at least trying to get it right.

Expatriate failure can be costly both for the organisations involved and the individuals concerned. The chances of failure are likely to be considerably reduced if one accounts for the following factors

- selection: managers need to be carefully selected for overseas missions. As well as having the appropriate job expertise they crucially need to have the ability to adapt to working in a different environment.
- training: as well as needing induction training, managers may need to have training to prepare them for new job responsibilities. As managers often get promoted when they go abroad, this preparation may need to include management training.
- domestic arrangements: if a manager plans to take other family members with them thought needs to be given to how well they are likely to be able to adapt. Key issues will include the career opportunities for the partner and education facilities for any children. Children may suffer from loss of cultural identity if they spend too much time away from their own country.
- length of assignment: the longer a manager works abroad, the more successful they are likely to be in adapting to local conditions. However, the more they do this, the more out of touch they may get with what is happening elsewhere in their organisation.
- organisational adaptability: organisations need to adapt their structure, policies and procedures to meet local conditions. It may help in making appropriate adaptations if local people are considered for senior positions. Unfortunately, many organisations seek to rigidly impose their own arrangements in cultures where actual variation is needed.

- repatriation: organisations often fail to consider the issue of the repatriation of a person sent to work abroad. Expatriates can find that it has been a case of 'out of sight and out of mind'. They may also suffer from reverse culture shock when they return to their own country.

The adjustments necessitated by inward investment are considered in chapter 14. These are considered from the point of view of both the employer and local employees.

NATIONAL CULTURE AND ETHICS

When working abroad managers may find that there will be differences in the criteria applied in situations where ethical issues have to be considered before decisions are made. What may be seen as unethical in one culture may be acceptable and even necessary in another culture. A common problem is what attitude to take towards questionable payments. In some societies, it will be common practice for bribes of some description to be paid when awarding contracts or when securing other people's services. Difficult moral and business decisions may have to be taken about the extent to which one adjusts to apparent local customs. The consequences of decisions may also be difficult to predict.

Example

Two Western companies were operating in the same market in Indonesia. One took the policy decision that it would not pay bribes. The other took the opposite decision and tried to bribe its way into the market. The first company found that virtue was rewarded as it found it was able to operate perfectly satisfactorily without paying bribes. The second company found that once it had become known that it would pay bribes the numbers of people soliciting them proliferated. Also, although a considerable amount was paid in bribes, it brought no apparent benefits. Whilst concepts of 'honesty' (according to Western definitions) may unfortunately not always be the best policy, this example shows the dangers of jumping to conclusions about what is appropriate local practice.

Assertiveness

Although managerial style needs to fit the situation, there is a strong case for managers needing to learn how to behave assertively. This is in contrast to being non-assertive or aggressive. Whilst there may be occasions when managers may need to be non-assertive or aggressive, in general being assertive is likely to achieve better results. In any case, managers need to know how to be assertive so that they have the option of using this style.

AGGRESSIVE, NON-ASSERTIVE AND ASSERTIVE BEHAVIOUR

Assertiveness training was originally particularly associated with developing the confidence and skills of women. However, the skills are equally relevant to both genders and work as well in personal situations (Back and Back, 1999). They involve consideration of the rights of the parties involved in a situation. The patterns of behaviour associated with aggressive, new and assertive behaviour are outlined below.

Aggressive behaviour

If a manager behaves aggressively they may be standing up for their own rights but behaving in such a way that the rights of others are violated. The assumption behind their behaviour is that their needs are more important than those of others, and that only they have something to contribute.

The consequences of aggressive behaviour may be that the manager concerned gets their way and is able to vent their feelings. However, this may be at the expense of worsening working relationships and even generating stress in the person who is being aggressive. Aggressive behaviour will sometimes generate aggressive responses. It can also lead to a pattern of subordinates concealing bad news which can lead to managers taking decisions on inadequate information. (See also chapter 8 on communications.)

Aggressive behaviour is often an emotional response to a situation and not one calculated to be effective. Managers may need to find ways of diffusing their anger before dealing with people who are the object of it. One way of doing this is to write something down and then rip it up with a view to writing, or doing, something that is more rational. If a manager is having to cope with aggressive behaviour by someone else, they will probably need to let them dissipate their anger and only then try and have a rational dialogue. To do this they will need to curb their own anger and remember not to descend to the level of the person behaving aggressively.

Non-assertive behaviour

Non-assertive behaviour is based on the opposite assumption to that involved in aggressive behaviour. It implies that other people's rights are more important than your own. It also implies that the manager has nothing to contribute. Non-assertive behaviour is a way of dealing with situations in the short-term to avoid initial or further conflict. It may also create short-term popularity. However, in the long term, subordinates may become frustrated because of the lack of direction. Also, whilst non-assertiveness may sometimes be appropriate, it may be a form of escapism. Managers normally need to face up to problems, whatever they may be. If they do not, they may internalise their anger which may not do their health or job performance much good. Non-assertiveness can also cause a manager to overreact on subsequent occasions and behave aggressively.

Assertive behaviour

Assertive behaviour involves recognising both your own rights and those of whoever else is involved. It also involves recognising the right of all the parties involved to speak in a direct, honest and open way. Subordinates are therefore encouraged to behave assertively. This enables the issues that need to be addressed to be identified. It also has the potential to enable issues to be addressed in a way that is satisfactory to all the parties involved and which develops constructive working relationships between them. Another potential advantage is that it may take much less emotional energy to deal with issues this way.

THE SKILLS OF BEHAVING ASSERTIVELY

Key aspects of behaving assertively are to concentrate on facts and not feelings, and on issues and not personalities. Questioning technique and the choice of language can also be important. It may be particularly necessary to phrase statements and questions in a neutral way. Leading statements or questions may discourage people from raising points that are necessary both for themselves and the manager. Managers also need to consider their tone of voice and body language.

Example

If a conscientious and heavily loaded employee is simply told to undertake a new urgent task they may behave in a non-assertive way and simply get on with it. This, however, may generate feelings of resentment on the part of the subordinate and lead to other important work being delayed. An over-loaded employee may also eventually suffer ill-health, causing a problem for themselves and also for the organisation. Even though it might be inconvenient for the manager to be told by the subordinate of the practical problems, they may well need to know of them before deciding to give the work to that particular person.

To obtain necessary information from the subordinate it will be necessary to approach them in such a way that they can explain their situation. This does not mean that the manager can't insist on them doing the work. However, it would give the manager the opportunity to explain why, having taken everything into account, the subordinate needs to do this task as well. It may also cause the manager to consider if there was another subordinate who would be better placed to handle the work.

If managers need to present a case, whether in writing or orally, they also need to consider the option of presenting assertively. Aggressive presentations can lead to aggressive responses, while non-assertive presentations can simply be ignored. A practical illustration of presenting assertively, as opposed to aggressively, concerns attempts to prevent the rundown of services at St Bartholomew's Hospital in London.

Example

The secretary of state for health at the time of the proposed closure of the hospital was Virginia Bottomley. In 1993 she said that she 'had paid no special attention to "noisy lobbies" and had listened at least as much to those who had made cases calmly and quietly'.

Evaluation of managerial style

Managerial style is not an end in itself but a means to an end. Ultimately, managers are judged by results. Different managers may achieve the same results by using different means. The key to effective management is matching the style to the situation. Despite the differences between management and leadership, evidence about who is likely to emerge as the informal leader of a group may nevertheless help in judging the effectiveness of the style that managers adopt. In analysing research findings of group behaviour, Homans identified six factors that were strongly associated with who would emerge as the informal leader (1975: ch. 8). These can provide a rough and ready way of evaluating the effectiveness of managerial style. Although this seems to be suggesting that there is a standard effective style, the factors do take into account the requirements of the situation in which leadership is exercised.

Assessment exercise

As a way of assessing managers and the appropriateness of their style, identify one or more managers and rank them on the following six-point scale.

1. Excellent
2. Very Good
3. Good
4. Meets the minimum standards
5. Does not meet the minimum standards
6. Should be dismissed

The next stage is to compare the rating or ratings on the above scale with the six points identified by Homans as being characteristic of the behaviour of informal group leaders. Answer yes or no to the following questions.

1. Do they represent what the group finds to be most important in a person at that time?
2. Do they make decisions which turn out, by and large, to be correct?
3. Do they keep their word?
4. Do they settle differences between members in a way the group believes to be fair?
5. Do they allow followers to go to them for advice and keep them informed about what is going on?
6. Do they give information to the group in the form of advice, orders, etc., and maintain two-way communication?

When the second part of the assessment is completed it is necessary to compare the number of 'no' responses with the initial rating of managerial effectiveness. Usually this correlates so that the fewer the 'no' responses to Homans's six points, the more likely it is that the manager or managers would have received a high rating in terms of managerial effectiveness. For example, a person with who received six 'yes' responses, and therefore zero 'no' responses, would have received a rating of 1 (excellent). Conversely, a person who was given 'no' six times would be rated as 6 (should be dismissed).

The above method of assessment can act as a means of identifying the reasons for managerial ineffectiveness as well as a means of assessing the level of performance. It can also be used as a method of self-assessment.

SUMMARY

✔ In this chapter the concept of managerial style has been explained as have the differences between the overlapping concepts of management and leadership. Managers are appointed but leaders often emerge as popular choices, particularly in representative structures. Managerial style is not an end in itself but a means to an end. The range of managerial styles has been examined. A key distinction is the level of direction that the manager gives. Examination of the various theories has shown that it is largely determined by the assumptions the managers make about why other people work and other variables in the situation. These variables are likely to include the organisational culture, the level of skill of subordinates and the extent to which their objectives converge with organisational ones. For managerial styles to be effective they need to match the situation. This may involve selecting people whose style fits a situation or people adjusting their style to the circumstances.

✔ National culture also does, or needs to, affect managerial style. This is an increasingly important issue because of globalisation and cultural diversity within countries. The work of Hofstede was examined and in particular the four key dimensions he used to differentiate between managerial styles in different countries.

✔ Whatever the style there is usually a case for managers behaving assertively rather than aggressively or non-assertively. Assertiveness involves respecting other people's rights to state their case but being prepared to firmly, yet politely, state one's own case. The associated skills in doing this have also been explained.

✔ Ultimately, managers have to be judged by effectiveness and not, for example, by their popularity. An exercise was included within the chapter so that readers can assess the managerial effectiveness of other people. Much depends on their relationship with their subordinates. A further exercise has been included as an appendix so that readers can examine their own managerial style and see if there is any need for adjustment.

SELF-ASSESSMENT QUESTIONS

1. How would you define the concept of managerial style?

2. Identify the main different types of managerial style.

3. Why does managerial style need to match the circumstances in which it is used?

4. What organisational factors can influence managerial style?

5. Identify key ways in which national culture can affect managerial style.

6. Explain the differences between assertive, aggressive and non-assertive behaviour.

7. How would you evaluate the effectiveness of a particular managerial style?

8. What is your own preferred managerial style? How effective is it usually?

 References

(Works of general interest in the specific references are marked with a star.)

Adair, John (1982) *Action-centred Leadership*, Gower.

* Back, Ken and Kate Back (1999) *Assertiveness at Work: A Practical Guide to Handling Awkward Situations*, 3rd ed., McGraw-Hill.

Belbin, R. Meredith (1981) *Management Teams: Why They Succeed or Fail*, Butterworth Heinemann.

Blake R. and J. S. Mouton (1978) *The New Management Grid*, Gulf Publishing.

Bottomley, Virginia (1993) 'Bart's Seeks Merger and Drops Fight', *The Guardian*, 18 February.

Fox, Alan (1965) 'Industrial Society and Industrial Relations', research paper no. 3, Royal Commission on Trade Unions and Employer's Associations, HMSO.

Garraham, Philip and Paul Stewart (1992) *The Nissan Enigma – Flexibility at Work in a Local Economy*, Mansell.

* Handy, Charles (1991) *The Age of Unreason*, 2nd ed., Business Books.

* Hofstede, G. (1994) *Cultures and Consequences*, Fontana.

* Hofstede, G (1991) *Cultures and Organisations: Software of the Mind*, McGraw Hill

Homans, George (1975) *The Human Group*, Routledge and Kegan Paul.

Hillary, Peter (1995) comments reported in *Evening Standard* (London), 23 August.

Lewis, Pamela S., Stephen H. Goodman and Patricia M. Fandt (1995) *Management – Challenges in the 21st Century – Annotated Instructor's Edition*, West Publishing Co., USA.

Local Government Management Board (1993) 'Managing Tomorrow', Panel of Inquiry report, Local Government Management Board.

* Mead, Richard (1998) *International Management, Cross-Cultural Dimensions*, 2nd ed., Blackwell.

* McGregor, Douglas (1969) *The Human Side of Enterprise*, McGraw-Hill.

Rees, W. David and C. Porter (1998) 'Employee Participation and Managerial Style (The Key Variable), *Industrial and Commercial Training*, MCB University Press, 30(5).

Tannenbaum R. and W. H. Schmidt (1957) 'How to Choose a Leadership Pattern', *Harvard Business Review*, 36(2).

General references

Belbin, R. Meredith (2000) *Beyond The Team*, Butterworth Heinemann.

Deresky, Helen (2000) 'International Management: Managing Across Borders and Cultures' in *Managing Interdependence – Social Responsibility and Ethics*, Prentice Hall: New Jersey, ch. 3.

Golzan, Godfrey (1999) *The Daily Telegraph's Guide to Working and Living Overseas*, Kogan Page, 21st ed. (for a wealth of information on the practical issues concerning working overseas).

Hall, E. T. (1987) *Hidden Differences*, Anchor Press/Doubleday.

Kandola, Rajvinder and Johanna Fullerton (1998) *Diversity in Action – Managing the Mosaic*, Institute of Personnel and Development.

Trompenaars, Fons (1993) *Riding the Waves of Culture: Understanding Cultural Diversity in Business*, Nicholas Brealey.

Appendix to chapter 4

1. Do you vary your style to match the situation?

2. Are you naturally Theory X or Theory Y in the assumptions that you make about employees?

3. Where do you fit on the leadership continuum?

4. Is your managerial style people-centred, task-centred or both?

5. Do your assumptions about conflict in organisations fit with those with a unitary or pluralistic frame of reference?

6. Are you generally non-assertive, assertive or aggressive?

7. Are you reactive or proactive in your managerial style? (See chapter 2 on identifying the manager's job.)

8. Is your orientation primarily managerial or specialist? (See chapter 1 on managers and their background.)

9. Do you generally get on with tasks yourself or do you generally see that they are done by others?

10. When you chair meetings is your orientation towards process management or substantive contribution? (See chapter 16 on meetings and chairing.)

11. How effective is your style?

12. In the light of your answers to the above questions do you need to alter any of your managerial behaviour in order to improve your effectiveness?

chapter five

Delegation

There are case studies and exercises at
http://www.thomsonlearning.co.uk
(for full details, see the listing at the
start of this book).

LEARNING OUTCOMES

By the end of this chapter you will be able to:

- Define, understand and apply the concept of delegation

- Identify the importance of delegation

- Identify criteria for deciding what should be delegated and what should not be delegated

- Identify and apply the key skills involved in implementing delegation

- Identify the main barriers to effective delegation and take appropriate remedial action

- Understand the differences between delegation and the overlapping concept of 'empowerment'

Introduction

Management has already been described in chapter 1 as 'getting work done through others'. It therefore follows that delegation is a part of every manager's job. It involves giving others the authority to act on your behalf. Criteria are given for deciding what might be delegated and what should not be. The managerial skills needed to delegate effectively are identified. These include risk assessment, consideration of the strengths and weaknesses of subordinates, and the establishment of appropriate control mechanisms. Managers also need to be prepared to spend time training their subordinates so that they are able to handle delegated authority.

Unfortunately, although the concepts involved in delegation are relatively easily explained, many managers are very bad at delegating. Consequently, the barriers to effective delegation are examined here. Whilst some of these managerial omissions are because of a lack of understanding of the nature of delegation, others may be of a more deep-seated nature. A particularly difficult barrier is psychological insecurity on the part of some managers. This can make it very difficult for them to give subordinates reasonable freedom to act on their behalf.

The overlapping concept of empowerment is also examined. It is important to try and identify what people mean by this term. Sometimes it is used interchangeably with delegation. However, empowerment often focuses on groups rather than individuals. Historically, it was a 'bottom-up' process whereby community groups in the USA took more control over their lives. Latterly, it has become more used in a managerial context as a 'top-down' process.

The nature of delegation

DEFINITION

Delegation may be defined as 'a person giving authority to someone to act on their behalf'. It should not be confused with the issuing of orders or giving of instructions to subordinates. Although the manager remains accountable for the actions of the subordinate, the essence of delegation is the conferring of authority on the subordinate. Thus, delegation is much more than just passing a task over to be executed. Like all management techniques it is neutral. It can be used to good or bad effect. What matters is that it is used appropriately.

ACCOUNTABILITY

When managers delegate they still remain accountable for the actions of their subordinates. Delegation does not involve abdication of responsibility. This has been illustrated by a number of important and well publicised cases.

> **Example**
>
> The owner and chief executive of the bankrupt Fire, Auto and Marine Insurance Company, Dr. Emile Savundra, was cross-examined in a fraud trial in Britain about the contrast between his personal wealth and the state of his former company. He responded by saying that he had practised modern management techniques – including delegation – and that such questions should be addressed instead to his former financial controller. The judge understood management better than that, and when sentencing Dr Savundra to a lengthy term of imprisonment, commented that whilst authority can be delegated, accountability remained!

ACCOUNTABILITY IN THE PUBLIC SECTOR

There is an extra dimension to the general concept of accountability in the public sector because of the issue of public accountability. At one stage in the UK it was the practice for government ministers to accept responsibility and resign if there was a serious enough error by one of their subordinates – regardless of whether the minister even knew of the action beforehand. The following examples explain how the concept has developed in the public sector:

Example

In 1955 it was found that land on Crichel Down, which had been compulsorily purchased by the government for military use during the Second World War, had been later used for agricultural purposes and then sold to a private buyer. This was despite an earlier assurance to give the original owner the first option of buying the land back. The minister was obliged to resign, even though he had not been personally involved in the decision and had had no reason to believe that his officials had acted in other than good faith.

This convention of public sector resignation, regardless of personal blame, was, however, later modified.

Example

The Aberfan disaster of 1966 occurred when a large slag heap of waste coal was dislodged by a swollen underground stream after heavy rain. It engulfed part of the village of Aberfan, in South Wales, including a school just after the children had arrived in the morning. A total of 147 people died, including 116 children. The owner of the slag heap was the National Coal Board, and its chairman, Lord Robens, offered his resignation. This was not accepted, however, on the basis that the disaster was not reasonably foreseeable. This was in spite of a tribunal of enquiry report that was highly critical of the Coal Board. The report concluded, in 1967, that 'blame for the disaster rests upon the National Coal Board' (McLean 1999: 12).

This modified concept of accountability was applied in later important cases involving the government. However, it was not enough to save a British Foreign Secretary from resignation.

Example

Both the British foreign secretary, Lord Carrington, and the defence secretary, John Nott (later Sir), offered their resignations after the Argentinean occupation of the Falklands Islands, a British colony, in 1982. In the event, the foreign secretary's resignation was accepted, despite his illustrious record, but not the defence secretary's. Presumably this was because it was judged that the Argentinean invasion should have been anticipated and preventative action initiated. It was also possible that it was politically necessary for someone to resign.

A dramatic reinforcement of the concept of accountability occurred with regard to the political responsibility of the members of the European Union Commission.

Example

An investigation by independent experts into fraud and mismanagement within the European Union Commission concluded that the president of the European Commission, Jacques Santer, and his team of 20 commissioners:

CONTINUED OVER ➤

CONTINUED FROM PREVIOUS PAGE

'has to bear responsibility for fraud, irregularities and mismanagement'. It also concluded that political responsibility 'cannot be a vague idea, a concept which in practice proves unrealistic… It is becoming difficult to find anyone that has even the slightest sense of responsibility.'

(Castle and Grice 1999: 1–2)

Despite the vigorous protests of Jacques Santer, the European Parliament also demonstrated their disapproval by passing a 'no confidence' motion in the work of the commission. Consequently all the commissioners, including the president, were obliged to resign. Only four commissioners were subsequently reappointed.

The cumulative effect of these cases, and others, is that, particularly in the public sector, policymakers are accountable for reasonably foreseeable and important failures. Failures of this nature may force their resignation. Consequently, it is important for them to set up effective control procedures so that they can either avoid major failures or take prompt action to limit their effect.

The need for delegation

One of the main reasons for delegation is that it is a means whereby a manager can, having decided their priorities, concentrate on the work of greatest importance, leaving the work of lesser importance to be done by others. Ironically, if delegation is set up effectively, the delegated work may, in time, be actually performed better by the subordinates. This also has the advantages of motivating and developing subordinates.

EFFECTIVE USE OF TIME

The time of managers is limited, thus it is important for them to tackle their work in some order of priority so that the most important tasks get the appropriate attention. If at the end of the day some work has not been completed, or has had to be passed on to others, this should be the work of lowest priority. Even if the work of lesser importance is not done, or is not done so well, this is appropriate behaviour for the person in charge. It would not be sensible for a manager to do their own clerical work because they thought they could do it better than their secretary or clerk. Running the risk of a slightly lower level of performance by a subordinate is a small price to pay for creating time to concentrate on the more important aspects of a job.

The lower the level at which a task is performed, the lower the cost of performing that task is therefore likely to be. Cost needs to be considered not just in terms of the salary of the person undertaking a particular task but also in terms of opportunity cost, i.e., the opportunity that is denied or created for the manager to do other work. Detailed techniques of prioritisation are explained later in this chapter.

EFFECTIVE USE OF SUBORDINATES

Many managers fail to make effective use of their subordinates. This can both reduce their own effectiveness and demotivate their subordinates. In some cases there would be a blatant disregard of the specialist expertise of a subordinate if the boss tried to do the subordinate's job. What would be the point, and the results, if, for example, a managing director tried to run the accounts department if they had a finance manager?

Arising out of this is the need for managers to seek to dovetail their activity with that of their subordinates. Everybody has relative strengths and weaknesses in their work. If a subordinate has particular strengths it may be appropriate to make use of those strengths rather than compete in that area or simply ignore those strengths. What matters is the effectiveness of the team as a whole rather than the direct performance of just the manager.

Further possible advantages of delegation are that the subordinate often has more time and readier access to the appropriate information than the boss. Also, what is routine work to the boss may be challenging to the subordinate, as well as carrying prestige. The more that subordinates are developed, the more they are likely to be able to undertake in the future.

Managers have to think carefully about the balance between managing by systems and through people. Detailed control procedures tend to be statements of lack of trust and can be unnecessary as well as demotivating if there are capable subordinates. Such systems may also inhibit healthy evolution and act as an organisational straitjacket. In any case, systems tend to be as good or bad as the people who operate them. A director of one civil service agency commented that the best legacy he could leave the agency was to see that the six key jobs under him were manned by capable people.

An example of the failure to use subordinates effectively is given in the following example.

Example

The chief executive of an organisation invested in the management training of those with managerial responsibilities. Jobs that were mainly supervisory or managerial were given the designation 'manager'. Remuneration was also improved for those with managerial responsibilities. However, simultaneously, more detailed central control was introduced and the number of senior managers at the head office was doubled. The newly designated managers became increasingly frustrated with their work. This was because the clarification of their managerial responsibilities and their management development coincided with a considerable reduction in their delegated authority. Their management training made them all the more aware of this contradiction.

DEVELOPMENT OF SUBORDINATES

A further advantage of effective delegation may be that a manager is setting the pattern for their subordinates to delegate in turn down the line. One adage about managerial assessment is that you judge a manager by the quality of their subordinates. This can also be important so that subordinates can deal with emergencies. Presumably, Philip II of Spain would not have rated highly on this basis, since it is alleged that he governed Spain in the 16th century in a manner which created 'apoplexy at the nucleus and paralysis at the periphery'.

Effective delegation can also help prepare subordinates for promotion. However, it is important that subordinates take advantage of the opportunities that may be presented to them. It may seem that promotion decisions are taken by the manager responsible for making the appointments. In reality, though, it may be much more the case that it is the managers being considered for promotion who decide for themselves whether or not they get it. Managers responsible for appointments do not make decisions in a vacuum. The existing pattern of behaviour of a manager is likely to influence any decision about their promotion. If a manager has got their pattern of delegation right, and because of that gets promotion, the onus may then be upon them to establish a new pattern so that they prepare themselves for even further promotion. The same reasoning can apply to people running small businesses. The expansion or non-expansion of a small business may depend less on external factors than is often imagined. Much may depend on the ability of the person running a small business to identify and concentrate on the key tasks, leaving the less critical, even if more enjoyable, tasks to others.

Example

Two small hospital groups had been merged, partly because of the ineffective management style of the chief executive of one of the groups, who was prematurely retired. He had operated on the classic Theory X assumptions about his subordinates, explained in the previous chapter. The chief executive of the other group now had to administer both groups. He was much more prepared to delegate and, interestingly, had attracted around him a much more capable group of managers than had his retired colleague, despite a common salary structure.

Initially, the chief executive of the merged group tried to cope with his own increased workload by increasing the delegated authority of the managers in the group which he had taken over. One of the unit managers tried to cope with his extra responsibility doing all the extra work as well as the work he had traditionally undertaken. However, this was too much for him and the work he left undone was most of the extra and important work which had been delegated to him. He was quite unable to identify his new priorities and to delegate down the line, as his new boss had delegated to him. Consequently, the chief executive had to take back most of the delegated authority, recognising that the unit manager had reached his limit as far as his capacity to assume responsibility was concerned. Ironically, the chief executive was then able to delegate even more authority to the managers in the other part of the group, as they were used to coping with increased responsibility. The unit

CONTINUED OVER ➤

CONTINUED FROM PREVIOUS PAGE manager, who had been relieved of part of his authority, had imposed his own limit. By demonstrating his inability to cope with increased authority and responsibility, he had not only restricted his own job but ruled himself out of consideration for future promotion. In ways such as this, people can set limits on their career without necessarily realising it.

The skills of delegation

The case for delegation is easy to make. However, people may rush into delegating without effective planning. The delegated work may then be mishandled, causing the boss to withdraw the delegated authority without realising that the problem lay in the lack of planning rather than the basic idea. The factors critical to effective planning of delegation need identification and explanation.

DISCRETIONARY AUTHORITY

The first critical factor is the need for clarity about just what has been delegated. A useful concept in this respect is Wilfred (later Lord) Brown's distinction between the prescribed and discretionary content of a manager's job (1965: 123). Prescribed work is that which must be performed in a predetermined manner. The discretionary element of a manager's job is where they are expected to use their own judgement. For example, a personnel officer could be told that they had authority to determine at what point on a given salary scale a recruit to an organisation would start. The salary range to be used, however, would be prescribed. Time and care need to be taken in defining a person's job in this way, particularly, for example, when a person has just started.

The use of discretion by subordinates must be tolerated, within reasonable limits. A subordinate cannot always be expected to perform in exactly the same way as their manager would. If that is the expectation, then the work concerned is prescribed content not discretionary content. If there is discretion, and it is used sensibly, it can be very demoralising for a subordinate to be told 'I wouldn't have done it quite that way'. If the discretion had been used unwisely, this may well reveal a weakness in the way the delegation was set up originally.

The appropriate use of discretionary powers may well involve considerable discussion between manager and subordinate. The access of the subordinate to the manager needs determining. If people are unsure of how to use their delegated powers, they may well act inappropriately or pass things back up to the manager. When items are passed up to managers, they need to consider whether they should do them or whether they should be passed back to the subordinate with a reminder about the subordinate's discretionary authority. When an appropriate discretionary area has been established, it is up to the manager to see that the subordinate gets on with their job and does not seek to over-involve them. It is important to clarify what the boss does and does not need to know.

PRIORITISATION

Managers need to develop criteria for judging what they do themselves and what they delegate. Useful criteria are:

- existing arrangements for the allocation of work;
- confidentiality;
- complexity;
- managers' strengths and weaknesses relative to those of their subordinates;
- speed of response required;
- availability of people to do a particular task;
- reversibility: if a decision can be reversed quickly and easily then it may be appropriate to delegate it. The consequences of error will not be great;
- repetition: if an issue or problem arises frequently it may be sensible to delegate it. There will be scale economies in investing time in setting up such a delegation;
- consequences: if the impact of a decision is small, the risks involved in delegating it will be small. The case for delegation will be stronger if no important precedents are being set;
- future commitment: future commitments can vary in resource implications and the time scale involved. The smaller the commitment and the smaller the time scale the greater the case for delegation;
- values and image: the impact of decision making on the image of an organisation needs to be considered. Representatives of an organisation may, for example, need to be much more carefully briefed about how they handle clients or customers, compared with their dealings with colleagues.

The use of these criteria may also help managers to avoid rationalising about why they need to undertake a particular task. It is all too easy to pretend that a particular task has to be carried out by oneself when that may not really be the case.

ROUTING OF WORK

Care has to be taken with work that is routed to the manager but which should be done by subordinates. In some cases colleagues will need to have it explained to them that they should go to the subordinates direct. On other occasions it will be entirely appropriate that the work should be routed to a manager, so that the chain of command is not bypassed. If a manager's boss routes something to them, it does not automatically follow that the manager must do the job themselves. The decision as to who does it is one for the manager. The real pattern of delegation is likely to be set by the way a manager handles routing decisions such as these. The critical question to be asked, before any work is undertaken, is 'whose job is this?' Obviously, authority can only be delegated to people who, in the long run, are going to be able to cope with the delegated powers. This may in turn become a criterion in selection, so that one chooses staff who will be able to integrate effectively with the work pattern of their boss.

CONTROL MECHANISMS

All delegated authority needs to be accompanied by effective control mechanisms, particularly in view of the accountability of the person delegating. It is difficult to envisage managers being given plenipotentiary powers, i.e. being allowed to decide crucial issues without reference to anyone. Control mechanisms can take many forms. These include:

- getting approval on specified issues before taking action;
- reporting back on issues after action has been taken;
- activity sampling by the boss;
- reporting by the subordinate on exceptional issues;
- appraisal systems, both informal and formal;
- visual observation;
- monitoring of results;
- inspection procedures by the boss, a separate inspection function or both;
- internal and/or external auditing;
- peer observation;
- internal and external complaints procedures.

Performance indicators are increasingly used in the public sector, in particular to monitor the progress of whole organisations.

Example

An example of the dangers of not having effective control procedures is illustrated by the case of Barings Bank. Nick Leeson was a market derivatives trader employed by Barings Bank at their Singapore branch. The derivatives market is highly speculative. Nick Leeson generated dramatic profits for the group which earned both him and his superiors large bonuses. Few questions were asked about his success and there was no effective check on his activities. Unfortunately, he generated his large profits by hiding his losses in a secret account. In an attempt to cover these hidden and mounting losses he speculated increasingly large amounts of the bank's money. Eventually the scale of the losses became unsupportable. The bank collapsed in 1995 with debts of approximately £900 million. Nick Leeson was sentenced to six and a half years in prison in Singapore following his breaches of local stock exchange regulations. In upholding one of the applications in Britain by the Department of Trade and Industry for the disqualification of the directors the judge described their lack of control as 'crass' and 'absolute'.

(Evening Standard 1998:4)

CONTROL OF PROFESSIONALLY QUALIFIED STAFF

There can be particular difficulties in trying to set up control systems for professionally qualified employees. This is sometimes because such employees see this as a slight on their professional independence. However, if they are funded by an organisation they are accountable for the use of those funds. Their activity needs to be integrated with the rest of the organisation. The employment relationship is quite different from a professional working in practice on their own. The dangers of specialists indulging in meeting their objectives, which may not necessarily be the same as the organisation's, were explained in detail in chapter 1.

A useful distinction is to hold professional employees accountable for end results but to leave it to them as to how they achieve results. In some cases, it is necessary to set up systems for monitoring the quality of professional work. This is an issue that is of particular concern in the National Health Service, because of the issues of public and legal liability and the potential seriousness of poor quality work. It has led to the concept of 'clinical governance'. The need for this was underlined following a report in 1998 of an investigation into the deaths of 29 babies, after heart surgery at Bristol Royal Infirmary. The need for further controls over the way general medical practitioners operate, in the UK at least, was dramatically emphasised when, in 2000, Dr. Harold Shipman was convicted of murdering 15 of his patients. These and other medical scandals led doctors themselves to pass a motion of no confidence in the work of the body responsible for monitoring medical standards, the General Medical Council, at the annual conference of the British Medical Association in 2000. The system of 'peer audit' has been developed in both medical and university teaching as one way of increasing the quality control of professionals working in these areas.

USE OF DEPUTIES

Delegation can be achieved by the appointment of a deputy or deputies. However, such arrangements need thinking through or they can be counter-productive. If a person is appointed as a full-time deputy, it begs the question of what the person does whilst the boss is available. It can be something of a luxury to have a permanent understudy available but not necessarily used. Such an arrangement would also be very frustrating for a deputy of any ability. If the arrangement of routing everything through a deputy is used, it raises the question of just what is the value of such a duplication of activity. This can generate rivalry and competition for what may really be only one job.

Normally deputies would carry ongoing responsibilities as well as being asked to 'act-up' when the boss is not available. However, there needs to be a very clear understanding between the boss and the deputy about the demarcation between their jobs. Other employees also need to know these arrangements so that they are able to route issues to the correct person.

There is a case for avoiding the title deputy because of the confusion it can cause. Instead, a manager may designate who is to act when they are not available. It may be appropriate to ask just one person to act-up or to have subordinates act-up according to defined areas of responsibility.

Sometime deputies are used to support a manager who is under pressure. However, before such an arrangement is used, thought needs to be given as to whether there are better solutions or not. This may involve other forms of work reorganisation or a review of the abilities of the manager under pressure. If the boss is replaced by a more capable person, there may no longer be any need for a deputy. However, the continuing need for a deputy may be a question people forget to ask in such a situation.

Example

The chief executive of a large hospital was overworked and a deputy was appointed to ease his workload. However, the deputy was not given enough work to do and soon left. Another deputy was appointed. He had turned down the chance of running a small hospital to gain experience in a large one. However, he also found that he was not given enough to do.

The chief executive encouraged people to come to him direct. Most mail was routed to him, even though it might take a day for him to look at it. He also sometimes countermanded the orders of subordinates, including those given by his 'deputy'. To compound these problems, the chief executive sometimes criticised his 'deputy' to others because of his lack of experience and because he maintained that he was not prepared to work as hard as he did.

The pattern of activity continued, and little long term planning or strategic thinking took place. The newly appointed deputy began to look around for another job. Heads of department were generally either frustrated by their lack of delegated authority or were content to let much of their work be handled by the chief executive. He was sent on a four-week management training course. This, however, did not lead to any change in his behaviour. He came into the hospital on Saturdays during this period to check what was happening and to deal with urgent business.

TRAINING

Delegating authority to others may well be accompanied by a need to train them in the way in which that authority is to be used. It is no good delegating authority to a subordinate unless they know what to do. All too often this stage is omitted and managers exclaim that people won't assume authority. There may be a need to start training well in advance of the delegation. Training needs to combine the substantive knowledge and skills required by the subordinate in their job with a careful definition of just what constitutes their job.

Training can be formal, informal or both. A useful convention in nursing management in the National Health Service is that when people with managerial responsibilities are absent their subordinates act-up. This is as opposed to the manager in charge of the person absent acting-down. Acting-up can leave managers free to concentrate on high priority work, develop subordinates and help identify promotion potential. Unfortunately, sometimes managers are only too keen to act-down because it enables them to engage in their historic and preferred specialist activity.

Obstacles to effective delegation

Even when people recognise the advantages of delegation and are aware of the skills involved in planning it effectively, they may still not delegate to the extent to which they should. There are a number of barriers to effective delegation – usually these are a lot easier to recognise in others than in oneself. Also, these are sometimes not so much barriers as genuine constraints. Sometimes it can by very difficult to disentangle imagined from real constraints.

TIME

Paradoxically, delegation may initially be time-consuming. In particular, significant time may need to be spent in:

- identifying what is to be delegated,
- establishing appropriate control procedures,
- briefing and training subordinates.

Delegation is like a capital investment: time spent setting it up may achieve substantial dividends – but only in the future. If the manager does not carefully think through the pattern of delegation, it may backfire and discourage them from further attempts.

LACK OF TRAINING

Many managers are not trained in how to manage. They may either lack formal training or the ability to learn and develop on the job under the guidance of managers. Even those managers who have received formal training may not have been trained in delegation. Despite its importance, it is often quite wrongly assumed that it does not need to feature in management training programmes.

FACTORS OUTSIDE THE MANAGER'S CONTROL

There can be a number of genuine constraints preventing or limiting the ability of managers to delegate. These include:

- lack of resources, particularly of subordinate staff — shortages of staff can be in terms of quantity, quality or both;
- an organisational climate that discourages delegation;
- their own lack of authority;
- lack of work to do anyway;
- jealousy between subordinates;
- over-ambitious subordinates;

- pressures to do particular tasks themselves that it would be counter-productive to resist;
- confidentiality.

MANAGERIAL INSECURITY

Although there can be genuine limits on the extent to which delegation can be implemented, some managers simply do not want to delegate. Often the greatest obstacle to delegation is the psychological insecurity of a manager. If this is the case, attempts to train a manager to delegate, or exhortations to delegate, may simply fail. One of the problems with management training generally is that managers have to integrate good management practice with their own personality.

Example

A college principal had all the college mail addressed to him personally. He would open the envelopes and, when rerouting mail to subordinate staff, instruct them on what action to take. This enabled him to complain that no-one else in the college worked as hard as he did or was prepared to assume responsibility. The fact was, of course, that he would not permit anyone else to take responsibility. One of the psychological pay-offs in this game was that if one starts with the assumption that one's subordinates are no good, this can then become a self-fulfilling prophecy – as good staff will be driven away. However, there was some progress in the case of the college principal. Eventually, his secretary was allowed to open the envelopes before the principal himself took out the enclosures!

THE INDISPENSABLE EMPLOYEE

Sometimes people can deliberately seek to make themselves indispensable. This may be a means of managers dealing with their feelings of personal insecurity. A rough guide to the competence of a manager is to see how well things work when they are absent. The effective manager should have developed systems and staff abilities so that people can cope in their absence. This may not be the case with the ineffective manager. The poor manager may even be glad that things have not gone well in their absence and even publicise that fact. The creation of a state of indispensability may be subconscious or carefully planned.

Example

An engineer in a local authority set out to make himself indispensable. Some of the maps of the local underground drainage system had been destroyed, and he was the only person who knew the exact locations of the drains in the relevant areas. He consistently refused to commit his knowledge to paper on the basis that as long as only he knew the complete layout the council would not dismiss him. When it was put to him that if he suddenly fell ill or died the lack of any record of the complete drainage system would cause obvious problems, he responded by saying that that would not be his problem!

Sometimes indispensability can happen by accident

<table>
<tr><td>Example</td><td>The head of the avionics division of an electronics company managed his division very effectively for 27 years. Unfortunately he became so good at his job that when he retired nobody could be found who could replace him. Ironically, had he been less good at his job a management system may have evolved that could have survived his retirement. As it was the division had to be closed down.</td></tr>
</table>

Empowerment

BACKGROUND

The concept of empowerment has become increasingly fashionable in recent years. The term seems to have originated in the USA when Democratic administrations in the 1960s were seeking to build 'The Great Society'. It was a response by government to the need for disadvantaged groups to have more control over their lives with a view to improving them. These groups particularly included ethnic minorities and the physically and mentally challenged. It was a bottom-up process.

Subsequently, the term empowerment was increasingly used in the business world. Authority was often devolved to lower levels of management to help achieve business objectives. However, this was a top-down process. It coincided with many other trends, which included de-layering, down-sizing, loss of faith in centralised planning and the introduction of TQM. These trends were associated with an increased pace of change because of globalisation and the increasing use of new technology. The practice spread to the public sector, partly as a means of devolving the difficult prioritisation that was necessary when expectations outstripped available funds.

DEFINITION

A problem with the term 'empowerment' is what people actually mean when they use it. Michael Armstrong defines it as:

> *ensuring that people are able to use and develop their skills and knowledge in ways which help to achieve both their own goals and those of the organisation. Empowerment is achieved by organisation and job design approaches which place responsibility fairly on individuals and teams, by recognising the contribution people can make, by providing mechanisms such as improvement groups to enable them to make this contribution and by training and development programmes which increase both competence and confidence.*

1991 :123

EMPOWERMENT IN PRACTICE

Even if people are clear what they mean by the term empowerment it may be implemented poorly or applied in situations where it is inappropriate. Unfortunately, the term is often used very loosely or applied with a messianic zeal as though it were an end in itself, instead of a means of helping achieve organisational objectives. It is not a concept that should be applied regardless of circumstances. A particular danger is that those seeking to apply it may ignore the potential for conflict between individual or sectional objectives and those of the rest of the organisation. This fundamental issue is explained under the heading 'unitary and pluralistic frames of reference' in chapters 4 and 14.

In many organisations that have introduced greater empowerment there is a strong internal social and cultural control to ensure that, for example, semi-autonomous work groups perform in a way that is congruent with organisational goals. Empowering people without thinking through the implications, however, could be disastrous. The example, given earlier in this chapter, of the lack of control of the derivatives market trader, Nick Leeson, dramatically illustrates this point. The tendency of specialists with managerial responsibility to go their own way has been documented in chapter 1. It is perhaps also worth making an analogy about the dangers of self-regulation by referring to groups such as doctors, lawyers, newspapers and the stock exchange, where it is arguable that the interests of the members have sometimes had a higher priority than that of other interest groups, including the public. Lloyds of London is an example of a self-regulatory body where many less influential members felt that their heavy financial losses had been caused by a rigging of the insurance risks against them.

Another aspect of empowerment is that it is sometimes associated with organisational down-sizing. This can create genuine opportunities for empowerment for the remaining managers. However, if the down-sizing is badly thought out, it can mean managers having to try and pick put the pieces of a restructuring exercise without the necessary resources, direction, or extra remuneration to adequately handle their new responsibilities.

KEY QUESTIONS

Key questions to ask to see if people are clear about actual or proposed empowerment arrangements are:

- Is it seen as an end in itself or as a means of helping achieve organisational objectives?
- Are management control procedures still required?
- Exactly what authority is being delegated and to whom?
- What resources are being allocated to the person or unit that is empowered to enable them to achieve their objectives?
- How does the empowered unit or person interrelate with existing authority structures?
- What happens if there are conflicts of objectives between the person or unit empowered and the overall organisation?

SUMMARY

✔ Delegation has been defined as 'a person giving authority to someone to act on their behalf'. However, whilst authority can be delegated, as has been explained, the person who delegates remains accountable for the actions of the person to whom they delegate. Delegation frees up time for the manager to concentrate on the key aspects of their job. It can also be used as a means of developing subordinates. Key skills that have been identified include:

- the need to clarify the discretionary authority of subordinates,
- prioritisation of work,
- routing work to the right people,
- establishing appropriate control mechanisms,
- selection and training of subordinates.

✔ Initially, implementing delegation takes time, and so it is time-consuming. As with all investments, the potential rewards are not immediate but evident in the future. The many obstacles to delegation have been examined. Some of them may be legitimate, such as a lack of staff. Unfortunately, the biggest obstacle can be the personal insecurity of some managers.

✔ Delegation overlaps with the concept of empowerment. A key difference between the two concepts can be that it involves conferring authority on groups of people. However, the term is often used very loosely and it is often necessary to find out exactly what people mean when they use the term. It is also necessary to recognise the potential for conflict between empowered groups or individuals and overall organisational objectives.

SELF-ASSESSMENT QUESTIONS

1. How would you define delegation?

2. Why is delegation a core management skill?

3. How would you decide whether a particular task should be delegated or not?

4. What are the key skills associated with delegation?

5. What are the main obstacles in practice to effective delegation?

6. Identify the differences between the concepts of delegation and empowerment.

 References

Armstrong, Michael (1991) *A Handbook of Personnel Management Practice*, 4th ed., Kogan Page.

Brown, Wilfred (1965) *Exploration in Management*, Pelican.

Castle C. and A. Grice (1999) articles in *The Independent*, 17 March.

McLean, I. (1999) 'Heartless bully who added to the agony of Aberfan', *The Observer*, 5 January.

Evening Standard (1998) 'Business ban on bungling Barings chiefs', London, 1 December.

chapter (six)

Motivation

There are case studies and exercises at
http://www.thomsonlearning.co.uk
(for full details, see the listing at the
start of this book).

LEARNING OUTCOMES

By the end of this chapter you will be able to:

- Diagnose the reasons why people perform effectively or ineffectively at work

- Explain the assumptions people make about why others work and analyse your own assumptions

- Explain key motivational theories

- Identify the role that money plays in motivation

- Develop strategies for matching individual needs to workplace requirements

- Explain the link between job design and job performance

- Evaluate the motivational problems caused by market turbulence and job insecurity

- Develop strategies for identifying and handling workplace stress

Introduction

In this chapter the variety of reasons why people work are examined. It is important to consider the range of reasons because it is all too easy for incorrect assumptions to be made. If the diagnosis of reasons for poor performance is inappropriate corrective action may be taken. Behavioural theories concerning motivation and the practical use that can be made of them are considered. The potential impact of national culture on motivation is also covered. The motivational implications of job design are examined, as is the concept of job distortion. A key issue is the extent to which job demands and individual needs can be reconciled.

Increasing market turbulence is causing some employers to introduce flexible employment policies. This can cause employer commitment to reduce whilst expecting an increase in employee commitment. The accelerating pace of change may be one factor causing increasing stress at work. Managers need to protect both themselves and their subordinates from undue stress. Whilst some attention is given to the role of money, it is considered in more detail in chapter 7.

Work performance

Motivation can be defined as 'providing the right conditions for people to work effectively'. It overlaps with the concept of morale, which is a measure of the extent to which employees feel positively or negatively about their work. While levels of performance and morale are usually positively correlated this is not always the case. There can be cases of people performing well under authoritarian but competent managers, perhaps out of fear, but who feel badly about their work. Similarly you can have instances of people doing as they please and enjoying it but not meeting organisational objectives. Ideally what is needed is a good match between the person and the job. Also, what most people may want is to have a comfortable amount of challenge, a good boss, good pay and security. Unfortunately, this is not always possible. However, often a better match is possible between individual needs and organisational requirements than is actually achieved.

DIAGNOSIS OF REASONS FOR POOR PERFORMANCE

If people are not working effectively, or in some cases not working at all, it may be the match between job and person that may need examining, not just one of those factors. Some people may never work effectively under any circumstances. Some jobs will always pose motivational problems, whoever is supposed to be doing them. However, it is also likely that there are circumstances under which most people will work effectively, just as there are circumstances under which the same people will not work effectively at all. Similarly, with most or many jobs there may be many people who will perform them effectively and other people who will perform them ineffectively. If there is a problem of ineffective performance it is necessary to establish if it is the person, the job, or the matching of the two. Remedial action depends on the diagnosis. It may be that, in the short term, neither can be changed. If that is, so attention will need to be paid to either the type of person selected in the future, the job structure or both, according to the diagnosis of the reasons for poor performance.

The need for accurate diagnosis has been stressed because it is all too easy for the diagnosis of reasons for poor performance to be faulty. It is a subjective area. The very criteria for judging effective work performance may be difficult to establish, as was demonstrated in the section on the definition of work objectives in chapter 2. It can be vital to analyse situations in role and not personality terms, as was explained in Chapter 3. If the blame is put on the person working ineffectively, then that absolves the boss, who may then fail to see the connection if the next person in the job also performs badly. In some cases the fault will be with the person doing the job. However, it is important not to automatically assume that this is the case. When the fault is not with the job-holder, there may be uncomfortable implications for the boss. The onus may then be on them to examine the job structure, or the support given to the job-holder.

The following checklist may be useful in establishing the reasons for poor performance:

- job design;
- work organisation: this can cover a wide range of factors, including lack of appropriate equipment, shortage of raw materials, poor work flow, inadequate support and incompetent management;
- selection: it may be necessary to examine the match between people's abilities and needs with job requirements;
- training;
- expectations: the expectations of both employer and employee may need reviewing and also the extent to which promises have been kept;
- pay.

ASSUMPTIONS ABOUT WHY PEOPLE WORK

Alternative sets of assumptions that managers may have about why people work were identified in chapter 4 in the explanation of Douglas McGregor's concepts of Theory X and Theory Y. The implicit assumptions that managers make may or may not be appropriate in relation to particular situations. As well as not necessarily knowing why other people work, managers may generalise on the basis of bad examples with particular individuals which may not even be very representative of the individuals concerned.

Questionnaire

To check your assumptions on why people work, complete the following questionnaire. Rank the reasons of why you think subordinates who work, or have worked, for you actually do work. If that is not possible, choose another group of people who you know. You may need to do some averaging to choose your rankings.

Reasons why people work
- Chance to use initiative at work
- Good working conditions
- Good working companions
- Good boss

- Steady, safe employment
- Money
- Good hours
- Interest in the work itself
- Opportunity for advancement
- Getting credit and recognition

When you have completed the questionnaire redo it, but this time identify the reasons why you work, also ranked in order of importance. When you have done this, compare the two rankings. What usually happens is that managers rank three factors more highly for themselves than for their subordinates. These are the chance to use initiative at work, interest in the work itself and the opportunity for advancement.

What also usually happens is that managers rank three factors more highly for subordinates than for themselves. These are money; steady, safe employment, and security. It may be that your responses do not conform to this general pattern. Even if they do, this may be for perfectly valid reasons.

When managers examine their own reasons for working they are in a position to make informed judgements because of their self-knowledge. This may not be the case when they make assumptions about why other people work, and they may consequently make uncharitable assumptions about the reasons for others working or not working. Even if they are accurate, other managers may make inaccurate assumptions, and this may affect motivational strategies. Sometimes, however, managers may make the reverse mistake. This can easily happen in small businesses. Proprietors may almost completely identify with their business and assume that their employees do, or should do, the same. The point may be missed that whilst the proprietor may make many sacrifices for the business, it is also the proprietor who will reap most of the financial and psychological rewards if the business prospers.

It is also necessary to take into account the concept of instrumentality. This can involve employers or employees carefully calculating the least they need to do to secure their objectives and then behaving accordingly.

Example

A firm making car components in the UK recruited a significant number of Asian immigrants for production work. The employees that they recruited were often of a high calibre and performed well. Many of the recruits had high educational standards and the firm, either knowingly, or unknowingly, had over-selected in terms of ability to do the job. After a while a serious and increasing problem of absenteeism emerged. Investigation revealed that many of the employees had understandable ambitions to better themselves in their new country. When they had accumulated some capital some of them took increasing amounts of time off in order to develop small commercial enterprises. This was with a view to developing their businesses sufficiently to work in them full-time. The more their businesses developed the more risks they were prepared to take with their full-time job.

It may be possible to classify managerial strategies for motivation into one of the four following categories:

- coercion;
- calculated compliance;
- co-operation: this is likely to include a problem-solving approach and some involvement in decision-making;
- commitment: this can overlap substantially with a co-operative strategy. However, it may also involve exhortation and strong financial incentives.

Which strategy is used will depend on managerial assumptions about why people work, organisational circumstances, or a combination of both.

Theories of motivation

It is necessary to have an understanding of some of the more important theories relating to motivation. Although the theories that will be examined are not particularly new, nor beyond methodological criticism, they are important and do have relevance to current problems and initiatives.

MASLOW

Abraham Maslow (1970) provides a very useful theory for examining individual motivation. He suggests that individual needs are arranged in a hierarchy. The lower level needs must be satisfied before people concern themselves with higher level needs. Hunger is seen as a basic need, even more important than safety. When one need is met, people proceed to try and meet their next need. The third level of needs is social, followed by status. The highest level of need is self-actualisation, which involves self-development by successfully responding to challenges. It is the next factor that can be satisfied that acts as a motivator, like a carrot being held in front of a donkey. If threats emerge to a lower level need that has previously been satisfied, individuals will refocus their activity to protect the lower level need.

Figure 6.1 illustrates the theory in a very simplified form. The actual pattern of needs will vary from person to person. There may be trade-offs between meeting needs at different levels. For example, some people may be prepared to take some risks with their safety in order to meet higher levels needs, such as self-actualisation. The level of need can also vary from person to person, e.g. the amount of status satisfaction that is desired. Also, needs are likely to vary over time and according to situational requirements. A person with considerable domestic commitments may not be too concerned with self-actualisation in their job. However, if their domestic commitments are met, they may then wish to achieve self-actualisation and to accept greater work responsibilities in an attempt to meet that need. According to McClelland (1961), the need to achieve self-actualisation may critically depend on social conditioning during childhood.

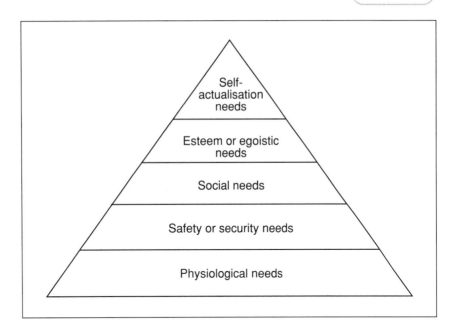

FIGURE 6.1 *Maslow's*
hierarchy of needs

Despite the qualifications inherent in Maslow's hierarchy, his ideas lend themselves to practical application. It can help to see that people's needs are matched to job requirements. Ways in which this can be done are job design, selection, training and promotion.

HERZBERG

The work of Frederick Herzberg (1960) complements that of Maslow. He conducted research into the motivation factors affecting engineers and accountants working in the USA. Herzberg grouped the responses into the factors that caused dissatisfaction. The factors that were found most likely to cause negative feelings (dissatisfiers) were generally external to the job. These are:

- company policy and administration,
- supervision,
- interpersonal relations,
- status,
- salary,
- security,
- impact of the job on personal life.

In contrast, the factors most likely to cause positive feelings about the job (satisfiers) were intrinsic to the job. These are:

- achievement,
- recognition of achievement,

- responsibility,
- advancement,
- interesting work,
- possibility of growth.

The absence of dissatisfiers was not enough to cause positive satisfaction. These tend to only operate in a negative way. For example, if office facilities are poor, that could cause strong negative feelings about the job. If the facilities were improved, that could remove a cause of irritation but would not normally be enough to cause positive feelings about the job. Herzberg termed the potential dissatisfiers as hygiene factors that related to the context in which a job was done. He argued that it is important to pay attention to these issues, but the opportunity for a measure of self-actualisation generally needs to be built into the content of a job if positive feelings are to be created. This requires people having the opportunity to be stretched in their jobs, through overcoming challenges. However, if the challenges are too high, this could cause negative feelings because of failure. Also, there is the danger that challenges that are too demanding interfere with domestic life.

The opportunity for success or failure can arise out of the same set of circumstances, and the dividing line between the two can be very small.

Example

The Indonesian captain of an oil tanker said that his most positive feelings about his job were when had had successfully and very skilfully navigated his ship through a typhoon off Hong King when many ships had been sunk. His most negative feelings about the job were experienced shortly afterwards when the ship's agent came on board and carefully checked all the damage but neglected to enquire or comment about the risks that had been experienced by the captain and his crew.

The role of money, according to Herzberg, is that it is primarily a hygiene factor. Inadequate salary could generate strong negative feelings and cause a person to leave their job. However, a good salary was found to generally not lead to strong positive feelings about a job. Paying people more money won't increase performance if organisational obstacles prevent them working more effectively. Also, there is a danger that paying people more money will increase frustration levels by increasing the difference between ability levels and job demands. This issue is examined further in the section on job design, later in this chapter. Account needs to be taken of variations in people's desire for money, their circumstances and the fact that some jobs may lend themselves, or require, financial inducements more than others.

The practical implications of Herzberg's work are considerable. The basic message is: don't ignore the hygiene factors but don't stop there. People may want considerable involvement in their job for their own self-development. Employers may find that this is a source of considerable energy that is available. Conversely, under-utilised employees may engage in potentially destructive activity.

Example	Traffic police in one part of the UK allegedly got so bored with their work that they booked vehicles in the same colour sequence as though they were playing a game of snooker!

It is necessary to be cautious in generalising about the relevance of Herzberg's work. There have been methodological criticisms of it, particularly because of his reliance on the critical incident technique which only established the highs and lows in the attitudes of employees to their jobs. Also his research was conducted some time ago and only with professional level employees working in the USA. Furthermore, not everyone wants to, or is able to, concentrate on meeting the higher level need of self-actualisation. This can be for a number of reasons, including preoccupation with meeting lower level needs. National culture can also be important, and the potential importance of this factor is examined in greater detail later in this chapter.

Herzberg's work, however, can provide a very useful framework for trying to match individual needs to job requirements. The distinction between intrinsic job factors relating to the job content, which can cause positive satisfaction and external factors relating to the job context, which can cause negative job attitudes, is important and can be put to practical effect.

If people want the opportunity for self-development, the most important thing for managers to do may be to set up their work so that it provides a challenge, and then help see that the challenge is met. Excessive help may be counter-productive. The main pay-off with human relations skills may to avoid unnecessarily upsetting employees. The control of the manager over work content will vary, but it is something that usually demands close attention. It may be one of the few important factors that managers can influence. Factors such as organisation policy, pay and working conditions may be outside their control. One of the problems for the prospective employee is that it is much easier to judge job context – for example salary, fringe benefit and working conditions – rather than more elusive factors such as independence within the job. Consequently, recruits may only find out after they have started whether a job really has positive motivational features or not.

EXPECTANCY THEORIES

Another perspective that needs to be integrated with the previously explained theories is that provided by the expectancy school of motivational theorists. The expectancy approach attempts to overcome one of the criticisms of other motivational theories by accounting for individual differences. The expectancy model of Nadler and Lawler (1977: 27) has three major components. They are:

- performance-outcome: this concerns the outcome that individual employees expect from certain behaviour;
- valence: this is the value that employees put on the outcome which they are expecting from particular behaviour – this will determine the motivating strength of a particular reward;

- effort-performance expectancy: these are the expectations of how difficult it will be to perform successfully and will affect people's reaction to a particular incentive. The logic is that employees will select the level of performance that seems to have the best chance of achieving an outcome they value.

It follows that it is necessary to check to see that the reward system in an organisation actually works in the way that it is intended to work. It is no good, for example, expecting to motivate people by offering incremental salary increases or promotion on the basis of merit if the reality is that such rewards are based on seniority or some other factor not connected with merit. Employees are likely to make judgements about what reward system really operates by what they believe is actually happening, rather than by statements of organisational policy. Even if rewards are based significantly on merit it is necessary to convince people of that, as motivation is likely to depend on what people perceive happens. It is also necessary to review how equitably rewards are distributed. Even if people are inclined to respond to a particular incentive, they may be discouraged from doing so by perceived unfairness in the way in which rewards are distributed. The relationships between the rewards given to different people may therefore need to be examined as well as the size of the rewards. The gap between intended and actual reward systems can be alarmingly high. As is explained in the next chapter, some can degenerate into arrangements for restricting rather than increasing performance.

SOCIO-TECHNICAL SYSTEMS THEORY

A number of writers have described the socio-technical systems that exist in workplaces. They have also commented about the disruptive effect that changes in work methods can have on social systems at work. Such changes can, in turn, affect motivation and levels of work performance. Seminal work in this area was done by Trist and Bamforth (1951: 3–38).

Example

Trist and Bamforth examined the impact of the new Longwall mechanised method of coal mining. This was far superior technically than the old board and pillar system. However, the new system involved people working in relative isolation from one another along a conveyor belt. The work was also made more specialised and repetitive. This was far less socially satisfying than the teams of two or three who had previously hand-cut coal in recesses in the seams and who had carried out a wider range of activities. The previous arrangement had also involved a high acceptance of responsibility for the safety of one another. Adjustments were made in the new system in order to try and build some social satisfaction back into the job. This involved forming small groups along the conveyor belt and giving them more authority. It was a move in the direction of semi-autonomous work groups. This had a significant and positive effect on production, time-keeping, absenteeism and safety. However, forming semi-autonomous work groups has to be a practical option both technically and economically.

Change in itself is neutral and can have positive or negative effects or a combination of the two. Sometimes the technical advantages of systems, such as vehicle assembly lines, outweigh the social disadvantages. Sometimes, though, it is possible to modify the technical system to take into account social and psychological needs.

IMPACT OF NATIONAL CULTURE

When considering theories of motivation and seeking to improve employee motivation via reward structures or redesigned jobs, the potential impact of national culture needs to be taken into account. Most theories of motivation are based in the United States. These theories are usually based on the assumption that employees have the same values as those in American society – high levels of individualism, low power distances, relatively high masculinity and a consequent emphasis on material values. Using Hofstede's (1994) terminology, those working in an individualist culture may value opportunities for individual promotion and growth while more collectivist cultures value opportunities to belong to an influential group. Employees in collectivist cultures may not be highly motivated by reward systems based on individual effort which undermine the importance of the group. In Western societies there is also much more opportunity for self-actualisation than in developing countries where, for those struggling for survival, concepts such as self-actualisation may be meaningless.

Examples

At Beijing Jeep, a joint venture between AMC and Beijing Automative Works, some workers willingly gave up their pay rises in order to appease the resentment of less productive colleagues.

(Mead, 1998)

In Thailand, the introduction of an individual merit bonus plan, which runs counter to the societal norm of group co-operation, may result in a decline rather than an increase in productivity from employees who openly refuse to compete with one another.

(Rieger and Wong-Rieger 1990: 1)

Mead points out (1998: 198) that as national cultures change due perhaps to economic advancement so the value systems may alter. He gives the example of changes in Chinese society where it was apparent that it had become acceptable to make money for one's own gratification rather than in the service of society.

Job design

One of the major implications of the theoretical perspectives, particularly Herzberg's, is that considerable attention needs to be given to human needs in job design. The tradition set by the advocates of scientific management, such as F. W. Taylor was, however, to simplify work as much as possible. This enabled employees to be selected and trained to undertake repetitive tasks. This approach later became known as Fordism. It did, though, ignore factors such as boredom and social needs. The Hawthorne experiments of 1927–32 demonstrated that social factors could play an important part in motivating employees to achieve high performance (Sheldrake 1966: ch. 11). (See also chapter 3 of this book.) Later approaches are taken into account in the rest of this section, particularly the need to reconcile individual needs with job demands to the extent that that is possible.

ERGONOMICS

Ergonomics involves looking at the job and person in relation to one another as a combined unit. This is in contrast to designing a job and then expecting to find someone who will be both willing and able to adapt to its requirements. A humorous way of explaining the concept is by the legend of Procrustes:

(Example)

Procrustes was a legendary figure in Greek mythology who had a special bed. He was obsessive about guests fitting his bed exactly. If they were too long for the bed he cut off their feet; if they were too small he stretched them on a rack until they fitted. Allegedly the Procrustean approach was used in the engineering industry in the design of some capstan lathe machines. This was because some were best operated by people who were 4 feet and 6 inches in height but with the arm span of a gorilla.

The use of the concept of ergonomics can be particularly important in the design of capital equipment so that, for example instrument panels and other signals are arranged so as to minimise the risk of misreading. It can also be of vital importance in the design of high performance military equipment. Good design can make all the difference in the achievement or non-achievement of objectives. It can also mean the difference between life and death for the personnel using the equipment on operational or even training missions.

MARKETING OF JOBS

A useful concept to apply to job design is that of marketing. Companies would soon get into financial difficulties if they designed products without regard to customer needs. Similarly with jobs, it is necessary to consider who would want to do them, or do them well. If jobs are particularly boring, for example, there may be problems in recruiting, motivating and retaining staff. Options may be to consider if they can be made less boring or automated out of existence. Jobs also need to have internal coherence and viability. They need to be assessed as a whole and the questions asked as to who would be able to and want to do such a job. Consideration may also need to be taken as to how long a job will stay in its present form. If it is likely to change significantly, that may affect the range of skills and adaptability of applicants. The problem of contradictory job demands also needs to be taken into account. This issue is considered in detail in the next section.

BASIC JOB STRUCTURE

Basic issues in job design include the range of skills required and the compatibility of the tasks. Many jobs contain a large element of routine activity but some demanding work as well. This is true in jobs as diverse as skilled manual workers and general medical practitioners. This issue is illustrated in Figure 6.2.

A motivational problem for jobs that have a large element of routine work and a small amount of complicated work is that the capable person may get bored with the routine work. It may also may be unnecessarily expensive in terms of their salary level. The capable person may also spend too much time on the work they find interesting. Conversely, the person who finds the routine work satisfying may not be very good at the complicated work. Unfortunately, some jobs need to be designed like this for safety reasons. Airline pilots, for example, have to be able to cope with emergencies that it is hoped will never happen. A way of reducing the boredom in skilled jobs can be to hive off aspects of the work so that auxiliary staff can undertake them under proper supervision. Examples of this are the use of practice nurses in general medical practices and dental hygienists in dental surgeries.

A related concept is that of skill mix. This involves comparing the skills actually needed to perform a job and those that job-holders actually have. There needs to be an accurate match so that people on the one hand have the skills to do their jobs but on the other hand are not performing work that could more cheaply and more satisfyingly, be performed by others.

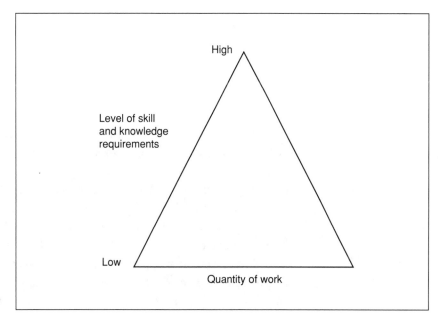

FIGURE 6.2 *The skill pyramid*

JOB DISTORTION

Job distortion can occur when a job is rearranged in a way that satisfies the needs of the organisation but not the individual. If, for example, a graduate is recruited to perform routine clerical work they may be initially glad to have the job. However, they may rapidly get bored because of the lack of intellectual stimulation. They may then expand the more interesting parts of the job and ignore the less demanding parts. If organisational equal-opportunities policies prevent managers from making judgements that a person is over-qualified for a job, job distortion is more likely. The greater the gap between the demands of the job and the ability level of the job-holder the more the temptation to try and alter the job. This process is illustrated in Figure 6.3. The continuous lines represent the boundaries of the job that the organisation requires to be performed, whilst the broken lines represent the boundaries of the job as it actually is performed.

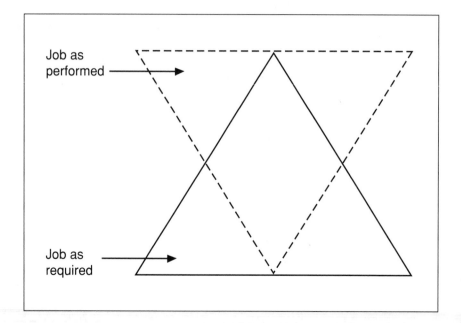

FIGURE 6.3 *Job distortion*

<table>
<tr><td>Example</td><td>The process and dangers of job distortion are particularly well illustrated by the example of a young man employed to collect and distribute the post in the directorate of a local authority. The mail in the directorate kept on being distributed later and later. Officers found that if they had to leave their offices before lunchtime, it might be the following day before they got their morning mail. Investigation revealed that the job-holder had been doing the job for five years and had got very bored with it. Consequently, he had taken to reading the mail before he distributed it. He also used the mail round as an opportunity to talk to friends and organise social events. Because of his reputation for being slow with the mail, no-one had been prepared to give him a more demanding job.</td></tr>
</table>

CONTINUED OVER ➤

CONTINUED FROM
PREVIOUS PAGE
The mismatch between individual and organisational needs should have been addressed long before. This could have been by restructuring the job so that it was combined with other work, limiting the time that a person spent doing that work, or employing a person who would have been less frustrated with the work. A further approach would have been to eliminate the job by requiring departments to organise the collection and distribution of their own mail.

Another pressure which can create job distortion can be the frustration of a person who considers that they should have a job more in line with their ability level within the same organisation. This can particularly happen if a person feels that they have outgrown their job.

Example

Some of the directors in an organisation concerned with the distribution of public grants were concerned about the lack of career opportunities for capable secretaries. It was proposed to upgrade some of them to positions as personal assistants to the directors. Juniors were to be recruited to undertake the more routine aspects of their work. However, it emerged that there was not enough of the more demanding work to justify having full-time personal assistants. The real solution was to encourage the more capable secretaries to undertake specialist or professional training so that they could apply for genuinely more demanding jobs, either in the organisation or elsewhere.

A further cause of job distortion can be differing views on what needs doing in a job. The dangers of managers spending too much time on their historic specialism and ignoring important managerial responsibilities was dealt with at length in chapter 1. People may even find that the organisation of activities that are clearly against their employer's interests provides both psychological and material rewards. The adrenalin can run for a person perpetrating a fraud just as it can for honest employees who develop themselves in their employer's interests instead of attempting to outwit the employer.

JOB ENLARGEMENT, JOB ROTATION AND JOB ENRICHMENT

Job enlargement

Job enlargement is a generic term used to indicate an increase in the number of tasks within a job. This can be achieved by increasing the range of activities, or increasing the responsibility level or both. Job rotation and job enrichment can be aspects of job enlargement.

Job rotation

Job rotation involves a horizontal broadening of the job without increasing the level of responsibility. It can be useful in reducing the monotony factor. One example is the rotation of staff working at leisure centres who may move from supervising one sporting activity to another every few hours. A potential disadvantage is when this is disruptive of social relationships at work. Also, it does not make jobs inherently more interesting.

Job enrichment

Job enrichment involves a vertical increase in the level of responsibility within a job. Sometimes this can be accomplished informally, for example, by a manager delegating more. The practice of having someone act-up whilst the boss is away is an example of a temporary form of job enrichment. The ability of managers to delegate varies considerably. The concept of delegation was examined in detail in chapter 5.

SELECTION, TRAINING AND PAY

When jobs have been sensibly designed it is then necessary to consider how people are selected, trained and paid for them. The danger of over-selection is a recurring issue. Ideally what is needed is a good match between the demands of the job and the abilities and motivation of the job-holder. Sometimes organisations recruit on the basis of status instead of trying to get a good match between person and job

Example

The newly appointed head of an engineering company's research department announced that he was only prepared to engage research staff who had good and relevant honours degrees. Investigation revealed, however, that much of the work that needed doing was routine and would more appropriately be undertaken by technicians operating under the guidance of more qualified staff.

When people have been selected it is necessary to consider their training needs. It can be highly demotivating for a person not to be able to perform effectively because they have not been trained adequately. This is also likely to be costly to the organisation. Adequate training is not only likely to improve performance and reduce labour turnover but also enhance the status of a job.

Sometimes employers respond to the problems of retaining staff on boring work by increasing their pay. However, a danger of doing this is that they attract more able staff who get even more bored with the job even more quickly. This can also happen when employees use their bargaining strength to force up their wages.

Example

Train drivers are one of the few groups of workers who still have considerable industrial power. This is because of the damage they can inflict by interrupting or closing down train services. However, as signalling systems develop and an increasing number of fail-safe systems are introduced, the job may become less demanding. These two developments can significantly increase job boredom. This may further increase due to the impetus given to even more fail-safe systems after the collision of two trains on the same track 2 miles outside Paddington station in London in 1999 in which 31 people were killed.

Vulnerability and stress

CORPORATE INVOLVEMENT AND CORPORATE LOYALTY

Increasing emphasis has been placed by some organisations and writers to treat the workforce as a valuable asset whose potential should be fully exploited rather than simply a cost. This is at the heart of initiatives such as TQM and quality circles. The impact of such initiatives may be reinforced by the social pressures that may be deliberately engineered by employers to obtain compliance with organisational goals. The concept of the quality of working life is also relevant. It has the broad aim of bringing together and satisfying both the goals and development of organisations and the needs and development of all their people (ACAS 1991). As explained in chapter 3, Peters and Waterman emphasised the need to release human potential – which is all the more important given the economic pressures on organisations and rising educational standards within workforces.

There seems little doubt that some organisations have consciously changed their policies to try and make much better use of their human resources. For this to happen there needs to be realistic planning about how this is to be achieved. Mere sloganising and exhortation won't produce much in the way of results. A major complication is that increased psychological commitment by the workforce may be expected when organisations are *reducing* their commitment to their employees. In commenting on the trend towards semi-autonomous business units one writer observed that:

> *This trend draws on the work of innumerable management thinkers who champion the idea of cutting corporate flab and 'empowering' teams of employees, which can then be judged by their performance. Some like America's Tom Peters and Britain's Charles Handy, sketch a future in which big firms will become little more than 'networks' of independent businesses. Most such gurus assume that employees will respond to their new responsibility with enthusiasm, even if their firm has just sacked thousands of workers and declared that no-one's job is safe.*
>
> *This seems naive. Even if many big companies sorely needed a shake-up, scrapping corporate cultures which evolved over decades is likely to be far more costly than many firms, or management theorists, imagine… Job cuts at Eastman Kodak, IBM and Philips have shattered morale and embittered many of those who remain, despite lavish redundancy payments.*
>
> The Economist 1993a: 81

Comment is also made in the article about the exodus of talent that can occur in such restructuring and the more instrumental attitudes that employees may develop about issues such as geographic moves within a group and selling their skills elsewhere. This is particularly important if one accepts the argument that the most important corporate asset is the intellectual creativity of its employees. Handy (1991) argues that this is crucial in his concept of the organisation based on intelligence, ideas and information, explained in chapter 4. Black (1993) has referred to the emerging concepts of just-in-time employment and the disposable workforce in the USA and the impact this has on corporate morale. Consequently, one needs to examine the impact of the flexible workforce on motivation and in particular developments such as the increasing use of fixed term contracts, especially for senior employees. A further complication can arise because of the actual generosity with which employers treat those who are being made redundant:

> *British Telecom spent some £1 billion this financial year (1992/3) shedding 33,000 workers. To tempt enough to go voluntarily, employees were baited with counselling, training and pay-offs as high as £100,000. Managers were miffed when 45,000 applied to leave. Morale crumbled, not because workers were forced out, but because 15,000 were forced to stay.*

The Economist 1993b

The reappraisals of commitment to the organisation caused by restructuring may be in tune with a general trend. Scase and Goffee comment that:

> *If, in earlier decades, managers were committed to their jobs to the extent that all other interests were subordinated to their work-related goals, they may now be developing more instrumental and calculative attitudes towards their employing organisations (Hearn 1977). Indeed, by deliberately cultivating personal identities that are separate and removed from organisational demands, they could be better equipped to cope with work-related stresses and to withstand the psychological challenges that can be posed by threats of redundancy and unexpected career changes. Accordingly, managers may cease to be psychologically immersed in their work roles and become less committed to their employing organisations. To do otherwise, in the light of increasing uncertainties, would be to make themselves more emotionally and psychologically vulnerable.*

1989: 13

Social trends, including changes in the role of women in the family and in society also have an impact on the work relationship. The custom of family commitments needing to be subordinated to the primary aim of promoting the career of the man in the home is breaking down. Almost half of the workforce is now female. The pattern of female careers is also changing – women are tending to have children later and to have shorter maternity leave. The growing number of dual career couples also imposes constraints upon both partners and lessens the dependency on the primary income. Also a significant number of employees are single parents (Foster 1988: 38–41).

Having explained the constraints that may exist with regard to attempt to improve employee involvement and develop corporate loyalty, it would be foolish to suggest that all attempts are doomed to failure. It is more logical to argue that, given the organisational turbulence that is often inevitable, it is even more important to consider how to try and get the best out of the workforce despite the difficulties. This is more likely to be done effectively if the nature of the difficulties is clearly recognised. It is necessary to consider the human dimension at the time that organisations are being restructured and to build in the direct and intangible costs of change before decisions are finalised. It is also important to have positive and integrated human resource strategies and the nature of these are considered in chapters 11 (in relation to training) and generally in chapter 14 (employee relations).

STRESS

The general point has been made that organisations tend to under-utilise and under-involve the human resources available to them but that there is an increasing recognition of the need to correct this. The point has also been made that a variety of factors are causing an increasing number of employees to try and set limits to their work involvement. Consequently, it is probably appropriate for both organisations and employees to consider what is the optimum level of involvement. This may be particularly necessary given the increasing potential intrusion of work into the home because of developments in information technology. Individuals may need to look carefully at their work in relation to their general life style and periodically conduct an audit on their total quality of life. Whilst the emphasis in the literature on motivation is on under-involvement, over-involvement may present risks for the employer as well as the employee. The dangers of workaholicism may include problems of employee replacement, damage to health and the loss of a sense of perspective and good judgement that comes from having other interests as a counterbalance. Workaholics may also seek to establish themselves as role models when they are really self-indulging or engaging in compensatory behaviour.

There is a distinction between pressure and stress. Some managers enjoy high levels of pressure and may perform more effectively when they are put under a certain amount of pressure. The pressure may relate to the volume or responsibility level of work or both. Other managers may react in a different way, and their inability to cope with pressure may result in stress. One could therefore define managerial stress as a symptom of being unable to cope with the workload. Unfortunately, this can precipitate a counter-productive chain reaction with those managers experiencing stress amplifying and transmitting it to those in their immediate circle. Stress may be caused by the problems inherent in a particular job, or the mismatch between the abilities of an individual and the requirements of a job, or a combination of the two. It is important to diagnose the causes of stress in particular situations because it is only when that is done that one can work out whether the appropriate remedy is to change an individual's behaviour, the pressures they are put under, or both.

It is also important to recognise that work stress is probably on the increase. This is because of the increasing impact of key factors which generate stress. These factors include the rate of change, pressures for cost-effective performance and job insecurity generated by change. Managers also have responsibility for monitoring the stress that subordinates are placed under.

Examples In 1994 John Walker, a senior social worker, won a High Court action against Northumberland County Council (IRLR 1994), because of its negligence in not doing enough to prevent him having a further nervous breakdown because of work overload. The council agreed to pay him £175,000 because of their breach of duty of care to him.

A related case was that of Beverly Lancaster, a housing officer employed by Birmingham City Council (*Evening Standard* 1999). She was promoted against her will, and the training and other support that she was promised was not provided. It was held that the unreasonable demands made of her helped precipitate a depressive illness which led to her early retirement. In 1999 she was awarded £67,000 compensation.

Whether managers are being submitted or submitting themselves to too much pressure or experiencing stress, the consequent work style may generate an excessive flow of adrenalin within the body. Dependence on physical stimulants such as nicotine and alcohol can prevent an individual from having an appropriate diet and sufficient physical exercise and rest. If the stress is self-induced it is perhaps just as well to face up to the medical implications in case there is any scope for personal adjustment. There is also the potential benefit that if stress is reduced for oneself it may also be reduced for those around you.

Doctors and stress consultants may be able to measure stress and advise on how the symptoms are treated, e.g. by relaxation techniques. However, managerial skills are likely to be needed to deal with the basic causes of managerial stress. The aim of this book is to do just that, by helping managers develop their basic skills.

SUMMARY

✔ The difference between motivation and morale and the wide variety of causes of under-performance has been explained. For effective action to be taken to improve performance, it is necessary to accurately diagnosis the reasons. If this is not done, corrective action may be ineffective or even counter-productive. One of the mistakes that can be made is for managers to make wrong assumptions about why their subordinates work. Even if there is a problem of poor motivation, it is necessary to consider what can be done to improve it. Relevant theories have been examined, particularly the work of Maslow, Herzberg, expectancy theorists and socio-technical systems theory. According to Herzberg, money is an important hygiene factor but not necessarily an important positive motivator. However, some care has to be taken in generalising on the basis of Herzberg's research. The impact of national culture on motivation was also considered.

✔ It is important to try and match individual needs and job demands as far as is practicable. This is an issue that needs to be considered when jobs are designed and marketed. One of the consequence of not doing this can be job distortion. Market turbulence and trends towards flexible employment policies can generate job insecurity and this may conflict with employer demands for greater employee commitment. Such factors can also increase the amount of job-related stress. Social trends also often aggravate the conflict between work and domestic commitments. The judgement, effectiveness and health of managers will be at risk if they experience too much stress. They also have a responsibility to see that their employees are not subjected to unreasonable amounts of stress. The development of managerial skills, such as prioritisation, can be an effective way of dealing with the causes of stress. The issue of pay is considered further in the next chapter, which is devoted to that topic.

SELF-ASSESSMENT QUESTIONS

1. Think of a group of workers you judge to be performing poorly. Identify the reasons for their poor performance.

2. Using the same group as you have in answer to the first question, what assumptions have you made about why these people work? How accurate are they?

3. Explain any one theory of motivation.

4. What do you believe is the role of money in motivating people?

5. How can you try and ensure a good match between individual needs and job demands?

6. Why is it important to take human needs into account when designing jobs?

7. Examine the conflict between flexible employment policies and employer expectations of greater employee involvement.

8. How can you try and reduce or avoid job-related stress both for yourself and others?

 References

ACAS (1991) *Effective Organisations – The People Factor*, Advisory Booklet no. 16 , ACAS.

Black, Larry (1993) 'Downsizing towards a disposable workforce – a view from New York', *The Independent*, 22 March.

The Economist (1993a) 3 April.

The Economist (1993b) 'Redundancies, Friendly Firing', 13 March.

Foster, Joanne (1988) 'Balancing Work and the Family', *Personnel Management*, September.

Handy, Charles (1991) *The Age of Unreason*, Business Books.

Herzberg, F. Mausner and B. Syderman (1960) *The Motivation to Work*, Wiley.

Hofstede, G. (1994) *Cultures and Consequences*, Fontana.

Maslow, A. H. (1970) *Motivation and Personality*, 2nd ed., Harper and Row.

McClelland D. C. (1961) *The Achieving Society*, Van Nostrand.

Mead, Richard (1998) ch. 9, 'Motivating Across Cultures' in *International Management,* 2nd ed., Blackwell.

Nadler, David and Edward E. Lawler III (1977) 'Motivation: a Diagnostic Approach' in Hackman, R. and Lawler E. (eds.) *Perspectives on Behaviour in Organisations*, McGraw Hill.

Rieger, F. and D. Wong-Rieger (1990) 'A configuration module of national influence applied to Southeast Asian organisations', Research Conference on Business in Southeast Asia: Proceedings, Southeast Asia Business Program, University of Michigan, p.p. 1–31.

Scase, Richard and Robert Goffee (1989) *Reluctant Managers*, Unwin Hyman.

Sheldrake, John (1996) 'Management Theory from Taylorism to Japanization' in *Elton Mayo and the Hawthorne Experiments*, International Thomson Business Press.

Trist, E. L. and K. W. Bamforth (1951) 'Some Sociological and Psychological Consequences of the Longwall Method of Coal-getting', *Human Relations*, no.4.

General reference

Earnshaw J. and C. Cooper (2001) *Stress and Employer Liability*, Chartered Institute of Personnel and Development, 2nd ed.

Cases cited

Lancaster vs *Birmingham City Council* (1999) County Court judgement reported in *The Evening Standard* (London), 5 July.

Walker vs *Northumberland County Council* (1994) IRLR 35, QBD.

chapter seven

Payment systems

There are case studies and exercises at
http://www.thomsonlearning.co.uk
(for full details, see the listing at the
start of this book).

LEARNING OUTCOMES

By the end of this chapter you will be able to:

- Identify the circumstances under which financial incentive schemes may improve performance

- Evaluate the potential long-term effects of financial incentive schemes

- Evaluate the nature of the main types of financial inventive schemes

- Analyse the objectives of job evaluation schemes

- Analyse how job evaluation schemes operate in practice

- Identify the main pressures causing change in the way organisations remunerate their employees

Introduction

Having considered the relevance of various behavioural theories of motivation in the previous chapter, it is now necessary to look more explicitly at the role of money as a motivator. The advantages and disadvantages of financial incentive schemes and profit sharing arrangements are therefore considered in this chapter. The issue of internal relativities is also examined, as is the way in which job evaluation may assist in establishing and maintaining a rational pay structure. The various types of job evaluation schemes are explained and the ways in which they need to be chosen, operated and maintained if they are to be effective. Consideration is given to the equal value regulations which stipulate that employees do not suffer pay discrimination on the basis of sex. The pressures for change in the way job evaluation operates and its changing role are examined. These include trends towards smaller and more flexible organisations and a greater emphasis on rewarding on the basis of individual performance. General trends are examined including re-examination of incremental salary scales and cafeteria-style fringe benefits. The issue of individual merit payment, especially performance-related pay is deferred until chapter 10, so that it can be considered in the context of appraisal.

Financial incentives

Probably the ideal arrangement for most jobs is that people have an interesting job, good supervision and an appropriate basic wage or salary. If the theories of Maslow and Herzberg mean anything at all, such arrangements should lead to effective work performance and satisfied employees. Unfortunately the achievement of such a happy state of affairs is, needless to say, not always possible. When this cannot be achieved financial incentives may be appropriate. However, it is most important for managers to ensure that their diagnosis of the reasons for under-achievement is correct before they try to improve work performance by the use of financial incentives. As part of this analysis they may need to consider the extent to which different individuals respond to financial rewards. There can be dangers in building systems around individuals as they and their needs may change.

DIAGNOSIS OF NEED

As has previously been explained, problems of work performance may be due to factors outside the control of the employee. Even when it would seem that employees could increase output by reasonable increases in effort, it is necessary to ask why the effort is not forthcoming. The structure of jobs and the matching of individuals to jobs should be examined. If poor performance is because of poor supervision, it may be that it is the supervision that should be changed and not the arrangements for payment. It is particularly necessary to check this, as the long-term effect of incentive schemes can be to diminish the role of the supervisor.

Employees operating under incentive schemes may see themselves akin to independent subcontractors, with the supervisor as an external figure who is likely to come into conflict with them over a range of issues concerning the operation of the incentive scheme. This can lead to the exclusion of the supervisor from the work group, because of attempts by them to monitor schemes in the interest of the employer rather than of the employee. Alternatively, the supervisor may be 'captured' by the work group so that, for example, they do not report on manipulations to the incentive scheme or show excessive concern about safety and quality standards. Unfortunately, either of these developments can lead to the continued erosion of first-line supervisors to a point, sometimes, where they act as little more than a conduit for messages between management and the workforce.

APPROPRIATE CONDITIONS

There are jobs in which the ideal arrangements identified above will simply not always be attainable. There will, for example, be situations when the structure of jobs is such that they are inherently boring and that, in the short-term at least, output will be best achieved by the use of financial incentive schemes. This can be particularly so with repetitive factory work where the pace of work is directly controlled by the operatives.

The circumstances under which payment by results schemes might be appropriate are identified in a checklist drawn up by the National Board for Prices and Incomes as part of one of their investigations (1968a: 11). Despite the length of time since their study was undertaken, their observations are still relevant. The four necessary conditions for the introduction of payment by results were stated to be where:

- the work can be measured and directly attributed to the individual or group; in practice this generally means highly repetitive manual work – as found in mass-production manufacturing;
- the pace of work is substantially controlled by the worker rather than by the machine or process they are tending;
- management is capable of maintaining a steady flow of work;
- the tasks are not subjected to frequent changes in method, materials or equipment.

Even under the above conditions and with proper monitoring, the NBPI commented on the inevitable slackening that occurs in schemes because of factors such as technological change. They found that, even under ideal conditions, there is likely to be an unavoidable wholly unproductive wage drift of at least 1 per cent a year (1968b: 50). It is to be regretted that there are so few independent studies on the effects of incentive schemes to warn employers of the ways in which they can be counter-productive. Much of the information available is either in textbooks explaining how schemes are supposed to operate in theory or in literature provided by consultants who make their money in selling and installing incentive packages.

LONG-TERM EFFECTS

Proposals for introducing incentive schemes and their short-term benefits can seem very convincing. However, managers need to review carefully their diagnosis of the real reasons for poor performance and the possible long-term effects of incentive schemes before committing themselves to this route to higher output. Figure 7.1 shows what can happen in the short and long term if, for example, a payment by results scheme is introduced.

Output may well increase by about one-third after the introduction of a scheme, with earnings going up in relation to output. However, as time goes on, even in relatively static production situations, there are likely to be improvements in work methods that are not entirely clawed back by the employer in terms of consequential reductions in

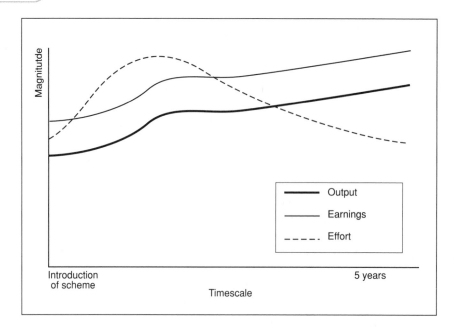

FIGURE 7.1 *The long-term pattern of incentive schemes*

time allowances. There may also be errors in initial time allowances and employees can be remarkably ingenious in manipulating schemes to their advantage. The most sophisticated manipulations involve capturing the supervisor and other potential enemies so that the higher levels of management are not aware that ultimately effort may decline whilst output and earnings increase. Schemes can degenerate to such an extent that they actually become arrangements for restricting production – for fear that, if normal effort is resumed, the output achieved would give the whole game away. The erosion of the position of the supervisor that may accompany these developments may facilitate, or be because of, the rise of shop steward influence.

Another problem can be the distorting effect that incentive schemes can have on pay structures. If, for whatever reason, the incentive earnings of one group rise this can create stresses with regard to pay relativities. Sometimes these can be acute and lead to a negative differential on the part of those, for example, who are supposed to supervise them. The introduction of new working methods may be accompanied by fear about the impact of this on earnings and may lead to resistance to the changes or haggling about any consequential adjustments to the incentive scheme. Another problem can be resistance to moving from jobs with slack times to those with tight times. The impact on quality of production or service also has to be examined.

Example

One of the innumerable examples of incentive schemes adversely affecting quality was the introduction of quotas and financial penalties by the contractors operating Westminster Council's street car parking arrangements on London This led to some traffic wardens issuing tickets in breach of the regulations so as to avoid penalties for themselves.

(Morton 1993)

The impact on safety also needs to be examined in case employees are actually rewarded for working dangerously. One of the many ways in which this can and does happen concerns some of the 'job and finish' arrangements for truck drivers. Such schemes may enable drivers to be paid at premium rates for trips done over and above their daily target. As well as encouraging unsafe driving this may also lead to excessive vehicle wear and fuel consumption.

The point that it is necessary to stress is that all the potential disadvantages of incentive schemes need to be taken into account before they are adopted. The trouble is that the short-term tangible benefits may be much more obvious than many of the long-term intangible, but nevertheless important, consequences. A policy of choosing 'horses for courses' is appropriate rather than any dogmatic assertion that one should always use incentive schemes or never use them. The matching of pay arrangements to situations can, however, be ill-conceived or the circumstances in which schemes operate can alter and make them invalid. A common example is when automatic production processes are introduced which predetermine the rate of production, which had previously been determined by operators. If the speed at which the now-reactive operators work consequently becomes an effect and not a cause of some other variable, it becomes pointless to reward them for something over which they no longer have control. The achievement of high levels of production may be related instead, for example, to ensuring that automatic process equipment is properly maintained and does not break down or operate in such a way that there are quality defects.

The importance of careful thought about the appropriate arrangements for paying employees is not confined to groups of manual employees.

Example

The method of paying dentists in the UK provides an apt example of some of the dangers. Initially, dentists, working under the National Health Service, were paid primarily on the physical services they provided. The financial incentive to extract or fill teeth, for example, may have discouraged time being spent advising about dental hygiene. This has led to financial incentives now being offered for dentists to employ dental hygienists.

The ramifications of incentive schemes are such that considerable thought has to be given, not only as to whether they should be used or not, but also as to how they should be managed if they are used. If incentive schemes are used, they may require just as much, or even more, managerial effort to see that performance targets are met, compared with the managerial effort involved when people are paid just a basic wage or salary.

GROUP SCHEMES

Most of the comments already made about financial incentive schemes also apply to group schemes. However, there are some specific aspects relating to group schemes that also need to be considered. Group schemes seem to work best when the group is no bigger than eight to 12 people, and the task is inherently a group rather than an individual task. If a plant-wide scheme is used, the relationship between individual effort and reward may be too weak for there to be an obvious causal relationship between the effort of the individual and overall output. Individual earnings may move in parallel with total output, but that does not prove that people are working harder because of a group incentive scheme. Employees may perceive that their earnings will be very much the same, however hard or little they work. They may also perceive that many factors other than their effort, or even the effort of themselves and their fellow workers, may affect total output, for example, workflow and technological change.

PROFIT SHARING

There are two main types of profit sharing arrangements – profit-related pay and employee-share option plans. The same issues concerning the weakness of the link between reward and individual performance emerge as with group bonus schemes. A fallacy about distributing profits in the form of shares is the assumption that once employees have a shareholder role, they will forget about the far more important wage-earner role and simply behave in the best interests of the shareholders. It is when 'weights' are attached to these two roles that it becomes apparent that any link between group performance and group profits may not actually be caused by a profit sharing incentive. If the roles come into conflict employees may behave in such a way that they protect their wage-earner role and subordinate any shareholder interests to this much greater primary role. Admittedly, often the roles will not be in conflict and there may be a general value in exposing employees to the shareholder perspective. However, variations in profits may in fact have little to do with the supposed motivating effect of a profit sharing scheme regardless of whether the rewards are in the form of direct payments or shares. Much may depend on market factors over which employees have little or no control.

At one stage profit sharing schemes were very popular in the UK because of the tax advantages they had. However, Chote (1991) and McLean (1994) suggested that there was little evidence of the positive effect on profits. In some cases, the pursuit of profit can cause those who stand to gain most to take unnecessary risks. They may also concentrate on short-term profits. A Bank of England study warned of the dangers with regard to traders in financial markets:

> ... large variable, bonuses that depend on some measure of performance can become a one-way bet for traders, who win if they generate profits for the business but do not have to pay out if they lose money.

1997

Example

In extreme circumstances such arrangements can threaten the survival of a business. Another lesson from the collapse of Barings Bank in 1995 (see chapter 5) was that the reckless and uncontrolled pursuit of profits and bonuses can destroy an organisation.

CONTINUED OVER ➤

CONTINUED FROM
PREVIOUS PAGE
An estimated £80 million was paid out in bonuses based on the false profits reported by Nick Leeson (Fay 1997). This may well have encouraged those responsible for supervising him to fail to examine his activities closely enough.

Job evaluation

PAY STRUCTURES

Another aspect of remuneration that needs careful consideration is the organisational pay structure. Pay structures need to meet a number of different, and sometimes conflicting, objectives. The main ones are likely to be:

- attracting, retaining and motivating staff who are competent in the jobs they are given;
- not paying over-generously, for reasons of cost;
- establishing internal relativities that minimise feelings of discontent about what other employees are getting;
- establishing differentials that encourage appropriate employees to apply for promotion;
- encouraging geographical and functional flexibility for employees where appropriate;
- reflecting the power realities so that the pay structure is not likely to be easily overturned by groups with strong bargaining power;
- compliance with the law, particularly minimum pay, regulations regarding hours of work and legislation and regulations regarding equal pay and equal pay for work of equal value;
- establishing a structure that is manageable, adaptive and cost effective in administrative expense;

Trade-offs may be necessary in determining which objectives have higher priority. Pay structures need to be synchronised with other organisational processes such as human resource planning and budgetary control. Such integration is necessary if overall organisational objectives are to be achieved.

PURPOSES OF JOB EVALUATION

Job evaluation schemes can provide a useful framework for creating an effective pay structure. The determination of wage and salary levels is a process that takes place after relativities have been established. However, job evaluation provides the basis for the allocation of money to different grades. It may also help with the process of salary surveys.

Job evaluation has historically been associated with the determination of white-collar pay structures in particular. However, occupational changes, the generally reduced bargaining power of trade unions and, in Europe, equal pay and equal value legislation have all been factors leading to the greater use of job evaluation schemes for manual workers.

Even if employees are paid well in comparison with similar work in other organisations, there can often be considerable dissatisfaction about perceived internal inequities. Job evaluation can be particularly useful in reducing discontent about this. Even if individuals do not always agree with the results of job evaluation schemes, they may at least accept that the employer has tried to resolve pay issues in a fair and systematic way.

TYPES OF SCHEMES

In considering the different types of job evaluation schemes particular attention is paid to important practical problems that are often overlooked in explanations of how schemes are *supposed* to work as opposed to the way they may work in practice. Few people argue that the process of job evaluation is scientific – it is essentially a systematic way of making a series of judgements about relativities. The use of scientific method is in making those subjective judgements, not replacing that judgemental process.

A basic distinction between the various types of schemes is between the non-analytical and the analytical ones. Examples of non-analytical schemes are job classification, job ranking and paired comparisons. A recent development has been to evaluate jobs in terms of competencies required or deployed by the person doing a job. This approach may be a factor in an analytical scheme or the basis of a complete scheme.

Non-analytical schemes
Job classification
Jobs are looked at as a whole and then grouped into families to which a grade is allocated (as in the civil service in the UK). Definitions are sometimes given of the basic characteristics of a classification or grade to judge where particular jobs should go. This can be a relatively cheap form of job evaluation. It also facilities the flexibility of tasks that are allocated, particularly if the range of tasks within a job grade is wide.

Job ranking
Job ranking involves arranging jobs in a hierarchy, and the vertical rank order can be split up into various job grades. This can also be a relatively cheap form of job evaluation.

Paired comparisons

The technique of paired comparisons is a more sophisticated way of arriving at a rank order. It involves comparing each job with every other job to identify the correct rank order. However, the greater the number of jobs, the greater the problem in making valid comparisons between jobs. Whilst the arithmetic may be handled by use of a computer, there remains the problem of people knowing enough about all the other jobs to make informed judgements.

The basic feature of all three of these non-analytical approaches is that the ultimate grading is achieved by comparison with other jobs rather than by systematically identifying the component elements in each job. They tend to be relatively cheap and easy to operate. However, it can be difficult to defend sex discrimination claims based on the equal value regulations with a non-analytical scheme. This is because it can be argued that the overall judgements contain an element of sex discrimination. The equal value regulations are explained later in this chapter.

Analytical schemes

The main analytical schemes often involve points rating, including many of the proprietary schemes offered by consultancy organisations. Points rating involves identifying the common factors in jobs and then allocating points to these factors according to the specific demands in each job. The points allocation, or weight, for each factor is established after systematic internal discussion about the relative importance of the factor to the organisation. Each factor in a job is then assessed and a total points score for the job obtained. The total points score indicates what job grade is appropriate. The proprietary schemes are often sophisticated versions of this points rating approach.

The job competence approach

Organisations may use competencies for part, or even all, of a job evaluation scheme, particularly if job competencies are also used for selection and training. The job competence approach is analytical in terms of the processes adopted. It involves a detailed examination of the range and varying levels of skills that can be brought to bear in a job. In more traditional approaches the focus of the evaluation is the job requirements. With job competencies the minimum competencies required in a person to do a job are specified but it is acknowledged that people may perform at a higher level than the minimum. This blurs the distinction between assessing the needs of the job as opposed to the performance of the individual. The approach recognises that some individuals can interpret and develop a job more productively than others. The level of competence displayed by a person doing a job can be used to determine the pay grade that they are given. Key advantages of the job competence approach are:

- it can link in with competencies developed for selection and training;
- employees can be encouraged to develop relevant skills;
- employees can be rewarded for showing initiative in their job, developing it and adding value to the work of the organisation.

Disadvantages of the job competence approach are:

- it focuses on skills not outcomes. If this approach is used, the extent to which objectives are achieved may also need to be considered;
- mundane but essential tasks may be ignored in favour of building up the more interesting parts of a job;
- it is a top-down process with little scope for employee or union involvement in the design of the scheme. This may affect the extent to which a scheme is felt fair;
- consistency of ratings may be hard to achieve, especially if the approach involves significant devolution of authority to line management;
- if a scheme is based completely on job competencies it may be extremely complicated.

CHOICE OF SCHEME

The dilemma for the individual employers is what, if any, scheme to adopt. No one scheme, or approach, is superior to all others; it is basically a question of choosing 'horses for courses' and then operating whatever scheme is chosen in a sensible manner. However refined and sophisticated schemes may appear to be, it must always be remembered that any statistical calculation is erected on a basis of subjective judgements of, for example, what factors should be chosen and what weights they should be given. Consequently, one should beware of spurious accuracy and of claims that everything is near perfect because ratings are very consistent. Ratings may be consistent in applying a scheme but as schemes rest on subjective judgements this can lead to consistent error.

Example

The complexity of some of the proprietary schemes designed by consultants can make them particularly difficult to understand. This can make it difficult to identify potential disadvantages. One ingenious personnel officer, however, discovered a way of finding out the potential weaknesses of proprietary schemes – to invite comment from rival consultants!

Key factors in deciding what type of scheme to have
Coverage within the organisation
Whilst it may seem convenient and fair to have one scheme for the whole of an organisation this is not always practicable. There can be so little in common between, for example, manual, technical and managerial grades that one may have to develop different schemes so that the jobs being compared and evaluated have a reasonable amount in common. There is not much point in having an overall scheme that seeks to assess a chief executive's job in terms of factors such as physical strength and monotony and boredom. However, a counter-argument that has emerged in favour of schemes covering all employees is that it may help in defending cases brought under the equal value regulations where comparisons are made between different parts of an employer's pay structure.

Cost

The costs of installing and maintaining a scheme need to be considered. The more sophisticated the scheme the greater such costs are likely to be. Another critical cost is the uplift in pay that usually results from the introduction of a scheme. Job evaluation is unlikely to leave the existing pay structure undisturbed, and the holders of jobs that are downgraded normally have their own salary protected. Consequently, an immediate effect of job evaluation is that as no-one has less pay and some will get more pay, the total wage and salary bill will increase. A rule of thumb for major restructuring exercises is that such an uplift will be in the order of 3 per cent of the total pay bill.

Size of organisation

The investment in a costly scheme for a small group of employees may simply be too expensive. Also it may be much easier to operate simpler schemes in small organisations because of the knowledge that people have about one another's jobs.

Rate of change

An important factor that often is ignored is the expected rate of change in an organisation. Job evaluation schemes are usually introduced on the assumption that the organisational arrangements are fixed. However, the pace of change is such now that one has to evaluate how well schemes will cope with projected change. There is not much point in having an expensive sophisticated scheme that is soon going to be out of date. This question also needs asking in a slightly modified form of existing schemes. It may be that existing schemes, which may historically have been sound, have become irrelevant through not being adjusted, or not being capable of adjustment, in line with organisational change.

| Example | A comprehensive proprietary job evaluation scheme was installed at an engineering factory in London. Unfortunately, it became obsolete within four months because of the rapidity of technical and organisational change. |

Employee involvement

Trade unions are likely to take more than a passing interest in job evaluation and their involvement in schemes has to be considered. They are likely to see job evaluation as a framework for bargaining. In any case, regardless of whether there is a trade union or not, one needs to consider the issue of employee involvement. If schemes are supposed to incorporate internal views about equity and fairness there needs to be some mechanism for taking employees' views into account with regard to the design and operation of schemes. The need to do this in the UK has been reinforced by developments in European law.

An almost inevitable consequence of job evaluation is that some jobs will be downgraded. Even if a person's salary is protected by the device of red-circling, it is arguable that such a change necessitates consultation with union or employee representatives if more than 20 employees are involved. This is because the requirement for statutory redundancy consultation was widened to over changes in contract terms. This requirement was incorporated in the Trade Union Reform and Employment Rights Act of 1993, bringing the UK into line with European law (Aiken and Mill 1994: 54–57). The remedies for a breach of these requirements though are just in relation to lack of consultation and not those for redundancy or unfair dismissal.

If anyone ever did design a perfect system, representatives would still feel obliged to try and bargain about the matter, as what trade union could countenance being told that it had no bargaining role? Unions also rightly query the basis on which schemes are based and the results they give. Unions may have to distance themselves a little from schemes, however, as otherwise they may seem to be implementing managerial policies. Once a scheme has been established they tend to acknowledge it and to retain and use the right to represent anyone who feels that they have a case for upgrading.

IMPLEMENTATION AND OPERATION

Job vs person

One of the basic issues is to remember is that unless job-holders' competencies are being assessed, it is the *job* and not the *person* that is being evaluated. If a job-holder has outgrown a job, the real answer is for them to be encouraged to seek promotion rather than to distort the pay structure by giving an upgrade that temporarily meets their needs but not the organisation's. One must also beware of the danger, explained in the previous chapter, that employees may distort a job to justify an upgrade. In contrast, if a person is not up to a job, it can sometimes be that this is because the job is not graded highly enough to attract people of the right calibre.

Choice of factors

Factors in analytical schemes have to be chosen carefully so that they don't overlap. Otherwise a job-holder can benefit twice under such factors as job complexity and education required which may be different ways of measuring the same requirement. Another complication can arise from the establishment of 'weights' for factors. Apart from the judgemental problems of doing this anyway, there is the statistical problem that the real weights depend not just on, for example, the points allocated for a particular factor, but also on the extent to which those making judgements use the full extent of the scale.

Example

There was once an attempt to introduce a new job evaluation scheme for nursing officers in the health service. It rapidly became apparent that for some jobs the only factors on which the scores differed were those related to the level of the unit in which a person was employed. The reality was that in practice the scheme for some jobs was based on a single factor – the one that was easiest to measure. A further explanation of these statistical problems is given in the section on recording and rating in chapter 10.

Upgrading claims

There can be misconceptions about the extent to which employees can be expected to change their duties without receiving any extra remuneration. Changes in the range of work at a given level do not normally constitute a case for upgrading. Work at a higher level of responsibility may provide a valid basis for upgrading, but even in this case it has to be remembered that job grades normally embrace a range of jobs and a person's increase in, for example, responsibility level may not be sufficient to lift them into the next grade. There is a common law requirement for employees to accept reasonable changes in job content and the prudent employer will reinforce this by the use of generic job titles and a flexibility clause in any job description.

Claims for upgrading can also be made on what may turn out to be basic job requirements rather than additional demands. Schemes need to be operated on the basis that there are minimum performance requirements which justify retention in a given job as opposed to justifying an upgrading. However, one cannot but admire the ingenuity with which some cases are argued.

Examples

One forklift driver applied for an upgrading at an oil refinery. His case rested on his responsibility for expensive plant and equipment as evidenced by the fact that he had recently fractured a fuel line and caused a fire costing over £1 million worth of damage!

Another such case involved a receptionist who was asked to elaborate on the decision-making elements in her job – which consisted mainly of routing telephone calls and visitors. She beamed and said she had to decide whether to come in each day or not. The argument advanced was that she had to decide if she was fit enough for work or not, as if she was not it would be bad for the external image of the firm if she came in and was grumpy!

Appeals

Irrespective of whether there is employee involvement in the design of a scheme or not, some sort of appeals mechanism is necessary. Appeals criteria need to be specified, such as a change in duties, and appeals bodies established. These may be managerial panels, joint management-union panels or involve the use of an outside arbitrator – either sitting alone or chairing a joint panel.

The knock-on effect

A crucial issue in establishing the grading of any job is its effect on the overall equilibrium of the pay structure. Serious inequities obviously should be corrected but not insubstantial cases for locating jobs in a higher grade. The key issue is not the extra direct costs this would involve but the knock-on effect. The danger is that by solving one person's perceived grievance you can create a host of repercussive claims.

External job market

Another key issue concerns the relationship of pay to the external job market. It is no good having a scheme that is out of line with the market. However, markets do not always operate so clearly and systematically that you can dispense with job evaluation. In making comparisons with pay in other organisations care has to be taken to ensure that you are comparing like with like. The use of job titles alone may be dangerous – for example a title such as 'fitter' can cover a wide range of different jobs in terms of actual duties and responsibility level. Sometimes there can be a marked conflict between internal relativities and the market rate for particular groups, for whom there is a strong demand. The realistic answer in cases like this is not to have a spurious re-evaluation of the staff concerned but to openly recognise and deal with the problem. It may be necessary to pay a market supplement for such staff or even take them out of the evaluation scheme altogether. This way at least the rest of the pay structure can remain consistent.

Using standard schemes

A further issue concerns the transferability of evaluation schemes to different organisations, countries and cultures. It can be tempting to do this as it may seem a short cut to copy someone else's scheme or use one's own in an overseas subsidiary. The usual rationale for job evaluation schemes is that they reflect the attitudes within an organisation about what is a fair set of relativities. However, the attitudes towards what is fair may be quite different in an organisation or country in which there is a different set of values. Consequently, such transfer of schemes may be an extremely hit-and-miss affair. This also applies to the use of schemes designed by consultants that have not been designed or sufficiently adapted to the needs of a particular organisation.

EQUAL VALUE

A further dimension of pay structures and job evaluation is the law regarding equal value. Employees have a broad right not to be discriminated against in terms of pay and conditions of employment on grounds of sex if their work is of equal value to someone of the opposite sex in the same organisation. This is a consequence in the UK of the government being obliged to comply with the requirements of the Treaty of Rome and the Equal Pay Directive of 1975. Under the Equal Pay Act of 1970, there was a limited right to equal pay but only for similar or broadly similar work, or for work rated as equivalent under a job evaluation scheme. The Equal Pay Act of 1970 was amended by the Equal Pay (Amendment) Regulations in 1983. The right to claim pay of equal value, like the right to claim equal pay, excludes comparisons with employees of the same sex. Guidance on the application of the law is given in a Code of Practice (EOC, 1997).

The right to equal pay for work of equal value exists where the job demands are the same in categories such as 'effort, skill and decision-making'. This implies a need for some sort of analytical job evaluation if the employer is to try and defend their position. Unless the tribunal decides that there are no reasonable grounds for the claim, and if the parties fail to reach an agreement, an independent expert is called in. The expert reports on whether or not the jobs that the claimant claims are of equal value are so. The tribunal subsequently decides in the light of the expert's report. All this may sound rather convoluted but the crunch comes if an individual claim succeeds. This may reveal that there is the basis for further claims and if any of these succeed the process may continue. The 'knock-on' effect can lead to the undermining of the whole of an existing pay structure.

The impact that a successful equal value claim can have means that employers must give some thought to this whole area. They may also feel that they should be doing this anyway to avoid sex discrimination. To do that it is necessary to review not just a pay structure but the processes by which pay rates and differentials are established. Implications for the operation of job evaluation schemes include ensuring that there is a fair cross-representation of any benchmark jobs and that there is adequate representation of both sexes on panels. If a points-rating scheme is used, it is necessary to ensure that the factors and weights used are not discriminatory. This may be all against a background where the internal 'felt fair' values represent, for example, dominant male values which may be in conflict with the legal requirement to avoid sex discrimination. Analytical job evaluation fairly applied will help avoid discrimination but not necessarily put a stop to argument. People sometimes think that the use of, for example, sophisticated statistical techniques enables *scientifically objective* decisions to be made about pay grades. However, what such techniques do is to provide elaborate means of establishing systematic *opinions* about job relationships. The judgements about how dissimilar factors or whole jobs should relate to one another can be carried out systematically, but the judgements are subjective. Consequently, an independent expert may well have a different view about job relationships from those who established a particular pay structure. The judgements of independent experts are also likely to vary according to which expert is asked to give evidence.

The case law arising out of equal value claims is proving a guide as to how the law operates in practice. The following important issues have been decided by case law.

- Claims have to involve comparisons with another job where employees are predominantly of the other sex (*Pickstone* vs *Freeman 1988*).
- Equal value law may be a powerful pressure for the harmonisation of the conditions of employment of manual and white-collar employees. Otherwise applicants may be able to point to just one element of the remuneration package where they think there is an unjustified difference and argue the case for parity (*Hayward* vs *Cammell Laird Shipbuilders 1988*).
- The practice of slotting-in jobs to outline structures without analysis of the jobs slotted in seems to be inadequate (*Bromley* vs *H.J. Quick 1988*).
- The existence of a separate collective bargaining structure is not an acceptable defence (*Enderby* vs *Frenchay Health Authority 1993*).
- The defence of a genuine material factor difference may include market rates, but only if that accounts for the whole difference (*Enderby* vs *Frenchay Health Authority, 1988*).

Employers have strong financial reasons for appealing against adverse judgements (as do unions). Consequently, it can be years before a case is decided. The lessons for employers include taking the basic steps already suggested to avoid obvious discrimination and hoping that they are not targeted for an important test case. If the pay structure is adjusted to take account of possible sex discrimination, the extra pay costs need to be taken into account when any general increase is considered. The response by the National Health Service in the UK to the loss of a number of cases has been to move towards a national system of job evaluation.

PRESSURES FOR CHANGE

The major changes that so many organisations have experienced, and which have been previously described particularly in chapter 3, are having a major impact on the way job evaluation is operated. The trend to less labour-intensive, more flexible organisations has been particularly important. Also, changes in job evaluation have been necessary in some cases to help bring about such organisational changes. Generally, there has been a move to fewer job grades, with less-detailed job descriptions and an emphasis on flexible working. In the case of Nissan, for example, this has involved the compression of manual jobs into just two different job titles with no job descriptions. The trend to multiskilling, as an aid to greater flexibility, also puts more emphasis on the personal attributes of the job-holder. This may include payment for additional competencies that the job-holder has acquired. These developments reduce the distinctiveness of individual jobs and encourage the concept of job families. Simpler schemes are more adaptive, more easily controlled in terms of pay drift, and less expensive in terms of administrative costs including the use of managerial time. Such costs savings are a particularly important pressure for change given the ongoing pressure to reduce costs in the private and public sectors. Computer-assisted schemes help reduce the costs of operating schemes further, provided the managerial politics are such that the results are viable.

The decline in union power has tended to give management more freedom with regard to job evaluation, and this has often been reinforced by more devolved patterns of organisational decision-making. The decline in union power has also facilitated more of an individual and less of a collectivist approach. This trend has tended to emphasise the link between pay and individual performance and to reduce the importance of grade levels. The traditional approach to job evaluation was that individual performance was discounted, but there is more acceptance now that the nature of the job may be shaped by the individual performing it. The concept of added value is important in this respect. All this has tended to reduce the need for complex schemes and high levels of accuracy, particularly as grade level is a less dominant factor in determining overall pay. The one contrary pressure arises from the equal value regulations which may cause organisations to consider retaining or introducing analytical schemes. Although few claims have been successfully established, organisations may also have to respond to claims during pay bargaining that their job evaluation schemes are sex discriminatory. Other trends include less emphasis on hierarchies and more use of overlapping pay scales.

A related development has been that of cafeteria-style benefits so that employees can have some choice in matching their benefits to their needs. However, this can generate significant administrative problems, particularly as a change in the level of one benefit can affect the relative worth of all the other benefits. This may be so even if computer programmes are used to help maintain consistency with the overall benefits package.

SUMMARY

✔ Employers need to consider a framework for remunerating their employees. Two main frameworks, which may complement one another, are the use of financial incentive schemes and job evaluation. Care needs to be taken before embarking on the use of financial incentive schemes. There are many potential reasons for poor performance and lack of financial incentive may be only one of them. Even if there is a lack of financial incentive, schemes that link pay to productivity or profitability don't always work. The basic conditions that have to be met for schemes to succeed were identified. Even when the conditions are right for the use of a financial incentive scheme, the right scheme has to be chosen and carefully implemented and operated.

✔ Schemes that are inappropriate or badly run may not only fail to improve performance but can be counter-productive and have damaging long-term consequences for an organisation. The main types of financial incentive are individual and group schemes related to output or performance, and profit-sharing.

✔ The conflicting pressures on organisational pay arrangements were identified. Job evaluation is a technique that may provide the basis for establishing a rational organisational pay structure. It may also be particularly useful in establishing viable internal pay relativities. However, schemes have to be carefully chosen, operated and monitored. The two main types of job evaluation schemes are non-analytical and the generally more complicated analytical schemes. A relatively recent innovation has been to grade jobs in part, or even sometimes completely, on the basis of the relevant job competencies that people need and/or display in a job.

✔ Despite the equal value regulations in the UK there are strong cost and organisational pressures for schemes to be simpler. The pressures for simpler schemes were identified and include the increased rate of organisational change, the desire for broader job banding to achieve greater job flexibility and more emphasis on individual performance in determining pay. The issue of performance-related pay is considered in chapter 10 in the context of appraisal generally.

SELF-ASSESSMENT QUESTIONS

1. What are the necessary preconditions for employee financial incentive schemes ?

2. Identify the potential long-term effects of employee financial incentive schemes?

3. If financial incentives schemes are to be used, how would you decide whether they be on an individual or group basis?

4. What are the purposes of job evaluation schemes?

5. What are the main operational problems in ensuring that job evaluation schemes remain effective?

6. What are the main labour market and organisational changes causing employers to review the way in which they financially reward their employees?

 References

Aiken, Olga and Cherry Mills (1994) 'No Escape from Consultation', *Personnel Management*, October.

Bank of England (1997) 'Financial Stability Review', as reported in *The Financial Times*, 3 March.

Chote, Robert (1991) 'Profit-related pay proves no panacea', *The Independent*, 24 May.

Equal Opportunities Commission, Code of Practice on Equal Pay, EOC, 1997.

Fay, Stephen (1996) *The Collapse of Barings*, excerpts and comments in *The Times*, 12 February.

McLean, Hazel (1994) *Fair Shares: The Future of Employee Financial Participation in the UK*, Institute of Employment Rights.

Morton, Ian (1993) 'Cheating traffic wardens curbed', *Evening Standard* (London), 8 September.

National Board for Prices and Incomes (1968a) Payment by Results Systems, report no. 65, Cmnd. 3627, HMSO, p. 11 of pamphlet summarising the above report.

National Board for Prices and Incomes (1968b), statistical supplement to Payment by Results report, para. 22.

General references

Armstrong, Michael and Angela Barron (1995) *The Job Evaluation Handbook*, Institute of Personnel and Development.

Institute of Personnel and Development (1996) The IPD Guide on Team Reward, IPD

Cases cited

Bromley vs *H. J. Quick Ltd.* (1988) IRLR, no. 249, CA.

Enderby vs *Frenchay Health Authority* (1993) TLR, 12 November, ECJ.

Hayward vs *Cammell Laird Shipbuilders Ltd* (1988) ICR 464, IRLR 257. HL.

Pickstone vs *Freemans plc* (1988) IRLR 267, HL.

chapter (eight)

Communication

There are case studies and exercises at
http://www.thomsonlearning.co.uk
(for full details, see the listing at the
start of this book).

LEARNING OUTCOMES

By the end of this chapter you will be able to:

- Identify the extent to which managers are involved in the communication process and the variety of ways in which communication takes place

- Identify and take account of the wide range of potential obstacles to effective communication

- Identify and apply the key skills involved in effective oral communication, particularly listening

- Identify and apply the key requirements for effective oral presentation

- Identify and apply the key requirements for written communication

- Evaluate the ways in which organisational structures can facilitate or hinder effective communication

- Identify and take account of the ways in which national culture can hinder effective communication

- Evaluate and take account of significant developments in information technology and the ways in which they can facilitate or hinder effective communication

- Evaluate the role of the media in communication and how to use it constructively

Introduction

This chapter is probably the most important in the whole book. The topic, as well as needing to be covered in its own right, serves as a foundation for much of the rest of the book. It also links back with material covered in previous chapters. This includes the link between organisational structure and the effectiveness of communication and the growing importance of electronic communication – both covered in chapter 3. Other phenomena that interrelate with communication are managerial style and culture – topics, which are covered in chapter 4.

The chapter starts with an explanation of why communication is such an important topic. Managers spend most of their time trying to communicate with others. This can be in a variety of ways, particularly talking, listening, writing, reading, attending meetings and sometimes by use of the media. Consequently, if readers are able to develop their communication skills as a result of reading this chapter, they can benefit time and time again. If the communication process is ineffective, the basis on which managers or others try and take decisions is likely to be faulty. Emphasis is placed on the importance of managers letting other people communicate with them as much of the time this is what is needed. Unfortunately, this is not always understood, and the whole process of communication is often assumed to be much easier than it really is. Other obstacles to effective communication are also examined. An understanding of these obstacles is a way of identifying the skills needed for effective communication. A key skill is active listening. Attention is also paid to presentational and written skills.

As organisational structure can facilitate or hinder effective communication, attention is paid to this issue. The problems in communicating between different national cultures are also considered. The growing importance of electronic communication and also some of the problems that it can create are examined. The final topic is the role of the mass media. This involves both the interpretation of media messages and presentational skills.

The importance of communication

Managers are likely to spend most of their time engaged directly in some form of communication process. Even when they are working alone – for example, studying or preparing reports – they are relying on other people's attempts to communicate with them or they are preparing to communicate with others. Accuracy in decision-making depends, in particular, on effective communication. If the communication process is faulty, then everything else can be affected.

Experiments, research and sheer personal observation show that most people are far too optimistic about the accuracy of the communication process. This applies not just to communication processes within employing organisations but to life in general. Even when errors are identified it may be too late, or the inherent faults in the process that will lead to further errors may not be recognised. The effective communication of factual information can be difficult enough, but often attitudes and feelings need to be communicated, and that can be far more complicated. The number and nature of the barriers are such that there is a strong case for communication skills training being given as part of the standard school curriculum. This is not yet generally the case, and in this chapter the attempt is made to give managers practical guidance on how to identify the communication processes in their organisations with a view to evaluating their effectiveness. This evaluation can then provide the basis for the development of the manager's own practical skills of communication.

In Rosemary Stewart's study of how managers spend their time , referred to in chapter 2, it was established that on average the 160 managers in the sample spent two-thirds of their time working with other people (1988: 50). It seems reasonable to assume that most managers spend the bulk of their working day in some type of communication activity. Even the 33 managers in the sample in backroom-type jobs spent about half of their time working with other people. This may be through attendance at meetings, the giving and receiving of instructions, discussions with colleagues and contact with customers or suppliers. Such contact may be face to face, over the telephone or a combination of both. Much of the remainder of the time is likely to be concerned with the assimilation or preparation of written information. If managers are to make the correct substantive decisions in their jobs, it follows that they need to be able to handle the communication process effectively. A problem of communication within organisations is that if it is faulty, everyone else in the communication chain can be misinformed. Also, the longer the chain, the greater the chance of further error creeping in.

It follows that the need to develop skills for effective communication may be a critical priority for many managers. Regrettably, this need is often not perceived, and managers may neglect the importance of, and the opportunity for, development in this critical area. Communication skills tend to be taken for granted and lack of skill far more easily recognised in others than in oneself. A consequence of blaming others is that people do not see the need to improve their own skills. The process of communication is often far more complex than people realise, and this is a further reason why skills development in this area tends to be neglected. It is only when people realise the subtleties concerning effective communication that they may become communication-conscious and start to develop their own skills. The complexities are such that those who are good at communication are likely to become even better if they systematically evaluate and consider their own effectiveness in this area.

Obstacles to effective communication

Having stressed the importance of the communication process, it is appropriate to develop further the hypothesis that communication in organisations is a great deal worse than most people realise. Explaining the nature of communication processes and the potential for breakdown will do this. Case examples are given to illustrate some of the major points.

TIME

Communication can be time-intensive. This can be either because of the need for prior preparation, giving people time to ask questions and the amount of listening that may be required. Time will also be needed to identify potential problems and ways of overcoming them. As managers are usually short of time, and often not as skilled as they think they are in communicating, insufficient time may be allowed.

LANGUAGE

Those involved in the communication process may not have a common language. Language differences can occur because of variations in technical understanding, general vocabulary levels and the use of in-house terms that are not familiar to others. This can be aggravated if there are significant differences in ability levels. The complications involved in communicating between different nationalities are dealt with later in this chapter in the section on national culture.

LISTENING PROBLEMS

It is appropriate to explain one major misconception about communication at this stage. This point is not only important in its own right but develops the argument that the approach of many managers to communication may not be sufficiently sophisticated.

Communication is usually seen as the need to brief other people. The reality is that most of a manager's time needs to be concerned with the receiving rather than the imparting of information and views. The reason for this is simple – in any conversation between two people there is a need to alternate between talking and listening. There is not much point in anyone talking if the intended recipient is not prepared to listen. If the two people involved in a discussion take equal turns talking and listening, they will obviously spend half of their time in the listening role.

As much of the communication in organisations involves face-to-face discussion between more than two people, it follows as a mathematical fact that most managers will need to spend more time listening than talking. There will be exceptions to this, but the very existence of exceptions reduces the time available for others to do the talking. Admittedly, managers may often need to take the lead in explaining things to their subordinates, but a statistically unequal share of talk in this direction may easily be counter-balanced by the time they have to spend in discussions and meetings involving a number of people when they talk only for a minority of the time. The basic point of this argument is that managers may fail to see that they will normally need to spend more time listening than talking.

Effective listening does not come naturally to all managers, particularly if they do not recognise the importance of it. People who set out to improve the quality of communication in organisations often assume that good communication is synonymous with the imparting of information. House magazines, letters from the chief executive, briefing meetings and training in public speaking are based mainly on the assumption that the problem is in disseminating information. The reality may be that it is more important to unblock the obstructions to information and views flowing in to the decision-makers. The problem may be that, until such time as communication is effective, managers may not realise that the obstructions are there. In any case, if everyone concentrates on imparting information and views, just who will be left to receive all these messages?

Example

A nursing officer attended a review meeting three months after he had attended a middle-management training course. When asked what had happened as a result of his training, the nursing officer explained that the area on which he had been able to concentrate was the development of his communication skills. He had worked on his listening skills and had put a chair by the side of his desk, on which people were invited to sit when they came into his office. He explained that he was amazed at the extra amount of information that he obtained this way compared with his previous pattern of letting people stand up or sit in a chair on the other side of the desk. He then realised the limited nature of the information he had been obtaining before and on which basis he had been taking decisions. Before, being unaware of the information that was available, he had not tried to get it. It was only after he had discovered his blindspot that he realised it existed.

It is also easy for people to be distracted from effective listening. They may have other problems on their mind, be physically distracted or simply lack the motivation to listen carefully.

LACK OF FEEDBACK

The problem of effective communication is unfortunately greater than just the recognition of its scale and importance and the comprehension that one needs to receive information as well as disseminate it. It is all too easy for people to assume that they have effectively communicated and be unaware that their attempts at communication have only been partially or totally unsuccessful.

Example

A way of demonstrating the undue optimism people have about the accuracy of the communications process is by use of the rectangles exercise. This involves asking one of the group to tell the rest, without any questions by them, how to draw a diagram consisting of six rectangles. The instructor is asked to sit facing the wall and convert a diagram, such as that shown in Figure 8.1, into words so that the group can reproduce the diagram from their oral instructions (Leavitt and Bahrani 1988: 103–112). In practice, one would not try to explain how to reproduce a diagram by oral instruction, but there are advantages in using this artificial example. It is easy to check the accuracy with which it is reproduced and it is no more complicated than some of the instructions that people actually try to explain orally.

CONTINUED OVER ➤

CONTINUED FROM
PREVIOUS PAGE

All the rectangles are of equal size and the angles either of 45 degrees or 90 degrees. The rectangles touch one another either at the corner or the midpoint. Invariably, there is considerable error in the attempts of the groups to convert the oral instructions back into the original diagram. Sometimes the results are devastating. On one occasion a zero score was achieved by a group of 16 managers because their instructor had unwittingly described the rectangles as triangles. Invariably, the instructor significantly underestimates the amount of error made by the group.

After the results of the attempt to explain the diagram using one-way communication have been recorded, the same instructor is asked to repeat the exercise but the second time facing the group and with unlimited opportunity for questioning. A similar type of diagram is converted into words and back into a diagram again by the rest of the group. There is a standard pattern to this second stage of the experiment. It takes longer, the accuracy is usually much higher, it is rare for there to be no error, and again the instructor overestimates the level of accuracy. The assumption is usually made that if people have queries they will raise them. The reality is that even in the relatively placid context of a training course, people may have inhibitions about asking questions. They may feel embarrassed about their inability to draw the diagram, be confused by the instruction, have wrongly thought that their reconstruction was correct, have failed to catch the eye of the instructor at the right time or simply lost interest. The instructor may fail to appreciate that there can be this variety of reasons for people not raising queries and make the common error of assuming that silence means that everyone has accurately reproduced the diagram.

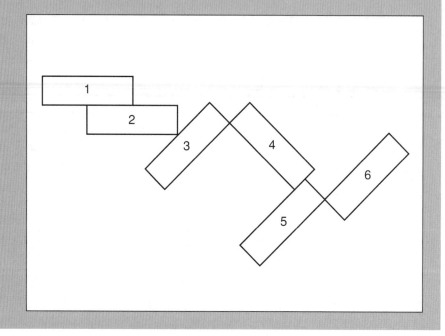

FIGURE 8.1

Communication

exercise

BOGUS FEEDBACK

When communication is initiated it is necessary for the initiator to consider both what the evidence is for their assumption that communication has been effective and the consequences of communication being defective. People can be very aware of their lack of understanding when they are on the receiving end of an instruction. It can be very tempting to create an impression of understanding through silence. The problem is that the initiator may be left with quite a false impression of their effectiveness. If a message is particularly important it is up to them to search for a more positive corroboration than mere silence that communication has been effective. They will need to consider other forms of feedback and to distinguish between accurate and bogus feedback.

Silence is not the only way in which people give false impressions about having understood explanations. There are occasions when people actually say they have understood when they have not. This commonly occurs, for instance, when someone asks for directions somewhere but are so confused by the instructions that they may say that they have understood when they have not. This type of breakdown can happen within organisations and for a variety of reasons. These include fear of embarrassment, inability to understand the person trying to help, politeness and impatience. Often people do not like to show their ignorance to people in positions of authority.

Examples

A student nurse was asked to give a patient an air ring. She apparently was not quite sure what to do but guessed that the appropriate interpretation was to move the patient's bed on to the verandah and remove the bedclothes. She had been expected to get an inflatable rubber air ring so that the patient could sit on it and receive a blanket bath. Another student nurse was given the same instruction but with slightly different phraseology – she was told to go and get an air ring. She returned three-quarters of an hour later saying how much she had enjoyed her walk!

A student nurse was expected to give a patient a warm drink of potassium citrate. As is so often the case, an abbreviation was used and she was asked to give the patient a 'hot pot cit'. Unfortunately her interpretation of this instruction led to the patient being sat upon a bedpan of boiling water!

In these cases the students' guesswork fortunately just led to comic results. That will not always be the case and such errors in the communication process may be picked up too late or not at all. The errors in the previous examples may be seen as stupidity or feebleness on the part of the student nurses, but such an interpretation is to miss the point. The fault really lies with the person who gave the instruction not ensuring that they had made themselves properly understood. Either they needed to make a positive check that the instruction was understood or to have had a working relationship with the student nurse such that queries would be raised if necessary. The objective with communication needs to be to see that it is effective rather than being able to lay the blame on someone else if things go wrong.

Nursing examples have been given to illustrate the need to get accurate feedback. However, such problems are likely in almost any organisation, particularly if the culture is authoritarian. Sometimes those in authority may go through the motions of obtaining feedback when in fact what they want is simply the pretence and alibi that people have had a fair opportunity to raise queries. Rhetorical questions may be used – such as, 'Is that clear?' – which do not really invite responses. The technique can be observed with lecturers, or after-dinner speakers, who leave the opportunity for questions until an impossibly late stage in the proceedings.

Example

When military orderly officers had to go through the routine of asking if there were complaints about the food some mastered the technique of asking if there were any queries in such a way that anyone who did complain deserved a medal. This enabled the orderly officer to maintain the fiction that people had been given an opportunity to complain about the food if they were dissatisfied.

Should subordinates nevertheless voice criticisms in situations like those described they may have the blame put back on them, however unjustly, to discourage further criticism. However, subordinates can also misperceive the response to their comments or questions. Sometimes it may be necessary and possible for them to raise sensitive issues. In doing this it may be as well to remember the skills of assertiveness explained in chapter 4.

RESISTANCE TO CRITICISM

It is important to recognise that any manager is going to prefer to hear good news than bad news, and the temptation for colleagues and subordinates is to tell people what they want to hear. In the long term this can be disastrous, and managers and political leaders alike need to consciously recognise the distortion that can occur in channels of communication and beware of succumbing to it.

Example

An illustration of the folly of not finding out what subordinates really think concerns President Saddam Hussein's invasion of Kuwait in 1990. It was difficult and dangerous for his advisers to warn President Saddam Hussein of the risk of a Western military response. Consequently, although his advisers are likely to have had a more realistic assessment of the consequences of invasion, they were unable or unwilling to try and dissuade him from such action. This communication failure may or may not have been compounded by the lack of a clear warning by the American ambassador, Avril Glaspie. Eight days before the invasion, she told Saddam Hussein that the US government had 'no opinion on the Arab-Arab conflicts, like your border disagreement with Kuwait' (Campbell 1991). However, Glaspie maintained that the part of the conversation containing the alleged assurance that there would be no invasion was not included in the tape that was released by the Iraqis when they subsequently claimed they had been misled by the Americans.

(Simpson 1991: 41–42)

The chances of blocking out critical or unfavourable news can be greatly reduced if the temptation to do this is consciously recognised and if modern-day equivalents of the ancient Greek tradition of slaying the messenger who brings news of defeat in battle is avoided. It may also be necessary to take independent checks to evaluate the information that is received. It was comprehension of this point which led some generals at the time of the First World War to say, 'If you want to know what's going on you have to go to the trenches.' Having said this, it is necessary also to make the point that there are few people, if any, who can cope with the whole truth all the time. Total exposure could be destructive to the individual concerned. What is needed is a realisation that the information fed to one in organisations needs careful evaluation, and other information may be needed but not passed on. Managers may need to seek out the bad news to the extent that it is necessary and to the extent that they can cope with it. An adage concerning delegation is that managers get the subordinates they deserve. The same adage can be used with regard to communication: managers get the communication they deserve.

SELECTIVE PERCEPTION AND BIAS

In considering barriers to communication, it is also necessary to deal specifically with the problems caused by selective perception and bias. The sheer volume of data that is available means that one has to have some basis for deciding what to look for and what to react to. However, careful judgement is needed in making these decisions. A totally open mind can simply mean that a person is swamped with data. A closed mind can mean that a person doesn't respond to what is under their nose. Particular dangers are seeing only what you want to see, making the 'facts' fit what has already been decided, and suppressing unpleasant facts.

Norman Dixon (1976), a former Army psychiatrist, explains a number of Western military disasters in terms of such selective perception on the part of the military leaders concerned. Three of the many examples he documents concern the Japanese attack on Pearl Harbour, the fall of Singapore and the failure of the Arnhem offensive in Holland. The pattern according to Dixon is clear and recurrent – the warning signs were there but, because they did not fit into the established thinking, they were ignored until too late. The extent to which people can be misled or even coerced into believing things, which are untrue, can be alarming.

Example

In one experiment conducted with American students by S. E. Asch it was found that a quarter of student groups could be coerced into stating that straight lines were of identical length when one was 25 per cent shorter than the other (Secord and Backman 1964: 304–307)) This effect was achieved by priming the seven other students in the experimental group to say that the lines were identical in length.

One must be careful not to over-generalise about the amount of social coercion possible from the results of a series of experiments in America with a particular

CONTINUED OVER ➤

CONTINUED FROM
PREVIOUS PAGE
group and at a particular time. However, if social pressure can have this effect on such obvious matters of fact, what is the scope for social pressure on matters that are more subjective or where people's self-interest is involved?

As well as having to cope with one's own subjectivity, it must also be recognised that much of the data which is available within organisations is subjective or actually misleading. In chapter 3 some of the reasons were given as to why department managers might be more concerned with protecting their reputations than with supplying objective data about their performance. Most people working in organisations are likely to be concerned with the pursuit of truth, but people in organisations, as in life generally, are under a variety of pressures to highlight some things and not others. There are also pressures to view events in a particular way. This means that managers need to evaluate carefully the information that is being fed to them. One of the themes of the British TV comedy series *Yes, Minister* (later *Yes, Prime Minister*) was that information was fed to the Cabinet minister by his permanent secretary in such a way that the minister thought that he was taking the decisions himself. One stratagem was that the options were put so that the minister was bound to choose the one preferred by his permanent secretary. This is why politicians at both national and local government level sometimes have political advisers and support staff to provide them with alternative viewpoints and other information.

It is also necessary to be careful in evaluating information that is fed down the line. Selective reporting and misunderstanding is not phenomena confined to upward reporting.

(Example)

Error and modification can also occur in downward communication. Corroboration of the existence and nature of these problems is given by a former civil servant, John Carswell (1981: 39).

Carswell explained that, when he was working on the administration of retirement pensions, an experienced superior said to him that there were three National Insurance schemes, not one: 'The scheme we put in the instructions, the scheme the permanent secretary talks to the minister about, and the scheme they administer in the local offices'.

Selective perception may be particularly likely if the parties involved in the communication process have different objectives. The greater the amount of the conflict the more likely that there are emotional blockages to effective communication. A major problem can be created by the frames of reference of the parties concerned. Managers with a unitary frame of reference may have difficulty in understanding that what is in the interests of an organisation as a whole may not necessarily be in the interests of all sections of the organisation. This concept is dealt with in detail in chapter 14 on employee relations.

GENDER DIFFERENCES

There may be obstacles of communication when a person is trying to communicate with a member of the opposite sex. It would seem reasonable to assume that just as cultures vary in their masculinity and femininity (Hofstede 1994) so also there are likely to be variations in the way that members of different sexes communicate, both with one another and with members of the opposite sex. The existence of different national conventions of communication between people of different genders is referred to in the later section in this chapter on national culture. The extent of the difference is likely to vary according to how much sex equality there is within a particular culture. Whilst there is an obvious danger of stereotyping, the implication of Hofstede's work is that men may tend to be more aggressive and individualistic than women. They may also tend to operate on a low-context basis whilst women may tend to rely more on non-verbal cues, which is high-context (Hall: 1976). Particular difficulties may arise when a person of one gender fails to adapt their style of communication, where appropriate, when communicating with a member of the opposite sex. For example, there may be a lower tolerance level for aggression in communication on the part of many women compared with men. Also the body language and body contact acceptable in communication between men may not always be acceptable in their communication with women.

Skills of effective oral communication

Much of the skill in effective communication lies in recognising the problem areas that have just identified. Effective communication is achieved as much as anything by avoiding these traps. One also has to beware of relying on information that is not in the form of original evidence. Groups such as research scientists, historians, medical doctors and lawyers are amongst those who are particularly aware of the danger of distortion – whether deliberate, subconscious or accidental – through relying on evidence that is not received first-hand. It won't always be possible as a manager to rely on direct evidence, but at least the dangers of relying on secondary sources can be recognised. Also, the quality of original or secondary source material provided by managers can be improved by the positive approaches explained in the rest of this section.

COAXING INFORMATION

It may be necessary for managers to work hard at coaxing information, particularly if people feel inhibited about discussing a particular issue. The lament, 'Why didn't someone tell me?' can be as much a condemnation of a manager's lack of skill in developing effective channels of communication as a condemnation of others for keeping them in the dark. It can be very hard for those in authority roles to realise the difficulty that others may have in communicating with them. The authority figure may feel totally relaxed and uninhibited and not appreciate that perhaps the very factors which create their security also create difficulties for others. The proprietor of a business may feel totally self-confident and secure and be amazed to find out, if they ever do, that people who are very dependent on them are reluctant to tell them anything unpleasant. Parents can encounter the same problem with their children. They may forget what it was like to be a child and be unaware of many of the thoughts and anxieties that their own children have and see any suggestion to the contrary as quite preposterous.

ACTIVE LISTENING

Adopting a listening role can be harder than taking the lead by talking. The problem with this can be that the more an authority figure talks, the less others may be inclined to talk. There can be a critical moment when people in the subordinate role might just start saying what they really feel, if only the authority figure stays quiet long enough. Once the subordinate has started talking, things may come out with a rush, to the amazement of the authority figure. One useful technique in any such situation can be to count silently to 10 before breaking the silence after you have asked a particularly important question.

Once a person has started to talk it can be relatively easy to get them to continue and for any others to join in. The problem is likely to be how to get them started. The authority figure needs to be aware of letting their ignorance, impatience or even their own nervousness prevent such a process starting. Care has to be taken with the timing of invitations for people to open up – it is not only the time and the place that can be important but also the stage in a discussion. It may be necessary to build up rapport gently before the invitation is given.

Thought also needs to be given to the way in which questions are put. They can be leading in nature, giving the impression that all that is required is confirmation of the questioner's obvious views, such as 'Don't you think this is a good idea?' Alternatively they can be probing and phrased in such a way as to encourage the respondents to state their own views. One useful distinction that is especially important in selection interviewing is between open questions, which encourage people to talk, and closed questions which limit responses to, for example, 'yes or no'. These issues are examined further in chapter 9 on selection and chapter 12 on counselling.

SCENE SETTING

The choice of time and place to invite people to talk can be critical. There are circumstances in which people may be prepared to 'open-up' and circumstances in which they will not. One of the skills of communication is picking up the cues as to whether a person is or is not prepared to talk about a sensitive matter. Even if the place cannot always be chosen, sometimes the geography of a room can be arranged to encourage, or for that matter to discourage, a person from talking. The more status symbols surrounding the authority figure, the less likely a subordinate is to feel free to talk. One relevant example is given below

Example

A personnel officer, who was over 6 feet tall, always made a point of seeing that he and the works superintendent were both seated if anything of consequence was to be discussed. The personnel officer had learned from experience that the superintendent was self-conscious about being short and so he did his best not to emphasise it.

A related issue is the use of open-plan offices. Originally these were found to be particularly useful in drawing offices and were meant to facilitate both monitoring of work and communication. However, the very openness can discourage people from speaking about confidential issues because of the fear of being overheard, or just being seen talking to a particular person. Consequently, open-plan layouts can actually create barriers to effective communication.

CHOICE OF LANGUAGE

Language difficulties can obviously hamper communication between people who have different national languages. Regional dialects can also complicate matters. However, there can be many other and more subtle language problems even between people who are from the same country, region and class. Technical language may be used in discussion, which is beyond the comprehension of some of the participants. In any organisation there are likely to be abbreviations, words with special connotations, and 'in-terms' whose meaning is taken for granted by those inside the organisation. Even when communication is between professionals of the same organisation there can be confusion about the meaning of words.

Example

Two nurses employed in the National Health Service in Britain were talking about sterilisation policies in their respective parts of the service. One was a midwife and the other a community nurse. It took a quarter of an hour before they realised that one was talking about sterilisation as a means of birth control and the other about sterilisation as a means of protecting babies from infection!

The recurring problem with language in communication is that the person who is trying to explain something may understandably use the language that is most convenient to them without perhaps realising that there is a choice of language. The person receiving the explanation may also, understandably, be reluctant to admit that they cannot understand the language that is used. The skill is in recognising that even when ordinary language is used there may be problems of comprehension. The initiator of any communication needs to get positive confirmation that the language they are using is one that can be understood.

In identifying the appropriate language for communication, attention needs to be given to the possibility of ambiguity. The more important the consequences of error, the more attention needs to be devoted to avoiding ambiguity. If stress is needed on this point, it can be provided by the ambiguous use of words which contributed to the world's worst air disaster at Tenerife in the Canary Islands in 1977.

Example

The pilot of a KLM jumbo jet, who was ironically also the head of their flight training department, was preparing to take off at Tenerife. He explained that he was ready to the air traffic controllers and in response was told 'OK. (pause) Stand by for take-off. I will call you.' In the pause after the word 'OK' there was radio interference because of a radio query by the captain of a Pan-Am jumbo about the intentions of the KLM captain. It seems likely that this caused the KLM captain to assume that the word 'OK' was the complete message. In any event, the KLM captain then took off and collided with the Pan-Am Jumbo killing a total of 573 people. The investigators commissioned by the American Airline Pilots Association concluded that this was the most likely explanation of events. They also commented on the ambiguous use of the term 'take-off'. Their comments on the use of the term 'OK' were as follows:

The word (or letters) 'OK' can be ambiguous also; to the controller it was either a word of acknowledgement or a delaying term to allow a moment to think. It can also mean a host of other things, such as a state of well-being, a check-off of a task accomplished, or a statement of approval. It could have had the latter meaning for the KLM crew.

(American Airline Pilots Association 1978: 22–24)

BODY LANGUAGE – GENERAL

The expressions, gestures and other body language that people may use, without necessarily realising it, can be important cues as to what they really think. Communication is not just imparting information; it often involves, or needs to involve, understanding people's attitudes and feelings which are not always clearly expressed in words. In some cases people may even feel obliged to say the opposite of what they really think. It is not uncommon, for example for people to say 'how interesting' in a tone of voice which indicates that they are in fact bored. An adage which makes the point that people sometimes accidentally misrepresent themselves is, 'Listen to what I mean not what I say.'

As words can be an inadequate or a misleading guide to what people really think, it can be important to look for other cues as to people's thoughts. A catalogue could be prepared of what particular physical cues could mean – fidgeting, that a person has other things on their mind; a glazed expression, that a person doesn't understand, and so on. Given that such a list could be very long and only be a guide anyway, the point that needs stressing is simply to watch for physical cues to a person's real thoughts, especially when it is likely that a person is not able to be, or does not want to be, frank about a particular topic. It can be very tempting to rely just on the words that a person uses, particularly if they give the answer that one wants to hear. To rely on words alone can be quite insufficient.

Interesting examples of how people can unwittingly reveal their true intentions are given by the American agent Mark McCormack, who negotiates on behalf of many international, particularly sports, celebrities. In his book he explains how:

> When I am meeting at someone else's office I have often noticed that people will sort of 'lean in' to the situation when they are ready to get serious, even unconsciously using their hands to push everything on their desk a couple of inches forward. Yet almost as often I have seen people at this same point lean back in their chairs and feign a totally relaxed position.
>
> McCormack 1984: 23–24

McCormack also explained in a British radio interview how one negotiator would unwittingly reveal his intentions by moving his chair back before making his final offer. The advantage of recognising such a cue is obviously to keep asking for more until the person moves their chair back.

An intriguing example of what might be learnt by studying a person's bodily behaviour concerns an allegation about Nikita Khrushchev's conduct during a famous debate at the General Assembly of the United Nations. Khrushschev interrupted proceedings by banging on the table with his shoe. This was part of his protest about American reconnaissance flights over the USSR in their U2 spy planes, which came to light when the American pilot Gary Powers was captured in 1960. The allegation is that TV cameras revealed Khrushchev had shoes on both feet and that the one he banged on the table just before he left the platform was a third shoe brought into the conference chamber expressly for that purpose. If the allegation is true, it reveals that the demonstration was a calculated piece of histrionics and not a spontaneous burst of anger.

The topic of body language is examined again later in this chapter in the context of national culture.

Oral presentation skills

LIMITATIONS OF DOWNWARD COMMUNICATION

Having emphasised the obstacles to effective communication and in particular the importance of upward communication, it is appropriate to say something about the presentational skills involved in downward communication. At the risk of being repetitious, it is first of all necessary to be aware of the limitations of downward communication, particularly in terms of volume, accuracy and commitment to that which is being communicated. There can be a role for devices such as mission statements and team briefings, but only in the context of the appropriate organisational culture and structure, and only if such devices are carefully thought out and competently implemented. Deming's approach to Total Quality Management (explained in chapter 3) deliberately avoided the use of slogans, exhortations and targets for the workforce.

SPECIFIC SKILLS

Having commented on the limitations that downward communication can have it is also necessary to emphasise how it can be very important. Managers have a responsibility to impart information and they need to do this effectively. They need to use time to optimum effect so that they influence the audience in the way they want to without wasting their time. The larger the audience the more the potential for wasted time. If the time available is limited, it is particularly important that the presenter makes good use of it. Crucial decisions can be made as a result of formal presentations, e.g. whether or not important business proposals are accepted or not. The reputations of managers may also depend on how effective their presentation skills are, particularly because people will be able to judge how good these skills are. As with teaching it is no good a person being technically competent if they cannot explain their ideas in such a way that others are motivated to listen and able to understand. Whatever level of oral presentation skills a person has it is usually possible to improve it by analysis, preparation and practice. The following checklist may be useful with regard to formal or informal oral presentations.

- Clarify objectives
- Identify the target audience
- Prior publicity
- Geographical and acoustic arrangements
- Structure
- Will the opening attract interest?
- Involvement of colleagues and audience
- Motivation and comprehension of the audience
- Timing, pace and duration
- Time control
- Beware of reading from notes as this reduces spontaneity and eye contact – prompt cards or an *aide-memoir* may be much better
- Visual aids, e.g. Powerpoint, overhead projector slides, prepared flip chart material, exhibits
- Clarity of expression and choice of language
- Eye contact and body language

- Volume of information – not too little, but beware of presenting too much and losing the audience in the detail
- Use of humour and dramatic pauses
- Pitch and variety of voice
- Use of examples
- Rehearsal
- Opportunity for feedback
- Back-up notes and sources of further information
- Evaluation of presentation
- Modifications for the future

Written communication

Written communication is a form of one-way communication. Forms of written communication can range from a memorandum to one person to a formal report that will be distributed to a large readership. Because of the lack of opportunity for immediate feedback, it is important that the writer expresses themselves clearly, concisely and without ambiguity. Time invested in doing this can avoid error, inappropriate responses, reduce queries and save the time of the reader. If a document is going to a number of people the organisational time that can be saved is proportionate to the number of readers. The need to invest time in writing was emphasised by the French writer Pascal (1657) when he wrote to a friend: 'I have made this letter longer than usual only because I have not had the time to make it shorter.'

USE OF LANGUAGE

The language used when writing needs to be convenient to the reader. There are a variety of reasons why writers may use inappropriate language. They may simply use the language that is most convenient to them. However, if this is too full of technical jargon or is unnecessarily complicated, the content may not be understood. However, if the writer wants to communicate and understands their subject, it should generally be possible to explain issues clearly. Written communication that is difficult to follow is often caused more by deficiencies of the writer than the lack of ability of the reader.

Sometimes matters have to be expressed in a precise technical way, and the use of particular language is unavoidable. This can be the case with legal documents, where the only way of achieving the necessary clarity is to use precise legal expression. However, even when technical language is used there is good and bad practice. There is no benefit in explaining matters in a more complicated way than is necessary. All too often sophisticated terms can be used unnecessarily because of a desire by the writer to impress, clumsy expression, or lack of clarity in the actual thinking. The use of many sociological terms, in particular, can be for these reasons.

FORMS

Particular care may need to be taken in the design of forms. One of the ironies concerning many government forms is that those who have to complete them may need a graduate-level ability to do so. Persons with that level of ability, though, would not often be applying for many of the services in question. Responses to completed forms also need to be in clear language.

Example

The need for clear written expression is illustrated by the reply quoted in the diary column of *The Guardian* newspaper by the Department of Social Security to a mentally ill 19-year old living on invalidity benefit who managed to get a job for two days, washing dishes at Olympia:

> The claimant is disqualified for receiving non-contributory invalidity benefit for 17.5.82 because he failed without good cause to observe the rule that he should do no work other than work which he had good cause for doing and from which his earnings were ordinarily not more than £16.50 a week – S.S. (Unemployment Sickness and Invalidity Benefit) Regulations reg 12(i) (a) (iii).
>
> As a result, an overpayment of non-contributory invalidity benefit has been made amounting to £2.95 as detailed below.* Repayment of this sum is required because it has not been shown that the claimant has throughout used due care and diligence in the obtaining and receipt of benefit to avoid over-payment (Social Security Act 1975 sec 119(1) and (2).
> *£17.75 ÷ 6 = £2.95.

The Guardian diarist went on to say that the reply could have been worded 'Please pay back one day's benefit because you worked.'

Attempts are being made by public servants in the UK to improve the clarity of expression. This is particularly so with regard to the legal system. Examples of changes include the replacement of plaintiff by claimant and respondent by defendant in civil law cases.

INTERNAL MEMOS

One of the most common forms of correspondence in organisations is the internal memorandum. Despite the relative informality of the internal memo and frequency with which it is used, there can be errors in the way they are used. The frequency of use, particularly now that memos are so easily sent by e-mail, is a strong argument for developing good habits about memo writing. Key issues are:

- the standard of presentation need not be as high as with a document that is meant for public consumption;
- memos still need to be thought out carefully. Mistakes are not as easily rectified as with two-way communication;

- memos can be sent to too many people, costing money and involving people unnecessarily;
- people can understandably take offence if memos are unnecessarily copied to their boss. The implication can be that they are not to be trusted or that an opportunity is being taken to show up their deficiencies;
- some memos are best not sent. They may be written in anger. The act of writing may have calmed the author down at which point consideration should be given to destroying or rewording the memo;
- critical memos can lead to memo wars. To avoid this, or to try and stop a memo war, it may be best to talk face to face with the other person involved. In a discussion it is possible to state your case point by point. If you get a positive response, a number of related issues may be best dropped. Misunderstandings can also be much more easily corrected in face to face discussion.

HELP-LINES

A growing practice with manufacturers and providers of some services is to provide a help-line telephone number. This enables clients to engage in two-way communication about the use of the product or service. It may be an important selling point. It may also give the provider of the product or service useful feedback about the quality of any written instructions. Furthermore, it may provide important market research data about customer responses to the product or service itself.

HOUSE MAGAZINES

Many organisations keep staff informed by way of house magazines or newsletters. This can be very useful but it has to be remembered that it is an exercise in one-way communication. It is important to devise complementary ways of checking on staff opinion, such as employee representative structures. Readership surveys are a way of judging the reaction to the actual magazines and newsletters. Care, however, needs to taken about the content of magazines and newsletters. Employees may have a quite different perspective of the organisation to that of senior managers. It may also be necessary to check that the messages don't have unintended consequences.

Example

In one national brewing company a copy of the house magazine was produced at a negotiating meeting. The employee representatives wanted to know why the company was only offering a low wage increase when the magazine included details of its healthy profits and major expenditure programme.

Organisational structure

The need for organisational structures to facilitate the accomplishment of organisational objectives was considered in chapter 3. As part of that process organisations need to be structured so that the right information gets to the necessary people at the right time so that any appropriate action can be taken. Unfortunately, the structure of many organisations does not, or no longer, fits with this need. There is no one correct model of an organisation. Structures need to fit the needs of particular situations. Even if the fit between the need for information flows and organisational structure is right, the way in which the organisation actually operates may obstruct necessary information flows.

OPTIONS IN ORGANISATIONAL DESIGN

A basic distinction between models of organisation is that between mechanistic and organic structures. Although the distinction between these two types of organisations was covered in chapter 3, it is appropriate to refer to it again in the context of communication. Features of mechanistic structures are that they are:

- bureaucratic,
- formalised,
- provided for upward reference for the resolution of differences,
- have a high degree of division of labour,
- have a clearly defined chain of command.

Organic structures in contrast provide for a greater use of initiative and for contact, co-operation and decision-making to be in accordance with the needs of the situation rather than the formal organisation. Mechanistic structures are better suited for stable, predictable situations, particularly where there are issues of public accountability. Organic structures are more appropriate for rapidly changing situations in which mechanistic structures could not react in time. The capability level of front-line staff needs to be greater in organic structures because of the greater decision-making responsibility at that level.

Organisations may need to have aspects of both mechanistic and organic structures. There are also other ways of classifying organisations. However, the basic point is that the basic structure of an organisation needs to facilitate necessary information flows and not obstruct them. Because the circumstances in which organisations operate change, it may be necessary to regularly check that the organisation has an appropriate structure. It may be that informal mechanisms have been developed to compensate for the weaknesses in the formal structures. Managers may need to use such informal processes to find out what is really going on.

OPERATIONAL PROBLEMS

Even if an organisation is structured in a way that facilitates appropriate communication flows blockages may occur. Principal reasons are as follows.

Size

The larger the organisation, the harder it is to achieve the necessary co-ordination. In small organisations it may be fairly self-evident what needs to be done and by whom. However, many small organisations fail to grow into large ones because of the difficulty in creating and managing a new organisational structure that can cope with the increased workload. The amount of co-ordination required as an organisation grows can increase the communication problems at an exponential rather than an arithmetic rate.

Lateral communication

Problems of lateral communication can be caused or aggravated by conflicts between departments. Internally competitive systems can emphasise the need to meet departmental rather than overall organisational goals. This may necessitate structural review of an organisation to see if such tensions can be reduced or overcome. The different value systems and interests between different occupational groups can also cause communication problems between departments. Also, people may find it much more congenial to work with people of a similar background. This may be reinforced by geographic boundaries. It may be necessary to develop remedial strategies to overcome such occupational boundaries. These can include project working, regular liaison meetings, interdisciplinary training and multidisciplinary teams.

Power

Personality factors can affect the way organisations operate. Some managers will manipulate the flow of communication and a variety of other techniques to develop and maintain their power even though this may not be for the good of the organisation overall. An aspect of this can be the use of power to frustrate necessary organisational change if it will reduce the power of the person concerned.

Managerial Style

The individual style of a manager can have a considerable impact on communication flows. Generally autocratic bosses are liable to receive much less in the way of accurate upward communication than more approachable managers. Worse than that, the information that they do receive may be doctored to humour them. Also, because they are not receiving accurate information they be unaware of what they are missing and of the need to evaluate the quality of their information flow.

National culture

Culture has many dimensions, including class, organisational, regional and national. The issue of organisational culture was given attention in chapter 4. The impact of national culture on communications is potentially so great that it is examined separately in this section. That impact is also growing for a number of reasons. Nations such as the UK are becoming more culturally diverse. Globalisation, ease of international travel and developments in information technology are making international collaboration in both the private and public sectors much more common. Managers are much more likely to have to deal with people of other nationalities, whether it be in their home country or working abroad.

Some potential obstacles to communication are obvious, such as language. A feature of language developments is the ever-increasing importance of English as a means of international communication. However, it may be important to use what has become known as 'offshore English' when communicating with people from other countries. This form of English can be defined as that spoken by people whose first language is not English and who have learned the language as adults from a practical rather than academic perspective (Guy and Mattock, 1991). Other potential obstacles to effective communication may be less obvious but nevertheless important. The very fact that they are not obvious can make them harder to deal with. These obstacles include cultural values and the varying use of body language in different cultures.

THE WORK OF HOFSTEDE

National culture can be shaped by many factors. These include history, religion, geography and climate. These in turn shape the behaviour of people, including the way they communicate with one another. The most important study to date of the impact of national culture on organisations was carried out by Hofstede (1994), which was examined in some detail in chapter 4. He found wide national differences in values and behaviour in four dimensions:

- power distance,
- uncertainty avoidance,
- individualism vs collectivism,
- masculinity vs femininity.

All four dimensions have an impact on communication. In high power distance cultures communication is hampered by long hierarchies and associated levels of high social inequality. It may be particularly difficult in such cultures to express views that are contrary to those of people in authority. In cultures where there is high uncertainty avoidance there is an emphasis on formality and on rules and regulations. In collectivist countries it is difficult for people to express views contrary to the group or organisation at large. Feminine cultures are in contrast to macho cultures and are characterised by high levels of mutual respect for one another's opinions.

HIGH AND LOW CONTEXT CULTURES

A related concept is the distinction between high-context and low-context communication (Hall 1987). Some low-context cultures, particularly the USA, are characterised by direct and specific expression, often reinforced by written contracts. Other cultures, particularly in Asia, are high-context and much more depends on the context in which communication takes place. People in high-context cultures will be much more used to interpreting meaning in accordance with factors such as personality, rank and body language. Language may be deliberately ambiguous. Demands for greater clarity may be seen as insulting and imply that a person is not to be trusted. The homogeneity, size and social control in a country may be important in determining whether the dominant culture is high or low-context. A large country with relatively low social homogeneity and social control will be more likely to be low-context. This may be why the annual output of lawyers in the USA is equal to the total stock of lawyers in Japan.

LEVEL OF FEEDBACK

In high power distance and high-context cultures managers may get little genuine feedback on their performance from their employees, particularly if they are not very effective. In such cultures local managers may realise this but not managers from other cultures.

| Example |

A British manager was anxious to impose his ideas on a group of Indonesian managers. Unfortunately he mistook silence for agreement with his suggestions and this led to him pressing his points harder and harder. He had not appreciated the need to carefully evaluate the meaning of silence or the problems the managers would have had in directly confronting him. The longer he went on the greater the resistance he created and the greater the barriers between him and his audience.

BUILDING AND MAINTAINING RELATIONSHIPS

It may take considerable time to develop working relationships between people of other cultures. It may not be realistic to discuss serious issues until an adequate level of trust is established. The distinction between roles and personalities is not as clear in some cultures as in others. When this is the case much time may be needed to develop acceptance as a person. Particularly in Asian cultures considerable care may need to be taken to save people's face as a way of maintaining relationships.

| Example |

At a meeting of Indonesian and British managers one of the Indonesians made an inappropriate suggestion and everybody, including the person who made the suggestion, realised its weaknesses. However, so that the standing of this person was

CONTINUED OVER ➢

CONTINUED FROM
PREVIOUS PAGE
not damaged in the eyes of his colleagues, great efforts were made by all those present to let him gracefully retreat from the idea and to thank him for his initiative. This process took far longer than it would have in many other cultures but was entirely necessary in the local situation.

BODY LANGUAGE – CULTURAL

The importance of body language has already been considered because of its general potential importance in communication. However, it is also necessary to specifically consider the cultural aspects. Managers need to pay attention to this, particularly in high-context communication cultures. It is also important that they do not assume that particular body language signals have the same meaning in all countries. The range of body language signals, conscious or otherwise, is very great. Illustrative examples of what they might mean are shown below.

Body contact
Conventions about body contact may vary considerably between cultures. Germans, for example, are renowned for shaking hands as a form of greeting. However, Indians traditionally clasp their hands together and bow. In France and Russia a traditional greeting is to kiss one another on the cheeks. As well as needing to understand these different conventions it may be particularly important to take into account potential problems about body contact between people of opposite genders.

Example

One of the Chinese political leaders paid a state visit to Iran at a time was revolutionary Islamic fervour was particularly high. A protocol problem arose because of the presence of a woman in the Iranian reception party. Unlike the men, and because of religious conventions in Iran, she could not be seen to be shaking hands with the Chinese leader, particularly in public and on national television. However, it was also essential for her graciously to acknowledge the visitor. The problem of how she should handle her greeting was resolved by her presenting the Chinese leader with a red rose so that each touched different parts of the stem. He was delighted with this gesture.

Eye-contact
In low power distance cultures there will be an expectation that people will look you in the eye when you are talking to them. In high power distance cultures this could be disrespectful on the part of the subordinate.

Facial expressions
In high-context cultures more of the message may be by way of facial expression. Conventions in the permitted facial expressions that are demonstrated to members of the opposite sex can be strict in some cultures.

Example

There was ill feeling by the female canteen workers in a West London factory because of the unappreciative way in which the Asian male production workers responded when they were served with their food. In particular, it was commented that the Asian men never smiled. When the Asian men became aware of this criticism they were bewildered. This was because, in their culture, it was seen as being unacceptable for men to smile at women they did not know. Far from trying to cause offence they had been trying to avoid it by their impassive expressions. When this story was told to a college receptionist in London she said she could now understand why she received such few smiles from Asian callers when she often received very broad smiles from other callers.

Cultural differences in smiling are commented on by Platt (1998: 23–29). She maintains that in the USA, for example, people generally smile when greeting someone. This is in contrast to the French who generally only smile for more specific purposes – to do otherwise would be seen as hypocritical and devalue the work of a smile. She also refers to 13 different types of smiles, each for a specific purpose.

Spatial relationships

People may have a preferred physical distance between them and the person they are talking to. Swedes and Scots tend to prefer a long distance; Arabs and Latin Americans usually prefer to be much closer (Argyle 1994).

Example

Americans and Europeans have been seen retreating backwards gyrating in circles at international conferences, pursued by Latin Americans trying to establish their habitual degree of proximity (Argyle 1994). This phenomenon has led to the story, apocryphal or otherwise, of the Latin American diplomat, frustrated at not being able to get close enough to British diplomats, saying that these British diplomats are very good – if only you can catch them!

Electronic communication

The impact of developments in information technology on organisations were examined in chapter 3. However, the overlapping impact on communication processes also needs to be examined in this chapter. Previous obstacles (such as time and location) are often being overcome or drastically reduced. The boundaries of organisations with their stakeholders can become increasingly blurred, with consequential effects on the way they operate. For example, databases and systems may be shared with subcontractors, suppliers and customers. There may also be some co-operation with competitors about sharing information and computer facilities. The skills required by employees are altering because of all these changes. However, interpersonal skills in communication are still required, and for organisations to function effectively there usually needs to be some social cohesion. A further dimension is the role of the media and the need for managers to know how to handle it.

THE NATURE OF DEVELOPMENTS

Range

Recent information technology innovations, which have been transforming both the structure and way in which organisations operate include word processors, fax machines, e-mail, software packages, shared databases, electronic markets and the satellite transmission of data. Organisations are also increasingly using integrated computer systems and data communication networks, such as the Internet and the World Wide Web, both for accessing and providing information. Video links and video-conferencing are also likely to become increasingly used.

Causes of Change

The above developments have been both a cause of and a response to globalisation. Markets have become more volatile, creating the prospect of large rewards for those who quickly exploit new market opportunities and considerable dangers for those who are slow to react. In both the private and public sectors there is the prospect of rapid access to detailed and accurate information. Time zones can sometimes be manipulated so that work can be sent to other countries at the end of the working day for processing and return by the start of the next working day.

Organisational impact

The effects on organisational structure and operation have been many and often radical. Offices have become more capital intensive and less labour intensive. The availability of data to front-line staff has often led to organisational de-layering. The gatekeeping roles of those that control the flow of and access to information are disappearing. Clients and customers are often encouraged to access data and give instructions directly to organisational databases. Production systems are sometimes so automated that people can complain of being lonely working in a factory.

Space

The easier storage of information enables space savings to be made, which in turn reduces the number of support staff needed to run a building. In some organisations this has led to hot-desking, an arrangement whereby staff use whatever desk, and associated electronic equipment, is available.

Start-up time

The speed with which organisations can be established has also been affected.

Example

When the USA granted diplomatic recognition to new countries in the former Yugoslavia, new Embassies could be set up and operating within a few hours. This was by a government representative using a laptop computer and satellite phone link. This enabled information to be inputted to and accessed from the databases in the USA.

Impact on staff requirements

The impact of these changes on organisational staffing requirements has been considerable. Staff increasingly need to be able to operate electronic communication systems. This can create a generation gap between older and younger staff. Those with direct access to databases can be empowered to use the information to take decisions. Even manual productions workers, for example, may need to have the skills to input data as part of monitoring and control processes. One commentator has gone so far as to say that:

> *A quadriplegic with good technical and communication skills is becoming a more valuable worker than an able-bodied person without these skills.*
>
> James 1996: 29

Given the increase in the ratio of employees to capital employed, there is a need to train people in how to use the information technology at their disposal. This can be critical given the tendency for technological developments in this area to race ahead of the ability of organisations to see that they are effectively used. A further aspect of the increasing use of information technology is that it is yet one more pressure for the use of English. This is because instruction manuals, software, relevant literature and general debate about information technology is so often only in English.

Employees also need to consider the impact of developments of information technology on their own career paths. Traditional career paths may disappear, and the organisational volatility caused by an increased pace of change may threaten their job security or offer exciting new prospects. The greatest individual security may come from developing marketable skills so that individuals can either capitalise on opportunities within their organisation or find work elsewhere. Core individual skills will generally need to include the ability to handle information technology.

DANGERS

Whilst great opportunities are created by the application of electronic communication there are also dangers in its use.

Information Overload

People can be so swamped by information that they are prevented from getting on with the key aspects of their job. The over use of e-mail, in particular, can lead to managers having to spend much time sifting the important from the unimportant. Consequently, careful consideration needs to be given as to when to copy information to people who are not directly concerned in an issue.

Evaluation of data

Electronically communicated data tends to be in quantifiable terms. Intangible factors, which are not easily quantifiable, can, however, also be important. Also, data can be manipulated or simply wrong. There is a danger that the emphasis on speed of access and quantification can lead to hasty decisions based on only some of the critical factors.

Error

Error may not be so quickly recognised or rectified when systems are automated.

Examples

A trainee stockbroker in London pressed an electronic button and effected a commercial transaction that caused his employer to lose millions of pounds.

A South Korean Airlines jumbo jet flying from the USA to Korea was incorrectly programmed to fly close to a sensitive Russian military installation by Vladivostock in 1983. The Russians shot down the aircraft killing all 269 people on board.

Security

The rapid access to detailed and accurate information in databases can create significant security problems. These include commercial espionage, release of confidential information and fraudulent financial transactions. Some unauthorised access may be in contravention of legal safeguards designed to protect the confidentiality of information held about employees and members of the public. Comprehensive security measures may be needed to control both unauthorised and illegal access and release of information.

The human factor

Some organisations may manage to become 'virtual organisations' operating entirely by electronic access to data. However, for most organisations some form of social interaction will be necessary. Users may demand human contact. Electronic communication may not be adaptable or sensitive enough to deal with all situations. The cohesion and synergy created by human interaction may be essential if organisations are to survive and develop. The increasing emphasis on computer literacy should not be allowed to obscure the need for employees, particularly front-line staff and managers, to have effective interpersonal communication skills. There is a danger that people who are naturally at home with computers will ignore the need to interact effectively with other people, both inside and outside the organisation. This needs to be taken into account in selection, appraisal, and training policies.

Media communication

The amount of time that people spend watching television and video cassettes and listening to the radio justifies a section on the media. Whilst this fits with a general consideration of communication, there may well be specific issues presented on the media that involve people in their role as managers. The material presented often needs to be carefully evaluated. Managers may also need to use the media to present information, so consideration is also given to the basic skills of media presentation.

SPEED OF REPORTING

The impact of television can be extremely powerful and pervasive. Strong visual images of dramatic events and human suffering can be brought quickly into the living room and in turn can have an interactive effect on those events. The coincidence of President Gorbachev being in Beijing at the outbreak of student demonstrations in 1989 meant that a mass of sophisticated television equipment was available to film the violent suppression of the student occupation of Tiananmen Square. Viewers can see events during wars either as they happen or shortly afterwards. The effectiveness of the satellite reporting during the Gulf War in 1990 was such that presidents George Bush and Saddam Hussein found that watching the networked television news reports gave them speedier coverage than their own intelligence agencies.

Technological media developments mean that it is generally much more likely that important issues are handled in public than in an unobserved or unrecorded manner. There can be great benefit in this, but there are also certain dangers. Those involved in publicly conducted events have to bear in mind the simultaneous impact of their statements and actions on those with whom they may be negotiating, those they represent and the general public. This may limit their room for manoeuvre and make it much more difficult for them to retrieve mistakes and errors of judgement. Also some developments have made both open and secret recording more likely. These include the miniaturisation of equipment, its reduced cost and its easier handling.

EVALUATION OF DATA

A further issue is the evaluation of material that is presented on the media. Issues of bias or misrepresentation are often easy to spot in advertisements. However, there are other causes of distortion that may be much more difficult to recognise. These include the balance of presentation, the advantages gained by a skilled presenter with a good acoustic background and the juxtaposition of items that are reported. A trade union official, for example, may, rightly or wrongly, have a hard time explaining the causes of industrial action just after a film showing vivid examples of the inconvenience that action may be causing.

There is an inherent conflict between the responsibility of media reporters and producers to present a fair and balanced programme and the pressure on them to attain high viewing or listening figures. This can lead to sensationalised reporting, emphasis on the unusual and the camera bias of dramatic visual images. Such problems led John Birt and Peter Jay to comment when they worked together at Independent Television's Weekend Word about the 'bias against understanding' with regard to television reporting of news and current affairs (Billen 2000: 29).

Presentation on the radio can be more balanced because it does not suffer from camera bias. Newspapers often have clear political affiliations but also offer readers the choice of which sections to read and the pace at which they read them. Although people can decide what programmes they watch on the television or listen to on the radio, the content has to be heavily filtered because the material has to be compressed and contained within a standard format. There cannot be the flexible use that there is with a newspaper.

The implication of the complexities of media presentation and the opportunity for distortion, deliberate or accidental, means that it is important to evaluate critically what is being presented rather than passively accept it. This is particularly important for managers if the information they receive from the media is likely to influence the managerial decisions they make. It is as well to remember also that a whole range of interest groups are concerned in providing information to the media in order to put over a particular point of view.

MEDIA PRESENTATION SKILLS

Pit-falls

Given the potential importance of the media it is important that managers know how to present themselves on it effectively if the need arises. The earlier section in this chapter on oral presentation skills may be particularly relevant. However, they also need to beware of the potential dangers in dealing with the media. Managers may have to face unexpected and hostile questions by a person well practised in the art of media interviewing. There is the possibility that they may be confronted by people with an opposing point of view without warning. Pre-recorded interviews can be selectively edited to the organisation's disadvantage and/or placed in an unfavourable juxta-position with other issues and images. Managers may also be misquoted, or have injudicious statements quoted out of context.

Counter-measures

Counter-measures that managers may wish to consider in dealing with aggressive or unfair media interviewing include:

- insisting on a live interview to prevent selective editing;
- issuing a press statement that can be read out in an interview;
- only saying what they want to say – there are no penalties, as in exams, for not answering questions exactly as the interviewer wishes, apart from whatever conclusions may be drawn from the audience; politicians can be particularly adept at not answering embarrassing questions;
- ensure that when answering questions that they use their own words and not ones put into their mouths by interviewers;
- before answering a question saying whatever it is they want to say;
- if managers do not want to give an interview it may be much better for them to issue a prepared statement rather than simply state 'no comment';
- managers engaged in potentially newsworthy activities may need to be able to react quickly to put over their point of view. Organisations may need to consider what in-house skills, policies, procedures and facilities they need to handle the media.

SUMMARY

✔ Managers normally spend most of their time trying to communicate with other people. Although the ability to communicate with others is important, it can be even more important to ensure that others can communicate with you. This is particularly so as managers usually need to spend more time receiving than imparting information. Accurate communication is necessary if decision-making is to be appropriate and implementation effective. Unfortunately, communication is often much less accurate than is appreciated. As was explained, this lack of awareness not only leads to error but means that people do not pay sufficient attention to the need to develop their skills in this area. However, communication skills are often easily developed and can lead to important recurring benefits.

✔ Identification of the potential obstacles to effective communication provides a foundation for developing skills in this area. Important obstacles can be poor listening skills, lack of time, lack of a common vocabulary, poor or false feedback and resistance to criticism. A key skill is that of active listening. The way in which oral presentation skills can be improved has also been examined; however, written communication is also important. The ways in which organisational structures can facilitate or hinder communication have been considered. It has also been necessary to look at the problems of communication between national cultures.

✔ Attention has been paid to the growing importance of electronic communication as well as some of the problems it creates. It has also been appropriate to consider the role of the media, including the evaluation of data and how to use it to communicate with others. It can be very important for managers to distinguish between their own agenda with regard to media presentation and that of media organisations.

SELF-ASSESSMENT QUESTIONS

1. Identify eight examples of communication that you have been involved in during the last 24 hours.

2. Taking the examples given in your answer to question 1 identify the main obstacles there have been to that communication being effective.

3. How could you improve your own interpersonal oral communication?

4. Identify six key skills in effective oral presentation.

5. Identify four key skills in effective written communication.

6. Comment on the ways in which organisational structure can help or hinder effective organisation.

7. Give examples on how differences in national culture can lead to misunderstanding?

8. In what ways can electronic communication both help and hinder communication?

9. If you had to give a presentation on radio or television how would go about it?

 References

(Works of general interest in the specific references are marked with a star.)

AirLine Pilots Association (American) (1978) Aircraft Accident Report: Engineering and Air Safety – Human Factors Report on the Tenerife Accident

* Argyle, Michael (1994) *The Psychology of Interpersonal Behaviour*, 5th ed. Penguin Books.

Asch, S. E. (1964) summaries in Secord P. F. and C. W. Backman, *Social Psychology*, International Student Edition, McGraw-Hill Kogakusha Ltd.

Billen, Andrew (2000) 'Banana skins and a bias against common sense', *Evening Standard* (London), 5 July.

Campbell, Jeremy (1991) 'Why Bush needs Saddam', *Evening Standard* (London), 2 October.

Carswell, John (1981) 'The slave of the lamp', *Sunday Times*, 29 March

Dixon, Norman F. (1976) *On the Psychology of Military Incompetence*, Cape.

Guy V. and J. Mattock (1991) *The New International Manager – An Action Guide to Cross-Cultural Business*, Kogan-Page.

Hall, E. T. (1987) *Hidden Differences*, Anchor Press/Doubleday.

Leavitt, Harold J. and Homa Bahrani (1988) *Managerial Psychology*, 5th ed., University of Chicago Press.

McCormack, Mark H. (1984) *What They Don't Teach You at Harvard Business School*, Collins.

Pascal, Blaise (1657) *Lettres Provinciales*.

Platt, Polly (1998) *French or Foe, Getting the Most out of Visiting, Living and Working in France*, 2nd ed., Culture Crossings.

Simpson, John (1991) 'Why Saddam went to war', *The Observer*, Review section, 21 July.

Stewart, Rosemary (1988) *Managers and Their Jobs*, 2nd ed., Macmillan.

General references

Dickinson, Sarah (1990) *How to Take on the Media*, Weidenfeld Paperbacks.

Galliers, R. D., D. E. Leidner and B. S. H. Baker (eds.) (1999) *Strategic Information Management Systems*, 2nd ed., Oxford University Press.

Gowers, Sir Ernest (1986) *Plain Words*, revised by Sidney Greenbaum and Janet Whinart, HMSO, also Penguin (1987).

Jones, Nicholas (1986) *Strikes and the Media, Communication and Conflict*, Blackwell.

Mead, Richard (1998) ch. 7, 'International Management', *Cross-cultural Management Communication*, 2nd ed., Blackwell.

Tammen, Deborah (1994) *Gender and Discourse*, Oxford University Press.

chapter (nine)

Selection

There are case studies and exercises at
http://www.thomsonlearning.co.uk
(for full details, see the listing at the
start of this book).

LEARNING OUTCOMES

By the end of this chapter you will be able to:

- Adopt a systematic approach to the selection process

- Analyse the nature of job vacancies, including the differences between short- and long-term needs

- Establish appropriate selection criteria for a job

- Assemble relevant and appropriate information about job candidates

- Structure and conduct an effective selection interview

- Understand the rationale for selection panels and their advantages and disadvantages

- Understand the rationale for equal opportunities policies and key aspects of relevant law

- Prepare for and present yourself to the best advantage when being interviewed for a job

Introduction

One of the most critical decisions that managers may have to make is the appointment of subordinate staff. Managers may also be involved in the appointment of subordinate staff for other managers – for example, by membership of interview boards. It is easier to exercise discretion at the appointment stage than later – it is much more difficult to remove staff once they have joined an organisation. The abilities of subordinate staff can have a critical effect on the performance of the manager concerned. Even though managers may only be involved in appointment decisions relatively infrequently, it is important that the selection decisions they take are the right ones. It is for this reason that a chapter has been devoted to selection.

One of the crucial issues with selection is to adopt a systematic approach. Therefore, topics covered in this chapter are arranged in a particular order according to a systematic approach that managers may wish to consider adopting. This approach includes the need to identify carefully the nature of a job that has to be filled. The long-term nature of the job has to be considered as well as the immediate requirements. The next step is to identify appropriate selection criteria. Two methods are explained – developing a person specification and identifying the necessary job competencies. The ways in which information can be collected about candidates are identified. So too are the actual skills involved in selection interviewing, including the skills that may be required at panel interviews.

The chapter includes a section on equal opportunities. This is important because failure to have effective policies can lead to poor utilisation of the human resources available and feelings of inequity. Also there are an increasing number of legal protections against unjustified discrimination. These protections are particularly important in the areas of gender, marital status, race and disability. Managers also need to be aware of their organisation's policies with regard to equal opportunities, as these may be more comprehensive than the statutory protections.

The rather different skills that may be required if one is the person being interviewed for a job are also considered. A self-assessment form is included as an appendix to help readers see how they might develop their own, or other people's, selection interviewing skills.

Defining the job

Whether a job is new or old, considerable care needs to be taken initially in defining the exact objective and scope of the job. The material in chapter 2 concerning the identification of objectives and key tasks may be relevant in this context. Even when jobs are well-established it is important to remember that the requirements may have changed. The actual tasks that have historically been performed may not be appropriate in changed circumstances. A manager may be unaware of some of the adjustments that have taken place in a job since they perhaps occupied that position. A starting point for identifying the requirements of a job may be to get the existing job-holder to prepare an updated job description. Other information may, however, also be necessary. A job may have been tailored to take account of an individual's strengths and weaknesses. It may be necessary, therefore, to consider the extent to which such tailoring should remain if a new person is being appointed. An account given by an employee of their job may be inaccurate or may reflect what is done rather than what needs doing. The manager concerned may need to consider what changes they and others think are necessary in a particular job. It may even be that the job does not need filling – either because there is no longer any purpose to it or because the individual tasks can more effectively be redistributed amongst other staff.

Example

> *For 20 years a large shipping company had difficulty filling one of its top jobs. It never had anyone really qualified for the position. And whoever filled it soon found himself in trouble and conflict. But for 20 years the job was filled whenever it became vacant. In the 21st year a new president asked: 'What would happen if we did not fill it?' The answer was, 'Nothing'. It then turned out that the position had been created to perform a job that had long since become unnecessary.*
>
> Drucker 1955: 320

Sometimes a job may be necessary but not of the nature originally countenanced.

Example

At a panel selection interview, the clear purpose and content of a job was only completed after all the candidates had been interviewed. The original reasoning about the job in question was inadequate and the questions asked during the interviews led to a more accurate assessment of what was really required. This led to a redefined job being advertised and the whole process of selection being started again. The consolation in this example was that at least the initial error of inadequate assessment of the real job requirements was not compounded by an appointment based on inadequate job definition.

SHORT-TERM AND LONG-TERM NEEDS

A potential problem area, which is often overlooked, is the distinction between the short-term and long-term needs in a job. A person may be recruited to fill a pressing but temporary need. The problem that may then arise is what to do with them when the need has passed.

Example

A person with accountancy and computer skills was recruited to establish a computer-based accounts system. When the new system was running smoothly it was found that there was no longer any need for him and he was made redundant. Exactly the same thing happened to him in his next two jobs. Each employer appeared to genuinely think that they needed him for a permanent position. None had thought through what to do with the person when the system was successfully established.

The pace of technological and organisational change, in particular, means that this is likely to be an increasing problem. Historically jobs were, and still sometimes are, seen as positions that will remain substantially the same during the working life of the job-holders. This can cause people to try freeze the activity of an organisation so that the demand for their existing skills is perpetuated. Once people join an organisation they become part of the political power structure. They are likely to take a lively interest in the prospects for security and promotion of people with their particular range of skills. Academic staff, for example, can take a ferocious interest in seeing that college departments run courses that provide the maximum prospects for advancing their particular specialism. This can lead to a conflict between the short-term interests of the individual and the long-term interests of the organisation. It may, therefore, be necessary to anticipate the pressures that potential employees will put on the organisation to develop in a particular way or remain in a particular mould.

In the engineering industry in the UK, the length of apprenticeships has been gradually reduced and opportunities for apprentices and skilled workers to increase their range of skills improved. The concept of the multicraft worker has also made some headway. The advantages that these developments can bring include the possibility of reduced resistance to technological and organisational change because the employees are more able to adapt to changed circumstances.

The dilemma of reconciling the need for specialist and generic skills was recognised by a large petrochemical firm in the UK. The firm recognised the dilemma of acquiring people with specialist skills for immediate problems, as well as needing people who would be prepared to adapt to the rapidly changing circumstances of their industry. The solution adopted was to recruit some graduate chemical engineers with specialised training to cope with immediate specialist needs. Other graduate engineers with a more general training were also recruited and were given either technical or managerial jobs. They were recruited with a view to being moved around the organisation so that they developed a range of technical and/or managerial skills. The reasoning was that as the organisation needed to adapt, so this latter group would be able to fill the emergent new jobs. Had only narrowly trained specialists been recruited, it seemed much less likely that the organisation would have been able to adapt to the rapidly changing circumstances of the petrochemical industry.

The dilemma of reconciling short- and long-term needs has also been recognised in the context of local government. The Local Government Management Board commented on the need for greater fluidity of organisational structures and job content. This 'could mean building into recruitment and assessment procedures a much more open and more generous estimation of capacity' (1993: 16). This is in contrast to the often very narrow and mechanistic methods by which employees are sometimes recruited and selected, with the criteria only relating to current needs.

The distinction between short-term and long-term needs has to be considered whenever appointments are made. The pace of technological change, in particular, is such that one has to ask whether a person will be prepared and able to adapt to the radical changes in job content that are increasingly likely. Admittedly, in some cases one may say that the short-term problems are those that have to take priority and that, if necessary, future inability to cope may have to be dealt with by redundancy. It seems prudent, however, at least to consider taking on a person with a temperament and range of skills that would make adjustment an easier process compared with applicants who may be over-specialised. Alternative approaches for dealing with short-term problems are to use short-term contracts or buy in consultancy expertise.

Selection criteria

Having defined a job and balanced the short- and long-term needs, the next stage is to identify appropriate selection criteria. One of the dilemmas in identifying criteria is that what is relevant is not always easily assessable. The criteria used to assess performance, more fully explained in the next chapter on appraisal, may help in establishing appropriate criteria. The headings are:

- validity (observability),
- reliability,
- relevance,
- discrimination,
- comprehensiveness,
- assessability.

Two specific approaches for identifying criteria are explained below – establishing a person specification and identifying the required job competencies. Other issues include the relevance of good and bad practice amongst existing job-holders, looking at the job as a whole, the dangers of choosing on the basis of historic performance, attitude and the particular importance of making valid selection in the case of those working abroad.

PERSON SPECIFICATION

A person specification identifies the personal attributes that the job-holder needs in order to do a job. These attributes can be divided into essential and desirable characteristics. One way of creating a specification is to use the Seven Point Plan described by Alec Rodger in a pamphlet published under the auspices of the former National Institute of Industrial Psychology (1970). The headings he identified for consideration were:

- physique, manner and bearing;
- attainments: (a) education, (b) experience;
- general intelligence;
- special aptitudes;
- interests;
- disposition;
- circumstances.

One may consider adding an eighth factor – the motivation to do a particular job. As is explained later in the chapter, motivational problems are particularly likely to arise if there is over-specification of the selection criteria. This is because of the boredom that can be created by selecting people who are over-qualified for a particular job. It may also be necessary to examine the extent to which applicants have stayed in previous jobs so that you do not take on job-hoppers who leave after a short while.

Care obviously needs to be taken in itemising the various requirements. Even though a job may have been carefully defined, the specification can be completed in such a way that it gives a spurious impression of accuracy and certainty. However, a major advantage of this method is that it is easy to grasp and therefore easy to explain to others involved in selection.

JOB COMPETENCIES

The alternative competencies approach sidesteps the issue of personal characteristics and identifies instead the job skills and knowledge that a person needs to have in order to adequately do a job. Sometimes competencies are split into levels. These can be used to identify the minimum acceptable level for a particular job. Potential advantages of identifying job competencies are:

- irrelevant requirements should be excluded – what will matter, for example, is whether a person has the technical ability or potential to do a job, not specific qualifications;
- the pool of candidates is likely to be increased;
- the approach is in keeping with equal opportunities policies;
- the established competencies may be useful in related areas – these include training and development, performance management, individual remuneration and pay grades.

Potential disadvantages of the competence approach are:

- it can be very complicated and therefore difficult to operate;
- the complexities can lead to inaccuracies and inconsistencies;
- it can be very time-consuming;
- there can be problems in applying generic competencies to specific jobs; important aspects can be missed, which can lead to important competencies being missed or unnecessary ones required;
- generic competencies can be difficult to alter in the light of changed circumstances, because, for example, of the time investment needed to change organisation-wide schemes.

OTHER ISSUES

The relevance of good and bad practice amongst existing job-holders

A way of identifying appropriate selection criteria may be to consider the extent to which people, satisfactorily performing the same or a similar job, fit the specification or competencies that have been identified. Examples of both good and bad practice in the job may also help.

Examples

One soft drinks company identified the main factors that were linked to good performance in service engineers who maintained and repaired drink dispensers. They found that the key factors were social skills and organising ability. Customers liked service engineers who were polite and who kept them informed about when they were coming and of any changes in appointments. The company had previously recruited people mainly on the basis of their engineering skills. It found it had over-specified in that direction, particularly as the relevant technical skills could fairly easily be taught in-house. As a result of this investigation, the selection criteria for the job were radically altered.

In an unpublished survey of the selection of lecturing staff it was found that for some years different criteria had been subconsciously applied regarding applicants who had not had previous contact with the department surveyed and those who had (e.g. as visiting lecturers or researchers). The former group had been primarily judged on their academic excellence, which was usually easy to assess. Different criteria had, however, been applied to those applicants who were known to panel members. This was because of the knowledge about the relative strengths and weaknesses of these applicants. The key attributes that emerged with this group were commitment, organising ability, teaching skills and motivation to do the job. It also emerged that the good performers in the department were mainly from those in this group and not in the group chosen primarily on the basis of academic excellence. However, previous knowledge of applicants did not always work in their favour. The different criteria used in their selection also often led to them being rejected.

The totality of a job

Another aspect of selection may be to look at the totality of a job and of an applicant so that one sees the applicant as a whole person and does not get lost in the detail. Practice may vary, though, as to whether this approach is considered too judgmental or not. This approach, though, may enable those responsible for selection to take account of issues that should have been included.

Over-specification

It is necessary to consider what constitutes a good match between a person and a job, as explained in chapter 6. A person of high ability may make a poor match for a routine job. A capable person may perform less well than a less able person who does not get bored with a routine job. The practice of discriminating against people because they are too able may vary, however, according to the organisational philosophy regarding access to jobs. Dangers of over-specification though are job distortion (see chapter 6) and being caught in the over-specification cycle. This phenomenon is explained in Figure 9.1.

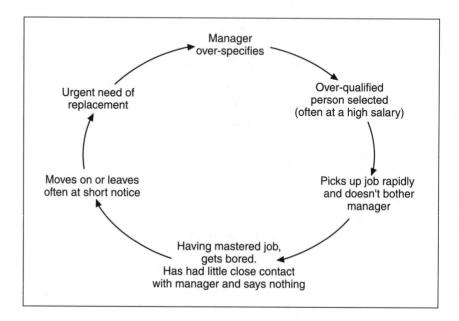

FIGURE 9.1 *The over-specification cycle*

Over-reaction to previous failures

A current or former employee may have a particular failing which blinds those responsible for choosing a successor to the other ways in which a person can fail in a job. In their anxiety to avoid choosing a person with such a failing, those responsible for selection may not pay sufficient attention to the other inappropriate attributes that candidates may have.

Choosing in one's own image

Particularly with senior positions, what may be needed is a person who complements, rather than replicates, the skills of the other team members. This fits with the findings of Belbin, explained in chapter 4, on how effective teamwork is achieved. One of the frequently voiced criticisms of British Civil Service selection, for example, has been the high degree to which those who enter at the administrative grade level replicate the backgrounds of those appointing them.

Emotional intelligence

For some jobs emotional intelligence may be particularly necessary. Broadly speaking this is the maturity of an individual. It is distinct from cognitive reasoning ability. Unfortunately, the possession by an individual of high reasoning ability does not guarantee that they will be able to use it wisely. Emotional intelligence may be particularly important in jobs that are potentially very stressful, such as in management or in conflict situations such as many in the military may have to face. What can be critical is the ability of people to use what reasoning ability they have sensibly rather than their ability to simply reason in the abstract. The ability to handle other workers constructively in conditions of stress may be particularly important (Goleman 1999, Dulewicz and Higgs 1999).

Dangers of selecting on the basis of historic performance

Particular care has to be taken in identifying the differences between a person's previous work experience and the job for which they are applying. A person who has performed admirably in one job will not necessarily perform well in a different job, particularly if that different job necessitates work at a higher level of responsibility. There is more than a grain of truth in Lawrence Peter's (1970) concept of people passing through their threshold of competence previously explained in chapter 1. His theory is that people are promoted on the basis of having done their last job well until they find themselves a job which they cannot do, which is when the basis for promotion ceases.

> **Example**
>
> In reflecting on when he was Minister of Munitions in 1915 during the First World War, David Lloyd George wrote:
>
> *I cannot claim that my first choices were always the best. They were, I think, the best available at the time. I found that some were admirable workers provided they were under the control and direction of others, but not equal to the responsibility of a supreme position. It was then that I realised thoroughly for the first time that men ought to be marked like army lorries with their carrying capacity: 'Not to carry more than three tons'. The three-tonners are perfect so long as you do not overload them with burdens for which they are not constructed by Providence. I have seen that happen in Law and Politics. The barrister who acquired a great practice as a junior and failed completely when he took silk; the politician who showed great promise as an under-secretary and achieved nothing when promoted to the headship of a department.*
>
> *1938: 149*

Attitude

Some organisations pay particular attention to attitude and try to ensure that those appointed 'fit' with the overall culture of the organisation. For example, Kirosingh (1984) reported that Sony said they would prefer a person to have the 100 per cent the right attitude and 90 per cent the right skills and never the other way around. However, the reliable assessment of attitude may not always be easy at the selection stage.

Selection of those working abroad

As was explained in chapter 4, it is particularly important to make appropriate selection decisions for those who will be working in a country other than their own. This is because of:

- the high cost of expatriate failure;
- the special problems that may be created by the impact on other members of a family, particularly a partner's career and children's education;
- the ability of the person selected to operate in a different culture;
- the extra responsibilities, managerial or otherwise, that a person may have in a new job which may be compounded by geographic distance from superiors.

Other advantages of having appropriate selection criteria

Further advantages about establishing appropriate selection criteria are that it can help with the recruitment and short-listing stages of the selection process. Clear and valid selection criteria encourage those who potentially fit those criteria to apply and may discourage those who don't. The more relevant information that is given about jobs, the more that selection process can be assisted by people *not* pursuing applications that would be inappropriate. Clear and appropriate criteria can also facilitate any short-listing process and provide a documentary base against any subsequent claim of illegal discrimination. Many employers issue their selection criteria in advance of interviews to candidates as part of their equal opportunities policies. They may also be prepared to give information to unsuccessful candidates about the reasons for their rejection.

FOLLOW-UP AND EVALUATION OF THE SELECTION PROCESS

To some extent the evaluation of selection procedures and the criteria used will always be speculative. Whatever follow-up investigations may reveal about the level of performance of people who join an organisation, one cannot really make judgements about how the people would have performed who were not selected. However, it would seem prudent to review selection procedures in the light of the performance of the people who are chosen, to test the validity of those procedures. Even then, care has to be taken in coming to conclusions. A person whose performance is poor may still have been the best of a bad bunch. There can also be other explanations for poor performance such as ineffective work arrangements. There is also the problem of whether you judge people by their contribution to short-term needs or by their long-term contribution to an organisation.

The systematic review of selection methods, whilst not leading to any magic answers, may reveal weaknesses which can be corrected in the future. One of the advantages of exit interviews is that personnel officers, in particular, can consider whether the pattern of people leaving indicates weaknesses in the selection procedure. The criteria for evaluating appraisal systems are also relevant to the selection process. These criteria are itemised in the next chapter in the section on rating and recording. However, the follow-up and evaluation of the effectiveness of the selection process is an integral part of ensuring that appropriate criteria have been used and sensibly checked out.

Consideration also needs to be given to the public relations aspects involved in selection. Quite apart from the considerations of natural justice, it would seem sensible for employers to leave unsuccessful candidates at least with the impression that their application has been considered fairly. It is also necessary to bear in mind the legislation concerning discrimination. A further issue is that the longer the selection process takes the more likely it is that able candidates will find jobs elsewhere.

The collection of information about candidates

The identification of realistic and clear selection criteria can be of great value in determining what information is relevant to selection decisions. Information about candidates can be collected from a variety of sources. Scrutiny of job advertisements indicates which employers have worked out the sort of person they want and the information they require, and which employers have not. A well-designed application form can present the relevant information to an employer in a way that they will find easy to follow. Examples of a person's work may help, as may references and testimonials from current or previous employers.

REFERENCES AND TESTIMONIALS

There is often confusion about the difference between the terms 'reference' and 'testimonial'. A testimonial is an open letter given by an employer to an employee to show to future prospective employers. As it is given to the person who is the subject of the testimonial, the writer may be reluctant to say anything detrimental about the person concerned. On the other hand, the fact that a person is prepared to praise a former employee in an open letter may be because the person deserves it. References are communications made directly with a prospective employer. They are given in confidence and are not normally revealed to the person who is the subject of the reference. This means that the current or past employer may be more prepared to be frank about the person concerned. However, care has to be taken in the interpretation of written references. A person writing a reference may feel reluctant to state the shortcomings of a person and mention just their good points. It is often the omissions that are the most important feature of a reference.

Oral references may be the most accurate, but it is important to beware of the employer who praises an employee they don't want in order to increase the chance of them leaving. It may be appropriate to approach an employer that a candidate has worked for previously, rather than a current employer, so that the candidate's relationship with their existing employer is not compromised. In evaluating a reference, whether it be good or bad, it needs to be remembered that the information received is about a person's performance in a job which may be significantly different from the job for which they have applied. The past record, although often useful, should only be seen as a guide in making selection decisions.

ACCURACY OF INFORMATION

Care often has to be taken in checking the information provided by candidates. Misrepresentation can vary from the gentle massaging of employment histories to outright fraud. Checking for inconsistencies in the information provided, such as dates of previous employment, can help establish how accurate the information provided is. Minor inconsistencies can be signposts for greater misrepresentations. Some organisations ask to see original qualifications and retain copies of these documents.

INTERNAL CANDIDATES

If a candidate is applying for a transfer or promotion from within an organisation, there may be a wealth of information available about them. Care needs to be taken in evaluating the information, but the quantity and quality of the information may mean that any interview is much less important than may be the case with external appointments. It can have a devastating effect on an organisation to promote people who are recognised by colleagues as being incompetent. However, practice varies about the extent to which internal reports are admissible. Sometimes the view is taken that it is necessary to rely primarily on performance at selection panel interviews. This issue is considered further in the section on selection panels.

The development of the flexible workforce, explained in chapter 3, means that people are increasingly likely to want to move from the peripheral to the core workforce, or in some cases, the other way around. Experience of employees in the peripheral workforce, and by them of the organisation, can provide invaluable information for both parties if there is ever the prospect of transfer to the core work-force. Another way in which relevant information may be obtained about internal candidates for promotion is to give them periods of acting-up at a more senior level to see how they handle the increased responsibility.

IMMIGRATION REQUIREMENTS

Under the Immigration and Asylum Act of 1996, UK employers need to keep documentary evidence, such as the national insurance number, of the right of employees to work in this country. Failure to do this is a criminal offence. Employers need to beware of refusing employment to applicants in case the prospective employee may be unable to provide such information as that could lead to an application for racial discrimination.

CRIMINAL RECORDS

In the UK it is proposed, under the Police Act 1997, to make three types of certificate available from the Criminal Records Bureau (CRB):

- The Criminal Conviction Certificate (CCC) gives details of 'unspent' convictions, if any, under the Rehabilitation of Offenders Act 1994. Registered employers will be able to require any prospective employees to apply to the Criminal Records Bureau for this type of certificate.
- The Criminal Record Certificate (CRC) consists of 'unspent' offences, 'spent' offences and cautions in respect of admitted offences. Applications by individuals will have to be countersigned by a registered person. These certificates would be relevant in occupations such as teaching, medicine and security.
- The Enhanced Criminal Record Certificate (ECRC) includes relevant non-conviction information. Again the application by an individual would have to be countersigned by a registered person. This type of certificate is particularly intended for people working with young children.

Fees will be charged for providing the information. Employers may offer to reimburse the cost of a certificate. A code of practice is to be issued regarding applications for certificates and use of the information obtained.

ASSESSMENT CENTRES

A way of increasing the available information about internal and external applicants is the use of assessment centres. These have become increasingly popular in recent years. They can be used both for selection and staff development. The process of assessment often includes group exercises, job-related exercises and psychometric tests.

Dulewicz (1991: 50) claims that small increases in the validity of selections can generate a handsome return on the investment in assessment centres. He also claims that the following factors are key to the design of effective assessment centres:

- adequate specification of target competencies,
- the design of relevant and valid exercises,
- adequate integration of results of competence exercises and of any psychometric tests that are used,
- assessor training,
- careful selection and briefing of candidates,
- efficient programming and management of the process,
- adequate feedback to participants and follow up of recommendations,
- monitoring of the validity and benefits of the process.

However, according to Fletcher and Anderson (1998) such criteria are only likely to be met in half of the assessment centres that have been established.

Example

One large company ran its assessment centre events for years before discovering that they had predicted nothing about future performance. Had the company done some monitoring it might have saved itself a lot of money.

(Fletcher and Anderson 1998: 44–46)

The need for caution expressed both by Dulewicz and by Fletcher and Anderson was confirmed by the experience of a large bank in the UK. The bank found that the competence profiles it had developed of staff at assessment centres did not correlate at all with the subsequent performance assessments made of the same staff. It found that the competence requirements had been applied mechanistically in selection and simply did not fit many of the key requirements. It also found that staff complained of an air of unreality of many of the exercises conducted at the centre. There were far more variations in job requirements than had been allowed for in the standardised competence approach that had been used. Consequently, the standard competencies that had been laboriously developed and applied in selection and development were abandoned. The basic data that the assessment centre had been working on was simply too unreliable.

Examples of bad practice do not undermine a good concept. The basic point is that much more care may need to be taken with the establishment of assessment centres than is often the case. Even when considerable effort is put in, however, wrong assumptions can still undermine the whole process, as evidenced by the example of the bank, given above. Conversely, sometimes some basic exercises can enhance a conventional selection process. Appropriate case studies, for example, can prove particularly useful as one of the ways of identifying managerial potential.

PSYCHOMETRIC TESTS

Psychometric tests have also become increasingly popular over recent years, both within the context of assessment centres and independently of them. The term is often used interchangeably with 'psychological testing'. Whilst such tests can provide useful information to facilitate effective selection and development, like any technique they can be misapplied. Dangers include irrelevant tests, incompetent administration, cultural bias, a belief that the tests can make the decision instead of facilitating decisions made in conjunction with other relevant information, and over-zealous sales promotion (IPD 1997).

DATA PROTECTION AND SUBJECT ACCESS

In the context of considering information on employees it should be remembered that electronic files on employees are subject to the provisions of the Data Protection Act 1998 in the UK. In general confidential information stored electronically must not be divulged without the employee's permission. Also, employees have the right to demand subject access to such files and correction rights. These rights are to be extended to structured manual files. However, at present it is not proposed to include confidential references in the subject access provisions. The 1998 act is being phased in over a nine-year period, and selection interview notes are likely to the covered by the subject access provisions if the European Data Protection Directive is to be complied with (Arkin 1997: 28). Restrictions are placed on the collection and use of sensitive personal information. There will also be restrictions on the use of automated decision-making in some areas, for example short-listing for jobs, unless the subject consents and the interests of the subject are safeguarded. Information is not to be kept longer than is necessary. The supervising agency is the Information Commission. Breaches of the legislation can lead to civil action and, in severe cases, prosecution, provided there has been material loss. The only defence for organisational data controllers is to show that they have taken reasonable steps to comply with the act.

The selection interview

Various studies have shown that the selection interview can be much more subjective and unreliable than people realise (Vernon 1953, Eysenck 1953). However, it is often an important or the only element in the process. Even if an employer were to dispense with the interview, they would need to consider how they were going to provide the candidates with information and answer their queries so that the candidates could make their decisions as to whether or not they should apply for or accept a job. The existence of clear selection criteria does enable an interview to be conducted systematically with the interviewer at least knowing what they are looking for. All too often the information collected at interviews is relatively worthless because the interviewer has not identified clearly enough what they wanted to know. Even when this has been done, a significant amount of skill may be needed to obtain the relevant information. The interviewer may have identified what they want to know, but a candidate may quite understandably be concerned with emphasising their strong points and with concealing their weaknesses.

There is a considerable amount of technique involved in obtaining information from a candidate. Readers are likely to have noticed the variation in skill demonstrated by people who have interviewed them for jobs. Appropriate training can improve the performance of interviewers both with regard to one-to-one interviews and selection panels.

PLANNING

The first stage in the interview is fairly obviously the prior preparation. Interviewers need not only to have established the selection criteria but also to have studied any relevant information before the interview starts, including organisational policies and procedures regarding selection. They also need to consider what information should be given to a candidate before the interview. The location of an interview needs to be considered, so that it takes place in surroundings that are as congenial as possible for the interviewer and candidate. It is also necessary to arrange for the interview to be free from interruptions.

If more than one person is to interview candidates it is necessary to decide whether the interviewing is sequential or joint. Generally, it is easier to coax information on a one-to-one basis. This may not involve any more organisational time as those involved in single interviewing do not have to sit through the questioning by other people. If more time is needed after the interviews to reconcile a variety of views about candidates this may be well worth the effort because the volume of data may be very valuable. However, the information so obtained may be selectively interpreted and reported and this needs to be borne in mind if this approach is used. The issues involved in joint interviewing are dealt with further in the section on selection panels.

Interviewers should have a good idea of what they want to find out during an interview. They may also want to identify the basic information that they will need to convey to a candidate. Checklists of information to be obtained and imparted can be very useful. It is also prudent to bear in mind that candidates are often understandably nervous and may not absorb much of what they are told. It is necessary to consider the structure and sequence of an interview so that the dialogue can be as effective as possible. If candidates are nervous it may be best to get them speaking as early as possible. It may be only when candidates have settled down that they are capable of absorbing important information.

One way of providing a clear and useful structure is to undertake a biographical interview. This involves the candidate being asked to explain their educational background and employment history in a chronological sequence. The interviewer can then concentrate on asking the supplementary questions that are needed to fill in any gaps. Such supplementary questioning may also need to focus on what the interviewee's actual achievements and skills are. Even if the biographical approach is not used, thought needs to be given to the structure of an interview and the agenda explained to the candidate. All too often interviews are conducted in a grasshopper style, with questions being asked at random with little if any thought being given as to how to lead up to sensitive issues. This can be caused not just by lack of skill on the part of the interviewer but also by their nervousness. The development of selection interviewing skills can have the advantage of giving the interviewer sufficient confidence to conduct an interview in a relaxed and effective manner.

INTERVIEWING SKILLS

Questioning

Considerable thought may need to be given to the way questions that are asked in an interview. The interviewer will want to find out if there are any reasons why they should not appoint a particular person. Interviewers may need to ask questions in such a way that they do not reveal what will be regarded as an acceptable or unacceptable answer. To do this they will need to frame their questions in a neutral manner. Even if one were to convert a leading question such as 'do you work hard?' into a neutral one, it would be fairly obvious what the interviewer was after. It may be more appropriate to ask what the tasks were that most interested a candidate in a previous job and which were the ones which least interested them, and why. It may also be appropriate to ask questions in an open-ended way so that the candidate may open up and talk freely. This is in contrast to closed questions which simply require a yes or no answer.

Asking the right questions in the right way can get a candidate talking freely. The more a candidate talks, the more the interviewer is likely to learn. The role of the interviewer may be to guide the interview gently, to look for leads that need following up and to be on the watch for inconsistencies in the candidate's answers. Nervousness or lack of skill on the part of the interviewer may prevent this. The issues of questioning technique, and getting people talking are both dealt with further in chapter 12 in the context of counselling.

Listening

One of the most common errors in interviews is for the interviewer to do most of the talking. This reduces the information that can be obtained from the candidate and on which the decision needs to be based. A useful rule of thumb is for the interviewer to spend no more than a quarter of the time talking, and to allow in any such estimate for the tendency to underestimate the amount of time that one speaks oneself. Listening carefully can require much more self-discipline and concentration than talking. If answers are unclear to the interviewer, it may be important to clarify just what an interviewee has meant. It may require considerable tact and patience to establish whether one has properly understood the point that a candidate is trying to make.

Interviewer confidence

A hidden agenda in interviews may be that the interviewer, in particular, is frightened of losing control and suffering one of the greatest punishments of all in the British culture – embarrassment. This may be a reason why interviews are often played far too cautiously, with important issues remaining unexplored. The development of selection interviewing skills may be the most effective way of overcoming this obstacle. This may particularly affect the close of the interview and the explanation to the candidate of just what the position is with regard to their application.

Time allocation between candidates

Many selection decisions turn out to be fairly straightforward. This is most likely to be the case with people who are clearly unsuitable. Much more time may be needed to identify the possible weaknesses with a candidate who turns out to be suitable. The greatest time may need to be taken with those candidates who are genuinely marginal and where extra relevant information may justifiably tilt the balance one way or the other. However, time allocation may be constrained by equal opportunities policies, which are considered later in this chapter.

Feedback on interviewing skills

The development of one's interviewing technique may not just depend on practice but on getting feedback on one's performance and adjusting future performance in the light of such feedback. It may be possible for readers to do this for themselves, and for this reason a selection interviewing self-assessment questionnaire is included as an appendix to this chapter. Readers can complete the questionnaire and identify any weaknesses with a view to seeing if these have been eliminated or reduced when they do their next interview.

COMMON PROBLEMS

Freezing

One of the major problems in selection interviews is that both the interviewer and the candidate may freeze into a set pattern of question and answer, with the candidate feeling fairly restricted about the information that they can volunteer. One way of trying to unfreeze both interviewer and interviewee is for the one to show the other around the prospective work area. A dialogue can then develop under much more relaxed circumstances.

Managers being taught interviewing skills have been known to relax and talk far more casually and usefully to people playing the part of candidates when the interview is apparently over. This can be built into training exercises. When the informal discussions have ended the point can be made that much extra information has been volunteered which should have emerged during the practice interview but did not. The amount of extra information obtained in this way can sometimes be astonishing.

Choice of selectors

Ironically, it may well be that the higher up an organisation selection decisions are taken, the less appropriate they may be. The peer group may often be in the best position to judge, because of their close knowledge of the demands of the job, on what is really required in a candidate. It may, therefore, be appropriate to consider whether the observations of the peer group should be sought, including their views on internal candidates. Factors such as seniority and length of experience tend to weigh heavily with selection panels in particular. This may be because they do not have the detailed knowledge of candidates and jobs that those closer to the situation have. Consequently, their decisions may be based on very superficial reasoning. More senior managers may not have to suffer the direct consequences of an inappropriate appointment. It is an understanding of this issue that has led some university medical schools to include a current student on the selection panels for prospective students.

The halo effect

Care also has to be taken to avoid the halo effect, where a particular strength in a candidate leads to over-generous assessments of their other attributes. A reverse halo can also develop where a particular weakness leads to a candidate being unnecessarily marked down in other areas. Obviously, employers also need to be aware of their own subjective views and biases and to allow for such factors in making decisions. A basic point is not placing too much emphasis on interview performance, whether before a single interviewer or a panel. This can unduly favour the fluent performer, whose subsequent actions on the job may not live up to their interview performance. This can be an important issue regarding selection panels. Their role and operation is considered next.

Selection panels

REASONS FOR PANELS

Selection panels are such a prominent feature of public sector appointments that they need examination and explanation. The presence of several people on a panel may be necessary because of the various interests that need to be represented at the selection stage. One of the historical reasons for the establishment of selection panels in the public sector was the need to see that jobs were not allocated on the basis of patronage. Subsequently, their structure and operation have often become key features of equal opportunities policies especially in local government. Even when there is no formal requirement for selection panels, there may be a preference by the representatives of an employer to see a candidate together rather than separately. Thus, a line manager and personnel officer may conduct a joint interview.

If there are clear policies and procedures about how selection panels are to operate, it is incumbent on panel members to understand and respect those policies and procedures. As was stated earlier in this chapter, organisational policies vary about the balance to be struck between asking candidates what may be deemed relevant and that which is relatively easily assessed. Basic issues concerning panel interviewing will now be explored. This is done to enable readers to understand the dynamics and to assist them with regard to any scope they have in their own organisations for interpreting or designing selection policies and procedures.

THE CONCEPT OF THE LEVEL PLAYING FIELD

In some organisations there is a strong belief that selection panels should be set up and operated in such a way that they provide a level playing field. In these circumstances the selection decision may be based primarily on interview performance. An alternative approach to providing a level playing field is to rely on the established selection criteria and to allow information from a variety of sources to be tested against those criteria. This will involve making subjective judgements on a wider base of relevant data.

A basic issue is that however much effort is put into attempting to create a level playing field, selection decisions in the end are subjective. The limitations of the objective approach need to be recognised. If, for example, standard questions are asked of each candidate at a panel, subjective judgements still have to be made about what questions are asked, their relevance and the quality and the weighting given to individual responses. Judgements can be influenced by a variety of factors including hidden interdepartmental rivalries. Questions may rightly or wrongly favour some candidates more than others. If questions are too rigidly standardised it may prevent members from following up leads about strengths and weaknesses that may be relevant to a candidate's application. There is also the danger that standardised questions may be anticipated, particularly by internal candidates, or even that prearranged questions are leaked to a favoured candidate.

POTENTIAL PROBLEMS

The problems of coaxing information out of candidates and probing for their strengths and weaknesses are likely to be much greater at panels compared with single interviewing. The amount of time available to each interviewer is much more restricted and the formality of the situation may inhibit candidates from making fluent responses. Sometimes it is argued that the ability to cope with panel-type situations is a critical aspect of the job. However, this is often not the case and this argument may be used as a rationalisation for a selection procedure which has been adopted for quite different reasons. Whatever method of selection is used it is necessary to remember that the prime purpose is to discriminate in favour of those who are best fitted to perform particular work. As explained earlier in this chapter because of the dangers of over-selection, this does not necessarily mean the most capable person. Selectors are likely to be looking for a combination of the person most likely to perform well and also the person who will perform consistently to the highest standard.

"Right, Mr Smith, just relax"

Source: Private Eye, 8 May 1992, no. 783, p. 12

Inappropriate or unlawful discrimination occurs when invalid criteria are used. Follow-up studies may be necessary to determine the validity of the process. If those involved with selection decisions then work with those appointed they will get regular feedback on the appropriateness of their decisions. Problems can arise if panel members make inappropriate decisions and fail to recognise what modifications in selection processes may be needed because of their ignorance of the consequences of past decisions.

THE ROLE OF PANEL CHAIR

The chances of effective decision-making at panels may be improved by careful chairing. If it is not possible to give training to panel members, the person chairing may be able to gently coach members in the skills of interviewing and selection – bearing in mind that often the worse interviewers are, the less they are likely to recognise their deficiencies. Where the information obtained by panel interviews is of little value at least it is best to recognise that and use what other valid information is available to panel members as a basis for decision-making.

Equal Opportunities

GENERAL FRAMEWORK

It is also necessary to consider the impact of selection processes in terms of equality of opportunity and the legislative rights that prospective employees and those applying for promotion have to protect them against discriminatory employment practices. As explained previously in this chapter the whole purpose of selection is to be discriminatory, in terms of choosing the person best fitted to do a particular job. Anti-discrimination law and policies are designed to prevent discrimination on an anti-social basis, not to oblige employers to choose people at random. Legal and contractual rights may be embraced in overall organisational policies for managing diversity, as explained in chapter 4. Key rights in the UK are embodied in the Sex Discrimination Acts of 1975 and 1986, the Race Relations Act 1976 and the Disability Discrimination Act 1995. The rights do not extend to religious discrimination and religious harassment within the UK apart from in Northern Ireland where they are covered by the Fair Employment (Northern Ireland) Acts 1976 and 1989. However, regard has to be paid in the UK to the Human Rights Act of 1998.

The issue of discrimination needs to be viewed not just in the light of the minimum standards set by the law, but what it is sensible for employers to do anyway. There is no merit or gain for organisations failing to make use of the talent and potential that is available by unjustified discrimination.

SEX AND RACE DISCRIMINATION

The provisions of the Sex and Race Discrimination Acts protect employees and prospective employees from discrimination in selection and other employment issues on the basis of sex and race. Protection is also given against discrimination on the basis of marital status. Women are also entitled to maternity leave some of which must be paid, the minimum level and time being equivalent to state sickness benefit for 18 weeks (Employment Relations Act 1999). It is illegal to refuse to employ women on the basis of pregnancy or to dismiss them for that reason.

Applicants who feel they have been the victims of illegal discrimination can pursue their case at an employment tribunal, claiming damages. Anti-discrimination orders about future selection practices by the organisation concerned can be issued by the relevant agencies and enforced in the courts. The relevant agencies are the Equal Opportunities Commission and the Commission for Racial Equality. The commissions may also assist applicants in pursuing claims at a tribunal. There is no ceiling to the compensation that can be awarded for the damages suffered. Individuals, as well as organisations, can be liable for damages. Employers are also likely to be sensitive to the public relations issues involved in losing a case.

The Equal Opportunities Commission and the Commission for Racial Equality have both published codes of practice advising employers on how to avoid discriminatory practices (1985 and 1995). A key method of doing this is by monitoring the composition of the workforce. Other important issues are the need to examine recruitment practices, including the pattern of applications and rejections, and promotion procedures. It is perhaps easier for employers to fall into the trap of indirect discrimination than direct discrimination. Indirect discrimination occurs when an unnecessary selection criterion is used which has an adverse effect on applicants from a particular sex or ethnic group. This can happen, for example, when too much importance is given to experience in job selection which may work against women who have the skills and/or potential to do a job but not have had the same opportunities as men to gain years of experience. The use of job competencies in selection can reduce the chance of such indirect discrimination by focussing on the actual requirements of a job rather than conventional views about what length of experience and qualifications are required.

Examples

An example of indirect discrimination was the use of an upper age limit of 28 for people applying for positions as executive officers with the civil service. This was held to be discriminatory against women because of the likelihood that family commitments would disproportionately reduce women's chances of applying for such positions (*Price* vs *Civil Service Commissioner 1977*).

Another example, this time concerning racial equality, was the requirement that unnecessary standards of English were demanded of applicants for manual work. The Commission for Racial Equality helped seven Bangladeshis pursue such a case against the British Steel Corporation. The seven were deemed to have failed a

CONTINUED OVER ➤

CONTINUED FROM PREVIOUS PAGE

language test when they reapplied for work after an extended holiday in Bangladesh. The corporation argued that the tests, for production workers, were necessary for safety reasons. The applicants argued that 'the test had an adverse impact on ethnic minorities whose language was not English and was not justifiable having regard to the job in question'. Under the terms of the agreed settlement the Bangladeshis were compensated and re-engaged, and the corporation also agreed to obtain professional help in reviewing its test procedures.

(IRS 1979)

Employers are increasingly obliged to demonstrate the fairness of their employment practices when challenged at employment tribunals. This may include providing a statistical analysis of their labour force and a reason for a particular mix. In cases of sex discrimination the onus of proof is on the employer to show that they have not behaved in a discriminatory way. However, whilst employers may adopt equality targets and positive action programmes to reduce imbalance, positive discrimination (such as recruitment quotas) is illegal with very limited exceptions. One emerging issue is the need to examine job structure, including terms and conditions of employment. Some jobs may easily be altered to increase their accessibility to particular groups. One example is the option of part-time work, especially to mothers returning from maternity leave.

DISABILITY DISCRIMINATION

Protection was extended in the UK to cover disabled people by the Disability Discrimination Act of 1995. This legislation currently affects employers with 15 or more employees. The rights and means of enforcement are similar to those with regard to race and sex discrimination. A Disability Rights Commission has been established with similar powers to the Equal Opportunities Commission and the Commission for Racial Equality. A Code of Practice (1996) has been published giving advice about the application of the act. There will be some problems in distinguishing between ill-health and disability. Some mental illness, such as schizophrenia, can be categorised as a disability. Under the act it is illegal to bar anyone from employment because of a disability, unless that disability would significantly impede their ability to do the job and the employer cannot reasonably overcome the problem. Employers need to make reasonable adjustments to enable disabled people, who would be otherwise suitable, to take up employment.

DISCRIMINATION ON THE BASIS OF TRADE UNION MEMBERSHIP

In the UK it is illegal to discriminate at the selection stage of employment on the basis of membership or non-membership of a trade union. This is one of the provisions of the Trade Union and Labour Relations (Consolidation) Act of 1992.

AGEISM

There is no legislation about age discrimination. However, as was explained in the section on sex and race discrimination, age requirements can constitute indirect sex discrimination (*Price* vs *Civil Service Commission 1977*). Indirect discrimination may also occur by undue attention being paid to health issues and in some cases may be in breach of the Disability Discrimination Act. The government has issued a voluntary Code of Practice on Age Diversity in Employment (1999). Ageism can involve unjustifiable discrimination against either the young or the old. The government has adopted the advice given in its own code in its role as an employer. An example of this is the banning of age limits on vacancies listed in job centres. The ageing of the work force and the general increase in life expectancy means that increasing attention is likely to be paid to the dangers of not making use of older workers in particular.

OTHER DISCRIMINATION

Some employers, particularly in the local government area, have developed their own comprehensive equal opportunities policies that cover other groups as well. Obviously, if one is employed in such an organisation it is necessary to know the details of such policies. It may also be important, and necessary in terms of the law, to review any services that an organisation offers to the public to ensure that they also are offered on a fair basis.

Being interviewed

POTENTIAL BARGAINING ISSUES

This chapter has so far been written from the perspective of the employer selecting candidates for a job. As readers will also inevitably be in the position of applying for jobs, it is appropriate to devote some time to considering the process from the perspective of the job applicant. As ever, it is necessary to be clear about the objectives of the process. The obvious objective is to secure a job, but there may need to be other objectives as well. It may be counter-productive to concentrate only on how to persuade an employer to offer you a job if it leads to you being offered a job that you cannot do, starting a job you find you do not want or accepting an offer on unfavourable terms. Consequently, the interviewee, as well as planning how to present themselves, also needs to plan to extract the information that they need to see if a job is worth having or to find out if there are any areas where bargaining can be conducted. It may be useful to bear in mind that you can at least ask for time to make your mind up if you are unsure whether or not to accept an offer. Also, the time when your bargaining position will be strongest is when the employer has made an offer and you have not given your decision.

If the offer is subject to conditions, such as a medical report or examination or satisfactory references you may wish to delay resigning from a current job until it is confirmed that these conditions have been met.

ANALYSIS OF THE PROCESS

Having clarified the range of objectives at an interview, it is now appropriate to concentrate on the skills relating to the prime objective – that of getting the employer to make you a job offer. One of the most important skills will be the ability to understand the selection process and get inside the mind of the interviewer in order to see things from their perspective. In order to do that it will help to be aware of the formal stages in the systematic selection process. In preparing for interview, the candidate should go through the same process as the interviewer, so that they can work out what the interviewer is likely to be looking for. In this the most important tool will be the job description which will be sent, more often than not, with the application form. As explained previously, the job description lists the main tasks and responsibilities that the candidate will be expected to perform. Some organisations, notably those with an equal opportunities policy, will also state their selection criteria. If the employer does not send selection criteria, then it is advisable for a prospective employee to try and identify them. Background research about the organisation will also help in getting a good approximation of this. When completing the application form and answering questions in the job interview the candidate should ensure that the information they volunteer is as relevant as possible to the potential employer's selection criteria. If the applicant feels any important aspects have been missed out, they can always volunteer more information at the end of the interview when they may be asked if there is anything else they need to say.

The above preparation has two advantages:

- the applicant will be presenting the most useful information to show that they are fitted for the job;
- the interviewer, or interviewers, will feel gratified because their questions actually seem to be eliciting the information they need to make a decision. In connection with this, it is likely that interviewers will feel better disposed towards those candidates with whom they feel they have conducted a good interview.

PRESENTATION

In presenting oneself at interview it is more important to concentrate on the content of what is being said than on peripheral issues like the positioning of one's hands or elimination of gestures. Having said that, prepared responses may sound too mechanistic, so it may be better to make notes on background information and leave them at home on the day, rather than have a scripted response. The questions probably will not come up exactly as envisaged, anyway.

As first impressions tend to be disproportionately important, dress should be on the conservative side. Bearing in mind that the prime objective of the interview is to secure an offer, it may be best to appear assertive rather than aggressive under any testing questions. Giving the interviewer, or panel, a difficult time may not increase your chances of an offer.

In seeking to demonstrate how well you fit the selection criteria it is as well to be clear that your purpose will be to demonstrate the strengths in your case whilst the employer should be probing for weaknesses. In demonstrating your strengths, clear and interesting responses are to be preferred – convoluted statements may be boring. Samples of work or other relevant evidence may help in presenting your case. Many people undersell themselves by being too deferential to the interviewer(s) or by volunteering weaknesses in their case that may have been better left unsaid.

Account also needs to be taken of the stress that can be present in job interviews. The stress inherent in such situations can be aggravated by problems involved in finding the location, being left waiting, changes in the arrangements and errors by the employer. The ability to cope with such stress before and during the interview can have a critical effect on the outcome. Particular reactions to avoid are talking too quickly and being aggressive.

LESSONS FOR NEXT TIME

If you are unsuccessful it may be appropriate to reflect on whether or not it was because you did not match the criteria as well as someone else did. In the last analysis, all you can hope to do is to present yourself as well as possible. If one application fails there are likely to be other opportunities where one can successfully demonstrate that you provide the best fit to an employer's selection criteria. If you have a run of rejections it is important to try not to let it lead to you going into an interview with a defeatist attitude and thus under-selling yourself.

You may want to ask for feedback from the organisation as to why you did not get a job, but often people are too demoralised to do this. If you are perplexed as to why you have not got jobs you feel you should have, one further piece of preparation may be to get a friend to give you a simulated interview and feedback on your performance. If this can be done with the aid of close-circuit television, so that you can see how you perform, so much the better.

SUMMARY

✔ As with most things the key to effective job selection is systematic and careful preparation. This is all the more so as selection decisions can critically affect the performance (or non-performance) of an organisation. It may also critically impact on whether one meets one's own work objectives. It is particularly important to work out the nature of a job and not to rely simply on historic and short-term needs. It is only when this is done that appropriate selection criteria can be identified. One way of doing this is by developing a person specification The Seven Point Plan is one way of developing such a specification. An alternative approach is to draw up a list of required job competencies. This is potentially a more rigorous approach but can be time-consuming and difficult for people not familiar with this method to handle accurately.

✔ Selection is likely to be assisted by the careful collection and examination of information about candidates prior to an interview. It is also important to identify what information candidates need to have. Working to sensible selection criteria with the appropriate information available creates a framework for an effective interview. However, interviewers need to develop interviewing skills, which particularly involve good questioning and active listening.

✔ The advantages and disadvantages of selection panels were also considered. These may form part of an equal opportunities policy. The volume of related law has steadily increased to ensure that the job selection process reduces or eliminates anti-social discrimination. Important protections and remedies have been introduced with regard to sex, race, and disability in particular. These may be supplemented by further protections provided by individual employers.

✔ There is a final section on the skills of being interviewed, which have as a starting point understanding the selection process from the employer's perspective. There is also an assessment questionnaire attached as an appendix to this chapter to enable readers to review their own performance as an interviewer.

SELF-ASSESSMENT QUESTIONS

1. Give an example and explanation of a particular job that you are familiar with that has been badly structured.

2. What criteria would you use for selecting a person for a particular job that you know about?

3. In the example given in question 2, what information would you try and collect about candidates in advance of the interview and how would you go about it?

4. How would you prepare for a job selection interview that you have to conduct?

5. What are the main potential advantages and disadvantages of selection panels?

6. What are the main areas of legal protection against anti-social job selection?

7. What basic steps would you take to ensure that you presented yourself effectively at a job interview?

 References

Arkin, Anat (1997) 'Secrets Out', *People Management*, 28 August.

Commission for Racial Equality (1995) Code of Practice for the Elimination of Racial Discrimination and the Promotion of Equality in Employment, CRE.

Department of Education and Employment (1996) Code of Practice for the Elimination of Discrimination in the Field of Employment Against Disabled Persons or Persons Who Have Had a Disability, HMSO.

Department of Employment (1999) Code of Practice on Age Diversity in Employment, DFEE Publications.

Drucker, Peter (1955) The Practice of Management, Heinemann.

Dulewicz, Victor (1991) 'Improving Assessment Centres', *Personnel Management*, June.

Dulewicz, Victor and Malcolm Higgs (1999) *Making Sense of Emotional Intelligence*, NFER-Nelson.

Equal Opportunities Commission (1985) Code of Practice on Sex Discrimination, Equal Opportunity Policies Procedures and Practices in Employment. (Revised to take account of the 1986 act.)

Eysenck, H. J. (1953) 'Uses and Abuses of Psychology' in *Each According to His Ability* Pelican, ch. 5.

Goleman, Daniel (1999) *Working with Emotional Intelligence*, Bloomsbury.

Industrial Relations Legal Information Bulletin No. 131, 21.2, 1979 (Industrial Relations Services), p. 12.

Institute of Personnel and Development (1997) The IPD Guide on Psychological Testing, Institute of Personnel and Development.

Kirosingh, M. (1984) *Changed Working Practices*, Allen & Unwin.

Lloyd George, David (1938) *War Memoirs of David Lloyd George*, Odhams Press, vol. 1.

Local Government Management Board (1993) Managing Tomorrow.

Peter, Lawrence and Raymond Hull (1970) *The Peter Principle*, Pan. Alternatively, see the Souvenir Press edition (1969) reissued in 1992.

Rodger, Alec (1970) *The Seven Point Plan*, National Institute of Industrial Psychology, London, 3rd ed.

Vernon, P. E., (1953) *Personality Tests and Assessments*, Methuen.

Cases cited

Price vs the Civil Service Commission, IRLR. Industrial Relations Services, 1977, p. 291.

Appendix to chapter 9

INTERVIEW ASSESSMENT FORM

When making your judgements try to relate these to specific acts or omissions on your part. Be sure you understand *why* you rate each item as you do.

++   Very good
+   Largely Satisfactory
0   Not so bad, could have been better
—   Not so good

	++	+	0	—
1. *Preparation:* Were you well prepared? Did you have clear and appropriate selection criteria? Were you aware of relevant organisational procedures and policies? Did you have a plan?				
2. *The opening:* How successful were you in opening the interview?				
3. *Putting the subject at ease:* Was the subject very nervous? Could they talk freely?				
4. *Facts:* Did you collect the relevant facts? Did you find out why and how as well as what?				
5. *Attitudes/feelings:* Did you manage to discover these as well as the facts (if appropriate)?				
6. *Questions:* Did you ask open-ended questions and probe where necessary? Did you ask leading questions or answer your own questions?				
7. *Listening:* Did you listen enough? Did you talk too much?				
8. *Giving information:* Did you give all the information the candidate needed in a way that they could understand?				
9. *Manner:* Were you courteous, factual, tactful? Were you tense, abrupt, argumentative? Did you make value judgements?				
10. *Discrimination:* Was there any invalid or illegal discrimination?				
11. *Closing:* In what frame of mind did the interviewee leave?				

chapter (ten

Appraisal

There are case studies and exercises at
http://www.thomsonlearning.co.uk
(for full details, see the listing at the
start of this book).

LEARNING OUTCOMES

By the end of this chapter you will be able to:

- Identify the range of purposes for which appraisal may be used

- Evaluate the reasons for failure of appraisal schemes

- Implement and operate appraisal so that the chances of success are optimised

- Handle appraisal situations, both formal and informal

- Understand the concept of performance management

- Handle individual performance appraisals

- Understand the potential advantages and disadvantages of performance-related pay

Introduction

In this chapter the various objectives of appraisal are identified and the point made that this is an area with many potential difficulties. One common problem is that if schemes are not thought out properly they may contain conflicting objectives. Another potential difficulty is the high level of interpersonal skills that can be needed in appraisal situations. Consideration of the likely pitfalls is necessary in order to decide whether a formal appraisal scheme should be used or not. Knowledge of the potential problems also helps to design and operate a scheme as effectively as possible. One important distinction is between informal ongoing appraisal and formal appraisal. Ideally these two processes should complement one another.

After the general issue of employee appraisal has been covered, attention is given to performance management. Sometimes individual performance appraisal is part of an overall strategy for performance management. Performance may be improved both by focusing on corporate and individual objectives and the development of key competencies. Sometimes performance-related pay is used as well. As with appraisal, considerable care is needed with their design, implementation and monitoring of performance-related pay schemes. It also needs to be remembered that pay is only one of the factors that determines the level of performance.

Objectives

There are a variety of reasons why managers may need to appraise their subordinates. The main reasons are likely to be:

- performance review,
- the identification of training needs,
- pay review,
- determining upgradings,
- determining promotion,
- probationary review,
- review of duties.

The distinction between upgrading and promotion is that upgrading normally means that a person is paid more because it is recognised that most of their work is, or will be, at the higher levels of responsibility within the existing job. Promotion, on the other hand, normally involves transfer to a different job that is at a higher level of responsibility.

Potential problems with formal schemes

It is necessary to explain the potential problems of formal appraisal to caution people against over-optimism about such schemes. Understanding of these problems is also necessary in order to decide whether or not to use a scheme and how a scheme might be designed. This knowledge is also necessary to know how to operate a scheme effectively or, in some cases, to minimise the damage that they can cause.

THE FAILURE RATE OF SCHEMES

Fletcher (1993: 34) refers to a study where 80 per cent of respondents were dissatisfied with their appraisal schemes – mainly because of the multiplicity of objectives. This fits with substantial anecdotal evidence about how managers view their own organisational schemes.

Watson provides an example from a large UK electronics company:

> *I get the impression that a lot of people are just going through the routine. Appraisal does not have the commitment of the directors. I have not been appraised in years. And nothing happens as a result of it and so employees regard it as a bit of a fag and the manager regards it as a bit of fag. So the two of them go though the sometimes embarrassing routine of something they know at the end of the day is… meaningless.*
>
> (1994: 158)

UNCLEAR OR CONFLICTING OBJECTIVES

The objectives of formal appraisal schemes need to be clearly defined. There is little point in appraising just for the sake of it or because it is fashionable. This may not only be a waste of time but may actually be counter-productive. If judgements are made and communicated for no apparent purpose, the people who are judged may rightly feel resentful. Unfortunately, there is a great temptation for people in organisations, as in life in general, to make judgements about other people simply because they like doing it. Superficiality in the judgements and tactlessness in the way any views are communicated may compound this.

The compatibility of appraising with different but simultaneous objectives also needs to be considered. Often this point is overlooked and organisations adopt formal multipurpose appraisal schemes not realising that some of the objectives may be contradictory. Some employers even carry this to the extreme of formally including the maintenance of discipline as one of the objectives of a multipurpose scheme. Including such an objective would be likely to discredit the rest of a scheme. Also, if a person being appraised sees their level of pay or future promotion influenced by the outcome of the exercise, they may be eager to demonstrate how good they are and to play down any shortcomings in their performance or training requirements. If the objectives of appraisal conflict in this way, it is much better to pursue the various objectives at different times rather than have the subordinate push in a single interview to achieve the objective they have singled out as being the most important.

The compatibility of appraisal with other organisational objectives also has to be considered. As explained in chapter 3 it may be counter-productive to introduce a Total Quality Management scheme with the emphasis on group performance alongside an individual performance scheme that stresses and may also reward people based on their individual performance.

OVER-OPTIMISM

Organisations may underestimate the resources needed for a scheme to operate effectively. The key cost is managerial time, but those being appraised also need to invest time, and the administrative expenses may also be significant. One of the reasons why multipurpose schemes with conflicting objectives are often established is to save on resources. Organisations may also be over-optimistic of the ability of their managers to handle a formal appraisal scheme. If the managerial structure and associated skills are undeveloped, appraisal may simply be too sophisticated to handle. In such circumstances, improvement in these other areas may need to be a higher priority anyway.

Explanations in textbooks about appraisal tend to suggest that formal schemes can be relatively easily implemented. Unfortunately this is often not the case. What is lacking in the literature is an appraisal of appraisal schemes explaining what actually happens in practice. A badly thought out scheme, or one introduced in the wrong circumstances, can do much more harm than good.

CONFLICT

Considerable conflict can be built into appraisal situations, particularly performance appraisal. A subordinate will not automatically accept that the criteria by which they are being judged are appropriate, or that the judgements made about their level of performance are accurate. This may be because of misperception by the subordinate of what is appropriate or because, in some cases, the subordinate has the best appreciation of what is required. The deployment of people in organisations cannot reach that level of perfection where the manager is always more competent than the subordinate. There is the additional problem that the subordinate may appreciate what is required, as far as the organisation is concerned, but recognise that this is not necessarily in their own best interests. This was a point that was raised in chapter 2, when considering management by objectives, and is sufficiently important to need reinforcing here. Organisational and personal objectives do not always neatly coincide. This can mean that at an appraisal interview a person finds themselves under pressure to do what they do not want to do. This could involve developing the job in a way they find inappropriate, or making cost savings that could affect their status, promotion prospects or even job security. The delicacy of these and the other issues that have been identified, which can arise during appraisal, is such that the manager may require considerable skill and sensitivity to handle the situation.

CONFRONTATION

Another danger of formal appraisal schemes is that managers may be precipitated into confrontations with their subordinates that they cannot handle. The simplistic answer to this is to train the managers in appraisal interviewing, but the reality is that many managers, however good they may be in other aspects of their job, will never have the interpersonal skills to handle sensitive appraisal interviews effectively. Many managers, in some cases wisely, just pay lip-service to formal appraisal and simply complete any necessary forms with as little embarrassment as possible. Others may simply upset their subordinates, often without realising it. Silence by the subordinate may be taken to mean agreement when the reality may be that the subordinate may just be managing to avoid losing their temper. Recognition of these problems does at least give the manager a chance of handling appraisal constructively, or of seeing when it is best to leave an issue alone. Sometimes confrontations may be quite unnecessary.

(Example)
A government agency had inherited a civil service practice of requiring employees to be assessed as suitable for promotion before they could be interviewed by a general promotion board. The practice of having general promotion boards was then stopped and employees were expected to apply just for specific jobs if they wanted promotion. Although there was no longer any need to formally assess whether employees were fit for promotion or not the practice still continued for some years. Approximately half of the employees were stigmatised each year by being classified as not fit for promotion when there was no longer any purpose in such an assessment.

LACK OF ONGOING DIALOGUE

In many organisations managers are required to undertake appraisal of their subordinates as part of a formal scheme. However, whether or not there is a formal scheme, managers need to have an ongoing dialogue with their subordinates. A formal scheme should supplement and not replace this. The absence of a formal appraisal scheme does not remove the need for the manager to consider systematically, for example, the performance, training, payment or suitability for promotion of subordinates. A formal appraisal between the manager and subordinate should not contain many surprises, rather the interview should review the ongoing dialogue that has taken place since the last formal meeting. Discussion is crucial, not only to check that any formal assessment is accurate but also to enable any need for change to be talked through and hopefully agreed upon by the two parties. For this to be productive, a manager needs to have clear ideas of what they are trying to assess and why, especially as this is an area where managerial thinking is often very muddled.

ILLEGAL DISCRIMINATION

It is necessary to monitor appraisal systems to ensure that they do not involve illegal discrimination. This is particularly important with regard to sex and race but can also involve those who are disabled and people engaged in trade union activities. The criteria used in appraisal schemes need to be examined to see if they directly or indirectly unfairly discriminate. Performance, merit payment or promotion criteria could, for example unnecessarily place a premium on aspects that disadvantage a particular group. This could happen, for example if experience was excessively weighted compared with the actual ability to do a job, which could disadvantage women applying for promotion.

<table>
<tr><td>Example</td><td>In 1993 London Underground made a £60,000 settlement in a case taken by the Commission for Racial Equality on behalf of 20 black station managers who had claimed that they had suffered indirect racial discrimination under a performance-related pay scheme between 1989 and 1992.</td></tr>
</table>

(Personnel Management 1993: 3)

NATIONAL VARIATIONS

Particular care may be needed in using performance appraisal schemes in international organisations. Schemes designed in one country but used in another need as a minimum to be adapted to take into account local conditions. The very concept of appraisal, giving feedback and encouraging employees to respond may be much less acceptable in some countries than others, especially where power distances are high. The process of appraisal may also be complicated by tensions between different ethnic groups. Account also needs to be taken of whether the focus in a particular society is the individual or the group. Individually focused performance appraisal may be much more suited to North American organisations than those in Japan where the focus is much more on the work group. The international manager conducting appraisal in a country other than their own will particularly need to acquire sensitivity to the norms and values of the country in which they are operating.

There is also the question of how international managers should be judged compared with their counterparts operating in their home environment. In commercial organisations, trading conditions may be very different overseas and the level of profitability may be considerably affected by factors such as internal transfer pricing. A job overseas may differ from a similar one filled by a manager operating in their home country. For example, the overseas job-holder may have to interact with governments and legislators in the host country but not at home. There may also be significant environmental constraints preventing the overseas manager from operating as effectively as they might have done at home. Also, the host country may have a more turbulent economic or political environment.

A manager can be evaluated according to operational, managerial or strategic criteria. Strategic criteria may be particularly important when a manager is operating overseas because they will have a significant impact on the subsidiary's performance. A fuller account of operating formal appraisal systems in an international environment is given by Dowling, Welch and Schuler (1999: 118–153).

LINKING PERFORMANCE AND PAY

Practice varies about linking between performance appraisal and pay. According to Armstrong and Barron:

Many employers believe in paying for performance and/or competence, but they feel that linking them too closely damages the development aspects of performance management.

1998: 41

Other evidence suggests that performance-related pay could actually be counter-productive. The issue of performance-related pay is covered in some detail later in this chapter. The issue of competence-based pay was covered in the context of job evaluation in chapter 7.

Strategies for effective handling

The rest of this section on appraisal is meant to show how schemes might be made to work effectively. The next chapter on training is also relevant. Effective training necessitates accurate diagnosis of training needs, and appraisal may play a critical part in the identification of these needs. Whatever purpose appraisal is used for and whether it be formal or informal, or both, counselling skills are required by the managers handling the process. The skills involved in effective counselling are explained in chapter 12.

ESTABLISHING THE RATIONALE OF A SCHEME

The need for clear and compatible objectives for appraisal schemes has already been stressed. What also needs stressing is that it is not enough to select one or more objectives and to assume that the logic of a scheme is self-evident. Care has to be taken to ensure that any objectives are realistically attainable and that the actual scheme devised will facilitate the achievement of objectives. It will be no good, for example, deciding to have a performance appraisal scheme that is based on unreliable, inconsistent and irrelevant judgements. Whatever the scheme, a considerable amount of intellectual effort is likely to be needed in identifying its precise objectives and the operational detail that is required if the objectives are to be accomplished. Specific objectives, and the circumstances in which schemes have to operate, are likely to vary widely from one organisation to another. It is unlikely that one can simply buy an 'off the shelf' scheme or copy someone else's. This may not stop people doing just that, which is no doubt one of the reasons why evidence of schemes actually working is so scarce. If schemes are to succeed, much patient effort is needed in developing appropriate in-house arrangements. The stages in the process include identifying and agreeing the objectives of a scheme with appropriate managers, the preparation of appropriate forms and briefing notes, and pilot runs to test the system. It is only then that the next essential step of training line managers in how to operate a system can be undertaken.

THE USE OF COMPETENCIES

As explained in the previous chapter on selection, organisations often identify the relevant competencies for a job. If competencies have already been established for selection purposes it may be particularly appropriate to use them for appraisal. They may also be useful in identifying training needs. Competencies can be divided into core and desirable ones. They may also be subdivided into different levels of performance. Employees may also be judged against the competencies necessary for the next highest grade to assess their suitability for promotion.

RATING AND RECORDING

A basic aspect of appraisal that needs to be explained is ratings – the way in which they and other material recorded are made. The first step at this stage is to ensure that the criteria used to judge the employees are the appropriate ones. Ratings also need to meet the following criteria:

- validity: ratings must relate to observable behaviour on the job;
- reliability: ratings made by different raters should be comparable (i.e. produce closely similar results), as should ratings made by the same individual at different times;
- relevance: the behaviour or qualities rated should be important to success in the particular job concerned;
- discrimination: the ratings should genuinely discriminate between above average, average and below average individuals;
- comprehensiveness: ratings should cover all main aspects of behaviour relevant to the purpose of the scheme;
- assessability: some factors such as loyalty and a sense of humour mean different things to different people – criteria need to be defined as well as needing to be assessable;
- attainability: any set targets should be realistically attainable.

Particular care is needed to ensure that ratings really are reliable. The dangers of inconsistency are considerable and can easily bring a scheme into disrepute. The hazards include the halo effect, where there is a spin-off from one desirable quality in an employee which causes overgenerous ratings on other factors. The reverse halo effect occurs when an undesirable quality causes other factors to be marked too harshly. Another phenomenon can be the blue-eyed child syndrome. This occurs when people are favoured for characteristics or behaviour unrelated to the job. It is concern over issues such as these that can arouse considerable trade union hostility to appraisal schemes. Another problem that can arise concerns the need to reconcile the ratings of managers who rate the employees either consistently highly or consistently badly. Other managers may create another problem – that of rating nearly everyone as 'average'. Sometimes managers are obliged to rate according to a normal statistical distribution to avoid such problems. However, this can create problems such as not discriminating between effective and ineffective departments.

Care has to be taken to ensure that any weighting of the various factors has the effect that the designers of a system intended.

Example

A merit-rating scheme was operated in which the most important factor in practice was punctuality. This was not the intention of the designers of the scheme but was a consequence of the way the raters operated. It was much easier to assess punctuality than other more important but less tangible factors. As the dispersion of ratings for punctuality was therefore much wider than was the case with the other factors, the result in practice was that the differences in the total scores for individuals were accounted for more by punctuality than by any other single rating.

(Gill and Ungerson 1984: 47)

Various methods of recording ratings and other relevant information can be used – some of which are aimed at producing statistical reliability and consistency. The methods include:

- comparison with established standards,
- rating on a graded scale,
- comparative rating of employees,
- paired comparisons of employees,
- forced choice questions,
- forced distribution of marks or grades,
- critical incident recording,
- written reports.

Combinations of the above methods are likely to be used, the exact choice depending on the specific appraisal scheme.

Another issue that has to be resolved is whether or not appraisal reports are shown to the employees who have been appraised. One consequence of having open systems is that, not surprisingly, they are likely to lead to only mild criticisms being made by the manager. Employees have rights of access to what is kept on file about their appraisal as a result of the data protection acts. The 1984 act had the effect of enabling employees to have access to appraisals and other information stored electronically about them. The 1998 act gives employees rights of access to such information stored on manual files (these legislative provisions were more fully explained in the previous chapter).

APPRAISAL INTERVIEW PREPARATION

One of the critical contributions that line managers need to make in operating an appraisal scheme is spending an adequate amount of time in both preparing for and conducting interviews. Their preparation needs to include thoroughly understanding a scheme and also being clear what it is they want to get out of an interview. All the managers involved require this commitment. The boss's boss (the organisational grandparent) may also need to be involved, and there may need to be inputs from other people with whom the appraisee interacts.

Preparation prior to an interview involves more than simply understanding the paperwork associated with a scheme. All relevant information should be assembled prior to an interview. There is no point in making judgements about, for example, levels of output or attendance patterns if objective data is available giving exact details. Judgement may be appropriate about the reason for a particular level of output or attendance pattern – but not to establish what the figures actually are. Care will be needed in deciding what judgements are relevant. Criteria also need to be established to ensure that the judgements are made systematically. Other relevant documentation that will need to be assembled includes details of any previous relevant appraisals – and particularly of any follow-up action that was planned. The job description and selection criteria are also likely to be needed.

Both the appraiser and the appraisee need time to prepare for the interview. The process should be seen as a two-way discussion and both parties need to think beforehand about how the interview can be constructively handled. It is hardly satisfactory if the appraisee is not given notice or, perhaps worse still, is told they have an interview but not told what it is to be about. A certain amount of tension and anxiety should also be anticipated which may affect both appraiser and appraisee. Appraisal interviews may reveal conflicts between the parties. This may well happen in performance appraisal interviews – as is explained later – but can happen in any type of appraisal situation. One implication of this is that the appraiser may need to consider what adjustments they need to make, either in their own behaviour or in organisational support, to help the appraisee accomplish their legitimate objectives. It is all too easy to see appraisal interviews as situations where adjustment just has to be made by the subordinate, but such a view is profoundly misconceived. A further way of endeavouring to secure a constructive outcome is to ensure that recent achievements by the appraisee are clearly acknowledged. All this means that a manager should not try and conduct too many appraisal interviews in one day. The interviews, as well as being likely to be time-consuming, may also be emotionally demanding. Time also has to be allowed for writing up and planning any appropriate action.

FEEDBACK

An extremely dangerous fallacy is that employees always want to know exactly where they stand and will always welcome feedback about their performance. The reality is that most people make a sharp distinction between receiving praise and receiving adverse criticism. Praise is invariably acceptable, but the extent to which people are prepared to accept criticism is limited.

Example

A principal nursing officer failed to distinguish between a senior nursing officer's capacity for receiving praise and constructive criticism. This led to considerable friction during the formal appraisal of the one by other. As a consequence the two people spoke to one another as little as possible after the interview.

When feedback does have to be given it may help to use the following checklist to decide what information should be given and in what way:

- presenting data rather than judgements,
- being specific,
- considering the needs of the person being appraised,
- praising strengths and achievements,
- offering appropriate support and recognising the need for appropriate adjustment by yourself as well as the appraisee,
- generally only giving feedback to people about issues, including their own personality, that they can do something about.

SELF-APPRAISAL

If one is to embark on the performance appraisal of subordinates, whether formally or informally, it is likely that the best results will be achieved by encouraging the subordinate, as far as possible, to engage in self-appraisal. This may necessitate the use of counselling techniques which are explained in chapter 12. Self-appraisal involves asking the subordinate to identify the appropriate criteria, the extent to which criteria have been met and areas of possible improvement. Employees may welcome the involvement this offers and may be more prepared to criticise themselves than have it done by others. People often tend to be their own harshest critics. Subordinates may also tend to overcriticise themselves for fear of seeming immodest. If this approach is taken, the manager may ironically find that they are in the position of telling the subordinates that they are being too harsh on themselves and explaining that their assessment is more favourable. However, there may be aspects of a subordinate's performance where the subordinate does not appreciate the need to improve. The manager is in a far stronger position, psychologically, to try to draw such aspects tactfully to the attention of the subordinate if they have previously been building them up, than if they had made such observations cold.

Careful judgement has to be made as to the extent to which a subordinate is able to benefit from criticism. If a person is simply going to reject it, there may be little point in pursuing discussion. Often, however, a person may be able to take a certain amount of adverse comment – the skill lies in recognising how much a person can take. If someone has volunteered three ways in which they will try to improve their performance and is able to accept direct comment about one out of three other areas in which they need to improve, it may be best simply to forget about the other two areas. If their attention is drawn to these other areas, they may become so defensive and demoralised that they refuse to accept the case for any improvement whatsoever.

INFORMAL GUIDANCE

The general philosophy of self-appraisal can be used in giving people informal guidance about how to improve their performance. It may be best to help people see for themselves how they can improve, but only to do this when it seems likely that the person will be able to benefit from such steering. The timing of discussion can be critical as well, with the manager needing to distinguish between when the time is right to help people improve and when such advice will be resisted. Often this will be best handled as problems actually occur. One of the further dangers of formal schemes is that they may be seen as a mechanism for bringing up old issues which are best forgotten. This practice has led some people to refer to the 'annual reprisal interview'. When problems do arise, a counselling technique may still be appropriate. If a subordinate has a problem, it may be best to start by asking how they think it should be handled. This may not only give the required result, but may develop the subordinate's capacity to work things out for themselves.

PEER AUDIT

A development related to self-appraisal is that of peer audit. This involves colleagues being assessed by each other. This has been used particularly in medicine and university teaching. The main benefit is that it can create a formal structure for critical self-appraisal and discussion where none existed before. It may also be more politically acceptable to professionals who often prefer to see themselves more as independent subcontractors than managed employees. Colleagues may be left to choose their partners. Alternatively, some people may be designated as auditors and employees choose which auditor evaluates their performance. This could involve some people carrying out several audits and others none. In the case of university lecturers, the audit would normally include sitting in on a teaching session with the person being audited. The technique is particularly appropriate for performance appraisal, maintaining quality standards and identifying training needs.

360-DEGREE APPRAISAL

The concept of 360-degree appraisal has increasingly attracted interest (Huggett 1988: 128–130). It involves the assessment of a person's performance by the parties particularly affected by it. The assessors may include not just the immediate boss but also other managers, immediate subordinates, internal and even external clients or customers. Sometimes information is collected by questionnaire. The theory is that this method will give a literally much more rounded assessment of a person's performance. Subordinates, for example, often have critical insights and information about a manager's strengths and weaknesses that the manager's boss does not have. However, although this form of appraisal has the potential to give a very thorough assessment there can be considerable practical difficulties in implementing it. These may include:

- the time and resource investment required;
- colleagues may be in competition with one another for promotion or other rewards and this may distort the feedback;
- it may be inappropriate to ask even internal clients to formally assess a person's performance;
- a manager's ability to control and, where necessary, discipline staff may be undermined if they also are under pressure to get good appraisal ratings from them.

The related concept of upward appraisal is often used to gain feedback about the performance of lecturers and trainers. Forms are completed anonymously and analysed either just by the person involved, their boss or client organisation as well. This can provide a useful source of information relatively easily. It is important, though, to carefully evaluate what has been reported. It may also be necessary to focus on the responsibilities of both the person who has taken a class and those who have been receiving instruction to play their part in benefiting from it.

Specific types of appraisals

Many of the points already made concerning appraisal generally apply to the range of appraisal situations. Performance appraisal is covered specifically in the next section of this chapter in the context of performance management. The appraisal of training needs is covered in the next chapter, and promotion was covered in chapter 9. However, it is appropriate to look at some of the specific issues involved in upgrading appraisals, the review of probationary employment and the review of duties.

UPGRADINGS

A particular issue that needs careful thought is the choice of the criteria by which upgradings are given or withheld. These criteria need to fit with organisational objectives and enable consistent and defensible decisions to be made. Upgrading arrangements should also motivate employees to acquire any extra knowledge and skills that are needed so that they can cope with their new pattern of work. Sometimes this is done by rewarding people for the acquisition of new and relevant job competencies. However, care also has to be taken to ensure that there is an appropriate balance of employees at the higher and lower grades, otherwise there may be a mismatch between people in a certain grade and the work available at that level. It would be somewhat counter-productive, for example, to upgrade everyone in a section leaving no one to do the routine work.

PROBATION

A particular point about probation appraisal is that arrangements for handling this often seem to be more honoured in the breach than the observance. Employees are frequently left to infer that their probation has been completed successfully by the absence of any comment whatsoever. It may even be that their performance has not been satisfactory, but the manager concerned has indicated otherwise by default, i.e. by not saying anything at the end of the stipulated period. Apart from anything else this may create difficulties in terminating the employment of an unsatisfactory employee. Even if a person does not have sufficient service to take an action for unfair dismissal to an employment tribunal, organisational procedures for dismissal are usually much more comprehensive for the person who has completed their probation. One useful device that can be used in the case of marginal performers is to extend their probationary period. This can give the probationer more time to improve whilst retaining the relative freedom of the employer to terminate if the required improvement does not materialise. However, once probationers have been employed for a year, they can contest a decision to terminate at an employment tribunal. In the case of people who have been promoted time spent in a previous job in the organisation will count towards this employment service requirement.

REVIEW OF DUTIES

The other appraisal situation that requires specific comment is where the duties of an employee are reviewed. Regular reviews of job content may be needed for a variety of reasons. Misunderstandings can easily arise about what actually is required in a job. Additionally, job demands change, and the capacity of employees to undertake particular tasks can also change. The motivational needs of employees also need to be considered, as was explained in chapter 6, as does the danger of employees wanting to do, or actually doing, work that is not in the best interests of the organisation. It is particularly necessary to remember the propensity of people to neglect managerial work in favour of specialist activity, as explained in chapter 1, and the pressures for job distortion, as explained in chapter 6.

Performance management

The concept of performance management is examined in relation to individual performance appraisal. It is also necessary to examine it in relation to setting objectives, key competencies and performance-related pay.

The term 'performance management', imported from the USA, has become increasingly fashionable, and it is important to identify its meaning. One definition of performance management is that it is :

A strategic and integrated approach to increasing the effectiveness of organisations by improving the performance of people who work in them and by developing the capabilities of teams and individual contributors.

Armstrong and Barron 1998: 38–39

Identifying training needs and appropriate pay arrangements are also usually an integral part of the performance management process.

The government in the UK has been anxious to introduce performance management in the public sector, particularly in the health service and education. Consequently, performance and quality standards have been introduced in these sectors. However, as explained in chapter 2, this can lead to an undue emphasis being placed on quantifiable measures of performance. Also performance statistics may be manipulated to show as favourable a picture as possible. For example, schools may use open or covert means of selection in order to have the best available pupils to teach in order to maintain or boost the school's performance standards. Hospital waiting lists may be reduced by giving a higher priority to minor conditions instead of more severe and resource consuming treatments. This means that performance criteria have to be selected carefully and performance results closely examined.

Whatever the problems may be in operating performance management, however, the concept is vital to the success of any organisation whatever way the performance or the organisation is managed. The emphasis on aspects such as organisational objectives, integration of activities and employee development are critical ingredients for success under whatever banner they feature.

SETTING OBJECTIVES

The process of improving performance by trying to integrate individual employee objectives with the organisation's strategic plan can be achieved via the appraisal process. To try and do this it is essential to have clear and preferably agreed upon criteria for judging performance. A methodology for doing this was explained in the context of management by objectives in chapter 2. Performance management has many similarities with management by objectives. However, performance management is a looser term than management by objectives and is not a brand name associated with one particular firm of consultants. According to Fowler performance management generally involves more emphasis on the definition of organisational mission statements aims and objectives, places less on quantification of performance and more on ownership by line management, particularly by the senior management team (1990: 47–51).

Because of the overlap between management by objectives and performance management it is as well to remember the main reasons for the collapse of formal management by objectives schemes. They were:

- their mechanistic nature,
- the lack of genuine involvement by line management,
- the ritualistic way in schemes were often introduced and applied,

- failure to recognise conflicts of interest between individual and organisational objectives,
- failure to recognise the conflicts of interest that change can create.

Objectives may be best specified in accordance with the SMART acronym:

- Specific
- Measurable
- Achievable
- Realistic
- Time-related.

Ideally objectives and any specific targets should be established at the start of the appraisal period. There should, however, be periodic dialogue about this. This is necessary because of any changes in circumstances. Also, if corrective action is necessary, it needs to be taken as soon as is practicable and not at the end of the appraisal period when it may be far too late. Even if everything is going smoothly, job-holders should be told so rather than left guessing if they are seen to be performing effectively.

When performance is assessed it is important to distinguish between work behaviour and personalities There is no point in making judgements about the people themselves unless such judgements are a necessary part of the assessment of performance. Any shortfall needs to be identified in objective terms relating to job demands and not in terms of personal failing.

The person who is normally best able to assess performance is the immediate supervisor or manager. It is prudent, though, to have someone review the assessment by the person making the appraisal. However, in the event of disagreement care needs to be taken not to override the judgement of the immediate boss who is best placed to assess performance. In the event of an appeal against a performance assessment those who hear the appeal must also be wary about imposing their own judgement. They may be well advised to concentrate on seeing the appropriate procedures were carried out. A way of handling performance appraisal is for the person conducting the appraisal to show draft reports to both the person being appraised and their own boss before the appraisal process is completed. This gives the opportunity to eliminate or minimise any disagreement by discussion before the process is finalised.

IDENTIFYING AND DEVELOPING KEY COMPETENCIES

Armstrong and Barron comment on the importance of the development of job competencies in performance management:

What is now emerging is a fully rounded view of performance that embraces how people get things done as well as what they have done. Inputs such as competencies, approaches and understanding have become as important as outputs such as products, goals attained and objectives achieved.

1998: 39

The job competence approach can be combined with objective setting by assessing the extent to which employees have developed both their job competencies and achieved their objectives. Whilst the development of job competencies can significantly enhance performance both on an individual and organisational basis there can be methodological problems in identifying and assessing them. These can include matching generic competencies with the actual key elements in a job. Also a certain amount of bargaining may take place about the extent to which competencies have been achieved or the levels of achievement.

Example

One subordinate insisted that high competence levels were essential in his job. His boss responded by saying he would agree to these high minimum levels but would take this into account when assessing the extent to which the subordinate met these high minimum levels. A knock-on effect of this was inconsistency in the minimum competencies that were set for similar jobs.

The issue of job competencies was examined in the context of job evaluation in chapter 7 and in the context of selection in chapter 9. The issue is also examined in the next chapter in the context of training.

PERFORMANCE-RELATED PAY

The increasing use of performance-related pay schemes necessitates some specific comment. This topic was held over from chapter 7, on payment systems, because of the need for performance-related pay to be grounded in an effective appraisal scheme. The distinction between general performance appraisal and performance-related pay is that with the latter there is a formal link between performance and pay. Merit payment can be viewed as a generic term that subsumes performance-related pay.

There are a number of reasons why performance-related pay has become more popular in the UK. These are:

- budgetary pressures combined with low inflation – this has caused some employers to question whether they should give both annual pay increases and automatic incremental increases within salary scales;
- the attempt to create more of a performance culture in the public sector of the UK;
- a greater stress on individual as opposed to collective terms of employment, particularly with regard to pay;
- greater fluidity and flexibility in jobs which has made the nature of many jobs more personalised;
- greater use of job competencies so that people are encouraged to develop their competencies within a job.

As with most management schemes, careful analysis is needed about both the wisdom of having performance-related pay schemes and the way in which schemes are actually operated. Important issues to consider are:

- the need for a management structure that is strong enough to operate a performance-related pay scheme – schemes place considerable responsibility on line managers;
- the need for clear and defensible criteria for awarding differential pay increases to people doing the same or comparable jobs;
- a sound appraisal scheme;
- whether increases should be given to the majority or a minority. Rewarding just the minority can have the effect of also punishing the majority. This can be exacerbated if the fixed distribution method allocating increases is used, particularly in small departments;
- whether or not there should be a fixed budget for performance increases. If there is, this can have the effect of only giving increases to those who increase their performance the most whatever the overall increase in performance may be;
- whether increases are one-off or permanent increases. Also, if increases are to be consolidated into the basic salary or not;
- whether the introduction of a scheme is to be preceded by a pilot scheme;
- identification of linkages with the identification of training needs and promotion;
- mechanisms for dealing with market shortages of particular skills. Schemes can be easily distorted by using them to increase the pay for people with skills in short supply.

The decision as to whether or not a person is to receive an increase and how much, needs to be taken in private after an informed discussion between the manager and subordinate. The discussion itself, or the subsequent communication of the decision, should not be allowed to degenerate into a bargaining session about payment. Performance-related pay is not a substitute for effective management but an aid to it. As explained in the context of performance appraisal appeal, procedures need working out, but one needs to beware of removing ultimate pay decisions from the immediate manager. The judgement of others, remote from the situation, could easily be less accurate. Consequently, appeals are best restricted to procedural issues with decisions referred back for review if the immediate manager has not handled the process adequately.

Trade unions tend to be unhappy about performance-related pay because of its emphasis on the individual employment contract as opposed to collective negotiations and the potential for divisiveness within a work force. However, they may not be in a position to actually prevent their members from having an opportunity to receive more money.

The use of performance-related pay involves risks as well as opportunities. It is likely to sharpen the interest in discussions about performance. Also, the case for trying to improve performance in organisations is self-evident. However, schemes need careful monitoring as well as designing and implementing. The increasing volume of evidence is that initiatives to introduce performance-related pay in the public sector in the UK have generally not been very successful. A key factor accounting for failure is organisational culture. Success criteria are not so easy to define. The concept of generating surplus or profit is alien to many public-sector employees. Also, management structures and management skills in the public sector are not usually as well developed or as acceptable as in the private sector.

The effect of a performance-related pay scheme introduced in the Inland Revenue in the UK was found to have the general effect of reducing motivation and teamwork (Marsden and French 1998). An investigation by the Treasury's public services productivity panel reported that:

> ... the bonus schemes in four agencies failed to increase either the commitment of staff or the quality of their work... [They are] ineffective and discredited... almost all individuals in the national office networks of the four agencies work as integrated team members, and their individual contributions are difficult to distinguish from that of the team as a whole.
>
> (Cooper 2000: 13)

Another particular problem in the public sector is the performance-related pay element is often such a small part of total pay that it has not had much motivational impact. However, part of the appeal to the Treasury regarding the public sector is that giving increases related to performance can reduce the size of annual pay awards.

Whilst performance pay schemes can work and in some cases are very necessary, there is a danger that employers concentrate either exclusively or too much on the pay element regarding performance. As explained in the chapter 6 in the context of motivation, there can be many reasons for poor performance. What is needed is an integrated and strategic approach to performance improvement that may or may not include performance-related pay.

SUMMARY

✔ Staff appraisal occurs for a variety of purposes. Unfortunately, despite the need for effective appraisal arrangements, the failure rate of formal schemes is high. Reasons include having conflicting objectives in schemes, the level of resourcing needed and the problems of giving constructive criticism as opposed to praise to those being appraised. Formal schemes need also to be supplemented by regular informal discussion and not be a substitute for ongoing dialogue.

✔ The way in which individual performance appraisal may be incorporated into an organisational strategy for performance management was examined. Performance management schemes increasingly involve focusing on employee development and organisational processes as well as achieving objectives and targets. Performance-related pay might be part of a performance management scheme. However, remuneration is only one variable affecting performance and the other variables need examining as well.

✔ As with appraisal schemes, performance-related pay can have unintended effects and examples of such effects were given. Performance-related pay schemes have tended to operate more successfully in the private than the public sector in the UK. This is particularly because of the generally different culture in the public sector.

SELF-ASSESSMENT QUESTIONS

1. For what main purposes are appraisal schemes used?

2. Why do appraisal schemes fail so often?

3. In what main ways can you try and ensure that appraisal schemes succeed?

4. How would you prepare for a formal appraisal interview?

5. What do you understand by the concept of performance management?

6. How might individual performance appraisal fit with an overall policy of performance management?

7. What are basic conditions need to be met in order for performance-related pay to be likely to succeed?

 References

Armstrong, Michael and Angela Barron (1998) 'Performance Management – Out of the Tick Box', *People Management*, 23 July.

Cooper, Cathy (2000) 'Civil Service Forced to Axe "Ineffective" Pay Systems', *People Management*, 17 February.

Fletcher, Clive (1993) 'An Idea Whose Time Has Gone?', *Personnel Management*, September.

Fowler, Alan (1990) 'Performance Management: The MBO of the '90s?', *Personnel Management*, July.

Gill, Deirdre and Bernard Ungerson (1984) *Equal Pay: The Challenge of Equal Value*, Institute of Personnel Management.

Huggett, Marianne (1998) '360-degree Feedback – Great Expectations?', *Industrial and Commercial Training*, MCB University Press, 30 (4).

Marsden D. W. and S. French (1998) 'What a Performance: Performance-related Pay in the Public Services', Centre for Economic Performance special report, London School of Economics.

Personnel Management (1993) 'Merit Pay Scheme Was Discriminatory', News section, May.

Watson, A. J. (1994) *In Search of Management, Culture, Chaos and Control in Managerial Work*, ITBS.

General references

Dowling, P. J., D. E. Welch and R. S. Schuler (1999) *International Human Resource Management: Managing People in a Multinational Context*, South-Western College Publishing , 3rd ed.

Fletcher, Clive (1997) *Routes to Improved Performance*, 2nd ed., Institute of Personnel and Development.

chapter eleven

Training

There are case studies and exercises at
http://www.thomsonlearning.co.uk
(for full details, see the listing at the
start of this book).

LEARNING OUTCOMES

By the end of this chapter you will be able to:

- Diagnose your own training needs and those of others

- Identify the main ways in which training needs can be met

- Understand recent developments in training

- Understand the need for and ways in which managers can be trained and developed

- Conduct a basic evaluation of the effectiveness of a training activity

Introduction

It is becoming increasingly important to have a well-trained workforce. The key reasons for this include the increased pace of change and greater competition. The various ways in which training needs can be identified are covered in this chapter. They include performance and training appraisal, ongoing supervision, changes in the external environment including the law, the identification of the training implications of change and identification of problem areas where training might secure an improvement. Training also needs to be implemented effectively. This involves considering the ways in which people learn and the options in training delivery.

Recent developments in training are covered and particularly include the radical changes that have occurred in the UK as a result of the establishment of National Vocational Qualifications (NVQs). These involve the identification of required behavioural outcomes in terms of competencies. NVQs are not courses in the traditional sense but standards by which people are assessed. Learning is seen as occurring in a variety of ways including that which occurs on the job. As well as replacing traditional arrangements such as craft apprenticeships, the methodology behind NVQ training is having an increasingly important impact on the whole range of occupational training and professional training and on the education provided in schools, colleges and universities. Other developments that are examined include the concept of the learning organisation and the Investors in People scheme.

Specific attention is paid in this chapter to the need for effective management training and development. The various obstacles to effectiveness in this area are identified. A particular problem with management training is that for it to be effective managers need to alter their personal behaviour towards others. Recent developments in management training and development are also examined. Finally, the ways in which training activities can be evaluated are considered. The key element in this is to try and identify what changes in behaviour have occurred as a result of training and to assess how appropriate they are. If training has not resulted in changes in behaviour it is necessary to question what the point of it has been.

There is often confusion and overlap between the terms training and development. The distinction used in this chapter between the two terms is that training is specific and formally planned. The overlapping concept of development is a wider one which involves exposing people to situations and giving them responsibilities where they will develop their work skills in a much more general and often more fundamental way.

Identification of training needs

IMPORTANCE OF TRAINING

Training has always been an issue that organisations need to take seriously and, if organised effectively, should be viewed as an essential investment and not an avoidable cost. The return on the investment involved should be such that employees reach an acceptable standard of performance more quickly than would otherwise have been the case. It is also a way of ensuring that employees perform to approved standards and avoid bad working practices. The standards achieved if training is properly organised are also likely to be higher than in organisations where training is neglected.

Training and development have become even more important as a result of recent developments. These developments include the accelerating rate of change and increased competitive pressures brought about by factors such as globalisation and the increasing development and application of information technology. The very ability of commercial organisations to strategically position themselves in the market place is likely to depend on them having the right permutation of often very sophisticated expertise in order to meet market needs. The existence of expertise, or the potential to develop it, can also create strategic options.

Public sector and non-governmental organisations have to take the identification of training needs seriously too. They are increasingly expected to learn from commercial organisations and to obtain value for money in their operations. They also need to be able to interact effectively with other organisations by, for example, keeping abreast of recent developments in information technology. Related developments are the concepts of continuous learning and the learning organisation. Both of these issues are examined later in this chapter.

Another important factor is the increasing amount of capital equipment at the disposal of employees. There is little point in buying expensive equipment and then not having it used properly because employees do not have the skills to operate it. An even greater danger is that employees will misuse equipment or facilities so that expensive mistakes are made. Another basic issue is that the willingness and the ability of employees to co-operate in implementing change may be considerably influenced by the extent to which they have been equipped to handle any such change.

The cumulative effect of the above developments is that both individuals and organisations have to increase their investment in training, including retraining, in order to remain effective. For this to happen it is crucial that managers regularly review their own training needs and those of subordinate staff. Individuals also need to take responsibility for identifying their own needs. The rate of technological change and the reduced predictability of career paths make it increasingly difficult to judge what the needs are and individual employees may be the ones best placed to make an informed guess about the nature of their training needs. This may involve them in identifying how they retain or develop their marketability in case they lose their jobs, for example, in a restructuring exercise.

METHODOLOGY OF IDENTIFYING TRAINING NEEDS

There are a variety of ways in which training needs can be identified. The methods used may overlap with one another. Key methods are:

- establishing the training needs of newcomers to an organisation: newcomers will normally need some induction training so that they are made aware of the context in which they work. Consideration may also need to be given to the remedial training that they may need to be able to perform the basic tasks in their job;
- identifying the gap between actual and potential performance: this may be done by a process of formal performance appraisal and/or ongoing informal managerial assessment of how training might improve performance. Such activities may be conducted on an individual or departmental basis or both;
- training needs assessment: again, this may be by a formal process of appraisal and/or ongoing informal managerial assessment of training needs. The focus may include the long-term developmental needs of individuals and groups to prepare them for the future. This may include preparing people for promotion and for them to be able to handle future organisational changes. Sometimes assessment centres are used as an element in this process. The way in which assessment centres operate was explained in chapter 9 in the context of selection;

- self-assessment: given the increasing pace of change, individuals may be far better placed than their organisation to map the career paths that may be available and the direction in which they want to go. They may also need to demonstrate that they are developing their knowledge and skills in order to retain membership of a professional body;
- peer audit: professional-level employees may be dependent on colleagues rather than managers for constructive comment about how they can develop their specialist skills. Such comment may also be more acceptable from peers, especially if the professionals concerned are resistant to a managerial culture;
- identification of problem areas: problems often centre around low levels of through-put and failure to meet quality standards. Many of these problem areas may be susceptible to training;
- identifying the training implications of organisational change: any organisational change has potential training implications that need to be identified. The greater the pace of change, the greater the potential training need. Such needs may arise from organisational restructuring, specific initiatives, new working arrangements, including the introduction of new equipment and changes in the law. Unfortunately, such training needs are often overlooked or inadequately met.

(Example) A national bank in the UK launched a major campaign advertising a new financial product. However, many of the branch staff did not have the details of the new product properly explained to them. Consequently, many potential accounts were lost because of failures by staff to handle customer enquiries effectively.

Great care has to be taken to ensure that training needs are realistically identified. The need for training can all too easily be used as a spurious alibi for explaining all short-comings in performance. Furthermore, performance problems are not always the fault of the individual concerned. What at first sight may seem to be a training requirement may, on closer examination, prove to be a case for changing work arrangements, amending policy or even buying-in particular skills. The problems of diagnosing the real issues can sometimes be so complex that the initial diagnosis has to be changed. Organisational weaknesses may emerge that need correcting instead of, or as well as, having a training intervention . Even if there is a training intervention, it may need to be with a different group of people.

Realism has to be used in judging whether a particular person will benefit from training – some individuals have a remarkable talent for emerging unscathed after the most rigorous of training. Training is not always about the acquisition of new knowledge or skills. Sometimes changes in attitude are needed. However, realism may also be needed in this area as employees may need convincing of both the need for and personal advantage to them of developing a different attitude. There may also be limits to the extent to which people can change.

(Example) A department head of a local authority had poor working relationships with his immediate colleagues. His boss decided that a training workshop on teamwork

CONTINUED OVER ➤

CONTINUED FROM
PREVIOUS PAGE
involving the members of the management team in the department concerned might improve matters. Unfortunately, it soon emerged that the abrasive managerial style of the department head was so entrenched that no significant improvement was possible. If anything, the workshop made matters worse by making the head even more defensive and dashing the expectations of improvement held by the rest of his management team. The realistic options were for the boss to move the head out of his job, for the people concerned, including the boss, to come to terms with his managerial style, or for people to leave.

Cost issues that need to be worked out include the marginal costs of releasing an employee, the other things the employee could be doing in that time and the time it will take for there to be a return on the training investment. Training should be geared to the major problems and issues facing an organisation – that way it is more likely to be seen as a necessary investment rather than an expendable cost. It also needs to be recognised that some needs can disappear, for example, when skills are transferred from operators and are handled automatically by new equipment. The development of the flexible organisation means that it is also increasingly important to consider the training needs of the peripheral workforce.

Meeting training needs

RESOURCE OPTIONS

There are a variety of ways in which training and developmental needs can be met. These include on-the-job coaching and planned job rotation and progression. Formal training arranged either externally or internally may also be appropriate. The better managers are likely to systematically identify opportunities to help subordinates improve themselves. If they do this, managers may find that, when the performance of those subordinates is assessed, there is often relatively little need for further improvement.

THE MANAGER AS COACH

Managers vary widely in their ability and willingness to undertake a coaching role. However, given the need for generally greater training investment, it is increasingly necessary for them to do this. Sometimes it may be more effective for managers to coach an employee on the job than for such training to be provided off the job. Coaching may be necessary not just because of the need for subordinates to develop but also to enable a manager to delegate.

The role of the coach also needs to be considered in the context of managerial style. Some managers may have a working relationship with their subordinates such that subordinates are encouraged to discuss work problems with their boss and in that way learn from them. The managers may also be able to treat mistakes more as learning opportunities than occasions for censure. It is necessary for bosses to see that formal training dovetails with on-the-job learning and is not an unrelated activity.

FORMAL TRAINING

Sometimes managers see training as something to be handled entirely by external providers, including an organisation's training department. However, there is only so much that can be handled externally, and even that may not be appropriate. People sometimes offer themselves for training that is not related to their needs. This can be for a variety of reasons, including an inflated view of the level at which they require training. A person may opt for a seminar on corporate strategy when their needs may be much more basic, such as the need to develop supervisory skills. External training may also be sought because of its prestige, enjoyment, or the prospects it offers for getting a job with a competitor.

Whilst it would be a dangerously parochial view to ignore what external training providers can offer, one must also be clear about the potential conflict of interests between an organisation selling training services and one considering buying those services. Standardised packages may be inappropriate for particular buyers, as can consultancy services generally. Also one has to beware of entering into dependency relationships with outside organisations that discourage client organisations from working out their own strategies for salvation. Other problems include the lack of responsibility of consultants for implementation and the lack of ownership of their recommendations by the client organisation. Care has to be taken too about buying in programmes that are related to the latest fashion and not the needs of an organisation. One sales technique can be to 'bounce' a senior manager into a commitment before those with the internal expertise to judge the appropriateness of what is on offer have had an opportunity to comment. However, external providers may have useful or even vital access to expertise and resources. Potential customers simply need to beware that what is on offer is not always aligned to their needs.

One way of checking the relevance of what courses are on offer is to examine the objectives, or intended outcomes, and to compare these with the actual, as opposed to imagined, needs of subordinates. If the objectives or outcomes of courses are not clearly stated, that in itself may tell you something about the care, or lack of care, with which the course has been designed. The statement of objectives or outcomes can also help in checking if a person has benefited from a course. It is this, rather than just asking a person what they thought about a particular course, that is the acid test. When external training is appropriate the manager needs also to help the subordinate to apply any relevant lessons, rather than let them suffer the frustration of seeing what needs to be done but being unable to do anything about it. A disciplined approach such as this should enable a judgement to be made as to whether the training activity has resulted in a worthwhile return on the investment made.

WAYS OF LEARNING

Whatever method of learning is used it is necessary to consider the ways in which people actually learn. This may vary from person to person and according to the nature of the knowledge to be acquired or skill to be developed. There may also be cultural differences in learning. People from authoritarian and collectivist countries may be more comfortable with prescriptive approaches whilst those from individualistic cultures may prefer to have a significant amount of experiential learning where they work things out for themselves. Whoever is responsible for organising learning for others needs to examine the fit between their training style and the learning style of the people concerned.

Example

A newly appointed lecturer in the UK conscientiously prepared his lecture material for the sessions that he took for a whole academic year. Towards the end of the year one of his students, who had attended regularly, explained that he would not be taking the examination. The lecturer was surprised at this as he felt that the student had been thoroughly prepared for the examination. After considerable private discussion the student eventually explained that it was because he had hardly understood a word the lecturer had said all year! This did, however, cause the lecturer to pay serious attention to his teaching methods in the future so that at least he learned from the error of his ways. It also caused him to question whether the term 'lecturer' was a helpful one as it carried an implication that the primary way in which people learn is from lectures.

The above example illustrates the need for checks to made about the effectiveness of training whilst it is in progress. The example also demonstrates the dangers of assuming that information that is imparted is actually absorbed, as was explained in chapter 8 on communication. If the learning process is ineffective, remedial action needs to be taken quickly. Early feedback on performance is necessary both for the instructor as well as those receiving training. Unfortunately, the authority system in many learning relationships is such that the blame for failure is often placed on those receiving the training.

Example

A student on a master's programme in the fine arts in the UK who had teaching experience complained about the lack of any obvious learning strategies for those on her programme. The response she got was that the institution had a policy of 'high ability intake', and those who could not cope with the programme as it was had no business being on it.

Strategies for effective learning

Strategies for ensuring that learning activities are effective include the following:

- Specify realistic learning outcomes that are clear to both the trainer and trainee. If standards are too high, less learning will occur compared with the establishment of lower but attainable targets. However, if standards are set too low this can create problems with regard to achievement and motivation.

- Ensure that learning inputs are aligned to the specified learning outcomes. Unfortunately, people responsible for learning inputs sometimes concentrate on 'talking at' people rather than identifying and then explaining what students need to learn.

- Try to ensure that those responsible for the learning of others pay attention to the manner in which learning is likely to be most effective. Many people automatically assume that the level, manner and language that comes naturally to them is equally convenient to others. Learning is much more likely to be effective if they identify the starting point of trainees and make regular checks to see how they are progressing. Trainers need to evaluate the effectiveness of their presentation skills. This was a topic that was covered in chapter 8 in the section on presentational skills which includes a comprehensive checklist.

- Trainers need to be aware of the concept of the learning curve. People may take a long time getting started but then accelerate. Learning targets need to be aligned to where people are on the learning curve.

- Many routine tasks simply involve getting people to do things in a specified sequence. It is necessary for those responsible for the training to invest time in identifying the most logical sequence before trying to explain it to trainees. Doing this may reveal illogicalities in existing work methods. Speed generally comes from people avoiding unnecessary movements rather than deliberate attempts to work quickly, which can create errors. When a routine sequence has been mastered by trainees, however, performance may fall because of boredom.

- Consideration needs to be given of the motivation of trainees to learn. They may need to be convinced of the benefits to them as well as to the organisation.

- Checks need to be taken on the effectiveness of the process: care needs to be taken to ensure that the explanation of theory is at a level and pace in line with the ability of people to absorb it. Theory may need to be interspersed with opportunities for practical application, which may also create theoretical insights.

| Example | A lecturer in photography used to give students feedback on their performance after every few photographs they took. However, it was found administratively convenient to get the students to do their fieldwork in much longer periods. Unfortunately this had the effect of each student often repeating basic errors in a hundred or more photographs instead of being shown how to correct these errors early on. |

- The link between theory and practice and the timing of feedback on performance is an issue that may need to be addressed in many other programmes. The training of medical students and nurses may, for example, suffer because of the long periods of theoretical college training before they see a patient.

- Consideration may also need to be given to the sequence in which theoretical explanation and practical application take place. The traditional approach is to explain the theory and then give those being trained the opportunity to apply it. However, this does not always work.

A series of courses were run on disciplinary handling in a large manufacturing company in the UK. Relevant law was carefully explained in as clear and interesting a way as possible. However, when the managers were asked to apply the law in a case study they were generally unable to apply even basic concepts. This was because they had not absorbed the legal information in a meaningful way. Consequently, the sequence was reversed and the case study given first. This focused the managers minds on what was really relevant and motivated them to ask appropriate questions to the tutor during syndicate discussions. They were also more receptive to a presentation of basic legal issues after the case study exercise. The reversal of sequence also made it a much more interesting experience for them.

- Sometimes it may be appropriate to reverse the process of theoretical explanation followed by practical application. This is because some people learn more after exposure to some of the practical issues. This reversed sequence may be particularly suitable for some subject areas and is often appropriate in management training.
- Some training may involve changing attitudes. This may be more difficult than the development of new skills. Trainees may need to be convinced of the legitimacy of the recommended attitudes before reviewing their own. The problems in doing this are often underestimated when attempts are made to change organisational culture, particularly if the benefits of the change to the actual employees are not obvious. Attitude change may be more easily accomplished in countries that have a high power distance and collectivist orientation such as Japan than in low power distance and individualistic national cultures such as the UK. However, such training may be much more likely to be effective if it involves group discussion and not just exhortation. This is because it will give the people concerned more chance to reason through the issues and develop a sense of involvement and commitment.
- Consideration needs to be given to organisational support and the reinforcement of learning. Good training practice needs to be reinforced by working practices and not undermined by them.

In one police station in the UK new members were told by some staff to forget what they had learned at the police training college and live in the real world. Unfortunately, the real world included corrupt practices which led to the prosecution of some of the police officers concerned.

TECHNOLOGICAL DEVELOPMENTS

Developments in electronics are significantly increasing the range of ways in which training can be delivered. This includes more opportunity for computer-assisted learning, interactive training videos and the development of the information super-highway using fibre-optic cabling that makes educational and training packages widely available. A related development is the need for the latest information and advice about governmental regulations. Needs in this area have increased because of greater governmental regulations in developed countries and European intervention in setting detailed standards and protections with regard to consumers, the public, the environment and employees. This increase in regulation has often coincided with a reduction in the number of specialist advisers available because of organisational de-layering. A way of managers coping with the extra responsibilities placed upon them is by having access to packages and Internet services explaining government regulations and how to comply with them. Such developments are increasingly making training providers the co-ordinators of training and information services rather than simply trainers.

A related development is the concept of a University of Industry in the UK. This is intended to operate as a virtual organisation offering flexible training packages via both home computers and work-based personal computers as well as those available to the general public. According to UK Chancellor of the Exchequer Gordon Brown:

> As the Open University achieved in the 1960s, this initiative has the potential to transform the way we view education. Small business owners, mothers and illiterate 16-year-olds can be reintroduced to training through the innovations taking place in information technology.
>
> *1996: 9*

Despite the potential of the concept of the University of Industry, it remains to be seen how effectively the political rhetoric is converted into practical reality. Key issues will be the relevance of training to organisational needs, funding, and the response both of users and employers.

THE EFFECTIVENESS OF TRAINING DEPARTMENTS

An issue that managers may need to carefully consider is the competence of their own training department, if they have one. Effective training is literally disturbing, as the whole point of it is to alter existing patterns of behaviour. Some training departments help identify and facilitate such change, whilst others either opt out of mainstream activity or are never allowed near it. This can result in the activity of a training department being anaesthetised. An indication of this phenomenon is the preoccupation of a training department with 'soft' options that do not contain a workshop element. Training may instead be focussed on prescriptive packages involving skills, such as report-writing, and time management that may be marginally useful to some of the individuals attending courses. A further feature may be that such activities are easily administered. However, such options are not likely to be part of a coherent strategy to address the key issues facing the organisation that require significant changes in individual behaviour.

Another measure of effectiveness is whether the training department is working in relative isolation from line management and engaging in training that is merely fashionable, random or token, or perhaps all three. Hopefully, managers who want a genuine contribution from their training department will encourage them to become involved with real issues that are relevant to the needs of the organisation and not connive in their relegation to dealing only with peripheral issues. Genuine training and development also involves those in senior positions considering what adjustments they may need to make in their behaviour and support.

Example

The chief executive of a financial services organisation that was experiencing trading difficulties arranged for all his managers to attend a two day residential management training workshop. However, he saw no need to stay after his introductory comments nor to meet the managers afterwards to identify what they had learned and to listen to what suggestions they had for organisational improvement. He believed that the only people who needed to change their behaviour were the managers. This is similar to one partner in a troubled marriage expecting the other partner to be the only one to receive marriage guidance counselling.

THE RESPONSIBILITY OF THE INDIVIDUAL

As explained in the earlier section on the identification of training needs, individuals need to increasingly take responsibility for managing their own training needs. They may be the best person to judge their own needs anyway. In addition, however, they can hardly expect their employer to take a keen interest in helping them develop if their objective is to move to another organisation. Continuing membership of professional bodies may also depend on individuals demonstrating that they have made adequate attempts to maintain and develop their expertise. This is explained in more detail in the next section.

Recent developments

THE LEARNING ORGANISATION

A number of developments have led to the concept of the learning organisation. This has been defined as 'an organisation which facilitates the learning of all its members and continuously transforms itself' (Pedler, Burgoyne and Boydell 1991). It overlaps with the concept of individual continuous development. However, it can be difficult to distinguish between good intentions and practical achievement. Some of the factors that have contributed to the practical and theoretical development of the concept have already been examined independently. These include the increasing rate of change, the greater need for flexible organisational structures, the concept of continuous improvement and the need to structure the pattern of interactions within an organisation so that there can be optimum interaction between its members.

The objective of the learning organisation is to enable those involved in an organisation to learn and thereby adapt in line with external changes and internal developments. This is meant to involve structuring the whole organisation so that such learning is facilitated, particularly in an experiential manner. This makes the approach qualitatively different from discrete 'bolted-on' training activities. The process ideally involves all key stakeholders, including customers and suppliers. The successful creation of a learning organisation is seen as the key to organisational survival and development. Other aspects are the importance of learning from those engaged in other functions so that a 'holistic' approach can be developed. Human resources are seen as 'elastic' and in need of effective motivation and development. The learning organisation also creates a learning climate that in turn creates and is reinforced by a social system that values and encourages learning.

The learning organisation also needs to fit with organisational culture and managerial style. It is much more likely to flourish in organic adaptive organisations than in mechanistic bureaucratic ones. Another basic requirement is that managers have an open style of management and are receptive to new ideas rather than adopt a prescriptive and secretive style.

The objectives of the learning organisation are praiseworthy. However, it is important that its practical implementation is thought out rather than create a climate where anything goes. Not all development opportunities can or should be followed up – otherwise organisational activity may lack coherence. There is the danger too that individuals may assume that personal developmental opportunities are automatically beneficial for the organisation. Employers need to be clear what the benefits of developmental activities are to the organisation as well as to the individuals concerned. In stable situations, or ones where risks need to be carefully controlled, strong central direction may be entirely appropriate. It may be very difficult to create an experiential learning climate when an organisation is restructuring or down-sizing.

CONTINUOUS DEVELOPMENT

The concept of continuous development is being gradually but unevenly applied to membership and training arrangements by professional bodies (IPD 1993). Some now make continuous professional development a condition of membership. This involves members being able to demonstrate that they are maintaining and developing their skills, particularly in core areas. A coherent strategy for self-development is also required. There is also a need for educational institutions to place an increasing emphasis on teaching people to learn how to learn and to help them manage such ongoing development. The pace of change is such that on long formal programmes a significant amount of material covered early on may be out of date before the programme is completed. Judgements about learning priorities and access to reference material are increasingly important because of the ongoing explosion in the quantity of information.

The UK government is also considering promoting continuous learning by the creation of individual learning accounts (ILAs) for vocational training. These accounts are aimed at adults and will be partly financed by tax concessions to both employers and employees. However, the size of the payments available for training activities are relatively small and developments are still at an experimental stage.

NATIONAL VOCATIONAL QUALIFICATIONS AND RELATED DEVELOPMENTS

Basic framework and purpose

There have been radical and comprehensive developments regarding the organisation of much of the vocational training in the UK. A new national framework for training has been created which replaces the former craft apprentice training arrangements and a large range of other occupational training arrangements as well. The comprehensive new framework includes business and administrative training. The certificates that are now awarded are National Vocational Qualifications (NVQs and SNVQs in Scotland). Vocational Advanced (A) level subjects that are modelled on the NVQ competence based system have also been introduced in schools and further education colleges. Much of the thinking comes from the German model where a paid job with workplace training was traditionally an option for school leavers (Rose and Wignanek 1990). The national policy in the UK is to increase the standing of vocational training, to reduce the divide between the vocational and academic areas and to make academically based training more rigorous. Universities are also encouraged by the government to include NVQs in generally widened admissions criteria.

Organisation of NVQs

NVQs are not courses in the traditional sense. They are national standards against which employees (or prospective employees) are assessed. Employers and training providers help people acquire the necessary knowledge and skill to reach the required standard. Training needs are expressed in terms of required behaviour rather than knowledge to be acquired. The standards are defined as occupational competencies and are set within a range of five graded levels by National Training Organisations (NTOs) in specific occupational areas. Supervisory and management skills are covered by grades 3–5. People wishing to acquire NVQs in these areas need to have some basic supervisory or management responsibility. Five key skills have been established that are common to all occupational areas. They are:

- information technology,
- application of numbers (numeracy),
- communication,
- working with others,
- improving your own performance (learning how to learn).

In order to qualify for an award, people need to demonstrate that they have the designated levels of key skills for the NVQ they are pursuing as well as the designated occupational skills. National traineeships are awarded at level 2. The requirement for a modern apprenticeship is NVQ level 2 and also level 3. Trainees are also required to have specified enhanced skills for some occupations.

These arrangements facilitate speedier progression than traditional training by providing for recognition of existing competencies, however acquired, and by excluding irrelevant knowledge. The national framework means that NVQs are standardised and not geared just to the needs of individual employers. Skills are therefore more easily transferred between employing organisations. Training, where required, takes place in a number of ways. It is likely to include coaching, supplemented by formal 'off the-job' training as and when necessary. Standards devised by the National Training Organisations have to be approved by the Government's Qualification and Curriculum Authority (QCA). The QCA also accredit awarding bodies such as the City and Guilds (London Institute) and industry specific bodies.

The accreditation process

The accreditation process typically involves specialist qualified occupational assessors regularly visiting candidates in their place of work to conduct reviews of work completed since their last meeting in accordance with the candidate's Individual Training Plan (ITP). A portfolio of evidence is developed to confirm the standards achieved. Trainees need to be able to demonstrate that they can actually perform whole work roles to appropriate standards in the workplace. Portfolio evidence is summarised on Candidate Assessment Record Sheets (CARS). The portfolios are subject to internal verification by the NVQ programme providers and external verification from the awarding body before an NVQ can be awarded. One of the roles of approved training providers is to simplify the administrative complexities to employing organisations

Financing

The incentive for NVQ training has been reinforced by the statutory right of 16- to 17-year-olds in the UK to have paid time off for NVQ level qualifications or their equivalent under the terms of the Teaching and Higher Education Act of 1998. Substantial funding is available for those in the age range 16–18. It can also usually be accessed for those in the age range 19–24. Some organisations have established comprehensive NVQ training for all age groups using accredited in-house assessors because of the innate benefits of the process and do not rely on public funding. The NVQ system does require significant public investment and considerable paperwork. However, it is the government's intention that 85 per cent of all young people attain level 2 qualifications, or their equivalent, by age 19 by 2002.

Impact of NVQs

The training developments outlined above represent a major break with tradition. Inevitably, there have been problems in introducing sweeping changes in the training field. Employers can find that NVQ standards are broader than they require for their organisational needs. This is likely given that the qualifications are awarded for the ability to meet national occupational standards. The balance between knowledge and competence can be skewed too much towards physical performance; it is often necessary for people to have a theoretical underpinning to a competence if they are to have versatility. The higher the level of the competence, the more this can be a problem especially with management competencies, as will be explained later in this chapter. The volume and validity of assessment can also present major problems, particularly pressures to generate a throughput of qualified students. Other issues are the complexity of the related bureaucracy and the need for more co-operation from employers. Hopefully, though, progress can be made in resolving, or reducing the scale of such problems as the new approach has much to commend it. The overall strategy is an essential element of creating a high value-added base for the national economy.

Impact of the NVQ process elsewhere in the UK

Some of the NVQ thinking is being adopted elsewhere in the education system. Standardisation of qualifications and national scrutiny of assessment procedures has taken place within the school system by the creation of the Schools Curriculum and Assessment Authority. Important innovations in Higher Education (including universities) and training for some professional qualifications include learning development contracts, modular course design, accreditation for prior learning (APL), and accreditation for prior experiential learning (APEL). The establishment of the Quality Assurance Agency (QAA) is also having a significant effect on university education. Individual subject areas are assessed under six headings and points awarded for each. Key elements in this evaluation process are examining the extent to which stated aims are met, the strategy for achieving these aims and the statement of explicit learning outcomes for specific academic activities. The results are published which helps prospective students make informed choices about which programmes at which university to apply for. This in turn creates a powerful pressure on universities to examine the effectiveness of their curriculum design and learning strategies.

Historically, in both craft trades and in the professions, the length and complexity of training was sometimes used as a means of restricting entry to an occupation in order to manipulate the labour market to their own advantage. The new approaches challenge such restrictive arrangements. Even in those professions where there has been no covert policy of restricting entry, some of them have yet to undertake a fundamental appraisal of their arrangements for training and membership. The new ideas are already having a significant impact on job design, occupational standards, syllabus structure and content and methods of training delivery of many professions.

LEARNING AND SKILLS COUNCILS

In the UK developments such as national vocational qualifications were boosted by the creation of 82 county-based Training and Enterprise Councils (TECs) in the early 1990s. They were particularly concerned with the development of a skilled workforce and economic regeneration. The TECs were subsequently reorganised and were replaced in 2001 by eight Learning and Skills Councils. This was in order to reduce administrative costs and achieve greater standardisation. Responsibility for retraining unemployed adults has been transferred to the Employment Service. The councils continue to give advice to employers on training issues and administer training grants. Business advice is also available from them.

INVESTORS IN PEOPLE

The councils still give advice about how organisations can obtain accreditation as members of the Investors in People (IIP) scheme. The central organisation is Investors in People UK. To gain accreditation employers must demonstrate that they have a coherent training policy and plan, which is adequately resourced and which delivers appropriate results. Organisations must also have an explicit commitment to equal employment opportunities. To retain accreditation employers need to either have an annual external audit or reapply every three years. Ideally, organisations use the scheme as a framework for identifying and meeting important training needs and not simply as a public relations kitemark to help attract more customers or clients. The IIP framework is best integrated with existing training arrangements, not as a separate set of policies and procedures.

Management training and development

THE NEED FOR EFFECTIVENESS

As explained in chapter 1, the effectiveness of organisations can critically depend on its level of managerial expertise. As also explained in that chapter, the biggest problem often facing organisations is the preference of those with managerial responsibilities to neglect these duties in favour of specialist activity. Effective management training and development can do much to rectify this.

OBSTACLES TO EFFECTIVE MANAGEMENT TRAINING AND DEVELOPMENT

There are many obstacles to achieving effective management training and development. These need to be recognised if effective strategies are to be developed.

Cost

Management training and development can be costly and the results difficult to verify. Some of the training on offer is poor, or may fail because it is given to the wrong people. There is also the problem that employees having received a substantial training investment may leave. This is much more likely in the UK than in a country like Japan where there is a strong tradition in many parts of the economy of people staying with the same employer. When there is pressure on budgets, long-term and speculative investments like management training are not likely to receive favour and training and development budgets are particularly vulnerable when short-term economies are required. However, if management training is carefully planned and targeted it is likely to be much more of an essential investment than an expendable cost.

Ineffective training

Management training and development can easily fail, and it is necessary to examine the processes involved carefully. Too often management training is undertaken on a random basis, without clear objectives, or delivered in an ineffective way. Particular causes of ineffective management training are:

- the people sent on management courses may fail to benefit because they were wrongly selected for their jobs;
- the training is not geared to organisational needs and developments;
- the organisational culture is not supportive to the training;
- inadequate attention is paid to both organisational and national culture; these factors may affect the environment in which people have to operate and the ways in which they learn;
- the timing is wrong – training may be offered too early or too late in people's careers for them to make effective use of it;
- training can be orientated around the needs of the individual, which are not always the same as the organisation;
- the diagnosis of need may be right but the training delivery may be ineffective – many training contractors, for example, provide programmes that are based around standard prescriptive packages, not around carefully diagnosed organisational needs;
- a wide range of topics can be passed off as falling within the definition of management education and training: training can switch to being about management instead of being for managers and be taught as a set of unrelated theoretical disciplines which can aggravate the problem of the compartmentalisation of management activity;
- undergraduate and other pre-experience management training needs to be reinforced by further training once those concerned have had greater exposure to management problems – such exposure is likely to lead to an increased awareness of what the problems really are and the concepts and skills that may assist in their resolution;

- The expectations of what management training can do are often unrealistic. Sponsors and managers may believe that there are easy prescriptive solutions to most management problems that can easily be learned and applied, but development in managerial expertise is often much more complicated than that;
- the skills of effective teaching are sophisticated and in short supply and the effectiveness of teaching in this area is difficult to validate;
- management training and development, unlike purely technical training, has to be integrated with personal behaviour. This is a particularly sensitive area, and egos can easily get bruised if people feel that their job performance is being criticised. Consequently, lessons that people need to learn may be blocked because they are too personally threatening. Also the mere acquisition of knowledge does not mean that people become better managers unless they are willing and able to apply that knowledge;
- even if training is effective one needs to ensure that the result has been achieved in the most cost-effective way.

ACTION LEARNING

One potentially useful approach to management training and development is action learning (Revans 1987). This can combine problem-solving with management development so that organisations gain a double benefit. It also ensures that development is focused on an organisation's real problems. A further advantage is that if it is conducted in-house on a group basis it overcomes the problem of managers being sent on external programmes and returning to a working environment that may be unsympathetic or unsupportive to any new ideas they have developed. Use of the technique of role set analysis in this context, explained in chapter 2, can prove particularly useful .

Action learning purists maintain that working in almost any other management area is likely to bring useful insights into one's existing job. Whilst there may be an element of truth in this, resource constraints mean that action learning needs to be focused on the issues most likely to yield benefit and not on a random basis. Consequently, it may or may not need to include the secondment of individuals into other management functions.

RECENT DEVELOPMENTS

The Management Charter Initiative and related developments

The publication of the Handy Report (1987) helped focus attention in the UK on the need for urgent action with regard to management training and development. This helped precipitate a lively debate about the improvements that were necessary. One of the developments was the Management Charter Initiative (MCI) in 1993. Many of the proposals contained in the original MCI were welcome and generally supported, such as the need for employers and the government to invest more in management education and training. Employers associated with the initiative were also committed to developing networks to achieve this. The mission of the MCI became clarified as 'to improve the performance of UK organisations by improving the quality of UK managers' (MCI 1993). The MCI organisation is the National Training Organisation for NVQs in management.

Whilst the case for improving the standards of management is overwhelming, there are specific problems involved in defining standards and in checking that they have been achieved. The competence approach adopted by the MCI has led to some difficulties with regard to definition and assessment. Competence is more specific than skill, as it is restricted to job performance standards based on an occupational analysis of the kind used in the NVQ approach. Competence definition and assessment is easiest when tasks have to be performed in an exact way. Concerns about the management competencies approach include:

- the competence approach lends itself more easily to the identification and development of manual skills which are relatively easily identified and assessed;
- the need for theoretical underpinning of managerial concepts;
- the need for a holistic approach to management. There is the danger of assessing competence or designing training on too compartmentalised a basis. A key attribute of managers may be the ability to synthesise knowledge and skills relating to a wide range of activities;
- the variety in managerial roles and expectations of what managers will do;
- the volume of assessments and the problems of making valid assessments anyway. The difficulties of doing this are of a completely different order compared with, for example, assessing manual skills. The skills (or competencies) of accurate problem diagnosis, decision-making and soundness of judgement may be crucial to effective management performance but be very difficult to assess. Valid assessments may also be resource intensive;
- assessment and learning can conflict, because of the volume of assessment that may be required and the inhibiting effect that assessment can have on experimentation and enquiry. This can be a significant problem in activities where both learning and assessment are expected;
- the competence approach does not provide a framework for teamwork and team development;
- the crucial distinction between people demonstrating competence in an assessment and securing appropriate performance outcomes. The observation of a person's behaviour during an assessment simulation or written evidence about their skills may not give an accurate indication of how they really behave in practice;

A further complication has been that specialists who have acquired management responsibility may also not see the need nor be prepared to study for management qualifications. The effective conversion of specialists into managers of specialists, however, needs to be seen in the context of the need for much more and much better management training generally. The competence approach can, however, help in the effective targeting of management training activity, although it is important that it is not used in an excessively mechanistic and bureaucratic way. Some of the criticisms apply to traditional methods of teaching management anyway. Also, whatever qualifications a person obtains, it is particularly necessary in the management area to use the selection process to check that people have the appropriate personal qualities to be able to perform adequately.

Constable and McCormick estimated that of the 3 million managers in the UK most received no formal training and that the average amount of time spent on training was only one day a year (1987: 3). Thomson *et al.* (1997) estimated that this had risen to 5.2 days each year. Also, as explained in chapter 1, there has been a substantial increase in the provision of qualification courses. However, because of the reasons explained above providing effective training is difficult. In commenting on the Thomson report, Caulkin stated:

> *By common consent, around half the £2 billion spent every year on UK executive development may be frittered away on jaunts, snake-oil remedies, or classroom theory with little relevance.*
>
> *1997: 4*

Thomson *et al.* (1997) also reported that whilst there was clearly no one appropriate model for management training and development in the UK there was a great need for organisations to develop consistent strategies that met their particular needs.

Mentoring

The concept of mentoring has begun to develop in the UK. Whilst some mentoring may take place by the immediate boss, formal mentoring involves the appointment of a more senior manager in a different, if related, department. The organisational distance this creates can reduce the political problems in the relationship. It can also bring detachment to the role and widen the experience of the person being mentored. Much depends on the enthusiasm of the parties and the process skills of the mentor.

Sometimes it may be appropriate to appoint an external mentor (Rees 1992: 20–21). Although this will normally cost more it can bring several advantages which may include:

- increasing the pool of possible mentors;
- an external mentor need not be involved in internal organisational politics;
- a suitable internal mentor may not be available. The more senior the manager, the more this is likely to be the case;
- appointment of an external mentor may enable a person to be developed when they cannot be released from their job;
- an external mentor may be able to develop a more confidential relationship with the person they are mentoring than would be possible with an internal mentor. This can assist with the development of a constructive counselling relationship. The skills of workplace counselling are covered in the next chapter.

Integration of individual training and development with organisational activity

An important issue is the need to integrate those who have received general management training into organisations. As explained in chapter 1 most organisations, because of their departmental structure, can only easily accommodate people with specialist skills. Thus, people with general management qualifications find it difficult to gain entry into organisations unless they have also acquired specialist skills. The general pattern remains one of grafting general management skills onto those who already have specialist skills.

Lessons from Japan

Management development in Japan provides some potentially useful lessons. As managers there often spend their entire careers with a single organisation, any benefits accrue to the employer who has made the investment. This also facilitates and justifies a long-term approach to management development. Much of the development is arranged by planned job rotation and career development, with individual commitment being to the organisation rather than the specialism. Extensive use is made of appointing in-house mentors to supplement the activity of the boss as coach (Storey, Edwards and Sisson 1997).

Evaluation and follow-up

Whatever pattern of training and development is adopted in an organisation, it is important that it be monitored to ensure that it is meeting the appropriate needs and giving value for money. As has already been stated, the identification of training needs in terms of objectives and/or expected outcomes makes it easier to judge whether training has been worthwhile. This is not just an activity that should be undertaken at the end of a learning activity. Interim evaluation may be needed so that adjustments can be made in time for those on a programme to benefit before the activity is completed. Follow-up studies may also be needed, though, to estimate the long-term impact of training particularly in areas such as management development. Such studies can be very useful as a means of improving future activity. The studies may also need to consider alternative ways of achieving required results. Line managers need to be involved in evaluation and follow-up activity in order to ensure that money spent on their behalf is achieving the desired results. Ways of doing this include interviewing people after they have completed formal programmes to discuss what can be applied in the workplace and reviewing the effectiveness of training during formal appraisal interviews. Sometimes follow-up interviews or questionnaires can give surprising answers.

An employee of a large manufacturing company in the UK said that the intensive induction training when he started had convinced him of his importance in his new organisation. He added that it had taken him three months to discover afterwards how unimportant he really was to the functioning of that organisation.

Training costs are often relatively easily identified, e.g. by aggregating the costs of releasing a person with the cost of the training provision. This can then be compared with the effect of the training on actual performance, which may be more difficult. However, this can provide the framework for a cost–benefit analysis to assess whether or not there has been a net benefit to the organisation. It can be particularly difficult to undertake a cost–benefit analysis with management training and development. The 'opportunity cost' of releasing managers has to be considered. Also it may be particularly difficult to measure changes in performance and to isolate those which have resulted from training. Estimates of whether a person is likely to stay, or be needed, in an organisation may also be necessary. Feedback forms can be used to obtain the views of those who have participated in training activities. However, the key issue is to find out what changes in behaviour have occurred as a result of the training activity.

One way of trying to overcome some of the above problems is to build in a follow-up session in a training activity. This may be particularly appropriate with management training. As well as asking people to comment on what has happened as a result of their training they may also be asked to report on a project designed to demonstrate the application of their learning. As well as helping assess the effectiveness of training this can also have considerable learning value. It may also further motivate people to apply their learning. Participants may also learn from one another's presentations at a follow-up event. However, one methodological problem is disentangling what people have done as a result of the training and what they may have done anyway. The follow-up of formal training activities may also reveal that people vary widely in their ability to benefit from the same programme. In some cases the methodological problems of assessing what benefits have derived from training and development activities may be insuperable. However, it may also be the case that activities such as management training and development are too important to be ignored and some investment is necessary as an act of faith.

RETENTION OF TRAINED STAFF

It may also be necessary to check on the extent to which organisations retain the people that they have trained and developed. This is more necessary in countries such as the UK where job mobility is generally higher than in countries such as Japan. Sometimes organisations make the mistake of having a considerable training investment in people that they then lose because they have not provided them with adequate opportunities to use their new found skills. This can also happen if pay levels get out of line with organisations that are competing for the same skills. It may be particularly necessary to review both the opportunities and pay levels in comparison with poacher organisations who invest little in training themselves but rely instead on recruiting people who have been trained elsewhere.

SUMMARY

✔ The increasing importance of training has been explained. Factors accounting for this increased importance include the accelerating rate of change, competitive pressures and the growing capital intensive nature of employment. Consequently, increased organisational resources need to be spent in identifying and meeting vocational training needs. Developments in information technology both generate new training needs and provide new ways of meeting them. Individuals also have a growing need to plan their own training and development. Traditional career paths are often disappearing, and individuals need to maintain and develop their expertise so that they retain their marketability. They may also need to be able to demonstrate their continuous professional development if they are to retain membership of a professional organisation.

✔ The overall pattern of training is changing radically. Recent developments that were examined include an emphasis on learning outcomes and the development of specific competencies. Initiatives taken at a macro level in the UK include the establishment of National Vocational Qualifications, the creation of a national network of Learning and Skills Councils and the Investors in People scheme. Another development has been the concept of the learning organisation. Whilst this concept is a desirable aim it is difficult to identify in a tangible form.

✔ Management training and development is particularly important because of the need to have managers capable of exploiting the potential opportunities for an organisation. This area has tended to be neglected. Also, there are many problems in ensuring that remedial action is effective. However, recognition of the difficulties can greatly increase the chances of management training and development being effective.

✔ Another important area is the evaluation of training. The establishment of clear learning outcomes can create a logical framework both for the implementation and evaluation of training. Follow-up studies can also be instructive in helping determine if the training investment has been worthwhile.

SELF-ASSESSMENT QUESTIONS

1. How would you assess the training needs of a subordinate member of your staff?

2. What are the main ways in which training needs can be met?

3. What do you understand by the term NVQ? Identify some of the impacts that this type of training has had in the UK.

4. Identify and comment on some of the difficulties in ensuring that effective management development takes place.

5. How would you evaluate the effectiveness of a training programme?

 References

Brown, Gordon (1996) as reported by Jilly Welch in 'Firms Query Labour's Virtual Learning Plans', *People Management*, 19 December.

Caulkin, Simon (1997) comments in *The Observer*, Business section, 13 July.

Constable John and Roger McCormick (1987) 'The Making of British Managers', a report for the British Institute of Managers and the Confederation of British Industry into management training, education and development, BIM.

Handy, Charles *et al.* (1987) *The Making of Managers* – The Handy Report, NEDO/HMSO.

Institute of Personnel and Development (1993) *Code of Practice, Continuous Development: People and Work*, Institute of Personnel and Development.

Management Charter Initiative (1993) MCI's Mission, 5th anniversary review.

Pedler, Mike and John Burgoyne and Tom Boydell (1991) *The Learning Company: A Strategy for Sustainable Development*, McGraw Book Co.

Rees, W. David (1992) 'Someone to Watch Over Me – An Experiment in Mentoring in Hackney', *Local Government Management*, Autumn.

Revans, Reg (1987) *The ABC of Action Learning*, Chartwell Brett, UK.

Rose, Richard and Gunter Wignanek (1990) *Training Without Trainers – How Germany Avoids Britain's Supply-side Bottleneck*, Anglo-German Foundation for the Study of Industrial Society.

Storey, John, Paul Edwards and Keith Sisson (1997) *Managers in the Making – Careers, Development and Control in Corporate Britain and Japan*, Sage.

General references

Bee, Frances and Roland Bee (1994) *Training: Needs Analysis and Evaluation*, Institute of Personnel and Development.

Bennett, Roger (1990) *Choosing and Using Management Consultants*, Kogan Page.

Bramley, Peter (1996) *Evaluating Training*, Institute of Personnel and Development.

Boydell, Tom and Malcolm Leary (2000) *Identifying Training Needs*, Institute of Personnel and Development.

Easterby-Smith, Mark, John Burgoyne and Luis Arajo (eds) (1999) *Organisational Learning and the Learning Organisation*, Sage Publications.

Siddons, Suzy (1997) *Delivering Training*, Institute of Personnel and Development.

chapter (twelve)

Counselling

There are case studies and exercises at
http://www.thomsonlearning.co.uk
(for full details, see the listing at the
start of this book).

LEARNING OUTCOMES

By the end of this chapter you will be able to:

- Understand what is meant by the term 'counselling'

- Identify the range of workplace situations in which counselling may be needed

- Understand the main skills involved in workplace counselling and the need to adopt a range of different styles of counselling

- Use counselling skills in grievance situations

- Use counselling skills in disciplinary situations

Introduction

Some reference was made to the need for counselling in the previous chapter on appraisal. It is now appropriate, however, to deal with the subject in greater detail. The nature of counselling is explained as are the range of work situations in which it may be needed. These situations include discussing work-related problems, personal problems that affect work, handling grievances and some disciplinary situations. The skills may be needed with colleagues, subordinates and customers. The basic skills of counselling are explained. These include recognising the various stages of counselling, identification of the actual problem and active listening. Counselling also particularly involves helping people work out their own solutions to problems rather than telling them what to do. This can be very time-consuming and managers may need to take a conscious decision whether they wish to or should get involved in particular situations. Counselling skills can be particularly useful and necessary when handling grievances and dealing with some disciplinary situations. Consequently, specific sections are included in the chapter on these areas.

The nature of and need for counselling

THE NATURE OF COUNSELLING

Counselling can be defined as a purposeful relationship in which one person helps another to help themselves. It is a way of relating and responding to another person so that that person is helped to explore their thoughts, feelings and behaviour with the aim of reaching a clearer understanding. The clearer understanding may be of themselves or of a problem, or of the one in relation to the other. The point of all this is to enable people to work out how they will handle for themselves issues, problems or decisions that have to be made. The technique is necessary because it may be that it is only by this process that an issue can be understood and/or the commitment created that will lead to an appropriate course of action being taken by the person concerned.

THE NEED FOR WORKPLACE COUNSELLING

The need for counselling can arise in a wide range of situations. Appraisal has already been mentioned, and the requirement for these skills in grievance and disciplinary situations is explained later in this chapter. The need for counselling skills can arise whenever a subordinate or colleague has a work-related problem. Sometimes it may be necessary to use these skills with clients as well. As well as managers needing counselling skills themselves, they also have to consider the extent to which their subordinates need these skills. It may be particularly important that any employee who has direct contact with clients or the public is trained in how to handle such contacts.

Given that managers spend most of their time in some form of communication and that much of it is oral communication, as explained in chapter 8, the need for counselling techniques can arise very frequently. The skills may not have the glamour of more high-status management activities but can nevertheless be one of the most critical of all management skills. The skills may also be constructively applied in one's personal life.

Usually, counselling discussions are initiated by the person who needs the help. However, there will be occasions when managers need to take the initiative and encourage employees to face up to issues that are having an adverse effect on their work. Whoever initiates discussion, some interpretation of an employee's responses will be necessary. Care needs to be taken about the level of discussion and analysis that is attempted. In-depth Freudian probing and analysis, for example, is better handled by those qualified to do it than by amateur psychiatrists. The requirement for counselling in work situations is usually for work-related rather than personal problems anyway.

Obviously, personal problems can affect behaviour at work, and counselling may be given by one person to another in the capacity of personal friend. There may well be situations, though, where it is not appropriate for a manager to get involved or where the best help that can be given is to refer a person to an appropriate agency or service.

Specific skills

Having explained the general nature and purpose of counselling, it is now appropriate to explain the skills in more detail. A particular feature of counselling skills is that managers will often have no advance notice of when they are going to need them. Consequently, if they are to act as counsellors they need to have sufficient mastery of the skills involved to be able to deploy them at a moment's notice.

CHOICE OF COUNSELLOR

The choice of who counsels and when is much more in the hands of the person wanting this type of help than with the potential counsellor. A person may choose not to speak about their problems to some people and may refuse offers of help that are made. So, the opportunity for counselling is likely to be determined by the person wanting help, but it is up to the manager, if invited, to decide whether or not to respond. The counselling that is required may be easily dealt with in a few moments or may involve several lengthy discussions. Those who have the opportunity to provide this type of help have to judge whether it is appropriate for them to give it and to assess if they are really likely to help, if they have the time to spare and whether there are other more appropriate ways of helping. A complication is that decisions on whether or not to counsel may have to be taken very quickly. If a person is rebuffed they may not ask again or, if counselling-type help is offered, it may be very difficult to stop once it has started.

STAGES IN THE PROCESS

There are normally several stages in a counselling interview. Part of the skill of counselling effectively is to identify the pattern an interview may take. The main stages are likely to be:

- identification of the problem,
- collection and exchange of information,
- checking that all the necessary statements have been made,
- establishing the criteria for a satisfactory solution,
- deciding on the appropriate solution,
- subsequently checking whether or not the solution has worked
- evaluating any outstanding problems.

The issue of the different stages in a counselling interview is not quite the same as the different styles of counselling. Each person who counsels may have their own style, which may vary from that of other people involved in intervention (or non-intervention) and the specific skills that are used. However, whatever basic style is used it will need to be varied according to the personality of the subject, the issue under discussion and the stage of the counselling process. See the appendix to this chapter for further explanation of this and a sample continuum of behavioural styles.

IDENTIFICATION OF THE PROBLEM

The problem that a person raises may just be a lead-in or a pretext for going on to discuss much more serious issues. Often the stated problem is rather like the tip of an iceberg. The subject may want to test that they are going to get a sympathetic response before being prepared to reveal the next part of a problem. Sometimes a person may not even be aware that the problem is much deeper than that indicated by them initially. This shows the danger of trying to deal with just the tip. The help that a person may need is to reason through the whole of a problem in such a way that they can cope with it, allowing for their own personality. It may be that there are also issues of which they are aware but which they deliberately keep secret. This is yet another reason for the counsellor to beware of seeking to impose a solution, as it may be based on an incomplete knowledge of the facts.

In order to discover the rest of the iceberg and to get the person to speak freely, the counsellor will find it useful to pay attention to their questioning technique. Open questions (i.e. those that start with an interrogative such as how, what, why, where) are more likely to help widen the conversation and explore the issues involved in a particular problem than closed questions. Closed questions are often phrased in such a way that they start with a verb: 'Do you enjoy your work?' If the interviewee is reluctant to talk, the 'yes' or 'no' given in answer to such a question may only help in a marginal way. There will, though, be situations when a straight yes or no answer is what is needed. Other skills that may be useful in building up rapport and encouraging the employee to talk include the processes of summarising, clarifying and reflecting back saying, for example, 'So that made you feel rather annoyed?'

ACTIVE LISTENING

Appearance of the counsellor

Active listening skills, which are also necessary in a counselling situation, involve two aspects. The first is being aware of appearing to be listening as well as actually hearing what is being said. Non-verbal skills in this situation include eye contact, leaning forward, not shuffling papers or making notes. The counsellor needs to be aware of the need for eye contact when appropriate throughout a counselling interview. That is not to say that they should spend all their time staring at the subject, but such contact can be helpful in showing that the counsellor is actively listening. It is also necessary to be aware of signals that are being given by a person's body language. This concept has already been explained in chapter 8. Premature intervention by the counsellor can prevent further disclosure by the subject.

Barriers to communication

The second aspect of listening skills which is important includes being aware of the source of barriers to hearing exactly what is being said. These barriers include some obvious ones like language differences, day-dreaming and environmental noise, but also selective perception (hearing what we want to hear), self-consciousness (the counsellor is more aware of the impression they are making) and behaviour rehearsal (the counsellor is busy working out what they are going to say next). There may also be a barrier when the counsellor has problems of their own which occupy their thoughts or where the content of what the employee is saying arouses anger or hostility in the counsellor. In many instances, simply being aware of the likely barriers can help the counsellor to make a conscious effort to eradicate them. These points on listening skills will also be relevant in other types of interview, as will the idea of open and closed questions. Some further points on questioning technique were made in chapter 9 on selection.

The pressure that people are often under before they speak needs to be kept in mind.

Example

An apocryphal story that demonstrates how worked up people can get before they speak concerns the person who had moved into a new house and knocked at a neighbour's door to ask if they could borrow their lawn mower. The newcomer had worked himself up into such a state about the legitimacy of his request to someone he hadn't yet met that when the neighbour opened the door he shouted 'you can keep your lawn-mower – I know you won't lend it to me!'

LEVEL OF DIRECTION

The amount of direction given by the counsellor will vary according to the situation and the personalities involved. It is the essence of counselling, though, that the person is helped to work the problem out for themselves. Not only may value judgements be inappropriate if made by the counsellor but, if they vary from the value judgements of the person requiring help, that person may see the counsellor as unsympathetic and consequently terminate any discussion. Nevertheless, even given all this, there can be a range of counselling styles (see the appendix to this chapter). At the one extreme a person may be totally non-directive and just give sufficient response, perhaps by ways of grunts, to let the other person know that they are actually listening. In other cases it may be appropriate for the counsellor to be rather more interventionist, whilst at the same time avoiding imposing their own views. This can be done in a neutral but friendly manner by positively encouraging a person to elaborate on an issue. Further interventions can be made to clarify what has been said and questions can be asked that are designed to get the person to talk more. It may be necessary for the counsellor to add information in such a way that the person being counselled feels free to make use of the information or ignore it. This represents a further stage in counselling intervention without sacrificing the neutrality of the counsellor. Another stage is to help the person concerned identify the options available to them – the critical point being that the choice has to be made by the person being counselled and not by the counsellor. This can involve a person taking a decision that is not necessarily in the interests of the organisation – for example, to leave (or in some cases not to leave). There is little point, however, in the counsellor seeking to impose the decision that is in the organisation's interests as the person would undoubtedly ignore it. If a person is going to decide to leave, for example, it may be just as well to help them come to that decision relatively quickly rather than to let the issue drag on. One problem may lead to another and perhaps much bigger area, and the counsellor needs to be aware that the closing of discussion on a particular topic is by no means necessarily the end of a counselling interview.

(Example)

A newly qualified personnel officer was appointed to his first job. Unfortunately, his formal training had not included counselling. Line managers and others, however, frequently asked his advice about human relations problems. Anxious to help, he made all sorts of suggestions about how these problems might be handled. However, he invariably found that for some reason his ideas were not practicable or acceptable. After a while he realised that the problem was that he was being too directive. He then encouraged people to talk through their problems with him. This enabled colleagues to frame solutions that took account of the facts that they had not disclosed and their own personality. They were also committed to the solutions that they developed. The personnel officer then found that people were often thanking him for helping solve problems that he had sometimes not even understood far less had a solution for.

CONFIDENTIALITY

Normally, the whole basis on which counselling takes place is one of complete confidence. Sometimes, however, the counsellor will need to warn the subject that information that may emerge, or already has, cannot be treated confidentially. If an accountant is told that their cashier has been systematically embezzling money it is hardly likely that they can, or should want to, keep this a private matter between the parties.

Grievance handling

Grievances may be raised by colleagues, subordinates, clients or members of the public. Commercial organisations are increasingly promoting customer grievance procedures in order to demonstrate their concern for their customers. This is reinforced by an increasing volume of statutory protection and provisions for processing complaints. Counselling may be needed in handling grievance situations. Before we look at the specific skills involved it is necessary to look at the framework within which grievances need to be handled and some of the problems that occur when grievances are being handled.

RIGHTS OF THOSE RAISING GRIEVANCES

There is a statutory requirement in the UK under the Employment Rights Act of 1996 for employers to give written details to employees of the grievance procedure if 20 or more people are employed. This must include the name or title of the person to whom an individual employee can complain and also the details of any appeals procedure. It may also, as explained in the next chapter on disciplinary handling and dismissal, be appropriate to use a grievance procedure as an appeals mechanism against minor disciplinary warnings. Employees in the UK are also entitled, under the terms of the Employment Relations Act of 1999, to be accompanied at a grievance hearing by a colleague or by a trade union representative, even if the organisation does not recognise trade unions. This right is restricted, however, to serious issues where the employer has failed to meet a contractual obligation or other significant duty towards the employee. Failure to respond to issues regarding sex, racial discrimination or harassment, or disability discrimination can also mean that employers are in breach of their statutory obligations and can result in proceedings at employment tribunals. The right to be accompanied was also extended, under the terms of the Employment Relations Act of 1999, to cover some categories of worker who are not necessarily employees. This issue is explained more fully in the section on the role of the representative in the chapter 13.

Other parties may also have contractual or statutory rights to raise grievances with organisations. Such rights can derive from commercial contracts, consumer protection legislation, or legislation protecting the public. In some cases there is the right of appeal to an ombudsman, either appointed by statute or voluntarily. Trading standards departments are increasingly active in responding to complaints by aggrieved customers. An example of the pressure for complaints procedures is that solicitors who are franchised to provide legal aid must provide clients with a written complaints procedure as a condition of being franchised. The increase in grievance and complaints procedures has been reinforced by the growth of a litigation culture so that people are more likely to use these procedures. A related development is the promotion of 'no win, no fee' legal services.

LEVELS FOR HANDLING GRIEVANCES

Counselling skills may be most useful in handling informal grievances, which constitute the great majority of grievances. Most issues should be settled at the informal level, and the chances of this happening are increased if front-line staff are selected and trained to handle grievances effectively. It is also important to examine carefully what is said when grievances are raised informally in order to examine whether there is any aspect of the grievance that can be addressed. If this is not done it can mean that the grievance festers and may become larger as time goes on; other grievances can then come along and become linked to the original grievance.

Example

A local government officer asked for two years why he was not being paid an acting-up allowance. After receiving no reply during that period he resorted to using the formal grievance procedure. Unfortunately, by the time the grievance was heard, relationships had deteriorated so much that he ended up being sacked and instituted proceedings against the organisation for unfair dismissal. Even if the employer felt justified in not paying the allowance, a patient explanation of the reasons at the outset may have prevented this breakdown in working relationships.

THE FALLIBILITY OF GRIEVANCE PROCEDURES

Unfortunately, the formal stages of grievance procedures covering employees tend to be little used, as the immediate boss is usually designated for the task of hearing the grievance but is normally also the cause of it. Consequently, the grievance procedure may only have a cosmetic effect.

Examples

Recruits at an engineering company were given a standard letter informing them of their right to take a grievance up with the managing director if necessary. On the one occasion that this right was invoked it turned out the managing director was quite unaware of this arrangement – the undertaking had been given by one of his predecessors.

Another example concerns the way in which information about a grievance procedure was given in a manner designed to prevent its use. Royal Air Force recruits were told the details of the grievance procedure that they could use if they felt they were being victimised. This was by their senior non-commissioned officer during their basic training. He also advised them that the last person to use the procedure was a recent recruit whom they could observe, if they looked out of the window, doing punishment drill around the camp!

People are generally averse to receiving no response whatsoever if they have raised a grievance. It would seem better, even if the answer is negative from the employee's or customer's point of view, to have the courtesy to at least tell them that. The problem with ineffective grievance or complaints procedures is that the opportunity is not taken to see if corrective action is necessary, both from the point of the person who may have been aggrieved and the organisation which may be failing in a particular respect.

SKILLS IN GRIEVANCE HANDLING

Identification of who needs grievance handling skills

Grievance handling skills may be needed by many levels of people within an organisation. It is not enough for managers to have the skills to handle grievances effectively themselves. They need to ensure that those people who work for them and who need the skills are also effective in this area. An audit may be needed of those who need grievance handling skills. This may include all those with managerial or supervisory responsibilities, sales staff and other front-line staff such as receptionists and switchboard operators. Airline staff, traditionally at least, compare favourably with railway staff in their customer handling. This is because of the effort put into customer handling including dealing with grievances. The same soft drinks company mentioned in chapter 9, for example, came to recognise that their delivery drivers needed to be selected and trained so that they acted as ambassadors for the company and not just as people who delivered goods. Often aggrieved clients or customers vent their frustrations on the first representative of an organisation that they come into contact with. In fairness to the front-line staff and those making complaints, representatives of the organisation need to be trained in how to handle such situations. Such training needs to include details of organisational policies and procedures so that representatives of an organisation are well briefed, which in turn helps develop confidence when dealing with employee grievances or customer complaints.

THE ROLE OF COUNSELLING IN GRIEVANCE HANDLING

There can be a variety of ways of handling grievances, including having a first-class row, ignoring it, referring it to someone else, or giving the person what they want. Often, however, grievances cannot, and should not, be ignored, yet there may be nothing that the person hearing the grievance concerned can do to resolve it. It may be that a person has a perfectly justifiable grievance, but nothing concrete can be done about it. It is in situations like this that counselling may be not only desirable but the only course of action that can be taken. This makes it all the more important that those who are likely to handle grievances are given some basic instruction in the skills of counselling.

In some grievance situations the answer may be simply to let people talk themselves out of their fury. Their frustration may require an outlet, and counselling techniques may enable them gradually to dissipate their anger. At the end of the discussion, an aggrieved person may actually thank the person at whom they have directed their anger for their help and go away reconciled to the situation. The dilemma for the person who has to handle the grievance is that, if they openly agree with the complaints, they may compromise their employer and, if they rebut the complaints, they may infuriate the complainant. Neutral yet sympathetic listening in many cases is not merely the only option but may be a complete answer. It may even be appropriate for the person at the receiving end of the grievance to take the initiative as the anger subsides and probe to see if there is any more anger that needs ventilation.

Sometimes the counselling of a person with a grievance will simply mark the end of the first stage of the discussion. It may then be necessary to see what, if anything, can be done about the person's complaint. It may be that a decision has to be deferred or the answer given that, whilst you are sympathetic, nothing can be done. It is crucial, however, that where feelings run high, this is only attempted after the counselling stage has been completed. It may only be then that a person can participate in a rational discussion of what can or cannot be done. Even if they still expect some action, a hearing of their case may have gone some way, if not the whole way, to providing psychological restitution. It may also emerge that their anger has prevented them from properly explaining their grievance and that the cause of their dissatisfaction is rather different from that which first seemed to be the case. Clarification of the nature of the grievance may be crucial, as otherwise decisions cannot be sensibly taken about what action should, or should not, follow – yet sometimes it may only be at a relatively late stage in the proceedings that this is possible.

When customers complain, organisations can sometimes seize the initiative by empowering front-line staff to make routine decisions regarding compensation and thus convert dissatisfied customers into people who praise the organisation instead. Enlightened organisations will also see that taking employee grievances and customer complaints seriously can be essential part of good employee relations, quality control and good customer relations. Sometimes organisations take a more proactive approach and have surveys of staff and customers.

The processes described above can be very necessary in confrontations between managers and union representatives, or with other special interest groups for that matter. It may be impossible to communicate effectively with representatives until they have ventilated their feelings about a particular issue. It may only be then that representatives are able to listen to the organisational side of a case. The problem for whoever is chairing such joint meetings is to prevent anyone on the organisation's side from retaliating and so inflaming a situation. This may be particularly necessary as the opposing interest group may have actually moderated their position after saying their piece.

Counselling in disciplinary situations

Counselling may also be applicable in disciplinary situations. As with grievance handling, it can be a necessary first stage and sometimes the only stage in resolving disciplinary problems. The best form of discipline is usually self-discipline, and the attempt to impose a pattern of behaviour on an employee should normally only be considered if the employee is unable to show the appropriate self-discipline. If it is appropriate for them to change their behaviour, one should normally seek to do this with the minimum amount of pressure consistent with that objective. If an employee's performance or conduct is inappropriate, it would generally seem sensible to encourage the employee to see this and work out for themselves the required change in their behaviour. As was stated during the section on performance appraisal, people can often be their own harshest critics. It would seem far better, therefore, to give an employee the opportunity to mend their ways voluntarily rather than to try to impose one's authority. Apart from the greater commitment that this may create, it may also save the employee's face if they are allowed to work out their own salvation. Again, as with grievance handling, even if counselling does not prove to be a complete answer, it may clear the way for appropriate action on any residual disagreement. The counselling stage may also be necessary to clarify the exact nature of the shortcomings, if indeed there are any. One of the problems of disciplinary handling is that there may need to be a considerable amount of discussion before it can be clarified whether there is a disciplinary problem or not. Counselling may, however, be just the first stage in the disciplinary process. The handling of further stages in that process is the subject of the next chapter.

SUMMARY

✔ Managers may often need to or be invited to counsel other people about their problems. These may be work-related or personal ones that may affect work. Many will be about minor operational issues that are dealt with quite informally. The essence of counselling is helping people work out their own solution to a problem rather than simply telling them what to do. Counselling techniques may be particularly necessary when appraising staff or dealing with grievances, customer complaints or many disciplinary issues. As managers often get little or no notice of when they may need to use counselling skills, they need to master the basic skills so that they can deploy immediately if necessary. However, they will also need to judge when it is appropriate for them to get involved in counselling situations and what style of behaviour to adopt at any particular point in the proceedings (see the appendix to this chapter).

✔ It is also necessary to consider which subordinate staff and colleagues also need to have basic counselling skills. It is likely to be particularly important that front-line staff in direct contact with customers or members of the public have basic counselling skills so that complaints are dealt with promptly and effectively. Even when counselling is not the complete answer it can help further discussion by defusing a situation and clarifying what the options are.

✔ Effective grievance handling strategies are important as a way of identifying when corrective action needs to be taken both with regard to the person who is aggrieved and ensuring that an organisation is functioning effectively. They are also increasingly important because of increased employee and customer rights. Counselling may also be important as a technique for helping employees change their behaviour in disciplinary situations.

SELF-ASSESSMENT QUESTIONS

1. What do you understand by the term 'counselling'?

2. In what work situations might counselling be appropriate?

3. What are the key skills involved in counselling?

4. How might counselling be of use in dealing with grievances?

5. How might counselling be of use in dealing with disciplinary problems?

 References

Advisory Conciliation and Arbitration Service (2000) Code of Practice on Disciplinary and Grievance Procedures, ACAS.

Summerfield, Jenny and Lyn Oudshoorn (1997) *Counselling in the Workplace*, Institute of Personnel and Development.

Appendix to chapter 12

CONTINUUM OF COUNSELLING STYLES

The following diagram shows the range of styles of counselling behaviour. The skilful counsellor may need to operate over a range of the continuum, and will decide which kind of behaviour will be most effective in each phase of any counselling situation.

OTHER-FOCUSED

Behaviour Style	Examples
Refuses to become involved	'Why don't you try to cope on your own first?' 'I'm too busy to help.' 'That is your problem to sort out.'
Listens	Remains silent, occasionally encouraging the other by eye contact, nods or saying 'uh huh' 'Could you say more?'
Reflects or clarifies	'As I understand it, you're saying…' 'You seem to feel… (e.g. encouraged, unfairly treated, confused, etc)'
Probes/questions	'Could you tell me more about it?' 'Why do you think so?' 'Have you tried to do anything to improve the situation?'
Interprets	'It seems to me that… (e.g. you feel insecure about the future, there is a status problem, etc)'
Adds new data	'I will tell you some of the background to… (e.g. the decision, the problem, etc)' 'There are several alternative courses of action you could take…'
Identifies options	'It seems to me that you could do… or possibly…' 'You could talk to Mr X before going ahead.'
Propose criteria for evaluating alternatives	'It seems to me that your choice should be guided by… (e.g. what is acceptable to the employee, the likely effect on the employee's work, the likely reaction from staff).'
Recommends/proposes solution	'I think you should do…'

SELF-FOCUSED

chapter thirteen

Disciplinary handling and dismissal

There are case studies and exercises at
http://www.thomsonlearning.co.uk
(for full details, see the listing at the
start of this book).

LEARNING OUTCOMES

By the end of this chapter you will be able to:

- Understand the objectives of discipline in an organisation, including preventative policies

- Understand and advise on basic law relating to dismissal, including redundancy, in the UK

- Identify the responsibilities of individual line managers regarding discipline

- Handle disciplinary issues informally and effectively when appropriate

- Present a case at a formal disciplinary hearing and also at the appeal stage

- Advise and/or chair a formal disciplinary or appeal hearing

In achieving the above outcomes readers will also be able to protect their own rights if they are ever threatened with disciplinary action or redundancy.

Introduction

In this chapter attention is paid to the objectives of disciplinary policies. Preventative policies are important to try and ensure that disciplinary problems are kept to a minimum. When problems nevertheless arise it is important that they are dealt with effectively and fairly. Often the term 'discipline' is seen as synonymous with dismissal but discipline is a generic term, and dismissal is simply the severest penalty that an employer may enforce. Also, some dismissals, for example on grounds of redundancy or ill-health, are not for disciplinary reasons.

Dismissal law in the UK is explained in this chapter because of the impact it can have on disciplinary policies and procedures. The consequences of legal actions alleging unfair dismissal have to be considered. However, most disciplinary action will involve less severe penalties or be best handled informally. This is explained by way of the disciplinary pyramid. This demonstrates that the greatest volume of activity is at an informal level at the base of the pyramid. It is crucial that line managers accept their responsibilities for maintaining discipline. Reasons why they might not are explained, as are strategies for encouraging managers to act effectively in this area.

The skills involved in formal disciplinary and appeal hearings are also examined. The need for clear role identification and separation at hearings are explained. Key roles are those of the case presenter, chair and employee representative. Important issues are the need for a logical sequence of events at a hearing and for an open mind on the part of the chair.

Three appendices are included in the chapter. The first contains the ACAS guidelines on disciplinary procedures. The second is a model sequence of events at a formal disciplinary hearing. The third is a checklist of the items that need consideration when writing disciplinary letters.

The objectives of discipline

KEY OBJECTIVES

The primary objective of discipline is to prevent or, failing that, to deal with inappropriate behaviour by employees that has an adverse effect on their work or the work of colleagues. The preventative aspect involves educating employees about the behaviour that is expected of them and reinforcing that with effective management control. Unless a person is dismissed, the aim needs to be to change a person's behaviour so that it becomes acceptable. Another important objective is to demonstrate that discipline is administered fairly. It is necessary to try to do this, not only to the person who may be the subject of disciplinary action, but also to their colleagues, whose attitudes can be considerably influenced by the action taken.

EVALUATION OF DISCIPLINARY EFFECTIVENESS

Just as with appraisal, so with disciplinary situations, managers need to work out quite carefully just what they are trying to achieve. Too often consideration of this topic simply consists of a discussion of an employer's track record at employment tribunals. It may be that an employer has never lost a case at an employment tribunal, or has never even had to defend a case but that may prove very little. The easiest way not to lose a case is never to dismiss anyone or to only do so when there is an overwhelming case. There is not much point in an employer always winning legal cases if, in the meantime, their line managers have opted out of their disciplinary role, possibly with a marked adverse effect on standards of performance. It is also necessary to look at basic performance criteria and check if any shortfalls are because of poor control. The areas that may need examining include:

- levels of cost-effective performance in an organisation,
- quality standards, including levels of customer service,
- the extent to which important disciplinary rules are observed, particularly in the area of health and safety,
- absence and timekeeping levels.

Weaknesses in disciplinary effectiveness may be a symptom of the wider issue of managerial effectiveness and control in an organisation. A wide range of factors other than discipline can also cause performance problems.

CIRCUMSTANCES WHEN DISCIPLINARY ACTION MAY BE APPROPRIATE

Dismissal may be necessary only if other, more appropriate means of dealing with a disciplinary problem, including attempts to alter a person's behaviour, have failed or are clearly pointless. Any formal intervention can, to some extent, be regarded as a sign of failure in that the more satisfactory approach of self-discipline may have failed. Disciplinary action may also only be appropriate if a person's behaviour is having a detrimental effect on their or other people's work. The objective is normally to try to get a person to mend their ways so that their behaviour is improved. If this is likely to prove impossible, then a manager has to make a judgement about whether to put up with it or to consider following the avenue that could lead to dismissal.

Judgements about when to intervene, and over what issues, may need considerable thought. People may have many irritating habits that they cannot or will not change, and it may be pointless trying to make them. Conversely, if managers are too lenient, they may find that events get seriously out of hand — the adage of 'a stitch in time saves nine' can be highly appropriate with regard to discipline. A small issue discreetly checked at the right time can prevent escalation into something far more difficult to contain.

DETERMINATION OF STANDARDS

There is a tendency for some managers to overestimate the extent to which standards in the disciplinary area are decided externally. It can be very convenient to assume that the responsibility for establishing and maintaining disciplinary standards lies elsewhere – either within the organisation or outside it. Organisations invariably have overall policies and procedures concerning discipline, but these provide a framework within which a manager should operate rather than devices for managers avoiding their own responsibility. It is only the manager in an individual department who can monitor and interpret the policies and procedures. If a person is not doing their job properly, it would seem to be a fundamental part of the manager's job to consider bringing the matter to the person's attention. The definition of standards within a department has to be undertaken, communicated and, when appropriate, enforced by the manager concerned.

The existence of overall policies and procedures does not take away the individual manager's responsibility in this area, however much some managers would like to pretend that it does. Often employees prefer a tighter discipline than actually exists and may resent seeing colleagues being able to behave in an inappropriate way. This tends to devalue their own job and may lead to them leaving or deciding that they may as well follow the lead that is given.

Inconsistencies in treatment, especially within a department, can create considerable resentment. Standards of attendance and punctuality can vary widely from department to department, even within the same organisation, according to the lead given by the managers concerned. Employees can also object to too harsh a regime, which is why managers need to think carefully what standards are appropriate and how they should be achieved, rather than avoid thinking about the issue at all.

The political judgements that managers have to make may be particularly difficult when dealing with professional-level employees. Some of them may find any concept of external control unacceptable, yet develop their work in a way that does not fit with the needs of the organisation. It is useful to distinguish between the professional's technical competence and their accountability for achieving objectives. It may be more effective, and acceptable, to make the point that discussion about the latter topic does not necessarily reflect on the professional employee's specialist competence.

The legal rights of an ex-employee to pursue a case for unfair dismissal are likely to have an impact on the disciplinary policies and procedures in an organisation. Consequently, it is appropriate to explain the legal position in the UK before considering the skills involved in disciplinary handling.

The law relating to dismissals

GENERAL FRAMEWORK

The current legal framework regarding unfair dismissal is contained in the Employment Rights Act 1996. However, there have been some amendments as a result of other later statutes. The key additions are incorporated in this section. Before statutory protection against unfair dismissal was first introduced in 1971, the only significant right of employees who had been dismissed was to take an action in the civil courts under common law if they had not received their proper entitlement to notice. Such actions alleging wrongful dismissal were, and are, restricted to considering the amount of notice, or money in lieu of notice, to which the ex-employee is entitled.

The grounds on which an employer can establish that a dismissal was fair are quite broad. The three main grounds that constitute fair dismissal are:

- capacity,
- conduct,
- redundancy.

Dismissal can also be for 'other substantial reasons'. This is when the employee has broken their contract of employment in a fundamental way which is not necessarily covered by the three main headings. An example could be a driver who has had their driving licence suspended and who it is not reasonably practicable to re-deploy. However, even in this example an employer might be able to justify dismissal on the grounds of lack of capacity.

For dismissal to be fair it also has to be reasonable in the circumstances. Judgement is on the balance of probabilities.

EXCLUSIONS

Not all dismissed employees can allege unfair dismissal at an employment tribunal. The main exclusions are:

- employees who have not completed one year's continuous employment,
- employees who have reached the normal retiring age.

The above exclusions are qualified. Employees who maintain that they have been dismissed because of illegal discrimination do not have to have any length of service requirement. This covers allegations of unfair dismissal on grounds of :

- sex,
- race,
- disability,
- trade union membership or non-membership,
- being an employee representative,
- activity as a health and safety representative,
- the first eight weeks of legal industrial action,
- refusal of a shop worker to work on a Sunday,
- exercise of a statutory right, for example whistleblowing, which is covered by the Public Interest Disclosure Act 1998.

If employers allow some people to work past normal retirement age they may face a claim for discrimination if they favour one group more than another (*Nash* vs *Mash/Roe Group 1998*). Local staff working in diplomatic missions may be able to take a case provided that they were not engaged on diplomatic work.

There is no requirement for employees to work a specified number of hours each week in order to be able to bring a claim. Employers were able to lawfully terminate the employment of those on fixed-term contracts of a year or more provided that the employee had signed an appropriate waiver and it was implemented on the agreed date. However, this option was removed by the Employment Relations Act of 1999. Further constraints on the freedom of employers to use fixed-term contracts are to be expected as and when a European directive on fixed-term contracts is agreed and implemented.

CONSTRUCTIVE DISMISSAL

Normally the act of dismissal is not contested. However, there can be cases where it is unclear whether the employee resigned or was dismissed. The sooner the employee clarifies the position the stronger their case. If an employer breaches a basic element of the contract the employee has the option of treating such action as a contract repudiation and therefore a dismissal. Such action can include severely unreasonable behaviour on the part of the employer. If the employee does not leave immediately, they need to make it clear that they regard the contract as having been broken. The longer they continue with the employer the more difficult it is for them to succeed in a claim that their position had become intolerable. One way of maintaining their position though could be to institute an action for breach of contract whilst continuing in their job (*Hogg* vs *Dover College 1989*).

It may be also be possible for an employee to withdraw notice if it was given in the 'heat of the moment' and after provocation. Relevant issues may be the extent of any provocation and the psychological make-up of the employee (*Kwik-Fit GB* vs *Lineham 1992*).

In the event of a case going to a tribunal the issue of whether or not there had been a dismissal would need to be decided first. In the event of there having been a dismissal it would then have to be determined whether or not the dismissal was fair. The weakness in an employer's case would be likely to be that no procedure had been followed before the dismissal occurred. This is a particular danger if employers try and circumvent the whole disciplinary process by putting pressure on an employee to leave.

CAPACITY

Dismissal on grounds of lack of capacity may be justified because of a person's poor performance. There are, unfortunately, occasions when people can be trying their best but nevertheless still fail to meet minimum job standards. Such situations are not really disciplinary situations, although they may still result in dismissal. Medical cases might also be dealt with as 'capacity' or under 'other substantial reasons'. Again, dismissal may result even though the person concerned may not be to blame. In some organisations separate procedures are established to deal with such cases, whilst in others the cases are handled within the disciplinary procedure. Guidance on this and related issues is contained in the ACAS Advisory Handbook, *Discipline at Work* (2000).

Whatever procedure is used it is important to investigate cases carefully and see what help the employer can reasonably give. In the case of sickness absence it is important to check on the prospects of an early return to work and to consider seeking medical advice. It may also be necessary to warn employees of the consequences of their not being able to resume normal work, or appropriate alternative work. Another important issue is the impact of the Disability Discrimination Act 1995. Case law decisions have resulted in a widening range of illnesses, such as schizophrenia, being classified as disabilities. This means that organisations with 15 or more employees need to be even more careful in demonstrating that they have taken all reasonable steps to help an employee who may be classified as disabled before considering dismissal.

CONDUCT

Dismissal on grounds of misconduct may be either because of a single instance of gross misconduct, which can entitle an employer to summarily dismiss (without notice), or because of cumulative misconduct, in which case the appropriate notice, or money in lieu, has to be given. Gross misconduct is not easy to define but legally occurs when an employee's (mis)behaviour goes to the root of the contract. It is prudent for an employer to clarify the position by giving predictable written examples of what is considered to be gross misconduct. These might well include theft or fraud perpetrated against the organisation and physical assault in the course of employment. This may have both an educative effect and make it easier to establish that particular behaviour constituted gross misconduct. However, lack of such advance publicity will not automatically prevent employers from treating other behaviour as gross misconduct if it is sufficiently serious.

There is a statutory requirement for disciplinary rules to be notified to employees and these need to cover basic requirements and not just examples of gross misconduct. If 20 or more people are employed these rules need to be in writing. It is increasingly important for rules to refer to the need to refrain from sexual or racial harassment. Quite apart from the inappropriateness of such behaviour, the obligations of employers to provide a harassment-free working environment have been underlined by a series of cases where damages have been awarded to applicants where employers have failed in this respect. Hopefully, though, the rules will have a powerful educative effect, so that the required behaviour is achieved without resort to discipline.

The basic expectations the employer has of employees should also be an integral part of induction training for newcomers. Also, if new rules are introduced, or if there are other changes in the expectations that employers have of employees, these should be communicated in advance. It is important that employees do not learn of the existence of rules or new expectations by being disciplined. Employers also need to demonstrate that they have systematically and fairly sought to enforce any such rules. Their position at a tribunal would be weak if a former employee were able to demonstrate uneven application of any such rules. Erratic attendance and time-keeping are particularly common examples of cumulative misconduct, and in cases like this the employer needs to be able to demonstrate to a tribunal that they have tried to operate policies fairly and in such a way that the pressure on an employee was gradually stepped up before any consideration of dismissal.

REDUNDANCY

Employers are able to fairly dismiss on grounds of redundancy, provided that it is genuine, that the selection is fair and that there is appropriate consultation.

Compensation

The statutory minimum payments are:

- for each year of service at age 18 or over, but under 22 – half a week's pay
- for each year of service at age 22 but under 41 – one week's pay
- for each year of service at age 41 or over but under 65 – one and a half weeks' pay

(ACAS 2000: 44).

These limits are subject, however, to an earnings cap which is adjusted annually on an index-linked basis. This means that the compensation is calculated on the basis of regular weekly earnings or the cap, whichever is the lower. The statutory entitlement is also limited to a maximum of 20 years service. Redundant employees are also entitled to a week's notice, or money in lieu, for every year of service up to a maximum of 12 weeks. Employees may be entitled to higher payments under their contract of employment. The first £30,000 of redundancy compensation is tax-free.

Employers can ask employees to sign waivers to fixed-term contracts giving up their rights to redundancy payments. Whilst at the time of writing there is no proposal to alter this, as has been explained above, the freedom of employers to engage people on fixed-term contracts is likely to be considerably reduced by a European Directive on this issue.

Employees faced with redundancy are also statutorily entitled to reasonable paid time off to look for another job and for training during the notice period.

Selection

A crucial test in establishing a redundancy is whether or not the dismissed employee was replaced. Selection for redundancy may be in accordance with a previously established policy which may also have been agreed with recognised trade unions. Length of service is an important criterion in deciding who should be retained and who should be dismissed, but other criteria, including capability, may need to be considered as well. Objective data may be necessary to demonstrate that selection criteria have been fairly applied. Employees are entitled to four weeks' trial in an alternative job without forfeiting any of their legal rights. It is necessary to ensure that redundancy selection does not unfairly disadvantage a particular group. This could happen, for example, if all part-timers were dismissed but a majority were women. An appeal procedure may be appropriate to consider appeals against redundancy and also against offers of alternative work within the organisation. In the event of the redundancy selection being deemed unfair by an employment tribunal, the former employee would be entitled to compensation for unfair dismissal as well as their redundancy entitlement.

Consultation

Employees are entitled to be consulted about redundancy on an individual basis. This should be done as early as is practicable if they are likely to be made redundant. Such consultation should include ways of avoiding the redundancy and also the opportunity for alternative work within the organisation.

Redundancies are also affected by collective law. Employers planning a redundancy of 20 or more employees are required to consult with relevant trade union representatives or, in their absence, with elected employee representatives with a view to reaching agreement. Such consultation would also need to include ways of avoiding or minimising proposed redundancy. The consultation has to take place 'in good time' – at least 30 days before dismissal with redundancies of between 20 and 99 employees, and 90 days before dismissal if the redundancies are expected to be 100 or over. Dismissal notices cannot be issued until that consultation process has been completed. The duty for collective consultation also applies when adverse contract changes are proposed but the employer does not propose to make people redundant. However, as explained in chapter 7, the remedy for breach of this requirement is restricted to failure to consult provided no actual unfair dismissal occurs. Employers are also obliged to give notice to the Department of Trade and Industry in line with the minimum time scales given above if redundancies of 20 or more are planned.

Failure to observe the requirements with regard to consultation can render a redundancy dismissal unfair. As explained previously this can mean that an employee is entitled to compensation both for redundancy and unfair dismissal. There are also financial penalties for breach of the provisions for collective consultation. A protective award of a normal week's pay for a maximum period of 90 days can be awarded by an employment tribunal if an employer is in breach of this requirement. The award can be in respect of every employee where it is held that there has been such a breach.

Employers acquiring new businesses, or even sometimes winning contracts for economic entities, must consult with employee representatives if the acquisition or the contract involves the potential or actual redundancy of acquired or existing employees. This is in addition to the legislation regarding the transfer of undertakings and which creates a further potential liability for employers. These regulations also necessitate collective consultation even if only one person is threatened with redundancy or if existing employees are likely to be significantly affected by the transfer. However, employees need to meet the one year's length of service requirement to take an action for unfair dismissal, unless they allege illegal discrimination.

REMEDIES FOR UNFAIR DISMISSAL

Employers are still, of course, able to dismiss – the application for unfair dismissal is made only after the employee has been given notice or dismissed. Normally, any tribunal hearing will only take place some months after a dismissal has actually taken place. If the decision is in favour of the applicant there are three potential remedies.

Reinstatement

Employment tribunals are obliged to consider reinstatement (or re-engagement) as a remedy if an application alleging unfair dismissal is upheld, but this can only be recommended and not enforced. Although tribunals can award extra compensation if a recommendation to reinstate is resisted by the employer, the normal remedy is financial compensation and not reinstatement.

In 1998–1999 only 28 (less than 1 per cent) of those applications actually upheld resulted in an award of reinstatement or re-engagement (Labour Market Trends 1999: 494).

Basic award

The basic award is equivalent to a person's statutory redundancy entitlement. This is based on age and length of service and subject to an earnings cap.

Compensatory award

The compensatory award is designed to cover any further loss suffered by the applicant. It will include loss suffered since the dismissal, loss of pension rights and an estimate of future earnings loss. The maximum award was raised from £12,000 to £50,000 in 1999 and index-linked. This may encourage more people to take cases to a tribunal, particularly those on higher incomes. Enhanced compensation for specified reasons are not subsumed within the maximum figure. The grounds for enhanced compensation are failure to implement a reinstatement order, dismissal for membership or non-membership of a trade union, legitimate trade union activity and legitimate health and safety activity.

In a range of cases there is no limit on the compensatory award. The range includes cases involving discrimination on the basis of sex, race or disability. There is also no limit if the dismissal was in contravention of the Public Interest Disclosure Act of 1998 protecting whistleblowers. However, people who have been dismissed have a duty to mitigate their loss by looking for other work. Also, compensation can be reduced by the proportion by which people contributed to their own dismissal.

General pattern of compensation

Unfair dismissal actions may also be associated with claims for breach of contract, for example failure to meet obligations with regard to money in lieu of notice. The average (median) compensation awarded by tribunals in 1998–1999 was only £2,388, but, as explained previously, this is likely to rise as those on higher incomes may be more likely to pursue cases given the increase in the maximum compensatory award to £50,000. The legal costs and managerial time involvement may be substantial whether a case is won or lost. Because of these factors employers often make conciliated settlements well above the level of the average tribunal award. In 1998–1999 34 per cent of cases referred to tribunals resulted in conciliated settlements (Labour Market Trends 1999: 494).

Conciliated settlements are agreements between the parties whereby the claimant waives their right to pursue a statutory claim. This is in return for concessions from the employer usually involving a cash payment. Such settlements are arranged by ACAS conciliation officers after a claim has been made to an employment tribunal. Agreements can also be negotiated directly between the parties whereby a settlement is reached without a case necessarily having lodged with a tribunal. The circumstances and manner in which such compromise agreements can be made are explained later in this chapter.

OTHER IMPLICATIONS OF DISMISSAL PROCEEDINGS

Industrial

Employers also have to consider the industrial repercussions of a dismissal. Irrespective of whether a tribunal judges a dismissal to be fair or unfair or if a tribunal even hears a case, sanctions may be applied by the remaining workers to try to secure the reinstatement of a colleague. Changed economic circumstances and access to tribunals have greatly reduced industrial action on dismissal, though. However, a dismissal may still have an effect on other employees and may have to be organisationally acceptable. This will particularly be the case where the employer is heavily dependent on employee goodwill.

Public relations

There may also be public relations implications involved in tribunal cases. Organisations with a high public profile might be particularly sensitive, for example, to discrimination cases. Even if they win some of the publicity they receive may be unfavourable.

Personal

Tribunal cases can be stressful and time-consuming. There may also be a temptation on the part of employers to look for scapegoats if any fault is found with the way they handled a case. However, witch hunts are likely to have the effect of discouraging managers from taking disciplinary action when it may be needed in the future. The checks and balances in internal procedures, particularly of separating the chairing of a hearing from case presentation and the right of internal appeal, should in any case mean that responsibility for dismissal is shared.

Precedent

Some issues may involve important matters of principle and employers may feel that they need to defend a case in order to demonstrate that they have behaved correctly. Employers may also want to demonstrate to their managers that they will back them when they have behaved correctly. A further issue is not to encourage former employees to pursue weak cases in order to get a conciliated cash settlement. Former employees may use this tactic hoping that employers will find it cheaper to make a financial settlement rather than have the expense of successfully defending a case at a tribunal.

EMPLOYMENT TRIBUNALS

Employment tribunals have three members – a person with an employer background, one with an employee background (normally from a trade union) and a lawyer who acts as chair. In some circumstances, when the issue is essentially a point of law, there is provision for the chair to sit alone. Appeals can be made against tribunal decisions, but only on points of law. Applications for cases to be heard normally need to be made within three months of a dismissal taking effect.

Tribunals have proved to be more formal and legalistic than was originally intended. This has been an almost an inevitable development, given the right of appeal through the legal system against the decisions of employment tribunals. The rising case load regarding unfair dismissal in particular and the continuing extension of the jurisdiction of tribunals in other areas of employment law has also significantly increased the time before cases are heard. The volume of case law has contributed to the increased use of lawyers. Applicants are not allowed to apply for legal aid at tribunals – although they can apply for aid with regard to case preparation and appeals to the Employment Appeals Tribunal. Costs do not go 'with the action' as in other civil cases, but in some circumstances an award can be made against unsuccessful applicants for frivolous cases. In some cases a preliminary hearing is held to determine whether a case is substantial enough or eligible to proceed to a full hearing.

The main costs to an employer can be the time spent in defending a case and any fees paid to professional representatives. Former employees can be deterred by the formality and legal complexity, although if they have the services of a union representative they have free representation. A further issue is the poor chance of former employees getting their job back, even if they win. Although the impact the law has had in improving organisations' disciplinary procedures has been constructive, it is not surprising that there have been criticisms of the way tribunals operate. A major response to the criticisms has been the introduction of binding arbitration as an alternative to employment tribunal proceedings. This option is explained later in this chapter.

In considering whether or not an employer has acted reasonably, a tribunal has to judge the employer's behaviour on the evidence available at the time. Even if evidence available after the dismissal (and any internal appeal hearing) proves that the employer was wrong, the dismissal may still have been 'reasonable'. However, in some circumstances the employer may be able to reopen a case. An employer, who had acquitted an employee on a disciplinary charge of misappropriating petrol did this. This was because fresh evidence had emerged about the incident when the person was subsequently successfully prosecuted at a criminal court. The employer dismissed on the basis of the fresh evidence and successfully resisted an application for unfair dismissal at the Court of Appeal (*British Gas plc* vs *McGarrick 1991*). Reasonableness is looked at from the employer's point of view and not the employee's, although a reasonable employer would be expected to take the employee's interests into account (*Chubb Fire Security Ltd.* vs *Harper 1984*).

In some cases where employers have suffered losses and been unable to identify the culprit, their actions in dismissing those who could have been responsible have been upheld (e.g. *Monie* vs *Coral Racing 1980*). Much will depend on the circumstances in such cases, but this emphasises the point that it is the employer's reasonableness that is the issue. In defining reasonable behaviour it is necessary to consider what a reasonable (not a perfect) employer might have done, the size and administrative resources of the employer, how genuine the belief was, the basis for the belief and the norms in an industry. Tribunals are obliged to accept that there can be a number of different ways of handling a situation, all of which can be regarded as reasonable. An employer's judgement does not necessarily have to coincide with the judgement that the tribunal members would have made in the same situation for it to be regarded as reasonable. The employer's behaviour needs to be 'within the range of reasonable options'.

The freedom of action of the employer to dismiss is often greatly underestimated. This may be because of misunderstandings about the legal position or because it may be a convenient alibi to maintain that the employer has much less discretion than is really the case. One of the common mistakes that is made is for people to confuse the burden of proof in civil actions before a tribunal with the burden in criminal cases. An employer does not have to establish their case 'beyond reasonable doubt', as is the case in criminal prosecutions. It is up to the tribunal to determine whether the onus of proof rests with the employer or former employee. Even so, the case has only to be established on the balance of probabilities. At the risk of oversimplifying the issue, it is useful to liken the burden of proof to being 95 per cent at a criminal case but only 51 per cent at an employment tribunal.

Of the 31.1 per cent of cases in 1998–1999 that were not withdrawn, or that resulted in a conciliated settlement, 68 per cent were decided in favour of the employer and 32 per cent in favour of the former employee (Labour Market Trends 1999: 494). Employers are more likely to be defending the defensible rather than the indefensible if they appear before a tribunal. The requirement for them to be 'reasonable' sets a maximum standard for behaviour as well as a minimum – they do not have to have acted perfectly.

Any well-organised employer should, almost by definition, be able to have a much better track record at tribunals than the national average. Successful applications against the employer occur particularly in the less well-organised sectors of the economy where managerial resources are limited. A convenient rule of thumb is for an employer to expect to win at least four out of every five cases taken against them. A lower success rate may indicate weaknesses that need attention. A very high success rate raises the possibility that the employer is being too cautious and only dismissing when they feel certain they will win. There will be some differences of opinion between employers and tribunals. Employers can always consider reinstating if they lose a case at a tribunal. It is important to recognise that, if employers are seen to opt out of dismissing employees, unless the reasons are overwhelming, this can create a climate where nobody tries to tell anybody what to do on the basis that nothing is likely to be done if the person refuses. The impact of decisions concerning dismissal needs to be seen in relation to the signals it is sending within an organisation and not in isolation, or just in terms of the track record at tribunals.

THE NEED FOR EFFECTIVE PROCEDURES

Regard has to be paid to the procedure that an employer has followed in dismissing an employee. The Code of Practice on Disciplinary and Grievance Procedures issued by the Advisory, Conciliation and Arbitration Service (ACAS 2000b) provides the guidelines that employers are expected to follow. These guidelines are rather like the Highway Code – a breach in itself is not actionable but, in the circumstances of a dismissal, a breach of the guidelines can lead to an application for unfair dismissal succeeding. The importance of following an appropriate procedure was heightened by the House of Lords decision in the case of *Polkey* vs *A.E. Dayton Services Ltd.* (1987). This decision ended the practice of justifying dismissals by arguing that, had the procedure been followed, it would have made 'no difference' and emphasised the statutory right of employees to a fair procedure. Consequently, although the specific circumstances of dismissal can be important, procedural failings are more likely to lead to a verdict of unfair dismissal at tribunal hearings. The 'no difference' concept can be very relevant however to the calculation of compensation. As previously explained, any compensation awarded to dismissed employees can be scaled down if their contributory behaviour warrants it.

Employers should have their own disciplinary procedures, and these should be the subject of consultation, but not necessarily agreement, with any recognised trade unions. They need to follow the pattern recommended in the Code of Practice. The critical recommendations concerning procedures are reproduced as appendix 1 to this chapter. Reference should also be made to ACAS's general advisory handbook, *Discipline at Work* (ACAS 2000). Though the rest of the handbook does not have the status of the code, it is full of practical and useful advice that employers would be rash to ignore. Employers have a statutory duty to notify employees of the disciplinary procedure, and if they employ 20 or more people the procedure needs to be in writing. However, the disciplinary (and grievance) procedure does not have to form part of the contract of employment. If employers do make it part of the contract, employees who have been dismissed can argue that a dismissal that has short-circuited the disciplinary procedure amounts to breach of contract and claim earnings for the period it would have taken for their case to have been heard (*Gunton* vs *Richmond-upon Thames London Borough Council 1980*).

The Achilles' heel of employers at tribunals often turns out to be their failure to follow a systematic procedure, even though there may be a clearly defined procedure within the organisation that the employer should follow. Individual managers may fail to deal with a disciplinary issue and then, when their frustration builds up, dismiss an employee in a moment of anger. The legal requirements are not so much aimed at preventing dismissal but at ensuring that, when it does take place, it is done for appropriate reasons and in a manner which preserves the rights of the individual concerned to natural justice. The guidelines in appendix 1 do not seem too difficult to follow but, as with so many areas of management, the problem is one of the application of existing knowledge rather than having some magic wand for dealing with problems. One particularly apt quote from a tribunal illustrates this point:

> *Mr G did not on that occasion give the applicant a serious reprimand, although he did mention that he would kill him if such a thing occurred again.*
>
> IDS 1976: 13

The observance of appropriate procedures is not just a technical matter but one which can affect the actual decision that is taken. The decision to dismiss a person before they have, for example, had the opportunity to state their case is wrong, not just because it is a breach of justice but also because the fact-finding process is incomplete. However, employers also need to beware of overcompensating in this area and having procedures that are unduly elaborate. In some organisations, especially with some public sector employers, this has led to the procedures being too complex for many of their managers to handle. This in turn may lead to managers opting out of discipline and/or the organisation repeatedly losing tribunal cases because they have not kept to their self-imposed elaborate requirements.

(Example)

In a study of unfair dismissal decisions by tribunals, 69 out of 165 cases were found in favour of the applicant. 'Where employees won their claims, their success related almost without exception to procedural shortcomings on the part of the employer, whether the dismissal was for reasons of conduct, redundancy or incapacity.'

(Earnshaw 1997: 35)

It is not sufficient for employers to have good procedures; it is also necessary for their managers to have the skills to operate the procedures appropriately. This is necessary for the handling of all disciplinary cases, not just the small proportion that result in dismissal. Consequently, the skills involved in disciplinary handling are considered in detail later in this chapter.

THE RELATIONSHIP BETWEEN DISMISSAL AND CRIMINAL LAW

A further source of confusion can arise if a person has apparently committed a criminal action. It is a fallacy to assume that such action can only be handled by the police. If, for example, a person has apparently stolen something, it may be appropriate for the employer to institute disciplinary proceedings about the employee's apparent unauthorised possession of property belonging to the employer. Any decisions about whether or not there should be a prosecution should be handled separately. The option of letting such an issue be handled just by the police may not be as easy as it seems. As has already been explained, the burden of proof in criminal law is much higher than in civil law. The procedural rules are much tighter in the criminal courts and it may be necessary to establish that a felony was committed or attempted. Added to this is the problem that, if no action is taken pending a court hearing, an employee may have to be suspended on pay for several months. In any case, the employer may find that, if the case is substantiated, the primary remedy they want is to be able to dismiss the person concerned. The point that needs stressing is that apparent criminal activity by an employee against their employer does not remove the employer's rights to handle an issue as a disciplinary matter.

The much higher standards needed to secure a criminal conviction compared with success in a civil action were dramatically illustrated by the O. J. Simpson case.

Example

O.J. Simpson had been a particularly famous American football star. In 1995 he was acquitted by a Californian court of the murder of his former wife, Nicole Simpson and her partner, Ronald Goldman, who had both been killed the previous year. However, in 1997 in a civil action for damages he was unanimously held to have caused both deaths. Initial damages were awarded against him of $8.5 million, followed by a later punitive award of $25 million damages.

Provided there is no specific procedural requirement that a prosecution should be resolved before disciplinary proceedings are taken, it is normally better for the employer to resolve the disciplinary issue in advance of a prosecution being resolved. Amongst other things, this avoids the dilemma of what to do if a person has already been acquitted in the criminal courts. Subsequent acquittal does not invalidate disciplinary action previously taken, because the disciplinary action should be based on the rather separate issue of the extent to which the employee, or ex-employee, fulfilled their employment contract. If the person involved is not prepared to state their case, because it may reveal issues they prefer were only raised at subsequent criminal proceedings, this does not of itself prevent the employer from going ahead with a disciplinary hearing. Documentation, including statements by those accused, may need to be prepared separately and to different standards in any subsequent criminal case. People may raise the issue of 'double jeopardy', arguing that a person cannot be tried twice for the same offence. However, this argument is fallacious as the law simply prevents people being tried twice under criminal law for the same offence.

Whilst it is not possible for a person to be charged twice with the same offence under criminal law, there is no prohibition on an employer taking the civil action of terminating a person's employment irrespective of whether or not prosecution is initiated based on the circumstances that led to the person's dismissal. However, employers may want to carefully consider the timing of any disciplinary action so that they do not jeopardise any covert police surveillance that is in progress. They should also not automatically assume that conviction for a criminal offence justifies dismissal. Much will depend on the circumstances of a case, including the relevance of the conviction to a person's job. In the event of a custodial sentence being awarded by the courts employers might decide to dismiss the employee concerned, if only because of their non-availability for work.

The responsibility of the individual manager

THE DISCIPLINARY PYRAMID

The introduction of unfair dismissal law has tended to concentrate attention on dismissal. Discipline is a generic term, and dismissal is just one aspect of the disciplinary process. Ideally, policies and practices should be such that disciplinary issues are contained, so that it is rare for a dismissal to be necessary. If there is effective supervisory and managerial control, disciplinary issues should be generally so contained. If this is not the case, too many issues may be allowed to spiral upwards before being dealt with. The main volume of activity should be in encouraging self-discipline, containment and low level penalties (see Figure 13.1).

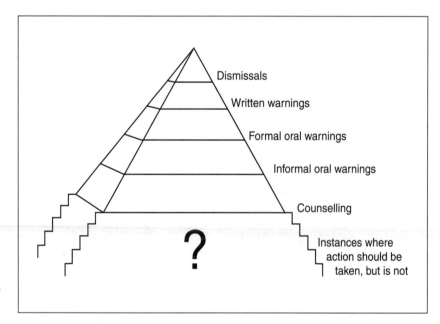

FIGURE 13.1 *The disciplinary pyramid*

A heavy emphasis on severe penalties may be indicative of ineffective control at the lower levels of the pyramid. This can happen all too frequently and what can emerge is that 'disciplinary problems' are a symptom of much deeper organisational problems, such as the lack of effective supervision and poor organisational structure. Contributory factors to this can be a general opting out of the management process and poor selection and training of supervisors and managers.

Sometimes supervisors either see themselves as not having any disciplinary responsibility at all or they are extremely vague about just what those responsibilities are. It may be particularly important to clarify exactly what the disciplinary responsibilities and powers are of the various levels of management. This is likely to be most needed with regard to the penalties that can be awarded at the base of the disciplinary pyramid where most action needs to take place and where the opportunity for confusion is greatest. The need to discipline subordinates is often an embarrassing and unpopular, if necessary, activity. The area where greatest organisational attention and clarification is often needed is the responsibility for investigation and follow-up of minor issues and the administering, where appropriate, of low-level penalties. This involves not just the drawing up of a clear procedure but also the training of supervisors and managers in how to handle their responsibilities. If these steps are not taken one is likely to have supervisors and managers intervening and getting it wrong or getting away with the potentially disastrous attitude that disciplinary control of their own subordinates is nothing to do with them but is some other mystery person's responsibility.

Even when responsibilities are clarified it is common for disciplinary issues to be referred upwards. It is important that managers do not get sucked into handling disciplinary issues that should be handled at a lower level. Instead they should coach those at a lower level in the managerial hierarchy in how to handle their responsibilities. This may involve junior managers keeping a diary note of informal warnings when appropriate. This may be useful if an employee later claims that they had not been told about a particular issue. However, such notes may be best kept in a general diary and not a diary or local file specifically about the person concerned. This is to avoid complications under the Data Protection Act of 1998 regarding subject notification, access and confidentiality. To make such entries on a central personnel file would also contradict the concept of an informal oral warning. The operation of discipline at this level is likely to overlap with general managerial control and the giving of work instructions.

A further reason for generally handling issues low down the pyramid is that any required change might as well be achieved with the minimum amount of pressure that will have the desired effect. If a quiet word will do the trick, there is little point in antagonising employees by using more pressure than is necessary. The informal oral warning may be the most important sanction in the disciplinary process. It may be convenient for people to argue that the only penalty is dismissal, but the reality is that most people do not like being corrected and that, psychologically, the informal oral warning is a sanction that managers may find they can use effectively. Only if this does not lead to the required change in behaviour does a manager need to consider more formal measures. In some cases employees may not even need reprimanding to change their behaviour.

Example
A technician wrecked a particularly expensive piece of equipment in a chemical works. The manager concerned took the view that that was one mistake the technician would never make again and that there was no need to take disciplinary action.

However, sometimes employees do need to have the error of their ways pointed out to them – either because they do not realise that they are in error or because they think that they can behave in a particular way with impunity.

THE ROLE OF THE PERSONNEL DEPARTMENT

Encouraging and helping junior managers to handle their responsibilities for discipline also leaves more senior managers free to be involved in more serious issues or in hearing appeals. A further danger is that disciplinary issues are referred to the personnel department for executive action. However, such involvement also encourages managers to opt out of their responsibilities. The general role of the personnel department should be to advise on the operation of disciplinary procedures rather than take a crucial element of management away from line managers. One of the ways in which this can be done is by having a personnel specialist as a member of a disciplinary panel, if only in an advisory capacity. Another specialist may then need to be assigned to give general procedural advice to one or both the parties about the case.

An issue where advice is often particularly needed is the level of penalty to be awarded when cases are upheld. This is often a grey area and it may be necessary to encourage managers to work through the implications of awarding particular penalties and the concept of the 'range of reasonable options'. The precedent effect of decisions and their impact on managers who are trying to maintain performance standards also have to be considered. The psychological aspects of discipline may also need to be taken into account. In many cases the very fact that a person has been called to account for their actions creates a considerable pressure. Also, the way in which an oral warning can be administered may make a marked impression on the person receiving it. It may also be necessary to encourage managers to focus on ways of getting employees to alter their behaviour, rather than simply establishing guilt or innocence. It may also be appropriate for a personnel department to arrange disciplinary skills training, particularly as this can be both necessary and very effective (Rees and Lee 1983: 42–45).

It may be necessary for an employer to dispel myths about the operation of the disciplinary process.

Example
In one health authority there was a generally held belief that there was no point in taking disciplinary action against employees because such action would only be reversed on appeal. On investigation it emerged that, in the previous 12 months, of the ten internal appeals against dismissal nine had failed and the one that had been allowed was generally felt to be the correction of an inappropriate previous decision.

CONTINUED OVER ➤

CONTINUED FROM PREVIOUS PAGE This simple statistic had not previously been established, and the myth was what people believed, not the reality. People may actually want to believe such myths, which is why it may be necessary to communicate what really does happen, as opposed to what people may prefer to think happens.

THE IMPACT OF OTHER MANAGEMENT ACTIVITIES

It may also be necessary to probe into other management activities to see what impact they are having on discipline.

Example

In the Social Services Department of a local authority, there was a particularly high need to employ staff who would take proper care of their clients, especially those in full-time care. Unfortunately, the screening process regarding the selection of staff was not very rigorous. As a consequence avoidable selection errors were made. The disciplinary problems that ensued were too great to be handled effectively by a weak management structure. These problems included the abuse of vulnerable people in care.

Disciplinary procedures and procedural skills

Any form of action needs to be preceded by careful diagnosis. There can be many reasons for inappropriate behaviour, including an inaccurate definition of what is appropriate. It is only when the facts have been checked out that one can begin to consider if disciplinary action may be necessary. Even if a person has behaved inappropriately, it may be that they see this for themselves and do not need to have salt rubbed in their wounds. When formal disciplinary proceedings appear to be needed, managers need to refer to the disciplinary procedures which their organisations should have or, failing that, the guidelines contained in the ACAS Code of Practice (2000b). It may also be necessary to refer to any disciplinary rules that exist or the need for such rules.

DISCIPLINARY HEARINGS

Perhaps the most crucial of all the distinctions that need to be made is that between a disciplinary hearing and disciplinary action. A common failing, revealed by a Department of Employment survey is for managers to assume that the outcome of proceedings is a foregone conclusion and to sentence the employee early in such proceedings (1975: 33–4). The word 'hearing' is as important as the word 'disciplinary', and one cannot be sure that disciplinary action is appropriate until the hearing has been completed. A formal hearing may not be necessary if relatively minor action is likely, but whatever the level of formality it is important that the employee is given the opportunity to state their case before any action is taken. At a formal hearing it is appropriate for whoever is conducting it to recess before communicating any decision. This gives the chair time to consider the position carefully or, if a panel is involved, to consider any differences of view, before any action is determined. Even if an employee's conduct seems quite inexcusable, there will be occasions when it turns out that an issue was not as straightforward as it first appeared. In any case, justice needs to be seen to be done, not just for the benefit of the employee concerned but for their colleagues as well. Although these points are obvious enough, unfortunately they are often neglected.

(Examples)

At one disciplinary hearing, an employee was listened to carefully, only to be handed a letter of dismissal which must have been typed before the hearing started. On another occasion an employee was asked to sit outside the room to await the decision of a disciplinary panel and was then given a letter of dismissal, which could have been typed during the recess apart from the fact that it was dated a week previously!

SUSPENSION

A predicament which employers can face is behaviour by an employee which necessitates them leaving the employer's premises immediately. This could be for a variety of reasons, including fighting, apparent drunkenness or apparent theft. The appropriate course of action in such situations is to suspend the employee on pay pending an investigation. Even if it appears that the employee has committed gross misconduct which justifies summary dismissal, such a decision should not be taken without there being a disciplinary hearing. If the case against an employee is established at a hearing, then dismissal may be given without notice from that point in time. If there is no such hearing, the employer will have fallen into the trap of prejudging the issue. Apart from giving an employee time to prepare their case, an interval between an incident and a decision can lead to a cooling of tempers all round and increase the prospects of a rational decision.

Suspension from duty is quite distinct from suspension without pay, which is sometimes used as a penalty after a hearing has been completed. Such unpaid suspension would have to be provided for in the contract of employment. This distinction may need to be made to employees who are being suspended, together with an explanation that nothing is decided until the hearing is completed and that there is no loss of pay involved. The important point is that managers faced with the problem of needing to get somebody off the premises immediately should do this by paid suspension and not instant dismissal.

THE ROLE OF THE CHAIR

When formal disciplinary hearings are held, consideration should be given to one of the managers acting as chair. A manager obviously will not be viewed as a totally independent person, but proper chairing can help ensure that proceedings are conducted as impartially as possible. The chair should not have been directly involved in the case beforehand. It is often appropriate for the chair to be the boss's boss. One of the dangers of the senior manager present putting the case is that they may then be seen as judge, prosecutor, jury, executioner and possibly witness all rolled into one. A further problem is that, if the senior manager gets involved in an argument, which would not be surprising given such a load of conflicting roles, then it is difficult for anyone else to keep the proceedings in order. A more satisfactory procedure is for the senior manager to concentrate on chairing, leaving other people to present any case and evidence. This is not only necessary for form's sake but to see that the proceedings are conducted in a systematic manner, so that no decision is taken until the arguments have all been properly considered. This role of chair should continue during a recess. Consideration also has to be given as to who should participate in the discussions during the recess. Managers who have been involved in presenting the case against an employee are best excluded at this stage. This is in order to reduce the possibility of collusion between those playing the roles of judge and prosecutor.

Perhaps the most awkward part of the whole disciplinary process for the chair is handling disagreements either about what happened or about what action should be taken. It is a fallacy that management is impotent unless an employee agrees to be disciplined, or that irrefutable proof has to be produced to substantiate any difference of opinion. The reality is that it is necessary for the manager acting as chair to listen carefully, consider the relevant points and then decide what action, if any, is appropriate. As with tribunals, the standard of proof, or the strictness of procedure, does not have to match criminal proceedings. The parties are in fact considering a civil issue – concerning the degree to which an employee has fulfilled their contract of employment – and not a criminal trial.

For proceedings to be handled effectively, a clear and preferably agreed sequence of events needs to be established. This should include arrangements for the exchange of any written documents and explanations of when each side should state their case, produce witnesses, cross-examine and sum up. The framework is essentially judicial, but sometimes the parties can mistakenly adopt a negotiating approach. If that happens, proceedings can degenerate into an unsystematic attempt by each side to browbeat the other, which can aggravate an already delicate situation instead of defusing it. The chair will also need to be aware of one or other party trying to take over the chair's role by, for example, giving procedural rulings (as opposed to raising points for the chair to rule on). Other dangers include the use of leading questions to the party's own witnesses, and attempts to intimidate witnesses produced by the other side. An example of a procedural sequence that will help a chair maintain control and facilitate a systematic hearing is given in appendix 2 to this chapter. The general skills of chairing are explained in the final chapter of this book.

Sometimes it is best to give any decision in writing to let tempers cool and allow the parties to come to terms with the fact that they might not win their case. Also the emotion involved in hearing a case and assembly of the parties involved in a case can create a potentially explosive environment. However, if the chair does give the decision orally it is essential that there should not be any further argument. If the proceedings have been conducted properly all the relevant points should have been made and considered anyway. If an employee disagrees with a decision, the appropriate way of handling the situation is simply to explain the rights of appeal. Often violent arguments break out at this stage simply because it is not made clear to an employee that there is an appeals procedure that they are entitled to use.

PRESENTING OFFICER

Managerial representatives presenting a case also need to prepare carefully beforehand. They may combine their role with that of investigating officer, or assign someone else to fill that role. A person's guilt may be self-evident, but the whole point of a quasi-judicial hearing is to enable the person or people sitting in judgement to decide solely on the basis of the evidence and argument that is openly presented. Consequently, patient work has to be undertaken in developing logical arguments and collecting relevant evidence. Consideration also has to be given to the presentational skills involved. All this is particularly important, as the skills of advocacy are often much more part of the 'stock in trade' of union representatives than of managers. This means that if managers fail to do their homework they may needlessly lose cases, and their confidence. Some of the basic issues concerning preparation and presentation are listed below (Evans 1983).

Preparation

- Select charge(s) carefully – pick the important one or ones you can sustain and don't use a scatter-gun approach;
- copy documents to the chair and employee's representative;
- organise witnesses.

Presentation

- Use an *aide-memoire* if it helps;
- speak clearly and to the chair or panel (you have to convince them rather than the opposing party);
- use logical argument and avoid 'purple prose';
- identify and see if you can destroy the main argument in your opponent's case – if you can do that the rest of the issues may fall into place;
- be assertive, not aggressive, and show conviction in your case;
- do not let yourself get riled by the other side;
- ask one question at a time;
- beware of asking questions to which you do not know the answer;
- keep cool under pressure.

If the presenting officer is making a case at an employment tribunal they will need to do it primarily by putting questions to their witnesses.

THE ROLE OF THE REPRESENTATIVE

Another critical issue concerning formal disciplinary procedures is the need for an employee to be accompanied. Under the terms of the Employment Relations Act of 1999 this is a statutory right. Breach of this right renders any dismissal automatically unfair, regardless of length of service. Those affected can also apply for interim relief. This right to be accompanied in disciplinary proceedings and proceedings regarding serious grievances also applies to certain categories of workers who are not classified as employees (Aikin 2000: 20–21). This could include:

- self-employed people who do not run their own businesses,
- home-workers,
- agency workers.

In practice the person who accompanies an employee is likely to act as a representative. It is difficult to see how a hearing can be fairly conducted otherwise. The representative can be a colleague or a union official of the employee's choice (even if the employer does not recognise unions). Employers may want, however, to consider restricting the rights of representation to colleagues or trade union officials. If there is no restriction they may find that an employee is accompanied by a lawyer who may introduce a greater level of formality and legalism into the proceedings than they wish to have.

There is a need for employees (and workers) to be represented regardless of their statutory right. A representative's function is to help a person put their case so that any decision is taken only after all the relevant arguments have been considered. The representative may have heard only the employee's version of events. A formal hearing can provide an employer with the opportunity to put over their version. This may influence the representative, whose views may be crucial if an issue is sensitive and likely to lead to industrial action. If an employer has a good case, it is appropriate that it should be explained; if the case is weak, then perhaps it should be dropped. Often managers fail to realise that the really critical audience in disciplinary proceedings can be the employee's colleagues.

The position of the representative has also to be considered. They may well feel that, whatever an employee has done, they have the right to have their case argued strongly, even if privately the representative does not condone the employee's behaviour. At the end of a hearing at least the representative can explain that they have done what they can for the employee concerned. If the representative does not agree with the action that an employer eventually takes, at least any subsequent disagreement need not be compounded by arguments about whether the person had a fair hearing. The crucial distinction is that, whatever an employee has or has not done, this should not affect their right to a fair hearing. Care should be taken to ensure that employees know their procedural rights and it is preferable that they have a copy of any relevant disciplinary rules and procedures. They do need to have copies of any written evidence that is to be used.

COMMUNICATING THE RESULT

Before any decision is taken after a hearing there needs to be a careful review of the options and of the need to communicate accurately what has been decided. The options include stating that the employee has been cleared. In cases of cumulative misconduct, it is appropriate to step up the pressure on an employee gradually, so that they either mend their ways or are made perfectly aware that failure to change their ways will result in more serious action next time. Care needs to be taken in deciding just what a person is to be warned about. If the grounds of the warning are narrow, for 'lateness' for example, an employee may be able to maintain that their lateness record cannot be taken into account if they are subsequently disciplined for absence. Thus it may be appropriate to broaden the base of a warning from lateness to general attendance. Warnings about other matters may need to include a proviso that repetition of a particular action or related misconduct can result in further disciplinary action. Too narrow a definition of what the warning is about can lead to the possibility of a person getting a number of 'final' warnings, all for different offences.

Consideration also needs to be given as to whether or not there should be automatic time limits for any penalties imposed. These are recommended in the ACAS Advisory Handbook (ACAS 2000: 30–31). However, one needs to be aware of the rigidities that specific time limits can create. Holidays, sickness, staff changes and other work commitments can cause procedural delays, causing a warning to be spent before it can be used as a platform for further disciplinary action. If fixed time limits are not used, consideration will have to be given when a penalty is imposed as to how long it is reasonable to take into account previous warnings. It is also necessary to consider just what previous warnings can be taken into account. There may be some semantic issues with regard to formal oral warnings. They differ from informal oral warnings in that they are a higher level penalty which were considered sufficiently serious to be confirmed in writing. However, they are one stage below written warnings. The authority for giving these differing levels of penalties may also be vested in different levels of management or supervision. If the distinction between an informal and a formal oral warning is seen as too obscure it may be best to eliminate the stage of a formal oral warning.

An advantage of having formal warnings in writing is to ensure that a person realises what is happening. It is all too easy for disciplinary interviews to be handled with so light a touch that a person comes away with the impression that they have been commended rather than rebuked.

Ambiguities and carelessness in communicating just what has happened as a consequence of a disciplinary hearing can result not only in failure to achieve the desired effect but also in confrontation, if a person is disciplined again, about what really was decided the last time. The representative of an employee should be given a copy of any written warning so that it is also clear to them what has happened. This may also help to prevent subsequent argument about whether or not an employee has received their copy. A further way of avoiding argument on that score may be to ask an employee to acknowledge receipt of a warning, making it clear that this is only an acknowledgement, and not meant to commit the employee either to agreeing or to disagreeing with a written warning.

The importance and number of points to be considered in drafting written warnings is such that a checklist of the potential issues is necessary. Such a checklist is produced as an appendix to this chapter.

APPEALS

Thought has to be given to the stage at which appeals can be lodged. It may not be necessary to provide for appeals against informal warnings, for example, especially as an employee can always use the grievance procedure if there is no formal procedure for handling appeals against minor penalties. It would seem appropriate, though, to build an appeals procedure into a disciplinary procedure when warnings get to the stage of indicating that dismissal is becoming a possibility. Appeals should be to managers not previously involved in the case. The grounds for an appeal should be clarified – they should not involve a total re-hearing of a case unless that is clearly appropriate. One set of circumstances that may be appropriate for a re-hearing, though, is where procedural defects occurred at the initial hearing (*Whitbread and Company* vs *Mills 1988*). If, however, an appeal is just against the disciplinary action that has been imposed, for example, it is just the level of penalty that needs to be considered. Another important issue concerns the admissibility of fresh evidence by either party. If it is relevant to the original charge it must be taken into account with internal appeals (*West Midlands Co-operative Society* vs *Mills 1986*).

An employee's right of appeal should always be made clear, regardless of whether or not they argue about the decision when they are told about it. Time limits need to be imposed, so that if an appeal is not lodged within a certain period of time it lapses. This can avoid subsequent disagreement about whether or not the employee accepted the decision. It may also be appropriate to specify the time within which appeals are to be heard. In cases where employees are dismissed, consideration also has to be given as to whether or not they stay on the payroll pending the hearing of their appeal. A danger of keeping people on the payroll pending appeal is that some people may appeal simply as a means of securing further payment.

Tribunals discourage the hearing of applications until internal appeals have been heard. They have the power to reduce any compensation awarded by a fortnight's pay if this is not done.

COMPROMISE AGREEMENTS

As was explained earlier in this chapter, in the context of financial compensation, employees who have made a claim to a tribunal for unfair dismissal often reach a conciliated settlement instead of proceeding to a tribunal hearing. However, there is also provision for compromise agreements to be made before an application is made to an employment tribunal, under which claimants waive their right to take a case to a tribunal. For such an agreement to be valid, it is necessary for the former employee to receive independent advice from a lawyer or other specialist who has a professional indemnity of insurance. The other specialist could be a full-time trade union official.

One of the outcomes of such a settlement could be that the case is determined by an independent arbitrator. It is normal for employers to include comprehensive waiver clauses to prevent any other action by the former employee, but these don't automatically prevent other actions that were not related to the specific dispute (*Lunt* vs *Merseyside Tec Ltd 1999*).

THE ARBITRATION OPTION

Under the terms of the Employment Rights (Dispute Resolution) Act of 1998 many unfair dismissal cases can be resolved by binding arbitration instead of being referred to an employment tribunal. This option requires the agreement of both the employer and former employee. Access to this arrangement would normally be via a conciliation officer of ACAS. The remit of arbitrators, who sit alone, is to decide whether or not a dismissal was fair on the basis of the facts and not the law. This distinction will determine whether cases are appropriate for arbitration or not. Cross-examination of witnesses can only be conducted via questions to the arbitrator. Parties will normally start their case with an oral presentation, rather than by the examination of witnesses, as with tribunals. Such statements may be provided to the arbitrator and other party in advance.

The remedies for successful applications are similar to those of tribunals. In practice the greater speed with which hearings can be arranged means that there is a greater prospect of reinstatement being a practical remedy. If an employer refuses to implement a reinstatement or re-engagement award, enforcement would be financial compensation via the courts. The only way in which a decision can be challenged is by judicial review. There is no provision for appeal on a point of law. Arbitrators do not have to be lawyers, though some will be. Because of these factors the nature of arbitration hearings will be significantly different from employment tribunals. They should be less legalistic, more quickly arranged, shorter and significantly cheaper because of the greatly reduced need for legal preparation, presentation and potential for appeal. The greater potential for use of written case statements may also help. Hearings are likely to be less stressful for the parties concerned and are held in private. They are intended to be conducted on an inquisitorial rather than an adversarial basis. Evidence is not given on oath.

Because arbitrators are not normally asked to determine points of law they are not bound by case law or the decisions of other arbitrators. However, they may take into account the reasoning that has taken place in decisions arising out of the tribunal procedure. An implication of this is that they may not feel constrained by the concept of 'the range of reasonable responses' and determine a case on the evidence and their industrial expertise. If this is the case employees may be more likely to win cases before an arbitrator than at a tribunal. However, arbitrators do not have the authority to substitute a lesser penalty, such as a written warning, for a dismissal.

SUMMARY

✔ The importance of effective disciplinary handling has been examined and the need for preventative policies and procedures. Sound management and education about what behaviour is expected of employees can do much to contain or prevent problems in this area. Relevant law has been examined, including the related area of redundancy dismissal. This is because of the statutory protections of employees regarding unfair dismissal and redundancy. Separate procedures may be necessary for handling cases of ill health and poor performance.

✔ As has been stressed, most disciplinary handling needs to be at the lower level of the disciplinary pyramid in terms of the level of sanction. Unfortunately, those with managerial responsibility often opt out of their responsibilities in this area. This can be for a variety of reasons. These include a general reluctance to manage, a lack of clarity about who has responsibility for control and discipline and the unpopularity that managers can fear from taking disciplinary action. This can lead to a general loss of control and to issues having to be dealt with more seriously than would otherwise have been necessary. On-the-job coaching and formal training can do much to train people about their responsibilities in this area and how to handle them.

✔ The need for an adequate investigation into potential disciplinary issues was explained. It is necessary to properly investigate the facts and to give any employee concerned the opportunity to state their case before any decision is taken. This not only helps to ensure decisions are correct but is likely to protect an employer from a successful action for unfair dismissal at an employment tribunal. In formal hearings it is advisable to separate out the roles of presenting officer and the person who has to chair the proceedings. Employees have the legal right to be accompanied in such proceedings. If a major penalty is imposed it is necessary for the employee concerned to have a right of appeal. Where practicable, this should be to a higher level of management and to people not previously involved in a case.

SELF-ASSESSMENT QUESTIONS

1. How would you assess whether or not disciplinary policies in an organisation were effective?

2. What are the three main grounds for fair dismissal in the UK?

3. Explain the concept of the disciplinary pyramid.

4. How would you handle a disciplinary issue at the informal level?

5. How would you set out to present a case at a formal disciplinary hearing?

6. What are the basic requirements for seeing that a formal disciplinary hearing is chaired properly?

 References

(Works of general interest in the specific references are marked with a star.)

* Advisory, Conciliation and Arbitration Service (2000) *Discipline at Work*, Advisory Handbook, ACAS.
* Advisory Conciliation and Arbitration Service (2000a) *Redundancy Handling*, ACAS.
  Aikin, Olga (2000) 'Strictly by Invitation Only', *People Management*, 6 July.
  Advisory, Conciliation and Arbitration Service (2000b) *Code of Practice on Disciplinary and Grievance Procedures*, ACAS.
  Department of Employment (1975) Manpower paper no. 14, HMSO.
  Earnshaw, Jill (1997) 'Tribunals and Tribulations', *People Management*, 29 May.
  Evans, Keith (1983) *Advocacy at the Bar: A Beginner's Guide*, Financial Training Publications Ltd.
  Incomes Data Services (1976) Brief 99, December.
  Labour Market Trends (1999) Employment Tribunal and Employment Appeal Tribunal Statistics 1997–1998 and 1998–1999, September. Office for National Statistics.
  Rees, David and Bob Lee (1983) 'Disciplinary Skills Training at Canada Dry Rawlings', *Personnel Executive*, February.

General references
Fowler, Alan (1999) *Managing Redundancy*, 2nd ed., Institute of Personnel and Development.
Incomes Data Services (1998) *Unfair Dismissal – Employment Law Handbook*, 3rd. ed., Incomes Data Services.
James, Philip and David Lewis (1992) *Discipline*, Institute of Personnel and Development.

Cases cited
British Gas plc vs *McGarrick* (1991) IRLR 305, CA.
Chubb Fire Security Ltd. vs *Harper* (1984) IRLR 311, EAT.
Gunton vs *Richmond-upon-Thames London Borough Council* (1980) ICR 755, IRLR 321, CA.

Hogg vs *Dover College* (1998) IRLIB 374, EAT

Kwik-Fit (GB) Ltd vs *Lineham* (1992) IRLR 156, EAT.

Lunt vs *Merseyside Tec Ltd* (1999) IRLR 459, EAT.

Monie vs *Coral Racing* (1980) IRLR 464 CA

Nash vs *Mash/Roe Group* (1998) IRLR 168.

Polkey vs *A. E. Dayton Services Ltd* (1987) IRL 503, H of L.

West Midlands Co-operative Society vs *Tipton* (1986) ICR 192, H of L.

Whitbread and Company plc vs *Mills* (1988) ICR 716, EAT.

Appendix 1 to chapter 13

Disciplinary procedures should:

i) be in writing;

ii) specify to whom they apply;

iii) be non-discriminatory;

iv) provide for matters to be dealt with without undue delay;

v) provide for proceedings, witness statements and records to be kept confidential;

vi) indicate the disciplinary actions which may be taken;

vii) specify the levels of management which have the authority to take the various forms of disciplinary action;

viii) provide for workers to be informed of the complaints against them and where possible all relevant evidence before any hearing;

ix) provide workers with an opportunity to state their case before decisions are reached;

x) provide workers with the right to be accompanied.

xi) ensure that, except for gross misconduct, no worker is dismissed for a first breach of discipline;

xii) ensure that disciplinary action is not taken until the case has been carefully investigated;

xiii) ensure that workers are given an explanation for any penalty imposed;

xiv) provide a right of appeal – normally to a more senior manger – and specify the procedure to be followed;

Appendix 2 to chapter 13

EXAMPLE OF PROCEDURAL SEQUENCE AT A DISCIPLINARY HEARING

1 Introduction by chair
  Explanation of charge
  Explanation of sequence of hearing

2 Presentation of case against the employee by the appropriate line manager
  Management witnesses
  Questioning of management witnesses via the chair

3 Union presentation and response to management submission
  Union witnesses
  Questioning of union witnesses via the chair

4 Further points by management
  Further points by union
  Further questions by chair/panel

5 Summing up by line manager
  Summing up by union representative

6 Recess

7 Decision – orally and/or in writing later

Appendix 3 to Chapter 13

CHECKLIST FOR DISCIPLINARY LETTERS

Item	Comments
1. Requesting attendance at hearing	
Specify charges.	The charges are allegations. They may or may not be proved as a result of a hearing.
Suggest the employee brings a representative if they wish, and relevant witnesses, if appropriate.	If a representative comes it will give you the opportunity to put your case over to them, as well as ensuring the arguments are properly examined.
Give appropriate information and time for the employee to prepare their defence adequately.	Failure to do this may invalidate the proceedings.
Refer to the disciplinary procedure.	The employee should have a copy. If there is doubt, send them one.
Indicate that disciplinary action could be imposed according to the result of the hearing.	
2. Disciplinary letter (given after the hearing)	
State what disciplinary action is to be taken, if any.	
State the nature of the offence(s).	You may wish to incorporate general terms, such as misconduct, in any warning letter. This may make it easier in the future to refer back to earlier offences.
Specify any conditions about future conduct. This may include any help you are prepared to give.	You may warn an employee about future conduct and any repetition or related offence may/will render them liable to further action.
Specify any time limits.	Sometimes procedures provide for warnings to lapse after a certain period of good behaviour. You do not have to put in time limits, it may be best not to – they can be rather rigid.
Specify the appeal procedure and the time limit for invoking it.	The more serious the penalty the more important it is to give a person the right of appeal.

Item	Comments

State if you want the employee to:
  i)   acknowledge receipt of the letter;
  ii) register dissent about any part of the letter they consider to be inaccurate.	

If suspension is involved, state if it is with or without pay.	If suspension is without pay, check if you have the contractual right to do this.
Send a copy of the letter to the person's representative and to any managers concerned.	

chapter (fourteen)

The manager and employee relations

There are case studies and exercises at http://www.thomsonlearning.co.uk (for full details, see the listing at the start of this book).

LEARNING OUTCOMES

By the end of this chapter you will be able to:

● Identify the objectives of both management and employees in organisations

● Locate the employee relations function within an organisation

● Identify the key variables in the labour market in which employee relations activity takes place

● Identify the legal framework of employee relations in the UK

● Understand the role of trade unions in employee relations

● Identify the causes of problems in the employee relations area and develop strategies for dealing with these issues

● Identify the role conflict involved in managers being members of trade unions and establish a way of coping with this if necessary

Introduction

In this chapter the objectives of both employers and employees are examined. Whilst there can be overlap in these objectives there can also be conflicts of interest. Conflicts can arise whether an employee is a member of a trade union or not. Employers need to have strategies for handling such key issues as pay and performance standards for all their employees, not just those in trades unions. That is why the term 'employee relations' is used rather than industrial relations. The term is becoming increasingly appropriate as most of the workforce are not members of trade unions, and there has been a steady decline in the number of employees covered by collective bargaining arrangements.

Employee relations activity in an organisation can be widely distributed and is an important activity whether trade unions are recognised or not. Maintaining cost-effective production or service is a key responsibility of line management. Personnel or human resource management specialists may also play a key role. The employee relations activity is significantly influenced by the labour market in which it operates. It is also influenced by the legal framework. Both these factors are examined. The role of trade unions is also examined, including their statutory rights. An important feature of employee relations over recent years in the UK has been the general decline in both the collective bargaining power and coverage of trade unions and the increase in individual statutory rights.

Identifying the causes of employee relations problems is not always easy. This is because weaknesses in other areas of organisational activity can have a knock-on effect into the employee relations area. However, an understanding of how this can happen can be essential to developing appropriate remedial strategies. Finally, the potential for conflict is examined if managers are also trade union members. Strategies for coping with any such conflict are explained. The related area of negotiating skills is covered in the next chapter.

Objectives in employee relations

MANAGERIAL VS EMPLOYEE OBJECTIVES

The primary aim of managers in the employee relations area is likely to be to obtain the co-operation of the workforce in achieving organisational objectives, such as:

- cost-effective performance (resulting in low unit labour costs),
- control of change,
- the avoidance of stoppages and other sanctions.

The pursuit of these objectives needs to be balanced as they may conflict with one another. This can also be the case with the objectives of trade unions (and/or individual employees) which are likely to be:

- the maintenance and possible improvement of the terms and conditions of employment,
- job security,
- control of change,
- the avoidance of stoppages and other sanctions.

The terms under which people work are negotiated either individually or between union representatives and the employer, or sometimes a combination of these two processes. The negotiated agreements represent a balance that provides sufficient incentive for both parties to come together. The parties will, however, take a continuing interest in the extent to which their concerns are being met. This may be done quite amicably – the resolution of areas of conflict through negotiation does not mean that sanctions have to be applied. Often the term 'conflict' is used in an industrial context synonymously with 'strike', ignoring the point that the application of sanctions is a way of trying to resolve conflict only when negotiations have broken down.

One has to be wary of the term 'good employee relations' as that begs the question, 'Good from whose point of view?' Each party will need to assess success according to whether or not they have adequately achieved their objectives. There can be win–win situations when, for example, an organisation is flourishing, wages are generous and there is job security. However, there will be occasions when this is not possible, and one needs to beware of adopting an unrealistic unitarist view of organisations, which ignores the potential for genuine conflicts of interests. This issue has been previously discussed, particularly in chapter 2, but is so basic to employee relations it needs further explanation in this chapter. It is also referred to in the next chapter in the context of negotiation.

FRAMES OF REFERENCE

Fox (1965) used the concepts of unitary and pluralistic frames of reference to classify managers into two groups. Unitarists view the organisation as having one common purpose with sectional interests needing to be subordinated to overall organisational objectives. Activity that detracts from this is seen as being illegitimate. Attempts to pursue sectional interests are seen as irrational because they damage the organisation overall. A relevant analogy is that of a sports team which has the overriding aim of winning. This view is in contrast with the pluralistic frame of reference which recognises that the objectives of the organisation and the various interest groups within it do not always coincide. An example of this is if there is a need for redundancy. The pluralist perspective provides a framework both for identifying potential conflict and dealing with it.

The unitary and pluralistic frames of reference can be a very useful way of analysing the way people approach employee relations. The two approaches highlight the fact that managers have to manage groups and people whose interests will not always coincide with organisational objectives. Sometimes employees or their representatives have a reverse unitarist approach which leads them to believe that anything that is for the benefit of the employee is automatically beneficial for the organisation. Managers don't choose to have a particular frame of reference; it is likely to be an inherent part of their personality and value system and not easily changed. Those with a unitary frame of reference may have difficulty in identifying the reasons for conflict generally, not just in the employee relations area.

The importance of managers having a frame of reference that enables them to recognise the causes and rationality of conflict is illustrated by the following two examples.

An engineering company in London had carefully built up a consensus model for decision-making with its employees. There were many areas of common interest where productive discussions took place. However, the model was not able to cope with significant areas of conflict. During a time of labour scarcity, management proposed that the factory be relocated to the West of England where labour was more plentiful and cheaper. However, employee representatives were understandably reluctant to agree to their members being made redundant or having to move to an area where wages were lower. Problems involving the transfer of council housing were another issue. The move did not take place. Similar difficulties had been experienced in getting the employee representatives to agree to progressive equal opportunities policies when there had been a large influx of immigrants into the area.

A consensus model of decision-making was also introduced into the National Health Service in the UK at one stage. Management teams were set up which were supposed to reach integrated decisions on a consensus basis. Unfortunately, this had the effect of giving each member of the team a veto. This caused such organisational paralysis that one of the ways in which decisions had to be forced was by employees taking industrial action (ACAS 1978). Consequently, the consensus arrangement had to be replaced by an orthodox line management structure.

Failure to recognise conflicts of interest can also make schemes of self-regulation ineffective. Examples of where it could be argued that the interests of members are allowed to override those of the public include disciplinary action against medical doctors, lawyers, newspapers and the stock exchange. The problems faced by front-line managers in dealing with conflicts of interest between managerial and employee objectives are dealt with later in this chapter. Strategies for supporting the position of the first line manager are also considered. The problems of trying to achieve consensus in employee participation schemes are also examined.

Employee relations in the context of the organisation

RANGE OF ACTIVITIES

Employee relations activity is likely to be widely distributed within an organisation. Activities in this area include:

- the determination of pay and benefits,
- work performance,
- disciplinary handling,
- individual and collective grievances,

- collective representation, including employee participation,
- health and safety,
- redundancy,
- other statutory rights of employees.

The involvement of a personnel department, if there is one, is often necessary to ensure that decisions form an integrated pattern and not a set of conflicting precedents. However, the individual manager is bound to have some responsibility within this framework, often at increasing levels. Even if all the financial and other formal agreements are determined outside their department, as a minimum line managers have to control labour costs and standards of performance.

Despite, or partly because of, the trend to greater devolution of authority to local management, there has been a tendency to integrate employee relations activity more closely with other organisational activity. When union power was stronger than it currently is, the role of personnel departments was often to act as trouble-shooters and take an executive role, leaving line management to concentrate on production and/or service delivery. This could have the effect of detaching policy in this area from policy decisions elsewhere. National bargaining and membership of employers' associations reinforced this tendency. However, a general decline in this historic type of trouble-shooting role has been offset by developments in employment law. The volume and complexity of the law have increased both the need for personnel specialists and the influence they have. The increased involvement of line management in many human resource management strategies has been another reason for a changed pattern of personnel management activity.

HUMAN RESOURCE MANAGEMENT

The term 'human resource management' (HRM), is subject to a variety of interpretations. It is sometimes subdivided into hard (quantifiable) and soft (intangible) areas.

Examples of hard areas include employee costs and head-counts. Soft areas include issues such as organisational capability, motivation, and training and development. It should involve a genuine attempt to integrate the various aspects of personnel (or human resource) management with one another as well as with corporate and other policy decision-making. This has always been the objective of progressive personnel management policies. The generally reduced bargaining power of trade unions, and cost and competitive pressures have created an impetus for more proactive policies in the personnel/human resource area. In the employee relations area this has often led to a change of emphasis by managers from trouble-shooting to an examination of ways in which more cost-effective working practices can be introduced.

HRM involves a tailoring of policies to fit the specific needs of an organisation rather than the use of a set of standard prescriptive remedies. As well as facilitating change, human resource management specialists should specify both the organisational objectives that exist and the constraints before strategic decisions are taken, rather than be expected to simply implement strategic decisions they have not been involved in. Both the options and the constraints may revolve around the capacity of the organisation and its staff to successfully undertake certain activities. An example was given in chapter 2 of the national charity that seriously overextended itself by an expansion programme and ignored its lack of managerial expertise and the legal obligation to retain 'acquired' staff. It also follows that human resource management specialists may also need to be involved in developing the organisational capability to handle potential new developments.

The type of HRM outlined above necessitates a specialist board member. For such a member to be effective they need to have sound general knowledge of the organisation as a whole, including its culture and the way in which it needs to develop from a strategic point of view. This may reduce the ability of specialist HRM staff to transfer their expertise between different types of organisation. This will particularly be the case if they try and impose a model that operated elsewhere in significantly different circumstances. For HRM directors to be effective they need to be involved in activities such as strategic planning, budgeting, organisational structuring and decisions involving major investment, acquisitions and divestments.

Specific ways in which human resource management has been developed include:

- the use of management information systems to facilitate staff planning and cost control;
- the development of individual rather than collective employment contracts;
- direct communication with the workforce rather than through trade unions;
- gearing of employment policies to increase customer or client orientation — this may involve attempts to change organisational culture and commitment;
- increased emphasis on the value added by individuals and activities — sometimes this has involved the use of performance-related pay;
- ensuring that training and development activities are closely aligned to corporate objectives;
- the development of internal consultancy skills and acting as a change agent;
- contracting out or sharing discrete activities such as payroll administration;
- internal surveys and benchmarking to help evaluate effectiveness;
- the adoption of flexible working practices either in terms of flexibility of function, flexibility of location or numerical flexibility. The concept of the flexible organisation was discussed in chapter 3.

Strategic HRM is often part of the management philosophy and practice particularly of Japanese and North American companies who have inwardly invested in the UK. Some critics argue that the concept is unitarist and that it ignores the potential conflict of interests between employers and employees. There is also potential conflict between the hard and soft variants of HRM. It may be difficult to expect commitment from employees, for example, who are on short-term contracts to suit the organisation's need for numerical flexibility. The alternative point of view is that sound strategies take account of such potential conflicts. Inevitably, strategic HRM requires the close involvement of senior management, and it is a process that is essentially driven by line management. Often, however, what is described as HRM is no more than routine personnel administration.

SUPERVISORY CONTROL

A crucial aspect of employee relations in any organisation is the extent to which managerial interests are safeguarded at the level of first-line supervision. This is the most junior level of management but also forms the largest part of the managerial pyramid. The term 'supervision' is used in this context to include managers with first-line responsibility for managing people. Managing at this level can often involve trying to reconcile the sometimes differing aspirations of the organisation and the employees with regard to issues such as work roles, working methods, and quantity and quality of production or service delivered. The problem of trying to reconcile conflicts can be intensified if the person in charge is also a member of the work group.

Unfortunately, senior managers may not understand the difficulties that first-line managers or supervisors have. This is particularly likely to be the case if senior managers have a unitary frame of reference. A potential consequence is that first-line managers or supervisors may give way to work group pressures and, in order to protect themselves, conceal this as far as possible from their superiors. Some people may not even want to accept or discharge their managerial responsibilities, as was explained in chapter 1. Also the advantages of being a supervisor in some organisations have been reduced by developments such as harmonisation of terms and conditions of employment with manual workers. Strategies to counter these issues include:

- judicious monitoring of what is really happening at this crucial level of management;
- examination of the impact of financial incentives on the role of the supervisor. As was explained in chapter 7, such schemes can undermine the position of the supervisor. This danger also needs to be taken into account when the use of such schemes is proposed;
- careful identification of the role of supervisors – e.g. what is the role of a supervisor if a separate team leader has been appointed?
- careful selection, training and development of supervisors;
- well-developed two-way communication between first-line supervisors and their work groups;
- the development of lateral relationships between supervisors as a means of mutual support;
- the delegation of appropriate authority to supervisors and care in seeing that this is not eroded, e.g. by unnecessarily overruling them, forgetting to consult with them and by letting employee representatives bypass them;
- building up the position of supervisors by enabling them to give rewards as well

as penalties. If any organisational favours are to be given, e.g. upgradings, merit increases and promotions supervisors need to be seen as being influential in this process.

EMPLOYEE PARTICIPATION

Another dimension of employee relations is employee participation. This can be defined as a way of involving the workforce in organisational issues that affect them. It is different from the concept of worker control where control is vested with the employees. There are few examples of worker control if only because of the reluctance of investors to forfeit control of their investment. In employee participation, the final decision rests with management.

The issue of ultimate control can create problems with joint regulatory mechanisms, such as supervisory boards. If the employer does not have the final say, major problems can be created. These include the financing of organisations, accountability to the general public and the veto that the employees can have on any change that is to their disadvantage. This can create major problems for the employee representatives who may have to handle conflicts of interest between the organisations and employees. These difficulties are often ignored by advocates of joint control who may focus on the constitutional arrangements for resolving such problems without actually examining what happens in practice. The problem may be compounded by those with a unitary frame of reference not being able to understand the potential for conflict between different interest groups.

Employee participation also needs to be seen in the context of organisational and national culture as a whole. Participatory schemes are not going to be very effective if the overall culture is autocratic and secretive. In chapter 4 reference was made to the study in which it was found that the success or failure of joint consultative schemes depended not on the constitutional mechanisms but on the style of individual managers. Those who were proactive in making their committees work were successful. Those who did not invest much time and thought in the scheme were predictably unsuccessful (Rees and Porter 1998: 165–170).

There are a number of different participative mechanisms. The main categories are direct, indirect and financial.

Direct

A basic characteristic of direct schemes of employee participation is that employees are directly involved rather than indirectly via a representative. Common arrangements are:

- self-managed work groups, where the group is left to determine its own way of working within paramaters set by management. These parameters include quantitative and qualitative performance standards;

- quality circles;
- total quality management by the involvement of employees in team meetings;
- briefing groups – but note the emphasis on downward communication which is a unitary model – also in-house magazines;
- attitude surveys of employees, particularly in non-unionised environments, and facilities for employees to submit anonymous letters about their organisation;
- job enrichment (explained in chapter 6);
- discussions with line management – this can be the most important factor of all.

Formal employee participation schemes can do little to compensate for the problems of working for an autocratic boss, particularly if the boss is incompetent as well.

Indirect

- collective bargaining with a trade union or staff association – these arrangements may include discussion with representatives over a wide range of issues;
- joint consultative committees;
- health and safety representatives and committees (examined later in this chapter);
- suggestion schemes – these are a combination of direct and indirect participation; suggestions are made directly by employees, but employee representatives may sit on the committee that considers them;
- works councils – there is a statutory requirement for European Works Councils that have to be established if a company has 1,000 employees in two member states with a minimum threshold of 150 employees in each country. The European Commission is considering whether there should be a directive for companies to have works councils even if they do not have employees in other member states and a draft directive is being considered.
- partnership agreements – these are formal agreements by employers and unions designed to increase co-operation between them on an ongoing basis in areas of common interest. The common interest areas normally include the success of individual enterprises, the encouragement of union membership and the need both for employment flexibility and job security. The Employment Relations Act of 1999 enables the government to make grants to help develop such arrangements.

Financial

- performance-related pay,
- profit-sharing,
- share options.

For further explanation of financial participation see chapter 7. The case of the John Lewis Partnership is interesting as the profits are distributed to the employees. However, the strong management hierarchy makes it more an example of the benevolence of the former owner than an example of employee participation (Flanders *et al.* 1968).

A concept that overlaps with employee participation is that of stakeholding. Stakeholders have an interest in and some responsibility for the success of an organisation and are distinct from external pressure groups which are simply trying to influence the organisation concerned. Thus an external group such as Friends of the Earth, which has general environmental aims, would not be classified as an organisational stakeholder. However, it is not always clear what stakeholding means in practice. The range of potential areas of application include pension arrangements, share options and profit-sharing. Representational arrangements may involve employee consultation, union recognition, employee directors, and mechanisms for involving suppliers and consumers or clients.

The labour market

KEY CHARACTERISTICS

There have been major changes in the nature of the employment market in the UK and in many other countries. This has mirrored changes in the economy in general. The market changed from being a seller's market with very low unemployment in the UK in the 1960s to being a buyer's market in the 1980s with nearly 12 per cent unemployment in 1986 and 1987. Although relatively full employment has returned, employment patterns have altered.

The characteristics of the labour market in the UK at present are as follows.

- Overall low unemployment, masks considerable regional and occupational variations. The north/south divide is very marked. Manufacturing is still in decline whilst areas such as services in general and computer services in particular are increasing.
- The alternative economy has developed in the UK. Some people work, don't pay tax but claim state benefits. Government policy is to encourage people to progress from welfare to work and to make unemployment benefit more difficult to obtain. There is also an underclass of unemployed people who receive minimum state benefits and who are not easily employable.
- The return of relatively full employment has *not* been accompanied by an upsurge in trade union membership or power. Less than one in three members of the labour force are union members. It is the areas of traditional union membership that are still in decline. Days lost through industrial action have declined dramatically. The ability of trade unions to control change in work practices is also greatly reduced. This is partly because of competitive pressures and the generally increased ability of customers to find other sources of supply. The pace of change also threatens jobs in their existing form.
- The trade union immunities withdrawn under successive Conservative governments have generally not been reintroduced. However, it has been the economic changes that have had more impact in reducing the general power of trade unions. A similar

decline in union power took place in the rest of the European Union where statutory trade union rights had not been reduced. The decline in bargaining power has to some extent been compensated by a considerable increase in the role of unions representing their members with regard to their individual statutory rights.

- The role of employers associations has changed significantly. National industry-wide agreements have virtually disappeared in the private sector. However, employers' associations remain important sources of information and advice for member organisations, particularly with regard to employment law. They often undertake representation at employment tribunals. Also, they have an important lobbying role in the UK and Brussels with regard to proposed changes.

- Inflation rates are low. This has reduced the impact of the annual wage round. Annual increases are in any case more likely to be based on individual performance or be given in exchange for changed working practices.

- People with scarce skills are likely to exploit their market position by moving to more highly paid jobs. Alternatively, employers may raise pay in order to stop this happening. They also need to avoid abrasive management styles with employees with scarce skills and to consider positive means of gaining commitment. Skills shortages are exacerbated by a general lack of training investment.

- The increased rate of economic and technological change has meant that jobs have a shorter shelf-life and the nature of jobs that remain alters more quickly. This creates economic insecurity for many despite the overall pattern of relatively high employment. It also increases the need for retraining and continuous professional development.

- There is an increasing tendency for pay to be partly determined by individual performance. Sometimes this is by formal performance-related pay schemes even though, as explained in chapter 7, the results have not been encouraging in the public sector.

- Complex job evaluation schemes are less in evidence. This is partly because they are not responsive enough to quickly changing labour market conditions. However, jobs are increasingly defined in terms of required competencies. They also tend to be defined in generic terms to assist flexibility at work.

- The labour market is affected by globalisation. Membership of the European Union and general reductions in tariffs have reinforced this tendency. So has the growth of multinational and transnational corporations. Production is more commonly outsourced or switched to other countries. This may affect components or complete products or both, and has also given international companies leverage in negotiations with trade unions about wage claims and working practices. Employee or union representatives may also have difficulty in getting access to the real decision makers.

- Excess global manufacturing capacity in areas such as vehicle production has intensified competition.

- Developments such as the flexible organisation have created more peripheral and part-time jobs. Sometimes employees are disadvantaged by this. In other cases, employees develop a portfolio of economic activities or find part-time work a convenient way of balancing work and domestic commitments.

- Outsourcing has become more common. This not only affects the pattern of employment within an organisation but creates a pressure for more efficient work practices to prevent outsourcing.

- Changes in organisational structures often have had significant effects on pay determination. Devolution of authority to managers in semi-autonomous business units has given them greater control over wages and working arrangements. Devolution of authority within what has remained of the public sector has also enabled the government to distance itself from cuts in services and to attempt to distance itself from pay bargaining. The level of funding, however, has indirectly but strongly affected the level of pay settlements in the public sector. National bargaining has generally survived these pressures in the public sector.

- Employment is often more capital intensive. An aspect of this is the increased computer technology available to a wide range of employees. This can increase the ability and logic of increasing wages to ensure that this capital is utilised effectively. This and the development of large capital installations, such as supermarkets and call centres, has led to an increase in shift and/or continuous working.

- There are contradictory pressures for deregulation and increased labour market regulation. Factors that have created a less regulated labour market include privatisation, compulsory competitive tendering in local government and the abolition of wages councils. More regulatory pressures include statutory minimum pay, anti-discrimination legislation, the reduction of the unfair dismissal qualification period to one year's service and a range of European directives. The directives include working hours, the employment of part-time workers, collective redundancy consultation and the transfer of undertakings.

- There are significant practical barriers to the free movement of labour within the UK. These include shortages in the availability of publicly financed housing and the high costs of private housing, particularly in London and South East England. The practical barriers are even greater with regard to the free movement of labour between the UK and other member countries of the European Union. These barriers include those of language and culture as well as accommodation.

- Executive remuneration has tended to increase as competition for executive talent in a results-orientated labour market has increased. Also shareholder and legal controls on executive remuneration and golden handshakes are weak. This is despite the growing practice of remuneration committees to advise on the pay of senior managers and directors.

- Fringe benefits in the UK are generally much lower than in other major European countries. This is because of national minimum provisions and collective agreements. An example of this is redundancy protection. Low levels of redundancy protection in the UK can encourage inward investment but discourage international companies from creating redundancies in countries with high levels of protection.

- Employees need to place more reliance on occupational or private pensions schemes. This is because of the long-term difficulty governments have of funding state pensions.

- About half of the workforce is female. Most women return to work after maternity leave. The dual income couple is often a powerful economic unit. However, this means couples placing limits on work involvement.
- Women are tending to break through 'glass ceilings' at work and increasingly achieve positions of responsibility. Both legal protections and cultural changes have facilitated this. To a lesser extent this has also happened with members of ethnic minorities.

A major unresolved issue about the UK economy in general that has major implications for the labour market is the role of the UK in Europe. Closer integration, including membership of the European Monetary Union (EMU), will stabilise exchange rates and encourage inward investment. However, a price to be paid for this is loss of control over interest rates and therefore a reduced ability to tackle inflation. Also, decisions taken at Brussels are more difficult to influence than those at Westminster. The two contrasting models are of an American deregulated labour market in an expanding economy but with limited employee protection and welfare provision; the other model is of a European regulated labour market with a high level of employee protection but with a less rapidly expanding economy. European integration may make competition easier within Europe but make it more difficult with the rest of the world. Another dilemma is that whilst the UK is geographically part of Europe, it is culturally much closer to the USA. For whatever reason the UK's economic cycle of activity is line with that in the USA rather than the mainland Europe. Also, the UK is much more influenced by American than European thinking about management.

THE IMPACT OF INWARD INVESTMENT

Another aspect of the labour market that merits consideration is the impact of inward investment. The UK has been successful in attracting investment from a number of countries, particularly Japan and the USA. This has been for a number of reasons. One is the low level of employment costs in comparison with other European partners, particularly with regard to fringe benefits. Other reasons include the convenience of using the English language, government grants, the availability of 'greenfield' sites and membership of the European Union. However, these advantages have to some extent been offset recently by the high value of the pound and the fact that the UK is not a member of the European Monetary Union.

The companies that have inwardly invested in the UK have mainly been sophisticated multinational organisations in capital-intensive industries. Given the scale of inward investment and the publicity about new-style employee relations, it is appropriate to try and identify the actual impact and to separate fact from media hype.

Many Japanese companies operating in the UK have introduced single status arrangements whereby there is a common scheme of fringe benefits for all employees.. However, there has been a mistaken perception that Japanese firms have also negotiated no-strike deals involving pendulum arbitration. The reality has been that few employers, including the Japanese, have been prepared to surrender decision-making about wages to outside arbitrators, regardless of whether the process involves pendulum arbitration or not.

A study commissioned by the Department of Employment into Japanese firms operating in Britain (Milsome 1993) reported that a distinctively Japanese model of working practices was only being used in motor manufacturing. This included total quality approaches and teamworking, 'just-in-time' production and flexible working. Even there it was being used in a modified form, partly because of the strength of local culture and tradition but also because policies such as lifetime employment could not be guaranteed. Also, attempts to introduce new practices at component suppliers had had little effect. Spectacular productivity levels have been reported at Nissan at Sunderland but critics also reported a downside for employees. This included a pattern of imposed consensus and employee dependency based on the marginalisation of unions, local unemployment and the lack of transferable skills (Garrahan and Stewart 1992). Care must also be taken in analysing productivity claims. The ratio of employees to cars is influenced by a number of factors. These include the level of capital investment and the amount of outsourcing of activities. A general conclusion of the Milsome study was that when new-style employment practices had been introduced there was no evidence that they had had much impact on productivity or profitability compared with traditional systems. The general pattern, however, appears to be that individual elements of the Japanese model have become more common, particularly total quality initiatives and flexible working, but one has to bear in mind that there were strong pressures for such changes anyway.

Legal framework

A number of individual and collective employment law rights in the UK have already been explained. These include the rights of employees when the ownership of their business is transferred (chapter 3), protection against discrimination on grounds of sex, race and trade union membership and activity (chapters 9 and 13), equal pay and equal pay for work of equal value (chapter 7) and unfair dismissal and redundancy (chapter 13). The issue of works councils was covered earlier in this chapter. Individual rights were consolidated in the Employment Rights Act of 1996, but there have been additions since then.

BACKGROUND

The whole issue of employment law is something of a political football. This is not surprising given the links between employers and the Conservative party and between the trade unions and the Labour Party in the UK. However, many of the restrictions on trade union activity introduced by successive Conservative governments in the 1980s and early 1990s were retained by the Labour government. These include:

- the illegality of the closed shop,
- the illegality of both secondary picketing and secondary industrial action,
- the requirement for postal ballots before industrial action,
- the liability of union funds in cases of illegal industrial action,
- the requirement that all members of trade union national executive committees be directly elected by postal ballot.

There have though been further additions to the employment law, arising out of initiatives by the Labour Government and Europe. These are outlined below.

UNION RECOGNITION

Where a trade union can demonstrate that a majority of the workforce are members, the employer may be obliged to grant recognition for collective bargaining. This is also the case if a majority of the actual workforce vote for union recognition, provided that the majority voting in favour represent at least 40 per cent of those entitled to vote. The regulatory agency is the Central Arbitration Committee. They organise ballots and determine jurisdictional issues. Some employers may grant recognition to avoid the use of statutory procedures. However, there are no powers to ensure that employers negotiate in good faith.

MINIMUM PAY

A national minimum pay rate of £3.60 was introduced in 1999 for those aged over 21. This is reviewed annually. The rate in 2000 for those aged 18–21 was £3.20. The rate initially set for adults receiving accredited training was £3.20. Minimum rates include some bonuses, but not premium rates for over-time and shift work. Payroll tips are included but not cash tips. It was estimated that minimum pay would directly affect 2 million workers. It has an indirect effect on many employers because of the impact on wage differentials and the costs of labour to outside contractors, particularly those involved in cleaning, catering and security work. Employers are obliged to publicise the minimum rates to employees. The Inland Revenue and Contributions Agency enforce this. Sanctions include fines and payment of back pay and potential publicity via legal action at employment tribunals or the courts. The establishment of a minimum wage has not had the effect of pricing significant numbers of people out of work, largely because of the modest level at which the rate was initially set.

WORKING TIME DIRECTIVE

Most UK workers are now covered by the Working Time Regulations. These were introduced in order to comply with the European Working Time Directive. It is planned to progressively increase the coverage so that groups currently excluded, such as junior hospital doctors and those transport workers not covered, are eventually included. Those who control their own hours of work are also excluded. Given the ambiguity about who this covers, e.g. managers, it will be left to case law to determine how senior a person needs to be to be excluded. Key provisions of the regulations are:

- the average working week is not to exceed 48 hours (calculated over a 17-week period). This limit can, however, be exceeded by mutual agreement. Given the existence of other restrictions this would mean a agreed maximum average working week of 78 hours;
- employees to receive one complete day's rest every week, though this can be averaged over a fortnight;
- adults are to receive 11 hours continuous rest in every 24 hours – normal not actual hours set the limit;
- a continuous 20-minute break within each six hours work, preferably away from the workplace. Whilst employers are not obliged to enforce this, the entitlement cannot be waived;
- night work to be restricted to eight hours each shift on average, but without averaging if there are special circumstances. Also free health assessments for night workers;
- four weeks' paid holiday a year. No payment in lieu unless the employment is terminated.

Some relaxation of the above arrangements can be achieved by voluntary derogations. These may be agreed with individuals, groups of workers and/or trade unions. Examples include averaging hours over a year and, when there are justified technical reasons for doing so, incorporating the rest allowance into the daily rest allowance. However, records of such agreed variations need to be kept. More detailed information is available from the Department of Trade and Industry (DTI 2000).

Monitoring is via the Health and Safety Commission and the local authority, who can institute criminal action for breaches. Employees can also raise claims at employment tribunals. Whilst some employers may take chances about observing the regulations, breaches may particularly come to light in the event of a serious accident investigation.

PART-TIME WORK DIRECTIVE

This requires employers to give equal treatment to part-time employees compared with their full-time colleagues. This is with regard to their terms and conditions of employment and stands unless differences can be objectively justified. There is some scope for ambiguity with regard to who exactly is covered by the regulations.

PARENTAL LEAVE DIRECTIVE

Under the regulations, parents with a year's service or more with their employer are entitled to unpaid leave for 13 weeks per child. This is not an annual allowance but exists over the entitlement period for the child up to their fifth birthday (or 18th birthday for disabled children). Both parents are entitled to the leave and for each child. There is also provision for reasonable unpaid time off to deal with dependents in emergencies.

SOCIAL CHAPTER

The above two directives were implemented as a result of the UK signing up to the European Union's Social Chapter, reversing the opt-out arrangement of the previous (Conservative) government. Membership of the Social Chapter also means that the UK will be bound by future directives which can be adopted under the arrangements for qualified majority voting. Qualified majority voting is a European Union arrangement whereby votes are allocated roughly according to the size of countries. A majority of approximately 70 per cent is required for a motion to be carried.

However, there appears to be a marked diminution in the number of directives affecting employment regulation. This may be because it is felt that reasonable *minimum* standards have been set. It may also be because of concerns about competitiveness with the rest of the world. The UK is also bound by case law developments regarding European directives. This includes case law in other member countries.

HEALTH AND SAFETY

Health and safety is an area that as well as being important in its own right has an important employee relations dimension. The framework legislation covering this area is the UK's Health and Safety at Work Act 1974. Basic features of the legislation are:

- the supervisory body with the responsibility for monitoring and enforcement is the Health and Safety Commission;
- employers are required to establish safe systems of work not just for their employers but with a view to protecting the public as well;
- there is an obligation on manufacturers and suppliers to provide safe products and systems;
- management in organisations employing five or more, including those operating on a self-employed basis, apart from private households, are obliged to have a written safety policy. Employers must publicise the policy and establish clear management arrangements for its implementation;
- accidents must be recorded and serious ones reported;
- employees must be briefed about any particular risks and changes;
- employers have an obligation to consult with any recognised trade union about health and safety issues and the union may appoint safety representatives;

- if there is a written request from two safety representatives to establish a safety committee, the employer must comply;
- the obligation to consult with a trade union has since been widened to an obligation to consult with the workforce in the absence of a union;
- employers must also provide free protective clothing, eyesight testing and safety training where appropriate. Codes of practice and regulations about substantive safety issues are regularly issued, the latter having the force of law;
- breach of the statute law makes organisations liable to criminal prosecution.

There are also obligations under common law, and organisations may be sued by those who have suffered injury through its negligence. Employers must also comply with European directives that can be approved on a qualified majority-voting basis. An example of how health and safety practice has evolved is the development of no-smoking policies in many organisations.

Under the Trade Unions and Employment Rights Act of 1993 protection for employees and safety representatives has been increased. Safety representatives cannot be lawfully disciplined for carrying out designated duties. Employees cannot be lawfully disciplined for taking reasonable steps to protect themselves or others from a danger they reasonably believe to be serious and imminent. Enhanced compensation is available for representatives or employees if they are dismissed in these circumstances. Also, employees taken off their job for health and safety reasons have to be transferred to suitable alternative work or suspended on full pay.

Unfortunately, despite the comprehensive nature of the legislative framework for the protection of employees and members of the public, the safety systems employers operate do not always work. Deregulation of the labour market and competitive pressures may have also increased the risks.

| Examples |

Safety dangers were highlighted by a series of disasters, mainly in the late 1980s, which included the capsizing of a P&O ferry at Zeebrugge, fires at the Bradford football ground and at Kings Cross underground station, rail crashes at Clapham and Purley, football spectators being suffocated at Sheffield's Hillsborough stadium, the sinking of *Marchioness* pleasure boat on the River Thames and the fire on the *Piper Alpha* oil rig. The sinking of the ferry *Estonia* off the coast of Finland in 1994 with the loss of 852 lives emphasises the potential scale of tragedy and its avoidability. More recent examples are the rail crash near London's Paddington station in 1999 in which 31 people died and the crash of an Air France Concorde at Paris in 2000 in which 113 were killed.

Preventative action is needed at all workplaces. Unfortunately, neglect can all too easily exist in this area. Consequently, consideration is being given in the UK to increasing the liability of individuals and organisations for health and safety failures. This may increase the likelihood of those responsible for future failures being jailed and organisations receiving substantial fines.

Unfortunately there can be major conflicts between pressures for production, service delivery and safety. As was explained in chapter 7, these pressures can be intensified by financial incentive schemes. In the USA, a multimillion-dollar lawsuit was instigated because of a person being knocked down by an employee trying to meet their employer's guarantee of the delivery of pizzas within 30 minutes of an order being placed. The road behaviour of many courier motor and pedal cyclists is another example of the potential conflict between commercial pressures and safety. Employers also need to be particularly aware of the danger of repetitive strain injuries and work-related stress. The issues of stress and its attendant legal liabilities was covered in chapter 6.

The role of trade unions

MEMBERSHIP PATTERN

The greatly reduced bargaining power of unions has been both caused and reinforced by other changes. Membership in the UK has fallen from a peak of 13.2 million in 1979 to 7.85 million in 1998, a fall of 40 per cent. However, for the first time since 1979 there was a slight increase in membership in 1998 (Certification Officer 2000: 20). The proportion of workplaces, employing 25 or more employees, where unions are recognised has fallen from 66 per cent in 1984 to 45 per cent in 1998 and only 36 per cent of employees at such workplaces were union members in 1998 (Department of Trade and Industry 1998: 14).

The key factor that has caused such falls has been structural economic change. Employment in traditionally important union areas, such as manufacture, mining, docks and railways has declined substantially. The abolition of the closed shop has also been significant. Density of membership is much higher in the public than the private sector. Factors accounting for this are the size of the employer, employer acceptance of unions and the tendency for pay increases to lag behind the private sector. Trade unions have had to cope with significantly reduced membership income. This has given a further boost to the pressure for amalgamations and mergers.

The reduction in union membership is not because of any great reduction in the logic of membership:

> *Traditional reasons for joining unions, such as 'support' should a problem arise at work, remain paramount. And management attitudes are among the most important sources of grievances*

Waddington and Whitson 1995: 47

RECOGNITION

It would also appear that there has been no general trend by employers to de-recognise unions. The Trades Union Congress (1998) reported that there were more recognition agreements being made than cases of union de-recognition. Account also has to be taken of the fact that negotiated agreements can determine the terms and conditions of non-union members as well as union members. However, there is an element of creeping de-recognition in many organisations with some grades being excluded, the range of issues reduced, non-recognition at new organisations and less notice taken of what unions have to say anyway. Another example of this erosion is the increase in the number of personal contracts and performance-related pay. Flexible working and generic job titles also reduce the opportunity of unions to make cases for upgrading. The increased tendency of employers to engage in direct communication with their workforce is also significant.

INDUSTRIAL ACTION

Union bargaining power has declined greatly from its post-war peak in the 1960s. Days lost in industrial action in the UK have declined in recent years and have been on or near the lowest since records were first kept in 1881. In the 12 months to February 2000 there were only 217,000 days lost. However, there are still areas where unions have significant bargaining strength. The most obvious area is transport. In 1999 nearly 150,000 of the 283,000 working days lost were in that sector (Labour Market trends 2000: S.93). Their power stems from the fact that they provide an essential service which cannot be run effectively without them. Trade union power is particularly noticeable with London Underground and railway company train staff. A feature of this power is the relative irreplaceability of the staff concerned. Railway unions are also able to use a good settlement with one regional employer to set the pattern with other employers.

Evidence of the potential power of staff in the transport sector is also illustrated by the dispute between British Airways and its cabin crew in 1997. This proved to be particularly costly because of lost revenue and may well have been a factor that contributed to the subsequent dismissal of the chief executive, Bob Ayling, in 2000. However, the most dramatic example of the vulnerability of the economy to transport disruption was provided by the impact of the popular demonstrations against increases in the price of petrol and diesel oil in the UK in September 2000. A feature of this was the unwillingness of tanker drivers to drive out of oil refineries past demonstrators. This rapidly caused major economic dislocation and mirrored similar action that had previously taken place in France and Belgium.

In assessing union power it is necessary to take into account the fact that it exists at the bottom of the organisation rather than at the top. The fact that unions have an organisational hierarchy can cause people to believe that they either do, or should, behave like organisations where power is much more at the top – as is the case with employers generally. Control in unions is ultimately in the hands of the lay members who pay their subscriptions and who elect their leaders. Elected groups of lay members have the ultimate formal authority in unions but, in any case, unions have to move in line with their members' wishes. This reality has been reinforced by the legislation introduced regarding ballots. Sometimes, though, affirmative industrial action ballots are simply used as a tactical device to encourage employers to be more generous in negotiations. The mistake that some people make is to see union officials as being akin to police officers with the responsibility and ability to instruct their members about what they should do. Even if union officials were to accept this debatable view of their role, they have little if anything in the way of sanctions to impose their will on their members.

CHANGES IN ROLE

Clearly, the ability of unions to serve their members and the way in which they serve them has altered. They are much more on the defensive now, often seeking to protect their members against redundancy and changes in working arrangements and employment contracts. The focus of bargaining is more localised which makes groups in weak positions more liable to be picked off. Local bargaining also creates resourcing problems for unions. It is also increasingly difficult for unions to gain access to the real decision-makers, particularly if they are based at headquarters in another country. One of the reactions of unions to these generally unfavourable developments has been to arrange for a range of discounts for members on the products and services provided by a range of commercial organisations. Another has been to pay increasing attention to the legal rights of members and unions, particularly given increases in these rights emanating from Europe. Consequently, trade unions lobby about proposed changes in the law in Brussels as well as in the UK.

COLLECTIVE AGREEMENTS

Relationships between employers and employees may to some extent be regulated by joint agreements. There are two main types of collective agreement which are:

● procedural, which stipulate the manner in which differences will be resolved;
● substantive, which contain the outcome of agreements negotiated via the appropriate procedure. Such agreements will normally cover matter such as wages and terms and conditions of employment.

Collective agreements may be about substantive or procedural issues. Substantive agreements cover matters such as wages and conditions of employment. Procedural agreements can be likened to the Queensberry rules for boxing – there can at least be rules regulating the manner in which arguments about substantive issues are conducted. Sometimes there may be disagreement about the nature of the procedural agreement as one party may feel that it will unduly help the other party achieve their substantive aims. If agreement about the procedure cannot be reached, the management may need to issue a procedure and say that this is the basis on which they propose to proceed.

The following issues are often covered by procedural agreements.

Individual

- Discipline and dismissal,
- grievances.

As explained in the previous chapter there is a statutory right for employee representation in both these areas if the outcome could be formal disciplinary action or if the grievance is serious. This means that outside trade union officials can be called in even if the employer does not recognise them.

Collective

- Disputes: these are for dealing with grievances affecting more than one person. Examples are the interpretation of collective agreements and changes in work arrangements;
- wage claims: there may be a standing procedure for handling annual wage claims;
- redundancy: agreements may cover consultation about redundancy, selection for redundancy and compensation. The legal obligations for consultation were explained in the previous chapter;
- health and safety: the arrangements for the maintenance of safe working conditions and for representatives and safety committees were explained earlier in this chapter.

Some employers enter into voluntary agreements according to the level of union membership. They may require a higher level of union membership or support for collective compared with individual issues. This is because of the greater coverage of collective issues. Employers may be anxious to keep to a minimum the number of unions that they deal with to avoid inter-union competition and friction. Japanese companies investing on greenfield sites often set up 'beauty competitions' to give potential unions the chance to tender for recognition before anyone was employed.

Procedural arrangements can provide a very useful framework for handling differences when they emerge. Managers and employee representatives can both be somewhat at a loss as to what to do when discussions end in failure. They can have a common interest in defining the area in dispute and agreeing on the next step and what, if anything, is to happen in the meantime. In this way a dispute can be processed without either party having had to give way, with the issue normally being referred to the next level so that it can be tackled afresh. The definition of the area of disagreement and time bought for fresh thought may help in the subsequent resolution of a dispute. If nothing else, procedures can get the immediate parties to the dispute off the hook, at least for a while. Ultimately, if discussion at higher levels does not produce agreement, the thorny issue of what happens next has to be considered. Either side may give way or consider imposing their will, which in a way is the final stage of procedure. Managers will have to weigh up carefully the disadvantages of risking union resistance and the impact on employee morale against the disadvantages of giving way. This needs to be a consciously taken decision.

Although the handling of differences via an agreed procedure will not guarantee a satisfactory resolution, it does at least provide an alternative to an immediate shoot-out, and gives the parties the opportunity to explore the possibilities for an agreed solution. Knowledge that, if there is no agreement, there may be resort to other means can in itself have a sobering effect on the parties. Sometimes arbitration is seen as the answer to unresolved differences, but if it is too readily available it may relieve the parties of the responsibility for settlement and lead to exaggerated claims and counter-claims with no movement towards a negotiated settlement. However, employers, including the state, are now generally reluctant to use arbitration for collective bargaining. The collective power of trade unions is still generally weak though skills shortages may cause employers to consider giving significant wages increases. Under these circumstances arbitration is perhaps more appropriate for differences about interpretation of agreements or the resolving of individual differences where there are no great financial implications to the decision.

One of the advantages of agreed procedures is that the parties can at least limit the area of disagreement by agreeing on what is in dispute and how the difference should be resolved, even if resolution can ultimately mean one side coerces the other. A further way of limiting the area of dispute can be the use of a *status quo* clause in a disputes procedure, which provides for the continuation of work on the basis that existed before a dispute began. This can be a useful device, but there can be occasions when it is difficult to identify just when a dispute arose and therefore what the *status quo* position was. Sometimes, too, employers feel that they are conceding too much opportunity to unions to block changes that are not to the unions' liking if such a clause is part of a disputes procedure.

| Example | The solution one engineering company adopted to resolve this dilemma was to introduce a ten-day rule. If management felt that discussions about changes in working practices were being unduly protracted they reserved the right to serve notice that in ten days the change would be introduced unless there was some other agreement in the meantime. |

Employers may also find other advantages in using collective agreements. It may be much more time-effective to negotiate many issues with representatives than with each individual employee. This is particularly so if many of the fringe benefits are or need to be standard anyway. Employers may also find that the representative structures are very useful for the two way flow of information about employee relations issues. Additionally such structures may be constructively used for improving co-operation in areas of common interest.

Diagnostic skills

It has been necessary to spend some time clarifying the framework within which managers operate in the employee relations area as the context has powerful implications regarding their behaviour. It is also necessary to spend some time examining the diagnostic skills that managers need. The nature of employee relations problems can often be easy enough to recognise – some of the most likely ones being interruptions to work, poor performance, resistance to change and restrictive practices. What can be much more difficult is establishing the actual causes of these problems and working out what, if anything, can be done about them. The emotional nature of the subject can hinder accurate diagnosis – if one has come to hate the sight of a particular representative it can be very tempting to go along with a stereotyped view to the effect that all troublemakers should be sacked or, according to some, imprisoned or shot. The reality is, of course, that whatever one's feelings, one usually has to live with particular representatives and they with their managers, about whom they may have equally strong views.

Bad personal relationships can exacerbate management-union relationships and in some cases conflicts can be no more than personality clashes. However, even if all the people involved were angels, they would still have to resolve issues where the interests of the parties are in conflict. One of the skills that managers need in this area is the ability to identify the basic conflicts that lie behind any personal issues. It is important, too, for the manager to judge the extent to which a representative is reflecting the views of their colleagues. Getting rid of the representative, even if this was possible, would not do much good if they were then replaced by someone else who behaved in a similar manner.

RECOGNISING CONFLICTS OF INTEREST

Perhaps the most critical ability needed by the manager with regard to employee relations is that of being able to recognise when managerial and employee interests come into conflict. Some people adopt a unitary perspective of the organisation and simply do not accept that this can happen. The line of argument can be that what is good for the organisation is automatically good for all its employees. Whilst this approach may present a simple and comforting philosophy for those who hold it, it does not help equip managers to deal with the genuine conflicts of interest that can and do arise about wage levels, working arrangements and job security, for example. Managers may be so preoccupied with the various pressures upon them that they neglect to consider the implications for their employees of particular decisions. If their employees see their interests being threatened by changes, they are hardly likely to be enthusiastic about such changes. It may, for example, be highly inconvenient for an employer to find that employees don't co-operate with the introduction of new processes because they threaten their career opportunities and job security, but decision-making needs to be based on an accurate assessment of the employees' views and not wishful thinking.

Resistance to change can blandly be ascribed to the innate conservatism of the workforce, but such an analysis may miss the point that employees may resist a particular change because it represents a threat to their interests. Other changes, such as pay increases, may be eagerly accepted. It is the nature of the change and its impact on their interests that employees are likely to consider. In a study of restrictive practices carried out for the Donovan Commission it was concluded that

> there must be few restrictive labour practices which are not genuinely thought by at least one of the parties concerned to be defensible in terms of their own interests
>
> *1967:52*

If diagnosis has been accurately undertaken, it is at least possible for managers to consider what, if anything, can be done. Acceptance that one just has to live with some problems may be much more constructive than time, money and effort being wasted on false solutions that will not work because the diagnosis was faulty. With some problems remedial action can be taken. It may be that effective communication can remove misunderstanding, or that it can pave the way to a negotiated answer which gives sufficient concessions to both parties to make a deal worthwhile. Anticipation of problems can lead to their being avoided or reduced in scale. Much can be achieved simply by managers thinking through the implications of their decisions as far as the employees are concerned. Managers may, for example, make apparently simple technical decisions blissfully unaware of the problems their decisions could create in other parts of the organisation. If production schedules, for example, are to be altered in such a way that people's earnings are affected, it is best to anticipate the likely reaction of employees, and to take that into account at the decision-making stage, rather than to take the decision in ignorance of its likely effects. Diagnosis also needs to take account of the power relationships. If a clash of interests is identified, it is then necessary to calculate the extent to which the respective parties are able to impose their views. It may seem regrettable that conflicts are determined by power relationships as well as by intellectual, technical and moral criteria, but it is hardly prudent for a manager to try to impose a particular decision if it can easily be resisted. Conversely, the mere fact that employees protest about a proposal does not automatically mean that the employer is unable to implement it.

THE INTEGRATION OF EMPLOYEE RELATIONS WITH OTHER MANAGEMENT ACTIVITIES

The emphasis in this chapter so far has mainly been on looking at employee relations as a subject on its own. However, for there to be any real understanding of the area it is vital to see the way in which employee relations interrelates with other management functions. This can be a crucial diagnostic skill. This is because often the causes of employee relations problems, and by implication any remedies, lie in these other areas. This basic point is often missed because of departmental boundaries. This may be compounded by lack of knowledge of those inside the employee relations area of what goes on outside it and, conversely, lack of knowledge of those outside the area of what goes on within it.

A sack manufacturing company in Guyana endured a strike of several weeks over a redundancy. The organisation had invested in equipment and labour to meet a large order from a sugar producer. The order was not met on time and was then cancelled. Subsequent investigations revealed that delivery had been promised for a time of peak seasonal demand for sacks and there had never been any prospect that the order could be delivered on time.

A children's clothing firm decided to switch the product range from long-run bread-and-butter production runs to a wide range of small-batch fashion garments. This failed because of the failure to take into account the learning problems for the production employees together with the impact of the change on their bonus earnings.

(Legge 1978: 45–46)

It is necessary to make this crucial point about the interrelationship of employee relations with other functions by way of examples because of their illustrative value and the lack of systematic study in this area. Unfortunately, there is an ongoing tradition of viewing employee relations as a self-contained activity. This is despite the potentially integrative approach involved in human resource management. The single dimensional approach was evident in the last state-initiated study of employee relations in the UK (The Donovan Report 1968) and is still very apparent in academic writing and much organisational behaviour. The Donovan Commission concentrated on the need for improvements within the industrial relations system. The main thrust of the report was that the way forward was the formalisation of procedures at plant level. The 'central defect in British industrial relations' was identified as being disorderly bargaining at factory level (Royal Commission on Trade Unions and Employers Associations 1968: para 1019). The narrowness of this approach may have been why so little was apparently achieved as a result of the Donovan recommendations (Singleton 1975).

The lesson for managers is clearly not to look for or expect progress in tackling employee relations problems to come just from initiatives in that area. Whilst effective procedures and employee relations expertise may be useful, they may not on their own enable basic causes of employee relations to be identified. Unfortunately, the training and background of those in employee relations is sometimes such that they may not understand that the causes of many of their problems lie outside their sphere. Conversely, those outside the employee relations area may know so little about the area that they do not appreciate the need to work out the employee relations implications of decisions they are taking. One answer to this problem is general management training for all managers. The case for this is all the more powerful when one realises that the way in which employee relations problems can be created by decisions or failures elsewhere is but one example of the way in which problems can be transmitted into any area of management. To take the analysis further managers need to see the implications of their decisions in other areas and also to recognise that plain incompetence in one area can easily precipitate crises elsewhere.

A positive development, covered earlier in this chapter is that genuine strategic human resource management initiatives linked to corporate policy should embrace employee relations issues in the context of an integrated systems approach to organisational issues. However, not all corporate and human resource initiatives are properly integrated and thought out. There are many examples of the human dimension being ignored or it being considered in a simplistic way without specialist advice at the design stage of policy. This topic was examined in chapter 2 and relevant examples are given concerning some TQM initiatives (chapter 3) and the high failure rate of performance-related pay schemes (chapter 10). This problem of narrowly based or superficially integrated initiatives unfortunately characterises the way many different types of organisational change are often handled.

The manager as a trade union member

REASONS FOR JOINING

One of the implications of white-collar unions is that managers may have to give serious thought as to whether or not they join or remain in a trade union. Public sector unions have traditionally included senior levels of management amongst their members. This has partly been because of employer acceptance of this and the size of the organisations concerned. Some managers, including some senior ones in the private sector are also union members. Reasons for this include people retaining membership when they are promoted, the specialist services offered by managers' unions and the use, or threatened use, of statutory recognition procedures. If managers are in a union, they may find that the possibility of industrial action by their own union leads to their greater interest in union affairs. The sheer size of an employee organisation may mean that union membership is the only way in which there can be proper discussions about a manager's terms and conditions of employment. Whilst the increase in the use of personal contracts and merit or performance-related pay increases has reduced the emphasis on collective negotiation, managers may still sometimes want the cover of a union to represent their interests. Concerns about job security and, in some cases, abrasive management styles are further reasons for joining unions. The legal insurance that unions offer and the services they provide at employment tribunal hearings can also be selling points to the potential managerial recruit. Some managers may join or stay in unions with the ulterior motive of using a membership as a means as of finding out what the union strategies and plans are.

CHOICE OF UNION

One of the decisions that a manager may have to make is just which union they should join. A specialist union, because of its specialised appeal, may not have many members and therefore lack comprehensive support services. Larger unions, whilst not perhaps offering the same degree of understanding about the individual manager's problems, may have a comprehensive range of services and specialists and the negotiating strength that can come from having a large membership, particularly if this membership includes large groups of key workers. Whilst some specialist unions thrive, others fail to last and merge with larger unions, often to the relief of the employer for this reduces the number of different unions with which they have to deal.

CONFLICTS OF INTEREST

Whilst it may be to the advantage of the individual manager to join a trade union, membership can bring with it a fresh set of problems. Managers may find that it is not always easy to reconcile their union and managerial roles. Sometimes the accommodation is fairly easy. The manager may join a managerial union, or the white-collar section of a manual workers' union. On the face of it there may be no problem in negotiating as a representative of the employer with employees who are in other unions, or even the same union but in a different section. However, sections of the same union can be bound by common policies and also some union branches can take in a large vertical section of the white-collar workers with a particular employer. This can lead to role conflict, such as a manager wanting to pursue a grievance against their boss, who may not only be in the same union branch but also one of its officers!

In the circumstances of industrial action, members may find that there is a conflict between the need to maintain production or services and a union desire to disrupt those services. Such conflicts have been most common in the public sector. The individual may find that they are damned by their employer if they do not keep services working and damned by their union if they do.

There is no easy answer to the conflicts that can arise for managers within unions. However, if the individual manager recognises the problems that can arise, this should help them make careful judgements about whether or not they should join a union, which union it should be, whether they should hold office within that union and the way in which role conflicts that occur for themselves and their colleagues within the union can be resolved. Many managers who are union members handle these potential problems by keeping a low profile within the union.

SUMMARY

✔ As has been demonstrated, the area of employee relations is potentially both complex and fluid. Even in a non-unionised environment there will still be conflicts of interest that need to be identified and managed. There may also be areas of common interest where co-operation can be constructively improved. Employee relations activities include pay, terms and conditions of employment, performance, working arrangements and job security. The greater pace of change means that working arrangements are changed with increasing frequency. It is essential that line management be actively involved in ensuring that working arrangements are effective and are reviewed in the light of changed circumstances.

✔ Key parameters within which employee relations exist are the labour market and employment law and these have both been examined. Whilst relative full unemployment has returned for much of the UK, this has not been accompanied by a general recovery in trade union bargaining power. Disputes are at a chronically low level and less than one-third of the workforce are union members. However, some people are able to exploit skills and geographic shortages of labour. Also, partly as a result of membership of the European Union, there has been a significant increase in individual employment rights in the UK. An increased role for unions is to represent their members in such issues.

✔ The difficulties that can exist in diagnosing the causes of employee relations problems were explained. This can be because problems can be precipitated by decisions in other areas of managerial activity. Weaknesses in line management can have repercussive effects in employee relations. Effective general management is a basic requirement for effective employee relations.

✔ Finally the role of the manager as a trade union member was examined. Various ways of handling potential conflicts of interest were identified. The related area of negotiation is the subject of the next chapter.

SELF-ASSESSMENT QUESTIONS

1. What are the objectives of both managers and employees in organisations?

2. What are likely to be the key employee relations issues in an organisation?

3. In what ways might the labour market determine the conduct of employee relations?

4. Identify six ways in the which employee relations in the UK is subject to legal regulation.

5. Identify the role of trade unions. Is the need for trade unions likely to continue?

6. Explain how failings in other areas of management can have a knock-on effect on employee relations.

7. Can membership of a trade union be reconciled with also being a manager?

 References

Certification Officer for Trade Unions and Employers Associations (2000) Annual Report 1999–2000, Certification Officer.

Department of Trade and Industry (1998) *The 1998 Workplace Employee Relations Survey – First Findings*, HMSO.

Department of Trade and Industry (2000) *A Guide to the Working Time Regulations*, DTI.

Fox, Alan (1965) research paper 3, 'Industrial Sociology and Industrial Relations', Royal Commission on Trade Unions and Employers' Associations, HMSO.

Flanders, A. *et al.* (1968) *Experiment in Industrial Democracy*, Faber.

Garrahan, Philip and Paul Stewart (1992) *The Nissan Enigma*, Mansell.

Labour Market Trends (May 2000) Office for National Statistics.

Legge, K (1978) *Power, Innovation and Problem-solving in Personnel Management*, McGraw-Hill.

Milsome, Sue (1993) *The Impact of Japanese Firms on Working and Employment Practices in British Manufacturing Industry*, Industrial Relations Services.

Rees, W. David and Christine Porter (1998) 'Employee Participation and Managerial Style – the Key Variable', *Industrial and Commercial Training,* 30(5).

Royal Commission on Trade Unions and Employers' Associations, The Donovan Commission, 1965–1968 Cmnd. 3623, HMSO.

Royal Commission on Trade Unions and Employers' Associations, The Donovan Commission (1967) 'Productivity Bargaining and Restrictive Labour Practices', research paper no. 4, HMSO.

Royal Commission on the National Health Service (1978) 'ACAS Evidence', ACAS report no. 12, 12 May.

Singleton, Norman (1975) 'Industrial Relations Procedures', Manpower paper no. 14, ch. 8, HMSO.

Trades Union Congress (1998) 'Focus on Recognition', trade union trends survey 1998, TUC.

Waddington and Whitston (1995) 'Interim Report', *People Management*, 26 January.

General references

Kessler, Sid and Fred Bayliss (1998) *Contemporary British Industrial Relations*, 3rd ed., MacMillan Business.

Legge, Karen (1995) *Human Resource Management – Rhetoric and Realities*, MacMillan Business.

Storey, John (ed.) (1995) *Human Resource Management: A Critical Text*, International Thomson Business Press.

chapter (fifteen)

Negotiating skills

There are case studies and exercises at http://www.thomsonlearning.co.uk (for full details, see the listing at the start of this book).

LEARNING OUTCOMES

By the end of this chapter you will be able to:

- Identify the range of negotiating situations in which you are likely to be involved, both formally and informally

- Understand basic theories relevant to the negotiating process

- Create a framework within which negotiations can be conducted

- Understand the different roles that either the same person, or different people, need to play during negotiations

- Identify realistic negotiating objectives

- Use tactical skills in conducting negotiations

- Take preventative action to reduce the chance of misunderstandings during and after negotiations

- Understand the processes of evaluation and implementation of agreements

Introduction

The range of formal and informal negotiating situations that managers are likely to be involved in are identified in this chapter. The accelerating pace of change means that this is an increasingly important part of a manager's job. Commercial and working arrangements have to be renegotiated to meet changed circumstances. Relevant theories are examined that help with both the analysis of the negotiating process and with skills development. The need to create a framework for negotiations is explained. This applies even in informal negotiations between two people. A key feature is the need for those involved in negotiations to understand the different roles that need to be played, sometimes by the same person. Often negotiations fail because people get so involved in the negotiations that they neglect to create a proper framework or allocate appropriate roles.

The importance of preparation is explained, as is the need to set realistic objectives. This is likely to involve an examination of the power realities and consideration of what to do if negotiations fail. Sometimes it is better to have no agreement than a bad one. In group negotiations a considerable amount of time may be needed to resolve internal differences. Often such internal differences are harder to resolve than differences with whoever the group is trying to negotiate with.

The various stages in the negotiating process are identified, including the concept of the negotiating ritual. The importance of effective chairing during negotiations is explained, as is the fact that often this sometimes needs to be done on an informal and discreet basis. The process skills of the chair, in particular, can be crucial in determining whether there is a constructive outcome or not. These skills are also necessary to avoid false agreements being reached based on misunderstandings of the parties on what was agreed. This can all too easily happen because communications during negotiations are often very fragile. Often the best results are obtained by the parties behaving assertively rather than aggressively. This way the potential for agreement can be explored and confrontations which threaten the process avoided.

Finally, attention is paid to the need for agreements to be evaluated, implemented and monitored. For the negotiating process to be effective formal and informal training may be necessary.

Negotiating roles and trends

ROLES

Negotiating is not something that is just the province of specialist negotiators. All managers are likely to be involved in some level of negotiations. Whilst most negotiations will be small scale, their cumulative effect can be considerable. Much of the negotiation managers are involved in is likely to be about operational matters, e.g. the implementation and monitoring of existing commercial contracts. They are likely to also be involved in a considerable amount of negotiation about how they meet other managers needs and how other managers meet their needs. Organisation of their own department may also involve much informal negotiation. This is likely to include allocation of work, logistical working arrangements and the quality control of what is done.

Negotiations do not cease when managers finish work. They will inevitably be involved with negotiations about, for example, their living arrangements and purchases. Social trends have created a much more egalitarian society which involves continuous negotiations about domestic arrangements. Some of the hardest negotiations can be with children about such issues as bed-time, homework, television and contributions to domestic chores.

A particular need for managers is to develop the habit of reflecting on the way that they and others negotiate. The increasing amount of time spent in negotiations creates a considerable opportunity to learn from the skills that are used and the mistakes made. The stereotype of the effective negotiator is the person who drives a very hard bargain. Whilst this can sometimes be appropriate it is not always a helpful image. Negotiators need to get the best that they can out of a given situation and often this may involve coming to a mutually satisfactory agreement. To try and drive too hard a bargain can sometimes mean no agreement at all. The key to effective negotiation is developing procedural and process skills so that the framework and conduct of negotiations is such that that which is potentially attainable is achieved.

TRENDS

The amount of negotiations that managers have to do seems to be significantly increasing. Whilst negotiations with trade unions are generally easier than they were when unions were more powerful, in many areas negotiations are becoming more difficult and more frequent. The increasing pace of change causes organisational arrangements to be reviewed more frequently. This can involve reviewing both commercial contracts and negotiations with employees about what they do, when and where. Failure to do this can affect the very survival of an organisation. A general excess of productive capacity in the world, boosted by technological development and globalisation, has turned many industries and services into a buyer's market. This has created chronic pressures for producers and providers of services to simultaneously increase quality and reduce costs. The mismatch between expectations and available resources in the public sector has also created increasing pressure to improve value for money.

Relevant theories

The process of negotiation is so complex that there neither is, nor can be, one theory that embraces all aspects of negotiation. However, there are two particularly useful theories about negotiation that cover key aspects. These theories can create an analytical framework for examining and developing your own skills and examining the behaviour of others. As with all theories, they need to be applied in the right context. Unsurprisingly the two theories are not recent. This is because the process of negotiation is so long established that writers have had plenty of time to study it.

INTEGRATIVE AND DISTRIBUTIVE BARGAINING

The seminal work on the theory of negotiation was written by Walton and McKersie (1965). They distinguished between *distributive* and *integrative* bargaining. In distributive bargaining one party can only gain at the expense of the other. This can be described as a fixed sum game, such as in the sale by one party and purchase of an item by another. In integrative bargaining there is the potential to increase the amount that can be distributed. This can be described as a varying sum game. An example of integrative bargaining from the employee relations area is productivity bargaining. Productivity bargaining can enable the value added by a group of people to be increased. In return they would expect to have some reward for their increased contribution. However, if the parties don't co-operate effectively they may not only fail to generate a mutual gain but they may actually undermine existing arrangements. In that event, the potential for a win–win outcome may not be achieved and instead there may be a lose–lose result.

Whilst the concepts of integrative and distributive bargaining are very clear in theory, in practice they may overlap. A negotiation can involve elements of both types of bargaining. Although the sale of a house, for example, is essentially a fixed sum game, there may be some potential for integrative bargaining. This could arise, for example, by agreeing a mutually advantageous completion date. In conducting negotiations it can be useful to identify what elements of integrative and distributive bargaining potentially exist.

UNITARY AND PLURALISTIC FRAMES OF REFERENCE

The concepts of unitary and pluralistic frames of reference were examined in the previous chapter because of their particular significance to the understanding of employee relations. However, these concepts, are also basic to an understanding of negotiations. This is because conflicts of interest are not always obvious. In internal organisation bargaining those with a unitary frame of reference may be unable to recognise conflicts of interest between different parts of the organisation. This is because they will apply a team concept and assume that everyone will or should subordinate their own objectives to those of the organisation overall. Those with a pluralistic frame of reference, however, will recognise that when sectional interests are threatened, people will not automatically co-operate for the common good. It is necessary to be able to recognise such conflicts of interest in order to develop a framework for dealing with them.

CONFLICTS OF RIGHT AND CONFLICTS OF INTEREST

Another useful concept is the difference between conflicts of right and conflicts of interest. Conflicts of right occur when there is a dispute about the interpretation of an existing agreement. Conflicts of interest occur when the parties dispute what an agreement should be as opposed to what it is.

The framework of negotiations

Whenever people negotiate there is a framework, however informal it may be. The framework relates to *how* an issue is being negotiated. The parties can be so involved in the substance of the negotiations that they can neglect to pay sufficient attention to the way in which the negotiations are being handled. This can reduce the chances of a positive outcome. This is particularly the case when the negotiations are complicated and/or a number of parties are involved. In team negotiations there may need to be a division of labour so that the different aspects of negotiation are handled effectively. Particular attention may need to be paid to internal differences between team members. As well as needing to structure negotiations effectively, it is also necessary for those involved to be clear about their objectives and tactics. Power realities also need to be carefully examined.

PROCEDURAL AND SUBSTANTIVE ISSUES

A basic distinction in negotiations is between the procedure that is used to negotiate and the actual substantive issues being negotiated about. If negotiations between the parties are part of an established pattern, the negotiations may have been formalised into a procedural agreement. If that is not the case at least the historic pattern will probably represent the expectations of the parties as to the *way* they wish to proceed. Even in small informal negotiations the parties need to consider the way in which they need to proceed and may also want to come to a joint understanding about that. There can be so much conflict and tension in negotiations about substantive issues that it can be in the interests of both parties to try and remove any misunderstandings about how the negotiations are to be conducted beforehand. This is a strong argument for having a procedure agreed well in advance of negotiations. It can be difficult enough trying to resolve the substantive issues without having to agree the procedure immediately beforehand, or having to make it up as you go along. To make an analysis with sport, the rules of the game are agreed well in advance of an actual game. Great care is often taken to ensure that the neutrals in change of sporting contests apply the rules in a consistent manner.

OBJECTIVES

Managers and others involved in negotiations need to carefully establish their objectives. Sometimes objectives are self-evident. On other occasions they involve patient diagnostic work. If a reactive style is taken it may be automatic to respond to a demand by saying 'no', prevaricating or making a less generous counter-offer. However, on some occasions it may be in both the parties interests if a demand is accepted. If, for example, there is a shortage of a particular category of staff it may be in management's interests to agree to a demand for a wage increase rather than reactively resist it.

In identifying objectives it can be crucial that the parties look forward and do not dwell on perceived historic injustices. Another important issue can be that demands may only be the symptom of a deeper underlying problem.

<table>
<tr><td>Example</td><td>In a former public utility there was high turnover of computer staff. When people left they said that it was because they were offered more money to work elsewhere. More money was given to the computer staff but the labour turnover remained high. The employer then asked people who were leaving what had caused them to look for another job. The clear pattern with the responses to his question was the poor interpersonal and management skills of their technical supervisors. The primary solution was clearly to do with the selection, development and monitoring of the supervisors of computer staff and not increasing wages.</td></tr>
</table>

PREPARATION

Once the negotiating objectives have been defined, it is then necessary to work out how those objectives might be achieved. One useful framework is the following:

- define objectives and rank them in order of importance;
- decide tactics to achieve objective;
- identify the maximum concessions you will make (the bottom line);
- decide on the action you will take if you do not achieve your objectives. This may cause you to rethink the concessions you are prepared to give.

It is particularly important to examine the power relationships. These may have far more impact on the outcome of negotiations than the intellectual or moral quality of a case. It involves asking such blunt questions as, 'Who can do what do whom and when?' A man with a knife at your throat may have a poor intellectual and moral case for robbing you but is likely to succeed. The Prussian military theorist Karl von Clausewitz explained the nature of power realities with reference to international politics in the 19th century. He stated, 'War is nothing but the continuation of politics with admixture of other means' (David 1997: 149).

Negotiations can take place at two levels. The surface element may be the intellectual presentation of a case supported by apparently relevant information. However, this can have a large element of charade about it. The parties may in reality be concentrating on what pressure they can bring on the others involved and how they might do it. However, whilst it is important to recognise and take into account the power realities, careful case preparation and presentation do sometimes significantly affect the outcome. Issues to consider including in a case might be:

- economic impact,
- legal impact,
- precedents and practice elsewhere,
- the precedent effect of accepting a demand
- ability of the parties to pay.

A further factor to consider is the nature of the relationship between the parties. Managers may be able to take much more on trust with a party if they have a long established relationship and a good reputation. They will need to be much more cautious in dealing with people they know little about, especially in a one-off negotiation. In a long-term relationship there is the factor of goodwill to be taken into account. It may also lead to the giving of face-saving compromises to the other side. If goodwill is not an issue there may be the temptation to use sharp practice to gain a better deal.

The confidentiality of information about bargaining positions can't always be taken for granted. Information can be leaked deliberately or accidentally. There is also often a grapevine by which people can gain information. However, care should be taken to try and avoid damaging leaks. Sometimes it is also necessary to beware of 'information' that is created or released to undermine the negotiating position of another party.

INTERNAL DIFFERENCES

Attention is often concentrated on the differences between the two sides in a negotiation. However, often the sides represent coalitions of interest groups. Members of a negotiating team can assume that because they are all on the same side that they have a common position. However, as well as personalities differing, there can be quite different pressures on different members of a side. Some team members may feel that other team members are being disloyal by not agreeing with their position. However, it is more profitable to try and understand the reasons why members of a team might disagree and explore what accommodations are possible. The worst thing to do is not to explore these issues beforehand and find that the internal differences only become obvious during negotiations with the other party.

The scale of the internal differences within a side can be greater and more difficult to resolve than the external differences between them and the other main party. This is not always obvious because of the much greater secrecy that may be involved in trying to resolve such differences. However, adequate time has to be given to establishing a party line. Sides can split into hawks and doves. Moderates are sometimes called doves because of the term 'doves of peace'. This is contrast to hardliners who are sometimes called hawks, hawks being birds of prey. It may be counter-productive to exclude hawks from the negotiating team. They may need to be exposed to the negotiating pressures and involved in any proposals for settlement. They may cause far more trouble shouting their opposition from the sidelines.

There are many examples from the world of politics of the problems of reconciling internal differences. In Northern Ireland and the Middle East the moderates on both sides could probably come to agreement relatively easily. Sometimes deals are made secretly between the leaders who then try to persuade their own side to accept them. The problem is getting their hawks to agree. Too many concessions to the other side, however, can destabilise the position of leaders and even lead to their death, for example, the assassination of the Israeli Prime Minister Yitzhak Rabin by an Israeli fundamentalist in 1995 following the Oslo Peace Agreement. An earlier example is the assassination of Michael Collins by Irish nationalists in 1922. This followed his conclusion of a peace deal with the British Government which involved independence for the south of Ireland but not the north.

Political parties often have formal party meetings before meetings of national and local government assemblies to agree the party line. This is where the real decisions are usually taken, rather than in public debate. The relationship between internal and external differences is illustrated in Figure 15.1.

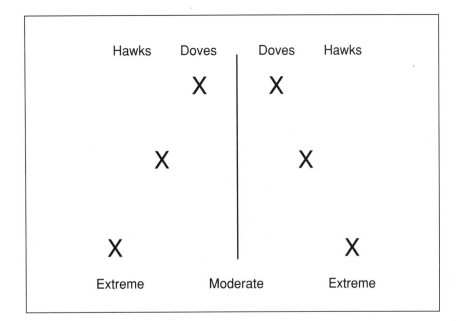

FIGURE 15.1 *Handling of internal differences*

ROLE ALLOCATIONS

Even in one-to-one negotiations there can be a number of different roles that the parties have to handle according to the stage they are in the negotiating process. A procedural framework needs to be established. This needs to include the time and place for negotiations, an agenda, and the preparation and presentation of any relevant documents. The parties will need to spend time both presenting and listening to one another during the substantive negotiations. It may be necessary to organise adjournments and further meetings. If a deal is concluded, attention then has to be paid to how it is implemented. Failure to pay adequate attention to these issues can jeopardise the negotiations. It may be necessary for one of the parties, however informally, to assume a chairing role in identifying and dealing with these issues.

In team negotiations the need for a division of labour between different members is more obvious than the need for one person to switch roles when they are bargaining on their own. However, even in team negotiations the need to arrange a sensible role allocation is often sadly neglected. This can lead to one person being quite unnecessarily overloaded, whilst their colleagues don't have enough to do. Key roles that have to be handled in team negotiations are:

Chairing

There can be three dimensions to the chairing role, chairing a team in the negotiations with the other party, chairing internal discussions and chairing the joint meeting overall.

Sometimes there are formal arrangements for handling joint meetings, e.g. by rotation or by having an independent chair handle it. Often there is no such provision and the chair of a team may need to handle this in such a way that an effective framework is provided without irritating the other side at this exercise of control.

The chairing roles can be of great importance and require significant skill and attention, as explained in chapter 16 on meetings and chairing. It is up to the chair to see that negotiations stay on course and to intervene if there is a danger of the process breaking down. This is much more easily done if they are concentrating primarily on this aspect and are detached from the argument about substantive issues.

Case presentation

A common practice is for the most senior person on the management side to handle all the chairing roles and be the lead negotiator. However, given the danger of role overload and the damaging consequences this can have, it is often best to have a separate person act as the lead negotiator. They can then concentrate on just the negotiating issues and leave the procedural aspects to the chair. It also means that if there is a deadlock in discussions, or if they get too heated, the chair can intervene. This may also create valuable thinking time for the lead negotiator.

Recording

Another way of easing the burden on the chair and lead negotiator is to have someone else take notes. The case is even stronger if that person does not have any other formal responsibility in the negotiations. Verbatim notes of a whole meeting are not necessary, but great care may be necessary to get an accurate record of key issues. The person taking notes will normally need to sit next to the chair so that they can liaise about note taking. The chair may to need to have the lead negotiator on their other side.

Observing

Much may be learnt about the other side's real intentions and internal differences by a careful study of their demeanour during negotiations. Points to watch can be:

- who people defer to within a team,
- body language, including facial expressions,

- signs of tension, e.g. in rate of talking, language used and pitch of voice,
- the issues on which they seem to need to refer back to their principals,
- cross-talk,
- contradictions in what is said.

It can be time well spent to have someone concentrate on observing. If necessary, this can be combined with another role, e.g. recording.

Example	When Hong Kong was a British colony people were employed there as China watchers. It was their job to make political assessments of what was really happening in the relatively closed and secretive country. They would do this by such devices as noting who appeared at public events and in what order.

Consideration may also be given to the need for expert witnesses during negotiations, who may stay for the whole meeting or just the relevant part.

SPECIALIST REPRESENTATION

Sometimes managers need to consider the case for appointing a specialist to lead negotiations. This will be logical if the costs of such representation are less than the potential gain in the negotiations. The specialist may be internally or externally appointed. Personnel managers often need to lead internal negotiations with employee representatives because of the dangers of line managers getting a poor or flawed deal. However, there are dangers of the personnel function taking over too much executive authority and in so doing preventing line managers from developing negotiating skills in the employee relations area. One option is to have line managers lead negotiations with a personnel representative present as an adviser.

Trade unions have long understood the need for specialist representation. The expertise of some employee representatives and of full-time union officials generally is such that they can often outmanoeuvre an inexperienced line manager. Also, union representatives may be appointed because of their negotiating ability whilst this may be a peripheral skill and issue for the line manager. The negotiating ability of managers is an issue that may need addressing by way of selection and training, a topic that is addressed later in this chapter.

Sometimes organisations need to consider the use of external specialists to represent them. This often happens with employment tribunal cases, although this is a judicial and not a negotiating process. Organisations that belong to employers' associations may get a specialist negotiator from the association to represent them on some issues. On commercial issues it may be necessary to consider using a commercial agent.

Advantages that specialist negotiators can bring include emotional detachment, knowledge of the substantive area, market trends and practice elsewhere, and contacts. Managers may be at a disadvantage if the person they are dealing with has specialist knowledge or specialist representation and they do not. However, conflicts of interests can sometimes emerge between the specialist negotiator and their client, such as the length of negotiations and fee arrangements. Also, agreements can sometimes be more satisfactorily struck by direct contact with the other side. This is because specialist representatives may strive too hard to get the best possible deal and ignore the need for ongoing relationship to be maintained between the parties. Dangers can arise if you negotiate without a specialist representative.

Example

Four young musicians who had formed their own group were offered a contract by a medium-sized recording studio. They were invited to travel to London to sign a contract. They told their accountant of this, and he advised them to take a lawyer with them. When the musicians entered the conference room they found that four *printed* standard contracts had been placed on the table for them to sign. The secretary who showed them into the room asked the members of the group who the fifth person was. When they introduced their lawyer the secretary responded by saying, 'You won't be needing these contracts then'. She then returned with four different *printed* standard contracts. It emerged that the original contract forms contained an open-ended costs clause, which would have enabled the recording company to offset costs against the income generated by the contract so that the musicians may not have received any money. The contract that the musicians eventually did sign had a fixed level of costs.

Negotiating processes

As well as there being a need for attention to be paid to the procedural framework for negotiations, care is also needed in managing the way in which people interact with one another during negotiations. Whoever is chairing a meeting or a team has a particular responsibility to manage these processes constructively. There can be considerable emotion and tension during negotiations, and careful management of the processes can make all the difference as to whether agreement is reached or not. Particular attention needs to be taken to the sequence in which events are handled, the many communication problems that can arise and the ways in which deadlock may be overcome.

SEQUENCE OF EVENTS

There are three particularly important aspects to consider in relation to the sequence of events during negotiations. These are the need for a negotiating ritual, including the issue of who should make the first bid, the need for the chair to stay in role and see that the other parties do the same and the need to focus on the important issues.

The Negotiating Ritual

It is probably best to try and agree the sequence of events with the other party before negotiations begin. If there is a procedural agreement, this may specify the sequence.

Invariably there is a ritual to negotiations. This usually consists of a series of offers and counter-offers and eventual compromise agreement. This ritual can fulfil a necessary function. This is particularly so if the parties negotiating have interest groups to whom they are responsible. The negotiators will need to demonstrate that they have got the best offer available in order to sell any deal to whoever they represent. Consequently it is important to avoid public displays of triumph if a good deal is obtained as this can undermine the position of the negotiators. Even in cases where the principals are negotiating directly with one another, they will also need to feel that they have got a good deal.

Thought needs to be given as to whether it is better to make the first offer yourself or try and get the other party to make the first bid. The pitching of an initial offer can have a crucial effect on the ultimate outcome. In the case of trying to buy something, too low an offer may mean that you are not taken seriously. Too high an offer can create the expectation that you can be persuaded to improve your offer significantly.

Parties to negotiations may have a recognisable historic pattern in the way they handle the ritual. It may help a manager in handling the ritual to try and identify that pattern. It may be necessary to take account of past patterns altering if a new and important person joins a negotiating team. The negotiating ritual needs to be handled with some skill. Sometimes mistakes can be elementary.

Example

At the start of annual railway pay negotiations the lead management negotiator referred to management proposals as 'the *first* offer'. This drew a swift response from the union spokesperson: 'We don't like the first offer – what about the second one?'

There is also a need to consider who makes their case first. Often it makes sense for the person who is trying to change a situation to be allowed to go first. If one side is particularly emotional about an issue it may be best to let them present first so that they can dissipate some of their anger. Having done that they may be more able to listen to the response and also may have even moderated their position through being given the chance to be heard. It is particularly important for the chair of the opposing team to prevent retaliatory comment from hawks on their own side at this stage as this could undo all the good work that may have already been accomplished. A further point is the need to consider what you should ask for in return whenever you make an offer. Opposing negotiators may be much more likely to make concessions if a trade-off is involved.

Keeping in role

The chair needs to ensure that the agreed procedure and sequence of negotiations are followed and that the parties keep to their allotted roles. It is all too easy for 'tennis matches' to develop whereby each side refutes what the other says and the discussions not only do not progress but get increasingly acrimonious (Rees and Porter 1997: 67). Understandably, both sides will want to concentrate on the strong and not the weak points in their case. It is up to the chair to let both sides make their case and then move on. Sometimes it may be necessary to agree to differ on a particular point and agree to return to it later. In order to navigate through these difficulties it is essential that the chair stays in role and doesn't get unnecessarily involved in argument about the substantive issues. If the chair is for some reasons involved in the substantive negotiations, e.g. if they are conducted between just two people, they may need to be adept at signalling when they are bargaining and when they are trying to manage the procedure and processes. This is akin to refereeing a sports match that one is also playing in and is a topic given further detailed attention in chapter 16 on meetings and chairing.

Tunnel vision

A further issue is the need for the parties to avoid tunnel vision. This can happen when the parties focus their attention on one aspect of negotiations and ignore other issues which may be far more important. Sometimes, also one or both of the parties may fail to see that the issue they are dealing with is a symptom of something more fundamental. This reinforces the need to think carefully about objectives, as explained in the section on the framework of negotiations earlier in this chapter.

Example	The managers in a manufacturing company became preoccupied with the earnings drift of a particular group of production workers who were receiving the benefit of a 'loose' group bonus scheme. They were benefiting because of changes in production methods that were enabling them to receive more money without any extra effort on their part. However, the real problem was not in limiting their increases but in getting rid of the bonus scheme altogether. It was no longer acting as an incentive for extra effort but just a way of paying more money and distorting the pay structure.

COMMUNICATION ISSUES

Communication processes can be fragile at the best of times, as has been explained in chapter 8. However, they can be particularly vulnerable during negotiations. This is because of the presence of factors such as conflict and emotion and the complexities that can arise during negotiations. Also, distortion is possible at each stage of the chain of communication. There is a need for people in chairing roles to pay particular attention to the potential for misunderstandings and to take preventative action to avoid them and the often very serious consequences that can flow from misunderstandings. Key areas involve listening and observing, taking account of any cultural differences and avoiding ambiguity.

Listening and observing

One of the dangers in negotiating meetings is that people get so involved in presenting their case that they do not listen carefully enough to what the other side has to say and then reflect on it. People in chairing roles need to give the other side adequate opportunity to present their case and ensure that it is listened to. A common problem is for people to use the time when the other side is presenting their case simply to rehearse the arguments they are going to use instead of listening to what is actually being said. Listening and observing are all the more important because a certain amount of posturing takes place during negotiations and it is necessary to get behind that to try and discover the other side's true intentions.

The style used in the negotiations can also be very important. There can be complications enough without the differences being personalised. The parties should try and behave assertively and not aggressively. The distinction between these two styles of behaviour has been explained in chapter 4. If a person is nevertheless aggressive, it is best to remain assertive and not make matters worse by responding aggressively. This can have the effect of calming the other person down. If it doesn't, it may lead to the other person losing the thread of their argument, making mistakes and losing sympathy with their colleagues.

Particular attention may need to be paid to the language that is used. Sometimes coded messages are sent between lead negotiators to indicate whether they are taking a hard or a soft line on a particular issue. On other occasions parties may unintentionally reveal their intentions by the use of particular words or by carelessness.

Example	At a consultative meeting about the possible merger of two units, the managing director of a company unwittingly revealed that the logistical arrangements to effect the merger had already been set in motion and that the consultation was meaningless.

Particular care must be applied to words that are used during negotiations. Words such as 'review', if used in the context of pay negotiations, are likely to be interpreted as meaning an increase. Much can be learnt by simply observing the behaviour of the other side, as illustrated by the example in chapter 8 about the American agent Mark McCormack's observances of body language during negotiations.

Cultural differences

Attention will need to be paid to any potential cultural barriers to understanding during negotiations, especially increasing cultural diversity within nations and globalisation (Mead 1998). It may be important to have a person to advise on how to handle the different negotiating conventions of those from other cultures. The impact of culture on communication is also considered in both chapter 4 on managerial style and chapter 8 on communication.

The rituals that people are used to from other countries may be different and sometimes much more prolonged. In countries such as the USA, communications are likely to be direct and often-reinforced by written contracts. In some Asian countries, for example, much more attention will have to be paid to the context in which negotiations take place. More may have to be taken on trust, as to ask for too much written clarification could be taken as insulting with the implication that the other party isn't trusted. In such cultures there also may be a higher need to save the face of the weaker party. Also, deference to elders can vary from culture to culture. In dealing with the

Japanese, for example, it may be important to recognise the deference shown to elder members on their team and to show politeness yourself. It may also be important to work out the effect that culture can have on power realities within a team.

The nature and importance of body language may also differ considerably from one culture to another. People from some cultures may be much more impassive than those with other cultural backgrounds. If a manager causes offence to people from some cultures, they be much less likely to realise it, however damaging it may be. The meaning of gestures can critically vary from one culture to another.

Example

Negotiations involving an international organisation in India were hampered at one stage by the habit of the people they were trying to do business with shaking their heads from side to side as if in disagreement. It then emerged that in this particular part of the country that gesture meant agreement and not disagreement.

Avoiding Ambiguity

It is crucial for negotiators to avoid unintended ambiguity during negotiations, especially in any agreement that is reached. Unfortunately, this can all too easily happen. Negotiators may remember the concessions that they have gained during negotiations far more readily than the concessions that they have made. Such selective perception may be compounded by the use of words that can have more than one meaning. Words such as 'may' can be interpreted as 'must, probably,' or 'possibly'. Those involved in negotiating are apt to make the interpretation most convenient to them, unaware that the other party may be doing the same thing in reverse. To make matters worse, when the difference in interpretations emerges, the parties may think that there has been deliberate deceit rather than genuine misunderstanding.

Example

In a series of experiments with simulated negotiating exercises with managers it was found that it was more common than not to have significant misunderstanding about what the parties thought they had agreed. This emerged when, at the conclusion of negotiations, each individual was asked to record the main items of agreement. The people involved were not allowed to confer with one another when recording their perception of the outcome. The managers concerned tended to misperceive the outcomes in their favour, i.e. managers would all tend to think that they had conceded less than other managers playing the part of employee representatives.

(Rees and Porter 1997: 68–9)

To avoid unintended ambiguity it is necessary for the chair and lead negotiator in particular to keep on checking during negotiations that misunderstanding has not occurred. Careful listening and observing is a way of helping to see if misunderstanding has developed or not. Frequent summarising of what has or has not been agreed may be necessary during a meeting. It may be necessary to repeat the same point a number of times to make sure that there is genuine agreement and understanding.

The following example shows how serious misunderstandings can easily and innocently arise.

Example

The payroll computer at a factory crashed on pay-day at a time when most manual employees were still paid in cash. Employee representatives demanded that each employee affected be given a cash payment because of this. The company refused to do this, and a three-day strike ensued. It was then discovered that the employees had simply wanted a cash advance which could later be deducted from whatever wages were due to them. The company had thought that the employees were asking for a cash payment to compensate for inconvenience as well as their wages. The problem then arose as to whether the men should receive any payment for the three days they had been on strike because of this misunderstanding. The nature of the confusion was only identified during talks convened to try and resolve the dispute when the two parties were asked to explain just what there differences were.

Recording the outcome of negotiations is a further way of preventing misunderstanding. However, the damage may be done by the time that a written document is issued. It is necessary to ensure that ambiguity does not arise during negotiations so that a written record confirms what was really agreed and not just what the person writing the document thought was agreed.

Sometimes there is a need for deliberate ambiguity. This can be the case when neither party wants to concede a particular issue but they don't want to contest it at that point in time. Providing there are no problems about implementing ambiguous wording, this can be a necessary device for getting agreement.

Reporting back

Particular problems can arise when negotiators report back to the groups they represent. This can be because of the pressure that negotiators may come under to say that they have obtained a better deal than they really have. If this is happening on both sides of a negotiation, perceptions of those in the interest groups of what was really agreed upon can get even more distorted. It is therefore important that those who receive reports from negotiators coax out of them what really happened at the negotiations. If there is a danger of distortion in reporting back from employee representatives to employees, managers may need to distribute written details to employees on the outcome of negotiations.

HANDLING DEADLOCKS

Handling deadlocks can be a key skill for negotiators. There are a number of ways of trying to prevent or resolve deadlock.

Agree on what can be agreed

It may be best to identify what can be agreed on and what can't. Finding some areas of agreement can create an element of mutual trust and become a platform for later agreement on more difficult issues. If necessary, more difficult issues may have to be left for another occasion.

Dealing with conflicting principles

Particular difficulties can emerge if the parties are pursuing different and conflicting points of principle. This may appear to rule out room for manoeuvre. Ways of trying to resolve this are to:

- make value judgements about the respective importance of the principles involved. In some cases it is necessary to let one principle override another because of its greater importance. This may involve giving way or standing firm;
- consider if the other party has simply run out of arguments and is clinging to a principle in order to save face. If so, it will then be necessary to try and find ways of saving the face of the other person so that they can discreetly withdraw from the issue of principle;
- examine if the principle involved has practical significance or is actually hampering the party that is clinging to it;

(Example) In the case of a six-week brewery strike, the management found that they were unable to negotiate with the people they desperately wanted to talk to because they had stated that they would not 'negotiate under duress'.

- devise a compromise deal that appears to leave conflicting principles intact, even though in practice that may not be the case.

Appointing a devil's advocate

It may help to have someone act as a devil's advocate. This may generate insights into the position of the other party. These may include an understanding of the concessions the other party may be able to make and the points that they will not be able to concede.

Identifying convergence and divergence

There is often a pattern in negotiations of the parties sometimes converging towards agreement and sometimes diverging. If the convergence is bringing the parties close to agreement, further small concessions may result in a deal. Once divergence sets in the opportunity may be lost. There may no point in making concessions when parties are moving apart. They may have to wait until there are prospects of convergence again before getting a constructive response to concessions.

Deadlines

Sometimes deadlines are set for agreement to be reached. If agreement is not reached, an offer may be withdrawn, change implemented or some other action taken. This can work, provided that the party setting the deadline has a viable plan of what to implement if there is no agreement.

Adjournments

If negotiations become acrimonious or if fresh ideas are needed, it may be best to seek an adjournment. Adjournments may also be necessary if one or other party needs to consider a fresh point or to resolve internal differences. It may also be necessary for one of the parties to report back to its interest group to receive fresh instructions. Sometimes parties need time to come to terms with what concessions have to be made. Delicate issues of timing can be involved in judging when it can be productive or counter-productive to arrange an adjournment.

Keeping the parties together

If agreement seems possible, it may be best to try and keep the parties together and clinch a deal. In marginal situations, factors such as fatigue may help encourage people to agree. If the negotiations are adjourned, people may have second thoughts or be urged to take a harder line by the interest groups they represent. This is the point at which a former chief conciliation officer of the UK Advisory Conciliation and Arbitration Service (ACAS) said that it may be necessary to provide 'cold fish and chips and warm lager'. However, any deal has to be realistic and not one that will be repudiated afterwards.

Separating interests and positions

An example of the constructive distinction between interests and positions occurred in the Israeli-Egyptian peace negotiations in 1978.

Example

It emerged that Israel's interests were security rather than its position of the continued occupation of the Sinai peninsula. Egypt wanted to regain sovereignty of the Sinai but did not have military objectives. When this was realised, it enabled a deal to be struck that satisfied the interests of both parties. This involved Egypt regaining the Sinai on the understanding that it would not base tanks there.

(Fisher, Ury and Patton 1997)

Back channels

Deadlock sometimes can be resolved by the use of back channels. These are secret contacts between some of the negotiators on each side. They may or may not involve the use of a third party. Back channels can be used to explore the possibility of agreement. If agreement is found to be possible, then the proposals can be presented to the respective negotiating teams. If the secret talks indicate that agreement is not possible, then they remain secret so as to protect the position of the parties involved.

(Example)

An example of the use of back channels is the secret discussions between representatives of the Israeli Government and the Palestine Liberation Organisation (PLO) in Oslo in 1993. These discussions took place whilst official talks were taking place in Washington. When it emerged in Oslo that agreement was possible, the main political leaders got officially involved and later signed a formal agreement.

Secret deals

Some issues may be so important and yet so sensitive that the parties may reach secret agreements about them. These may involve mutual understandings or formal secret protocols. There are dangers in this, particularly if a key negotiator is replaced or one party fails to honour their side of the bargain.

(Example)

During the Cuban missile crisis in 1962, President Kennedy secretly agreed to withdraw nuclear missiles from Turkey. This was in exchange for the Russian public withdrawal of nuclear missiles from Cuba. President Kennedy needed secrecy about his concession because of greater dependence on public opinion than the Russian leader, Nikita Khrushchev.

Third parties

Sometimes third parties may be able to help resolve deadlock. In the case of employment disputes in the UK, the services of the Advisory Conciliation and Arbitration Service (ACAS) are available free of charge. Conciliation is provided both for trade disputes and individual employment rights disputes that have been first referred to an employment tribunal. ACAS has considerable experience and expertise in providing conciliation services. In the case of trade disputes they may be able to smooth the waters and in so doing help the parties explore the possibilities for an agreement. They may also be able to act as a back channel for exploratory suggestions by either party. Many other countries have similar arrangements. In individual employment rights issues in the UK conciliation officers may, and often do, facilitate negotiated settlements that avoid the need for the parties to have an employment tribunal hearing.

Independent arbitration can be provided in both trade disputes and in individual applications for unfair dismissal in the UK. Both parties need to agree to the process. However, the party in the more powerful position in a trade dispute may be reluctant to accept arbitration if they think that this will give them a less favourable outcome than using their negotiating power. Arbitration awards in trade disputes are not legally binding but are invariably accepted. Trades disputes arbitration lends itself particularly to conflicts of right, i.e. issues relating to the interpretation of agreements. The issues may not be as great as those involved in conflicts of interest and it can be seen as a fair way of settling an issue. Alternatively, arbitrators can be appointed as mediators to see if they can suggest ways as to how the parties can resolve their differences. This process is not binding. In practice, elements of mediation may be present in the conciliation in trade disputes.

If recourse is made to arbitration, it is essential to have clear terms of reference.

A privately arranged arbitration panel was appointed to resolve a dispute between a London-based company and its employees. The issue concerned the car mileage rate to be paid to employees who had to drive to work during train strikes. The company wanted to pay a different and lower rate than that given when employees had to use their cars for company business. The terms of reference were to confirm that the company practice of paying the lower mileage rate during train strikes was correct. Once proceedings had started it emerged that the company's interpretation of the terms of reference was such that the panel could only rule in its favour. The panel had no authority to vary the company practice. When this became apparent, the union side promptly withdrew from the proceedings.

As was explained in the previous chapter, the role of arbitration in unfair dismissal cases was greatly extended in 2000. The parties can jointly agree to refer appropriate cases to independent arbitration instead of employment tribunals. There is no right of legal appeal, apart from an application for a judicial review.

Accepting failure
Not all deadlocks can or even should be broken. Managers need to consider their bottom line, as explained in the section on objectives earlier in this chapter. No deal may be better than a bad deal. However, the consequences of not having agreement may need to be reconsidered before breaking off negotiations. If agreement is not reached there is always the possibility that the matter can be reconsidered in the future. In that respect, a 'no' is not as final as a 'yes'. Also, other opportunities may arise in other directions for progress.

Even if a negotiator fails to achieve their objectives, it can be possible to put up markers for the future. This can be about issues to be raised at a later date. If negotiators make predictions that are ignored but which later turn out to have been correct, this is likely to enhance their personal reputation. They are also likely to enhance their reputation by the dignity with which they accept failure.

Negotiating outcomes

COMMUNICATING THE RESULT

Once an agreement is made it may need to be written up and communicated to all the parties concerned. Employers may want to see that each employee is given details of any agreements affecting them. Care needs to be taken to see that there are no misunderstandings about the content and interpretation of an agreement. In some cases it may be appropriate to issue press releases or hold press conferences.

EVALUATION

It may help to do a cost–benefit analysis of an agreement to see what lessons there are for the future. This can help decide whether there should be further negotiations in an area or if it should be left alone.

IMPLEMENTATION

The terms of an agreement need to be achieved in practice. The practicability of being able to implement the terms of an agreement need to be considered very early on in the negotiating process. Historically, there were many cases in the UK of productivity deals between trade unions and employers at a national level which were not implemented locally. Consequently, employers were paying for productivity gains they were not getting. Attention needs to be paid to arrangements for monitoring and control and the need for safeguards if promised concessions are not implemented. Sometimes phased payments are made in accordance with progress made.

DISPUTES

It may be necessary to provide a mechanism for resolving disputes about the interpretation of an agreement. This may be handled by internal procedures. If internal procedures do not result in agreement, sometimes there is provision for reference to an outside party. In the UK there is increasing use of an ombudsman, for example in national and local government and in the banking and travel industries. In the case of employment disputes there can be reference to ACAS for voluntary arbitration. Other independent parties include lawyers and commercial arbitrators.

The way in which disputes about the interpretation of agreements are to be resolved needs to be taken into account when agreements are written. In collective employee-relations agreements in the UK the tradition is often to abide by the spirit rather than the letter of the agreement. This is in contrast to the USA where such documents are legally binding between the parties and interpreted according to the letter of the agreement. Agreements that are binding in spirit may be difficult to interpret by outsiders because of ambiguities and mutual unwritten understandings. However, there is always a case for expressing agreements as clearly as is practicable. The ease with which disputes can arise about what was agreed and the difficulties that can arise in settling such disputes underlines the need to ensure that negotiations are conducted and concluded in such a way that there is no room for subsequent disagreement.

VARIATION OF AGREEMENTS

Provision may need to be made for the variation of an agreement. The duration of an agreement may need to be specified as well as the procedure for seeking to vary it. There may also need to be provision for inflation and escape clauses in the event of specified circumstances. Building and construction contracts usually allow for renegotiation of the price if extra work is requested. It is necessary to beware of open-ended commitments, especially if they can be manipulated by one of the parties. An example of how this can happen was given earlier in the chapter. This concerned the open-ended costs clause in a contract offered by a recording studio to four young musicians which could have enabled the studio to offset whatever costs they liked against the revenue generated.

TRAINING

In evaluating negotiating outcomes attention may need to be paid to the skill with which the negotiations were handled. This may reveal training needs. Training needs may also be created by reorganisation, particularly if that involves giving more responsibility to line managers for negotiation. This often happens when business units are created and the authority of central functional departments, for example personnel, is reduced.

The development of negotiating skills can be achieved by the gradual exposure of managers to negotiating situations. They may learn much by watching experienced negotiators in action. Skills can also be developed on formal training courses. Participants can develop their diagnostic skills by identifying objectives and tactics in a graded series of exercises. Simulation exercises involving role plays can provide the opportunity for people to practice their negotiating skills and gain feedback on their performance in a risk-free environment. Feedback can be given by other participants, observers and, if appropriate, closed circuit television replays of critical incidents. It can be particularly useful for participants to identify misunderstandings that arise during simulated negotiations and the causes of these misunderstandings. It can also be very useful for participants to experiment with different role allocations during team negotiations (Rees and Porter 1997: 65–68, 153–157).

SUMMARY

✔ Managers spend much of their time in negotiation over a wide range of topics, much of it informal. The pace of change is such that negotiation and renegotiation is becoming ever more important. A key theoretical distinction is between integrative and distributive bargaining. In integrative bargaining the parties may be able to co-operate in such a way that they make their objectives complementary to one another. In distributive bargaining one party can only gain at the expense of the other. The importance of the frames of reference of the negotiators was also considered in this chapter. Managers with a unitarist perspective may be handicapped by failing to understand the rationale of those with whom they are negotiating. Those with a pluralist perspective are more able to understand the rationale and even the legitimacy of the claims of other parties.

✔ The need for managers to develop a framework for negotiation, even in informal situations was explained. This involves preparation, identification of objectives and a rational sequence of events during the bargaining process. Often the internal differences within a team can be more difficult to resolve than those with the external party with whom negotiations need to be conducted. Consequently, considerable time may need to be taken to try and resolve internal differences before negotiations can start. It is also important to examine the power relationships in a bargaining relationship. Power relationships are likely to have much more influence on the outcome of negotiations than the debating skills of the parties involved.

✔ The need for clear roles to be allocated to those involved in team negotiations was stressed. The complexity and pressures involved in negotiations can be such that misunderstandings easily arise. Anticipation of communication problems is important to ensure that real agreement is reached. Division of labour within negotiating teams is one way of avoiding such problems. Key roles are chairing, case presentation, recording and observing. In one-to-one negotiations these activities will all need to be covered by the same person. Sometimes the cost of hiring a specialist negotiator may be a sound investment.

✔ Consideration may need to be given as to how deadlock is handled, e.g. by the involvement of a third party. Acceptance of the need for a negotiating ritual, including a series of offers and counter-offers, may be necessary if agreement is to be reached. However, no agreement may be better than a bad agreement. Consideration was also given to the effective implementation and monitoring of agreements. It may also be necessary to make arrangements for variations of agreements and resolving disputes about the interpretation of agreements.

✔ The way in which negotiating skills can be developed was also covered. The skills of negotiation can be systematically identified. Managers can develop their ability to apply these skills by observation, practice, reflection on their own negotiating behaviour, coaching and formal training. The use of simulation exercises can be a useful way of developing negotiating skills in a risk-free environment.

SELF-ASSESSMENT QUESTIONS

1. Identify the issues you had to negotiate both at work and elsewhere in your last working day.

2. Explain one theory relevant to negotiation.

3. Why is it necessary to have a procedural framework for negotiations?

4. What are the different roles that people may need to play during team negotiations?

5. Why is it necessary to identify the power realities of the parties involved in negotiations?

6. Explain the term 'negotiating ritual' and its potential importance.

7. Why are misunderstandings likely during negotiations?

8. How can you try and ensure that agreements are kept?

References

(Works of general interest in the specific references are marked with a star.)

David, Saul (1997) *Military Blunders – The How and Why of Military Failure*, Robinson Publishing Ltd.

* Fisher R., W. Ury and B. Patton (1997) *Getting to Yes, Negotiating an Agreement Without Giving In*, 2nd ed., Arrow.

* Fox, A. (1965) 'Industrial Sociology and Industrial Relations', research paper no.3, Royal Commission on Trade Unions and Employers Associations, HMSO.

Mead, Richard (1998) 'Negotiations', *International Management*, 2nd ed., Blackwell Business, ch. 11.

Rees, W. David and C. Porter (1997) 'Negotiation – Mystic Art or Identifiable Process?', parts 1–2, *Industrial and Commercial Training*, (29: 3,5).

* Walton, R. E. and R. B. McKersie (1965) *A Behavioral Theory of Labor Negotiations*, McGraw-Hill: New York.

chapter sixteen

Meetings and chairing

There are case studies and exercises at
http://www.thomsonlearning.co.uk
(for full details, see the listing at the
start of this book).

LEARNING OUTCOMES

By the end of this chapter you will be able to:

- Identify the need for and range of informal and formal meetings in which one is likely to be engaged at work

- Identify the objectives of meetings and, if they include decision-making, the decision making mechanisms that operate within a particular type of meeting

- Identify the nature of key roles at meetings, particularly that of chair and secretary

- Prepare for meetings effectively

- Employ key skills for the effective conduct of meetings

- Understand the role of conflict at meetings and how it can be managed

- Identify the necessary follow-up action that is necessary after meetings, particularly implementation and monitoring

Introduction

In this chapter the role of meetings in organisations and the associated skills in seeing that they are conducted effectively are examined. Meetings, whether formal or informal, are an integral part of organisational activity and attendance at them can occupy a considerable part of a manager's time. The different types of meetings are explained and the need stressed for those attending a meeting to be clear about their objectives and any decision-making arrangements involved. It is particularly important that the chair and secretary of formal meetings prepare beforehand to ensure that the time at meetings is used effectively. Other members may also need to prepare beforehand, particularly if they want to influence any outcomes. Prior preparation may also be necessary for informal meetings.

The differences between procedures, processes and tasks are explained. Attention is also given to the need for the chair to avoid getting over-involved in discussion and the way in which they may need to handle conflict at a meeting. The importance of follow-up action, including implementation and monitoring, is covered. The appendix to this chapter explains the main rules relating to formal committee procedure.

The term 'chair' is used throughout the chapter rather than the alternative expression 'chairman' to emphasise the point that the chair can be a man or a woman.

The need for meetings

PLACE IN ORGANISATIONAL STRUCTURE

Meetings can be an indispensable part of an organisation's structure. In some organisations, such as local government, policy decisions must be taken by a committee-type structure with various committees or subcommittees reporting to the council as a whole. In commercial organisations the need for meetings below the level of shareholders' and directors' meetings may not be obligatory but may still be very necessary. Meetings may be necessary as an aid to the running of departments. They can also be vital in promoting interdepartmental co-operation which otherwise might not be achieved. The growing complexity of decision-making, caused partly by the diffusion of knowledge within organisations, means that very often decisions can only be taken effectively by groups of people coming together and pooling their knowledge and expertise. Globalisation and developments in information technology mean that some meetings involve simultaneous multi-lingual translation and/or electronic conferencing. If meetings are ineffective it can mean that a vital aspect of organisational structure is failing.

THE CONSEQUENCES OF INEFFECTIVENESS

There are many reasons why attention needs to be paid to the effective conduct of meetings. The decisions that are taken in meetings can be very important. The quality of decision-making may correlate with the skill with which meetings are conducted. Small improvements in the effectiveness of meetings can lead to considerable savings in time because of the multiplication of the time saved by the number of people present. Meetings can also have functions other than decision-making, such as providing briefing for those present or ensuring that decisions are taken in an open way. The quality of decision-making and the efficiency with which business is conducted can also affect working relationships outside meetings and the credibility of the role of meetings for future occasions. Managers should also be aware that they are in the spotlight when chairing meetings and that the effectiveness of their performance is likely to enhance or damage their reputation, often before critical audiences. However, if others are responsible for the poor conduct of meetings, at least managers can learn by their mistakes. By contrast, effective chairing is not so obvious as bad chairing simply because things go so smoothly. It is for that reason that the best sports referees are often the ones who are least noticed.

Activities in meetings

LEVEL OF FORMALITY

Meetings can vary in importance and formality, from the proceedings of Parliament to the informal discussion of a temporary problem between colleagues. Whatever the type of meeting, it is necessary for the participants to be aware of the methods by which the business is conducted. Crucial distinctions follow.

PROCEDURAL ARRANGEMENTS

These may be formally embodied in the constitution or terms of reference of a committee, or agreed by the parties present or, in some cases, imposed by one party on another.

PROCESS CONTROL

This is the interpersonal interaction between those present. For meetings to be effectively handled there needs to be constructive management of these interactions. Even in very informal situations there is always a process aspect to the discussions, and the skill with which this is handled can affect the quality and acceptability of any outcome.

SUBSTANTIVE CONTENT OR TASK

Substantive content or the task can be defined as the business of the meeting. For the business to be conducted effectively there needs to be a sound procedural and process framework.

PURPOSES OF MEETINGS

Meetings can be for a variety of purposes. Important types of meetings are:

- decision-making (which may be part of a constitutional decision-making process),
- negotiating,
- consultation,

- briefing,
- fact-finding,
- exchange of views, sometimes this may involve brainstorming,
- problem-solving,
- bonding – this may be between individuals or by a group to other parts of an organisation.

The above classification is a very broad one, and there can be subdivisions within the general headings. Also, some meetings may involve a number, or even all, of the above activities.

DECISION-MAKING

In the case of decision-making meetings there are a number of ways in which decisions may be taken, these are by:

- the most senior person present,
- voting,
- consensus
- negotiated agreement,
- recommendation to another body.

It is important for people to be able to distinguish between the different purposes and decision-making arrangements of meetings. If the members of a meeting fail to see the distinction it can lead to confusion; if the chair does not see the differences it can lead to chaos. This can happen if people have a stereotyped view of meetings and start applying the wrong conventions in a particular situation. Managers may assume that they have to operate by consensus or majority vote, when the reality may be that an organisation has vested them ultimately with the sole decision-making responsibility within a particular area. Management chairs at joint consultative meetings can, and sometimes do, use voting procedures and short-circuit established management structures because the chair has not appreciated that a consultative meeting literally means just that. It is an aid to decision-making via established management procedures, not a substitute for those procedures. During formal negotiations there can be three different centres of decision-making: at the pre-meetings of two separate groups, before a joint meeting and during a joint meeting. All three discussions require effective chairing.

Roles in meetings

Even in small informal meetings it may be necessary to identify the roles that members need to play and have an appropriate division of labour. In some cases people can change roles in a meeting, for example from presenting a case to acting as a chair so that others can put their case. Particularly important roles are those of chair and secretary.

THE ROLE OF THE CHAIR

Attention to procedural and process issues

A chair needs to understand the substantive issue under discussion but also needs to devote some time to a consideration of how the meeting is to be handled effectively. A common error is for the chair to be so immersed in the substantive issues that they neglect the procedural arrangements and the issue of process control. This is especially likely to happen if the chair is anxious to achieve particular outcomes with regard to controversial issues. This can lead to a further complication, which is that a chair may seek to manipulate or cut through any inconvenient arrangements about decision-making in order to secure a particular result. They may get their way in securing a particular outcome, but this may be at the expense of reducing the quality and/or acceptability of a decision. If the case for a particular decision is that strong, it may be that there is little to fear from open and fair discussion. The danger is, though, that the manager concerned is so involved substantively and emotionally that they fail to consider the procedures and processes adequately.

Poor quality decisions for which there is little commitment may stem not so much from a desire to manipulate decision-making procedures and processes as from a failure to consider the relevance of these issues to the business in hand. If the decision-making process requires the pooling of information and elements of negotiation amongst colleagues, the chair needs to ensure that just that takes place. If conflicts have to be resolved, the chair may also need to ensure that discussion takes place in an atmosphere in which those with opposing views each feel they have at least had a fair opportunity to state their case. Whilst a chair will need to understand the substantive issues, it may be best if they refrain from taking a partisan line as far as possible. There are those people who have the skills to referee, for example, a football match in which they are also playing – but it does require a high degree of ability, and it is best for a chair to avoid doing this as far as is practicable. The person with the greatest knowledge of the substantive issues will not automatically have either the time or the aptitude to chair discussions.

A complication concerning the chairing of meetings is that the chair may be the person with the greatest knowledge of the substantive issues. Even if that is the case, the chair still needs to recognise that they must find time to give adequate attention to procedural and process issues. The chair may find that they are also fiercely committed to a particular outcome. In such cases they need to pay considerable attention to seeing that their commitment to a particular view does not prevent them from giving those people who have a different view a fair opportunity to state their case. Some people have or can develop the skill to explain a partisan line yet at the same time chair a discussion fairly. It may be important that they do both, so that the substantive decision is based on a consideration of all relevant views, including the chair's. If, however, the chair finds that they cannot combine these two tasks, then it could be that they should consider letting someone else take the chair, at least for the duration of discussion of a particular topic. The role of the chair is examined later in the chapter with particular regard to resolving conflict during meetings.

Division of labour at meetings

It is critical to recognise that there needs to be a division of labour at meetings. Otherwise, for example, a group of people may be invited to a meeting and find that their views are not sought or are ignored. The chair will need to ensure that they obtain the necessary contributions from those present at a meeting, and may want them to concentrate on resolving, as far as possible, the substantive issues at hand. The chair, sometimes assisted by a secretary, will have to concentrate on the procedural and process issues so that there is a framework within which the group can operate.

It is only when the chair has satisfactorily created the framework for a meeting that they should consider taking time off from their chairing role to get involved in the substantive issues. Even then it may be best to do that to the minimum extent as, if the framework of the meeting is right, the rest of the group may be able to resolve the business themselves, looking to the chair only for procedural and specialist guidance when appropriate. Meetings do not automatically keep on the rails and, if the chair becomes so involved in the discussion that they neglect to consider how the meeting is handled, the discussion may be inadequately guided. An appropriate division of labour is whereby the chair spends perhaps most of their time on procedural matters and process control, someone else takes the minutes and the other members concentrate exclusively on the substantive issues. A meeting where no one concentrates or even bothers about the procedural and process aspects is the one most likely to be ineffective.

THE ROLE OF THE SECRETARY

If a meeting is of any size it may be necessary to have a secretary. This can be a very influential role. This may be a legal or other formal requirement. The secretary can take much of the load off the chair. This may be particularly important if the chair has extensive other commitments. It will also enable the chair to concentrate on the important issues that need attention. Much of the preparatory, administrative and follow-up work may need to be handled by the secretary, including preparation of the draft agenda and distribution of relevant papers including the agreed agenda. The chair and secretary should spend time together before a meeting to plan how it can be most effectively handled. This can increase the influence of the secretary, but one should beware of the business of a meeting being pre-empted by such discussions. A preliminary meeting should be in order to facilitate the smooth running of the main meeting, not to ensure that it acts as a rubber-stamp for the chair and secretary.

The secretary will also take responsibility for keeping a record of a meeting. They may do this themselves or alternatively have another person operating under their control taking notes. The minutes will need to be checked by both the secretary and chair. Even in small informal meetings it may be best if one of the parties identifies and carries on whatever secretarial activity is necessary. This may include a note of any significant outcomes including what follow-up action is needed and by whom. This topic is considered further in the section on recording the outcome of meetings later in this chapter.

Preparation before meetings

The amount of preparation required before meetings will vary according to the type of meeting – its formality, importance, predictability and what role that the individual who is attending the meeting is going to take there. There can be few meetings, however, to which people do not need to give some prior thought. Perhaps the most important issue to consider is what your own objectives are going to be at a meeting. It is only when these have been clarified that it is possible to establish what other prior preparation is required. It is also necessary to consider what is likely to be expected of you at a meeting. This may indicate the preparation you need to make so that other people's needs can be satisfied.

Any procedural rules or constitutional statement about the powers of a meeting not only needs to be to hand but also thoroughly understood, so that such issues can be dealt with immediately and reassuringly if they emerge during a meeting. One would not be reassured by a football referee who had continually to refer to a book on the rules of football whilst a game was being played. The more formal the meeting, the more a chair may rely on the secretary to handle procedural matters before a meeting and to be a source of information during it. It may be expected that the meeting will be run not just in accordance with its constitution but also by the normal conventions of committee procedure. Consequently, a list of these conventions is included as an appendix to this chapter. The chair will also need to understand the substantive issues and their history sufficiently to guide the discussion effectively.

THE AGENDA AND ITS MANAGEMENT

Clearly, meetings need a structure for the consideration of substantive items. This is normally provided by an agenda. However, it is necessary to be proactive in thinking about an agenda and not simply list the items in the order that they are received. Both the chair and the secretary may have to think carefully about what items need to be considered. If decisions are to be taken at a meeting, the degrees of freedom available need to be identified and explained.

The frequency of meetings and their duration need to be related to the volume of business. The volume of business may also need to be managed by combining items. Thought should also be given to logical sequence of items. A further issue is the need to allocate time for discussion of individual items. It is all too easy to spend an inordinate amount of time on easy and relatively minor items with key issues being left to the end when people may be in a hurry, tired and a meeting not even quorate. Approval may be needed from a committee as a whole about issues such as sequence, time allocations and deferment of items. Exceptionally, the order of business may need to be varied because, for example, a key person has to leave. Other items may be introduced under 'any other business', but not if they are controversial and should have been identified on the original agenda. The chair also needs to beware of the agenda being hijacked by a member or members raising items 'on the back of' other items instead of tabling these issues beforehand with written reports if necessary. Another issue for the chair to beware of is a meeting being used as a dumping ground for issues where responsibilities lie elsewhere or for problems that simply can't be resolved.

WHO SHOULD ATTEND MEETINGS?

Thought may have to be given to who should be invited to a meeting. This may be totally prescribed by the constitution of a committee but, when the constitution is first established, the matter has to be examined. In any case, constitutions sometimes need amending, people may need to be specially invited to attend meetings and, on occasion, people may need to be excluded from meetings or part of the proceedings because of conflicts of interest. A balance usually has to be struck between having the interested parties present and not involving too many people because of the varying levels of interest and the costs involved, particularly in terms of time. A system of subcommittees can be a way of getting the optimum balance between differing interests and economy of time. Sometimes it will be appropriate to establish *ad hoc* subcommittees that can enable the detail of a particular issue to be examined without holding up the main business of a meeting.

It can be particularly dangerous to exclude a person from a meeting primarily because they are likely to take a controversial position, or controversial as far as the chair is concerned. To exclude on this basis may lead to charges of unfair chairing, which may then mean that the chair is under procedural challenge as well as being challenged on a substantive issue. Controversial issues tend to surface anyway, and it may be best to see that this happens via the established machinery for resolving conflict rather than in another way, particularly if the chair would otherwise lose respect in the process.

OTHER PREPARATION

Other issues that may require forethought include the exact nature of information that people attending meetings need to have beforehand so that they can contribute effectively and the seating arrangements at a meeting. The type of room and layout can affect discussion, as can seating arrangements. Seating arrangements can be controlled by providing place names, which has the added advantage of identifying those present.

There may be premeetings before the main meeting. In national and local government it is customary for political parties to meet to agree on a party line before engaging in public debate at the formal decision-making body. It is usually the case that the real decisions are taken by the majority party in their pre-meeting. Other pre-meetings may be of groups of people forming a caucus to try to agree the line that they will take during a meeting. A small minority who prepare in this way can have a powerful influence on the outcome of any discussions. They will be primed and create a certain amount of momentum for the views that they express during a meeting. If they vote together at a meeting, they may find that the natural divisions amongst the other people present make it relatively easy to get a majority in favour of their point of view. This may lead other sub-groups to have pre-meetings as well, in an attempt to counter such tactics. One way of dealing with an attempt to force a minority point of view through a committee or other meeting is simply to alert other members as to what is happening beforehand. The chair or any member of a committee may wish to forestall a particular proposal. It may be a matter not so much of converting others, which is sometimes difficult, but of alerting people as to what is happening, so that they are on guard as far as their own interests are concerned. This may also be necessary when there is an attempt to conceal information.

The importance of preparation before meetings was illustrated by the example given in chapter 4 concerning the former Wales Gas Board. Those managers who prepared for the consultative committee meetings with employee representatives found that the committees played a constructive role. Those who did not prepare and who perhaps also did not take the committees seriously found that the employee representatives simply stopped attending, causing the committees to collapse.

Conduct by the chair during meetings

THE CHAIR AS A FACILITATOR

It has been emphasised that chairing a meeting effectively involves adequate preparation and the ability of the chair to distinguish between substantive issues and procedural and process issues. Consideration will now be given to some of the potential problems that may arise during a meeting. A key job of the chair is to see that they actually use the knowledge of the people who are present. It is up to the chair to see that the appropriate issues are identified and then ensure that the collective knowledge and skills of the members are used to resolve the issues. If further information would help, the chair needs to consider releasing or obtaining it. The chair may contribute to the substantive discussions, but should only do so when the issues have been properly identified. The position as chair should not be used to exclude members from discussion who may have important contributions to make or who may feel neglected if they are not given the opportunity to contribute. This may seem an obvious point to make, but in practice chairs vary considerably in the skill with which they use the abilities of the people present. Good and bad examples are obvious on radio and television programmes, just as there will be good and bad examples of chairing in most organisations. Some chairs are very adept at drawing out the views of those who have been invited to speak and at controlling subsequent discussion. For example, others lacking this skill invite people to contribute to on media programmes and then use their procedural position and studio confidence to talk too much themselves, and in so doing wreck any discussion.

THE CHAIR'S ROLE IN RESOLVING CONFLICT

One of the key roles of meetings can be as a way of resolving conflict. Ironically, one of the key roles of a chair can be to identify what the conflict is in the first place. Unless this is done, agreement may be reached before the basic issues have been adequately considered. Another general problem is the need to handle conflict in such a way that the mechanism for resolving it is not destroyed in the process. Sometimes there is little or no conflict, and the exchange of specialist information leads to a decision to which all contributors are equally committed. On other occasions the conflicts can be so bitter that the decision-making process collapses. The range of potential conflict within national government assemblies is such that members do not risk having a chair who is not neutral: the speaker, who chairs the proceedings, has a neutral procedural role. Non-executive mayors fulfil the same function in meetings of local government councils. Many trade unions appoint a president who fulfils a similar function.

The conflict between providing leadership on substantive policy issues and in the procedural and process areas is sometimes obvious within the British Cabinet. Prime ministers need to provide leadership in all these areas, but run the risk that, if they fall out of step with the majority of Cabinet members on policy issues, their position will become threatened. The problem of achieving balance may influence the choice of party leader in the first place. Party leaders have to be careful not to be identified with too extreme a position for fear that they are seen to frustrate the democratic process within their party, particularly in countries which pride themselves on their democratic traditions. It is also necessary for party leaders to demonstrate that they can distinguish between their own views and those of the party, particularly as the views of the party which they will have to present will sometimes differ from their personal views. Neglect of these issues may well have contributed to the replacement of Margaret Thatcher as Prime Minister in the UK by John Major in 1990.

Examples of the problems of reconciling these different types of leadership are particularly easy to give from the world of politics because of the blaze of publicity that surrounds political activity in democratic countries. A balance still has to be kept within less democratic structures, as few leaders have so much power that they can afford to ignore totally the views of their supporters. In any case, a balance is necessary so that decisions are taken after the relevant information has been considered and not imposed by one person regardless of what information is available from others.

One of the ways in which the chair can retain credibility and acceptability when they are involved in securing a particular outcome is by avoiding getting involved in controversial discussion unless it is as a last resort. They may find that the conflict resolves itself satisfactorily without their involvement or that the residual conflict between themselves and the majority of those present at a meeting is so small that accommodation between the two views is relatively easy. Even when the residual conflict is large, the chair may then preserve their position by demonstrating that, after providing for fair discussion of a particular point, they will resolve the outstanding conflict by whatever method is agreed. If the decision-making process is democratic, this may mean that the chair is outvoted, but the defeat on the substantive issue need not affect the chair's credibility to lead procedurally if they have shown that their views have not affected the quality of their procedural and process leadership. In a more hierarchical structure, the chair may ultimately say, 'I have heard you all but disagree' and impose their own decision. Resolving conflict in that way means at least that the chair is fully aware of the arguments against their particular decision and has demonstrated that colleagues have had a fair opportunity to state their case before the final decision is taken. What is likely to be counter-productive is the chair appearing to be willing to listen or to share decision-making powers when they have decided what to do anyway. What is then likely to emerge is that the members have complete freedom to come to the decision that the chair has already determined.

The need for process leadership may exist even in informal discussions between relatively few people. It may be important to think carefully about how such meetings are handled, as so much business can be conducted in this way. Sometimes the level of informality, the competitive nature of relationships or the sensitivity of the issues being discussed is such that it is inappropriate for a formal chair to be appointed. It may nevertheless be both useful and necessary if one person, perhaps quite informally, deals with the process aspects of discussion. This may involve taking a purely neutral role and asking such questions as 'What is the problem?' or 'What are everyone's views?' The other parties may be quite prepared to let one person emerge as the informal chair, particularly if it is seen that they are confining themselves to a neutral role. It may later be possible for that person to enter into the substantive discussions – but only so long as they demonstrate that this is not going to endanger the process control arrangements that have evolved. Otherwise, the person may find that their substantive contributions are not welcome or that process leadership is challenged.

DANGERS OF OVER-INVOLVEMENT BY THE CHAIR

It is very easy for the person chairing a meeting to underestimate the extent to which they get involved in discussion and to overestimate the extent to which other people are involved. This is also a problem that can confront lecturers who have responsibility for leading discussions. One system for training lecturers in the technique of discussion-leading is to chart the pattern of contributions during a discussion. The resultant chart or 'sociogram' can reveal a pattern of which the discussion leader was unaware. A typical pattern is shown in Figure 16.1.

An examination of the flow of discussion shows that most of it was centred around the chair or discussion leader. There was little cross-discussion, and one person did not contribute at all. If this was appropriate, and the chair was aware of what was really happening, it may have been perfectly satisfactory. However, it is very easy for a chair to assume that, because they are involved and interested, so is everyone else. This is not automatically the case. It is possible for a person to sit through a meeting, seething with frustration, but not contributing. Others may remain passively silent though able to contribute. Meanwhile, the chair may be quite unaware of all this. It can be instructive for a chair to be shown a flow chart (or sociogram) of a meeting they have chaired and mentally try to build up a picture of the actual pattern of discussion during their next meeting. Regular checks on the body language of those present can provide important clues as to their feelings about particular topics and about the conduct of the meeting generally.

> **Example**
>
> [A] story is told about a brand new judge who took his place on the bench determined to achieve standards of self-restraint. At the end of his first day he thought he had done remarkably well and went round to his old chambers to see a friend who had been appearing in front of him all day. 'How did I do?' asked the new judge confidently. 'Not bad at all dear boy,' said the other. 'But you really must stop talking so much.'
>
> *(Evans 1987: 87)*

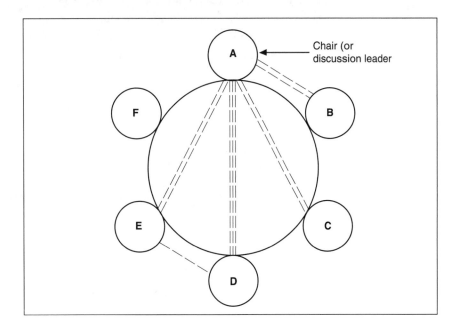

FIGURE 16.1 *Chair-centred discussion*

INVOLVING MEMBERS

Often the flow of discussion that is actually needed is more like that shown in Figure 16.2. In this second chart it is much less obvious who is the chair. Everyone has contributed and there is more cross-discussion than was the case in the previous chart. The flow of discussion may need to be routed more through the chair in large formal meetings, but even in that situation it may be appropriate to allow some cross-discussion provided it is not disruptive. In large formal meetings it may still be necessary for the chair to check out the attitudes of members to the way meetings are handled. There may be major misperceptions of the dynamics of meetings.

The attitudes of the various members of a hospital management committee towards the way in which meetings were handled were established by observation of the meetings and interviews with key participants. There were some surprising differences in perception. The chair and secretary appeared convinced that everyone had ample opportunity to contribute. This was in marked contrast to the senior member of the nursing staff in particular who was clearly of the opinion that she was only permitted to speak when invited to do so. In this particular case, open discussion was not helped by the fact that meetings were conducted in a long rectangular room. The higher the status of a person, the closer they sat to the head of the table. Discussion was confined to those sitting close to the chair. The nursing representative sat at the far end of the table, away from the chair and secretary.

At another hospital in the same group, management committee meetings were held in a room which permitted seating arrangements to be in the form of a semi-circle, which seemed to permit a more genuinely open discussion. The different seating arrangements, whether by accident or design, reflected the very different managerial styles of those organising the meetings.

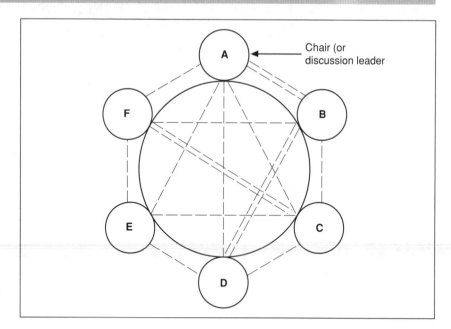

FIGURE 16.2 *Group-centred discussion*

OTHER ISSUES

Control by the chair

There are other important points to note. These include the need for the chair to protect the position of the member who is being ridiculed, particularly if they have a potential contribution to make. Conversely, it is important to see that the authority of the chair is not used against an individual, unless there is very good reason. Members may feel much more keenly about opposition to their views expressed from the chair than from ordinary members of a meeting.

Careful judgements have to be made about the amount of control exercised by the chair. If the chair is seen as being primarily concerned with organising discussion so that the group can resolve its differences and proceed with its business, control by the chair is likely to be accepted. This is in comparison with a situation where there is suspicion that the control is being used to establish particular policy decisions. If exchanges become too heated, that may be the time to insist that all contributions be routed through the chair, even if subsequently that convention is dropped. The routing of all contributions through the chair may only be necessary when the group lacks the self-discipline to evolve a means of taking it in turns to speak. If the chair is ignored, or if people talk whilst the chair is speaking, the pointed silence may be a more appropriate way of re-establishing control than by the raising of one's voice. The use of humour may also be an effective way of relieving tension and progressing a meeting.

Pace of discussion

Chairs also need to strike the right balance concerning the pace of discussion. People may be very concerned to state their own views but impatient of the right of others to do the same. Too quick a pace may leave many people with the feeling that they have not had adequate opportunity to state their views, whilst too slow a pace may leave many people with the view that their time has been unnecessarily wasted. The ease with which points at issue can simply be misunderstood should never be underestimated. It is important that the chair clarifies and summarises whenever there appears to be any doubt or whenever decisions are taken.

Cultural issues

It is increasingly necessary to take account of any cultural diversity within meetings. This is more common because of globalisation, ease of international travel, greater cultural diversity within countries and developments in technology. It is also more likely because or organisational developments such as multi- and transnational companies, joint ventures, greater intergovernment co-operation on a regional and national basis and developments such as European Works Councils. Sometimes such developments necessitate simultaneous translation into a number of different languages.

Video-conferencing

Meetings can now take place without all members being physically present by video link-up. Whilst video-conferencing can have many advantages it is also necessary to be aware of its limitations. Considerable technological resources are needed to set it up. The quality of interaction cannot be as great as if members are physically together. Also, a key aspect of meetings can be the informal exchanges between members that often take place before, during and after meetings.

RECORDING THE OUTCOME OF MEETINGS

The possibility of confusion about the content and outcome of a meeting will be reduced if there are adequate minutes or whatever other record is appropriate. However, for this to be undertaken effectively, meetings need to have been conducted properly in the first place. One does not, for example, want misunderstandings about what was really decided to be left to surface when the minutes are distributed. As was explained in the previous chapter in the context of negotiation, there are many factors which can cause confusion. These include selective perception, poor listening skills and the use of ambiguous language.

Recording can take a variety of forms, but verbatim records are rarely necessary or useful. A circulated minute is the most common type of record but, if this is inappropriate, as a minimum the chair should make an *aide-memoire* even in many informal situations. Other parties involved may also find it prudent to record an *aide-memoire* where there is no formal minute.

A record of the outcomes of a meeting is what is crucial. A record of the whole course of discussion may be counter-productive. In the heat of discussion people may say things that it is in no-one's interest to record. Consequently, considerable tact may be needed in writing up minutes so that the outcomes are accurately recorded without rekindling arguments that have been settled. The responsibility for action also needs to be carefully identified to help ensure that action that is agreed is actually implemented. Where the scale and importance justifies it, one may need a note-taker who is separate from the person advising the chair on procedural matters.

SUMMARY

✔ Informal and formal meetings are an integral part of organisational activity. Consequently, managers need to know the various purposes of meetings and how they are or should be structured. As managers are often likely to chair meetings it is particularly important that they develop effective chairing skills. The effects of badly organised meetings were examined. These included poor communication and decision-making. Badly conducted meetings can also waste a lot of people's time and damage the reputation of those responsible for their organisation. The need for chairs not to get over-involved in substantive discussion at meetings was stressed as this can damage the procedural framework within which discussions need to take place. Their over-involvement can also lead to inadequate process control during a meeting.

✔ The need for prior preparation was explained, even with informal meetings. This affects all those involved in a meeting but particularly the chair and secretary. The preparation involves the drawing up on an agenda and arranging a division of labour at a meeting so that the chair in particular is not overloaded.

✔ The role of conflict at meetings was examined as was a strategy for handling it. Usually it is best for chairs to facilitate a fair discussion about the issues and then using whatever mechanism is appropriate for resolving it. Members may be far more likely to be upset about not having had the chance to raise legitimate concerns than by having a decision go against them. Decisions are in any case likely to be more balanced if they are taken after a full examination of the issues. The need for effective recording was also considered. It is important that responsibility for any action is clearly identified and that implementation is monitored.

SELF-ASSESSMENT QUESTIONS

1. Identify the range of meetings in which you are likely to be involved in any one day or week, both formal and informal.

2. Identify the purpose of these meetings and any decision-making mechanisms.

3. Select up to three meetings that you have recently attended and consider whether roles were properly allocated and kept to or not.

4. Did any of these meetings you identified in answer to question 3 suffer from lack of preparation on the part of those involved? Identify any lack of preparation.

5. With the meetings you identified in your answer to question 3, consider how well they were conducted.

6. How might the chair of a meeting best handle conflict? If possible, answer with reference to meetings you have already commented on.

7. What follow-up action may be necessary to ensure that meetings are effective?

 References

Evans, Keith (1983) *Advocacy at the Bar: A Beginner's Guide*, Financial Training Publications.

General References
Forsyth, P. (1998) *Making Meetings Work*, Institute of Personnel and Development: London.
Janner, G. (1990) *How to Win Meetings*, Gower.
Tropman, J. E. (1996) *Making Meetings Work: Achieving High Quality Business Decisions*, Sage.

Appendix to chapter 16

DEFINITIONS AND EXPLANATIONS OF SOME TERMS USED IN FORMAL MEETINGS

Ad hoc: this Latin phrase literally means 'to this'. Its meaning has been extended to 'set up to serve a particular purpose'. Thus, an *ad hoc* committee is one which has been set up to serve a particular purpose and which will cease to exist as soon as this purpose has been served.

Agenda: Latin meaning 'things requiring or deserving to be done'. It is really plural in form but is now used as a singular word and means simply 'a list of the items of business to be dealt with at a meeting'.

Amendment: when someone moves that a proposition should be altered in some way, they are moving an amendment. It should be noted that an amendment proposes an alteration of a proposition, not a direct negation of it nor a completely different proposition.

Ballot: 'a secret vote'. Members register their votes on paper and not by a show of hands.

Casting vote: the chair is allowed an ordinary vote as a member of the meeting. Sometimes, however, the standing orders allow them an extra vote which is called a casting vote, because they may, if they so wish, use it to decide on an issue on which the voting is equal.

Co-opt: if a committee feels that it would benefit from the services of some person possessing special qualifications or experience, it may decide (if it has been given such powers) to co-opt that person, i.e., to make them an additional member of the committee. The committee has exercised power of co-option and the person has been co-opted.

Ex officio: a person may claim to be a member of a committee, not because they have been elected but *ex officio*, that is 'by virtue of their office'.

Minutes: a brief but accurate record of what took place at a meeting.

Motion: anything that is moved or proposed at a meeting. Thus, a proposition is a motion but an amendment is also a motion.

Nem. con.: an abbreviation for the Latin phrase *nemine contradicente* and means 'no-one speaking against'. Thus 'carried *nem. con.*' does not mean the same as 'carried unanimously' which means that every one present voted for the motion.

Next business: when a motion is being debated it may appear to some member or members that it would be unfortunate for the meeting to reach a decision on the matter in question or that it would be a waste of time to continue the debate. One device to stop the debate is for a member who has not already spoken to stand up and say 'Chair, I move next business'. If this motion is seconded, it is put to the vote immediately, without discussion, and if it is carried the meeting does in fact move on to the next business. If the motion is defeated, the meeting then resumes the debate on which it was already engaged.

Nominate: to propose someone for election to an office. Usually a nomination does not need to be seconded.

Other business: this may appear on the agenda of a meeting to allow members to raise items which have come to light after the agenda has been prepared. However, any items the chair allows under this heading must be agreed by the meeting to be urgent and to have come to notice so recently that there was no time to have them included in the agenda.

Point of information: sometimes a member who does not wish to take part in a discussion, or who is preparing to speak later, may wish to ask a question on relevant facts. They may do this by saying 'Chair, on a point of information, can you tell me, etc.'

Point of order: a member may rise at any time and say something on a point of order, but they should soon be told to sit down if what they say is not in fact on a point of order. The member must be able to prove that, or reasonably to question whether, another member has spoken or acted, or something has been done, or is going to be done not in accordance with the rules, standing orders or terms of reference or other regulations which govern the conduct of the meeting. A point of order relates only to procedure – if the point raised is really part of the subject under discussion, it is not a point of order.

Previous question: that the question be not *now* put. If the motion is carried, no more discussion of the main question can occur, and it is shelved. If it is not carried, then the original motion must be put to the vote at once. Previous question can only be moved for an original or substantive motion.

Quorum: this is a Latin word meaning simply 'of whom'. Its meaning in meeting procedure is extended to the number of members who must be present before the proceedings can be valid. The quorum for a meeting is usually laid down on the rules or standing orders which apply, but if it is not laid down it is generally taken to mean a minimum of approximately one-third and never less than three.

Reference: when a task has been delegated by a meeting to a committee or by a committee to a subcommittee, the committee or subcommittee will eventually report to the main body and will probably recommend some action. If a member of the main body does not agree with any action reported or recommendation made, they should move the reference back to the report. This motion is discussed and if it is carried it means that the committee or subcommittee must reconsider the subject in question and report again later.

Resolution: it is wrong to talk of moving or proposing a resolution. One can move or propose a motion or proposition and either of these becomes a resolution if it is passed. In other words, a resolution is something that a meeting has resolved to do.

Right to reply: it is customary to allow the mover of a proposition (but not of an amendment), who will have spoken first in the debate the right to speak again at the end of the debate. In the second speech, however, they must not introduce any new material but merely reply to points already raised by other speakers.

Standing orders: organisations which hold regular formal meetings (e.g., trade unions, councils, clubs) often have rules which stipulate the manner in which the business of their meetings shall be conducted. These are called standing orders, and they deal with such things as the length of time for which speakers may speak, the order in which speakers shall speak, the manner of conducting elections of officers, the order in which items shall be taken. Standing orders may be in addition to, or may even override, the general rules of meeting procedure. If there are any, the chair and the secretary should be very familiar with them. A member may at any time move suspension of standing orders and have this motion debated. For instance, if standing orders stipulate that a speaker may speak for only five minutes, it may occasionally be desirable to allow someone to exceed this limit in order to complete an important statement. Suspension of standing orders, if carried, will allow them to do this.

Substantive motion: when any amendments to a motion have been passed, the motion has its wording altered accordingly and is then called the substantive motion.

Teller: this means a member who has been appointed to count the number of votes cast on any question.

Terms of reference: these are instructions given, generally to a committee, defining clearly the nature and the limits of the task which it has been set.

That the question be now put: this may be moved at any time during the debate on a motion but must be moved by someone who has not already spoken. If it is carried, the matter under debate is immediately put to the vote; if it is not carried, the debate is resumed. Clearly this is a useful device to stop unnecessary or useless discussion (see also 'next business').

Conclusion

The aim of this book has been to help those who have, or expect to have, managerial responsibilities. Readers may have found that the content is relevant to the problems they see or face to a surprisingly large extent. The reality is that many other people have had to face similar problems and one may as well profit from their experience. There is little point in rediscovering the wheel on your own if such rediscovery, or rather the managerial equivalent, is unnecessary. The coverage of the book is not intended to be exhaustive. However, anyone with managerial responsibilities must be confronted with many of the problem areas that have been identified and need to have, or to develop, the conceptual understanding and related skills to deal with these issues.

The skills of management are not a mystic art which people either do or do not have. Neither are they a pattern of behaviour which can only be acquired in a mysterious way which defies analysis. As with so many skills, careful study and practice can lead to substantial improvements in performance. Admittedly, some people will have more potential than others, but perhaps the most important requirement for the conscious development of managerial skills is the realisation that this is possible.

Some readers are likely to have had little in the way of formal management training, and those who have may have found that not all of it has helped improve their managerial performance. This book is intended to provide a sound base for the development of a range of critical managerial skills. The conceptual understanding that is required is the vital first stage. That needs to be followed by the conscious development of skills and evaluation by the reader of the extent to which they have been able to able to apply them. It may well be that readers are already proficient in some of the areas that have been identified, but there may be other areas where there is the potential for significant development.

A key feature of this book has been the stress on the need for managers to develop their diagnostic skills. The book is not intended to provide a set of prescriptive remedies to be applied without thought. It is only after careful analysis has been undertaken to identify the nature and cause or causes of problems that it is appropriate to consider solutions. The range of techniques explained in the book, or any other techniques for that matter, should only be applied after adequate diagnosis. Careful thought may also need to be given as to the sequence in which various problems are tackled.

The self-development of the individual manager and improvements in job performance may hinge on the identification of realistic objectives. This may necessitate not just concentration on one or two key areas but also the setting of attainable standards. It may be quite counter-productive for a person to set out to change the world in managerial terms, either in the range of improvements they attempt or in the level of performance which they set. Setting unrealistic standards of performance may confirm the adage that the 'excellent is the enemy of the good'. It is far better to achieve a good improvement than to fail in attempting the impossible. A gradual approach to development of managerial skills may also help in the assessment of what improvements are politically possible. It is no good for a manager identifying improvements in an organisation, however desirable, if they are not politically attainable. It may also be appropriate to identify short-term and long-term objectives for improvement, both in oneself and in organisational performance.

The development of the reader's managerial skills is likely to result in their advance up the managerial escalator. This is likely to lead to a need to pay even more attention to the managerial aspects of their job and to the relevant areas of skill. This also emphasises the constantly changing pattern of work in organisations. Just as the individual is not a static creature, so organisations change and also the environments in which they exist. Individuals may also move from one organisation to another. The reader may not only have to cope with a fairly continuous pattern of change but may find that much of their work is concerned with implementing change that affects other people. This is likely to be both the continuous everyday changes and the more spectacular one-off changes caused by, for example, the development of specific new technologies or markets. In short, the manager will find that they have continuously to adapt to changed circumstances and also to help other people adapt. The realisation of this, and the development of appropriate skills, should help the individual not only to handle such change more effectively but also to influence events as well as simply be influenced by them.

One of the particular problems likely to be encountered as a person acquires increasing managerial responsibility is greater exposure to criticism. Backseat advice can be very annoying, particularly if it comes from people who are neither particularly well informed nor competent. It can be all the more annoying if sometimes the advice turns out to be correct. As the importance of the decisions that the manager has to take increases, it is inevitable that those affected will comment on those decisions, either openly or covertly. This is a cross that just has to be borne – hopefully somewhat more easily if it is recognised in advance. It is the price to be paid by almost anyone who accepts responsibility. What is particularly needed is the ability to react sensibly to criticism – neither overreacting to ill-informed comment nor ignoring what may be sound advice.

This book is not intended as a substitute for decision-making but as a means of helping managers develop the ability to take appropriate decisions for themselves and to acquire the ability to implement those decisions effectively. The more that managerial problems are consciously identified and tackled and the more that the individual works at their managerial skills development, the more effective they will be. This should generate confidence and create the opportunity for even further development. Ironically, one of the ways in which managers may learn most is when they make mistakes. This can cause them to question their pattern of behaviour with a view to improving their performance. The critical need is for managers to use such incidents as opportunities for learning, instead of letting them affect their self-confidence.

One of the biggest adjustments that a successful manager may have to make is that of continuously outgrowing their job. In coping with that, however, they may not only gain substantial material rewards but develop as a person and make a powerful contribution to the particular organisation in which they work and to society in general.

Index